This description of European higher education is unequaled for its clarity and comprehensiveness. Today, 100 years later, Matthew Arnold's observations are as timely as when first written. Inspector of schools as well as poet and critic, Arnold watched democracy breed self-satisfied Philistines and realized that not all the liberty and industry in the world could insure the rule of right reason. In 1865 he left England to investigate higher education in France, Italy, Germany, and Switzerland.

In this volume Arnold traces the growth of schools and universities on the continent, examines the role of government in their development, and argues for organized public education and state schools in England. Included are the 1868 and 1882 Prefaces to *Schools and Universities on the Continent,* a newly discovered essay entitled "German and English Universities," and three letters written to the editor of the *Pall Mall Gazette.* This book makes clear the goals and achievements of European higher education and their relation to 19th-century and modern standards of learning.

Schools and Universities on the Continent is the fourth volume in the complete and definitive critical edition of THE COMPLETE PROSE WORKS OF MATTHEW ARNOLD prepared by R. H. Super. It includes critical, explanatory, and textual notes and an index especially prepared to help the reader follow Arnold's concepts through all his prose works.

R. H. SUPER is professor of English at The University of Michigan. He was educated at Oxford, B. Litt., and Princeton, A.B., Ph.D., and is the author of a number of articles about Matthew Arnold. His *Walter Savage Landor: A Biography*, published in 1954, was warmly received by British and American critics.

MATTHEW ARNOLD

SCHOOLS AND UNIVERSITIES ON THE CONTINENT

Edited by R. H. Super

ANN ARBOR   THE UNIVERSITY OF MICHIGAN PRESS

Second printing 1979
Copyright © by The University of Michigan 1964
All rights reserved
ISBN 0-472-11654-1
Library of Congress Catalog Card No. 60-5018
Published in the United States of America by
The University of Michigan Press and simultaneously
in Rexdale, Canada, by John Wiley & Sons Canada, Limited
Manufactured in the United States of America

Editor's Preface

Schools and Universities on the Continent, written first as a report to the Schools Inquiry Commission of 1865–67, is the longest book Arnold ever published. To it are added, in the present edition, four short anonymous contributions to the *Pall Mall Gazette* on educational matters, three of them previously published in Fraser Neiman's *Essays, Letters and Reviews by Matthew Arnold* (Cambridge: Harvard University Press, 1960), and the fourth, "German and English Universities," a discovery of the present editor's, here first reprinted from the files of that newspaper. When Arnold in 1874 republished part of his report on Continental education as *Higher Schools and Universities in Germany,* he wrote by way of new Preface a long essay on Bismarck's handling of the religious problem in the newly united Germany and its relevance to education in England and Ireland; this Preface is so little an introduction to the description of German education in 1865, and so closely tied to the immediate problems of the year it was written, that it will appear more appropriately with other works of the same year in volume VII of the present edition. The very brief Preface to the 1882 edition of *Higher Schools and Universities in Germany* is printed in this volume.

When Arnold republished the chapters on Germany separately he made slight textual changes, some to take into account the lapse of time since he had conducted his investigation, some to avoid reference to parts of the book not reprinted, and a few to improve the clarity of his expression. To have kept most of these alterations in an edition that reunites all the original report would only have made the reader uncomfortable, and rather than produce an eclectic text by adopting the two dozen or so purely stylistic modifications of 1874, I have followed the text of the published book of 1868 (not the official report of that year) throughout. Variant readings in the other editions are recorded in the Textual Notes, though alterations in punctuation and spelling are generally ignored. Obvious misprints are usually silently corrected, and so are a few misspellings of foreign words and place-names. Notes at the bottom of the page are Arnold's own, but the editor has occasionally amplified them, in square brackets.

In his earlier report on the elementary education of the Continent, Arnold recorded his sources with great thoroughness; in the present report he was at much less pains to document his work. The Critical and Explanatory Notes indicate the sources insofar as they have been accessible to the editor—quite completely for the German section of the report, less fully for the Italian (where the principal source was clear enough but not available), still less fully for the French, and hardly at all for the Swiss. Still, it is evident enough how Arnold worked. The notes also identify those names whose familiarity in the nineteenth century Arnold might perhaps take for granted, but which are much less known today, and attempt to give other information that will make Arnold's book clearer to the modern reader. The Glossary may be of some use, especially for the American reader.

Professor Arnold Whitridge has supplied some mementos of his grandfather's Continental tour, Signora Giuliana Artom-Treves has given important help in the identification and location of Italian materials, and Miss P. M. Downie and her staff at the Ministry of Education Library, London, have searched out their own resources for the editor's use and suggested helpful new lines of inquiry.

The volume was prepared while the editor was on sabbatical leave from the University of Michigan and enjoying a fellowship from the John Simon Guggenheim Memorial Foundation. Expenses arising from the preparation of the volume were met by a grant from the Horace H. Rackham Fund at the University of Michigan.

Ann Arbor, Michigan

Contents

Education and the State [I]

TO THE EDITOR OF THE PALL MALL GAZETTE

Sir,—The recent meeting at the Culham Training School and
the comments of the *Times* upon it, Mr. Lingen's letter and
the Culham rejoinder, afford a happy opportunity for placing
in a point of view where they are intelligible and interesting
to all the world the policy of the Revised Code, and that   5
policy's inevitable results.

The Culham speakers say that by the storm of the Revised
Code they were suddenly deprived of resources which were
absolutely necessary to the maintenance of their students.
They were thrown upon themselves, and appealed to those   10
who, like themselves, "felt the importance of the Church education of the people of the land," who "desired to see all
classes of the people well trained in Church principles." Their
appeal was successful. They are getting, in consequence,
"schools far more independent of any Government influence   15
than they had ever been before." The action of Government
upon the whole educational system of the country has been,
they say, eminently hostile. The tendency of the action of
the Government towards the Church of England has been
eminently hostile. But whatever the intention of what has   20
been done, they believe it will turn out for good. The desire
"to have all classes of the people well trained in Church principles" stands a much better chance of being gratified than
it did before the Revised Code.

The *Times* is enchanted. You are wrong, it says (and says   25
truly enough) to the Culham speakers, in supposing that the
recent proceedings of the Privy Council were animated by

1

any spirit either of hostility or friendship, whether to the Established Church or to other religious bodies. The plain tendency of those proceedings is simply *to restrict the aid of the State in the work of education;* and that not merely in
5 matters of religion, but in every particular. The policy that dictated them is a general policy of limiting the pecuniary aid of the Government. But it is precisely in this general view of the question that the policy of the last two or three years is to be regarded with so much satisfaction. You have easily sup-
10 plied the resources which Government withdrew. You have got, or are getting, independent schools. When aid comes to schools from the State, its application is necessarily fettered by restrictions; when it comes from the noblemen and gentlemen of the diocese, it can be applied exactly as the donors please.
15 There can, we should think, be little doubt that the latter is the more desirable method; for this method gives us schools supported by spontaneous effort instead of State agency.

And Mr. Lingen confirms, if it wanted confirming, the interpretation put by the *Times* on Mr. Lowe's policy in his educa-
20 tional reform. "Such meetings as the one at Culham," says Mr. Lingen, "afford satisfactory evidence that their lordships' hope of more active local support to these institutions will be fulfilled." He, too, is well pleased, the *Times* is well pleased, the Culham speakers are not ill pleased—they, at any rate, smile
25 through their tears—and who, then, has any reason to be ill pleased? Only the *corpus vile*, on which all our educational machinery is to operate; "the people of the land," as the Bishop of Oxford calls it.

For what are, in truth, the "trammels" which State aid im-
30 poses, and from which the Duke of Marlborough, the Bishop of Oxford, and the *Times* are so eager to deliver schools? They are these, as compendiously exhibited in M. Guizot's education law, in one clause, worthy to stand as a model to legislators wishing to impose "trammels" of this kind: "Le voeu des par-
35 ents sera consulté et suivi en tout ce qui concerne l'éducation religieuse de leurs enfants." These are the "trammels." The parent is to determine whether his child shall be brought up a Protestant or a Catholic, a Churchman or a Dissenter. But

such trammels the "noblemen and gentlemen of the diocese" desirous to have "all classes of the people well trained in Church principles" find very objectionable. A clause imposing them, a *conscience clause*, "involves a principle," says the Duke of Marlborough, "to which no clergyman of the Church of England can conscientiously agree." Such a clause the State, if it aids schools, must sooner or later enforce. But if the aid to schools comes from the noblemen and gentlemen of the diocese, why then of course "it can be applied exactly as the owners please." Trammels which prevent "all classes of the people from being well trained in Church principles" can be dispensed with. "There can be little doubt," as the *Times* says, "that the latter is the more desirable method."

The Privy Council Office wishes, of course, to discharge its paramount duty of justice, and to have a conscience clause. If it had continued to take an increasing part in the establishment of schools, this conscience clause must sooner or later have become the rule of the elementary schools of this country. One would think, therefore, that the Privy Council Office should sedulously have pursued its work of intervention; the "people of the land" would have been great gainers. They would have been able, for instance, to educate their children, without necessarily, if Dissenters, paying to the noblemen and gentlemen of the diocese the admission fee of a sound training in Church principles. But no; here Mr. Lowe stepped in. It is right, no doubt, for the State, if it aids schools, to be just; but it is still more right for the State not to aid schools at all. The particular policy of giving to the people of the land schools with the protection of a conscience clause must yield to the general policy of limiting the pecuniary aid of the Government. So the grand thing for the Privy Council Office is to cut the schools adrift, and to leave them to the noblemen and gentlemen of the diocese. Mr. Lowe and the *Times* may be a little sorry that these donors, exercising their indisputable right of applying their aid exactly as they please, should think that to let a Dissenter's child attend school without learning the Church catechism "involves a principle to which no clergyman of the Church of England can conscientiously agree." But then they are very glad "to have restricted the aid of the State in the work of education, and that not merely in matters of religion but in every particular." And "it is in this general view of the question that the policy of the last two or three years is to be regarded with so much satisfaction."

So our elementary schools are to go as fast as possible to the noblemen and gentry of the diocese, "who have the great interests of the Church and of Church education at heart." And we are all to be very glad of it. The State may still, in any cases where it offers aid, propose to protect religious liberty by a conscience clause. But very soon, as soon as the policy of the Revised Code shall have borne its full fruits, the nobility, clergy, and gentry of the diocese will give the State this answer:—"Why trouble us with your talk of a conscience clause? *The school question is taken out of your hands.*" And Mr. Lingen will have to be charmed with this "satisfactory evidence that their lordships' hopes of more active local support to these institutions have been fulfilled."

For the professors of some better liberalism than the sterile liberalism of the past, with its pedantic application of certain maxims of political economy in the wrong place, this school question is one of the most vital questions of the future. The notion that to establish elementary schools for the "people of the land" is the State's duty—that it has no right to hand over this duty to the "noblemen and gentry of the diocese"—that the people suffers in its liberty, its self-respect, its education, when the State's duty is so handed over—this notion suits the prejudices and preponderance of some persons very ill, and therefore they would gladly extinguish it if they could. But it is sound; and therefore, in spite of hostility, it will live. It will thrive, it will strengthen. Tons of regulation claptrap about the "colossal official education of continental countries," about "the local diversity and independent energy which are such vital characteristics of our national life," will not be able to crush it.—Your obedient servant,

                                    A LOVER OF LIGHT

Education and the State [II]

Sir,—This subject is of such capital importance that you will allow me to return to it for one moment after your leading article of last night.

You say that I am misled by the fallacy—a very common one —that a thing or person called the State probably lives in Downing-street, or its neighbourhood, and is burdened with duties of the utmost importance towards the nation (which is another person living elsewhere), among them that of providing for the education of the people at large, and protecting them against the bigotry of the clergy and the nobility and gentry. But this State, you say, is a mere phantom. The State is only a collective name for the inhabitants of the country. The State means Parliament: the bishops and the nobility constitute one House of Parliament, and the gentry have a good deal to do with the other; so that the State turns out to be, in fact, a mere *alias* for the very people who manage the matter as it is.

It could not possibly be better put. And yet, let me ask you, do you see no meaning in these lines of Wither, quoted by Coleridge?—

> Let not your King and Parliament in one,
> Much less apart, mistake themselves for that
> Which is most worthy to be thought upon,
> Nor think they are essentially the State.
> But let them know there is *a deeper life*
> *Which they but represent;*
> *That there's on earth a yet auguster thing,*
> *Veil'd though it be, than Parliament and King.*

Do we not all desire, or at least are we not ashamed not to profess to desire, that the collective action of the community should aim at expressing the better reason of the community, and should aim at something higher than the everyday practice, deformed by stupidity and passions, of the common run of all of us who compose it? Is not Parliament on any but the coarsest theory of delegation meant to try and give effect to this better reason? Are not the nobility, clergy and gentry, if, as you say, they pretty much constitute Parliament, bound to be, as constituting Parliament, something more than a simple *alias* for themselves as private managers of schools?

This, you will say, is mere transcendental talk, and concerns the State in its idea. We have to do with the State in practice. Well, I think I can show you in this very matter of education that the State in practice has a sense of the duty of being something more than an *alias* for the very persons who manage education as it is, a sense of the duty of interposing between the people at large and bigotry, of serving as the organ of that "deeper life" of which Wither speaks. Mr. G. Shaw Lefevre has lately published in the *Fortnightly Review* an account of the conscience clause dispute between the Privy Council Office and the clergy. In one or two points Mr. Lefevre's information seems not quite perfect, but on the whole his sketch of the dispute is excellent—most clear, temperate, and trustworthy. He quotes Lord Granville's evidence, given before a Parliamentary Committee last session, as to the reasons which had prevented him from bringing the conscience clause dispute before Parliament. Lord Granville says:—"I think that if I were to lay before the House of Commons a conscience clause now, exactly in the shape in which it is, with rather a difficult and wavering rule as to the number of Dissenters, the first question of the House of Commons would be, 'Why are any number of Dissenters to be forced either to violate their religious feelings or to be excluded from the benefit of the education which is partly supported by the State?' I believe that our conscience clause does not go far enough now to satisfy the House of Commons." Lord Granville's ground for such forbearance is, that "it is very desirable that the Privy Council should be on good terms with the Church of England;" and undoubtedly it is one of the strongest traditions and instincts of an aristocratic Government like ours to deal tenderly with a powerful kindred and conservative order like the clergy: but surely here is proof that Parliament, that the State, has an impulse prompting it to protect the people of the land against the exorbitant pretensions of the "noblemen and gentlemen of the diocese" to have them all "well trained in Church principles;" prompting it to be something more than a mere *alias* for the squires and clergy who manage education as it is. And why, then, should you fix yourself in the disheartening conviction that, whatever may be the duties of the State in this matter, its chance of fulfilling them is very remote indeed?

Remote it is, and will be, if we are to wait for the poor to agitate before the State fulfils those duties to them. No civilization is possible on such terms. You say that you wish for a system like that of the common schools of the United States; but show me, anywhere, such a system owing its origin to the clamour and agitation of the poor who need it. Such a system must owe its first establishment to the intelligence and patriotism of the educated class; it educates the poor to prize it, to be no longer "neutral and indifferent;" they will defend it, they will not demand it. I do not deny that the actual oppressiveness of our present system may easily be exaggerated, nor that, in a measure, the education given by it humanizes, civilizes, and does good; but have you enough considered how humanizing and civilizing a thing in itself is the contact with reason and justice? how much more service instruction conjoined with these is likely to do the poor than instruction divorced from them? how much better is its hope of rescuing the poor from always "remaining much as they are"?—Your obedient servant,

Dec. 21, 1865. A LOVER OF LIGHT.

The Mansion-House Meeting

Sir,—The Mansion-House meeting on Middle Class Education has been held. The plan of Mr. Rogers and his friends for furthering this education has been announced; the subscription list has been made public. Any one who doubted that Englishmen were wonderful people at a subscription will have found out his mistake. Any one who doubted whether they were equally wonderful people at organizing on the wisest plan a great public service will perhaps retain his doubts still.

Let us in the amplest manner do homage to the liberality which the subscribers have shown. Let us declare, with the *Times,* that "there is something admirable in the facility with which large sums of money can be raised in this metropolis." Let us boast ourselves, with the *Star,* that "there is probably no other city in Europe in which, upon private application, thirty-three gentlemen would have subscribed a thousand pounds each to any object of this kind." And then, having duly rejoiced, let us ask how the end for which all this money is given is really being served.

The end is to provide schools for the middle class, in London first, afterwards in the suburbs. The *Star* hopes "that the provinces may follow the example of London, and that a movement which is now metropolitan may prove general throughout Great Britain." And evidently from the language of Mr. Freshfield and other speakers at the meeting, the promoters of the scheme have this development of it in view. The middle-class children, for whom these schools are meant, are "the children of clerks, of tradesmen, and other persons in the same rank of life, for whom no adequate system of education exists." Mr. Gassiot put the income of the sort of London clerk that wants these schools at from £200 to £300 a year; let us say, taking the country through, they are meant for the children of people with from £100 to £300 a year. The proposed schools are to be day schools, and the yearly charge for a boy's education is not to exceed £4.

In London and all over the country there are numerous charitable endowments, many of which, it is thought, might be made available for middle-class education. Some of these endowments do not easily at present find proper recipients, and have an unappropriated balance. Mr. Rogers and his friends went to the Charity Commissioners. They were told that all proceedings in connection with ancient charities were so embarrassing that the Commissioners could not promise them any immediate support. They went to the Court of Chancery, and were told the same thing. Mr. Rogers and his friends, the *Times* tells us, never contemplated seeking the assistance of Parliament, so as to compel a diversion of these surplus revenues; they only wished to invite the trustees to help them. When they found that even this invitation would be attended with difficulties, they came to what the *Times* calls the very wise conclusion to throw themselves upon private liberality. Hence the subscription and the plan of operations now announced.

Now, Mr. Rogers and his friends give their money and service, and merit due honour; and we are all ready to cry out triumphantly that now the thing is started, and that it is thus we manage these things in England. But let us look what this mode of managing these things really comes to. We are all agreed that middle-class education wants mending. But we have a favourite catchword that the State must not meddle with these things. So a philanthropist like Mr. Rogers, who sees that there is a great want to be met, comes forward. He takes to him a number of City gentlemen, whose clerks cry out that their children's schooling, if good, is very dear; if cheap, is very bad. They call meetings, raise money, and come forth with a programme. They define the middle class in their own

way, they fix the school charge in their own way, they arrange the plan of studies in their own way. It is left to them
to do, and they do it. Now I wish to speak with the greatest
respect of Mr. Rogers and his coadjutors; their intentions are
5   excellent; their liberality is great; Mr. Rogers has had great
experience of schools for the poor, and the City gentlemen
have had great experience of the wants of their clerks. But
it is no disrespect to them to say, that for fixing, in general,
the bounds of middle-class education, its cost, and its plan of
10 studies, they are hardly an adequate body. Well, but see how
the thing goes on. They get a splendid subscription; they begin a big school in Finsbury; and then they go to Government
for a charter and for facilities for getting at the funds of
charitable endowments. "What can be more proper?" cries
15 the Government. "God forbid that we should have to deal
with middle-class education ourselves; we hate meddling; our
Education Department hates it more than any of us; these
excellent people are in the field; this is individual enterprise
and self-reliance as the country likes to see it; by all means
20 let them have a charter." It is clear that the people who gave
the money and started the scheme have the right to manage it.
So of course Mr. Rogers and his shower of aldermen are the
Corporation by the new charter. Their functions are pretty
much those of the Superior Council of Public Instruction in
25 France. This Council consists of the Minister of Public Instruction and of eminent representatives of the different religious
communions, of the law, of the Institute, and of education,
public and private. Our Council will be Mr. Rogers and his
aldermen, who will settle what schools are wanted, what the
30 scholars are to pay, and what learn. No public establishment
of middle-class education will be attempted, no stringent
scheme for applying charitable endowments to school purposes
authorized; but "facilities" will be given for dealing with
trustees; a certain number of schools will be built, a good many
35 trustees will be negotiated with, and a good many charities
pecked at. Meanwhile to all plans for reforming middle-class
education the answer will be: "These good people are in the

field; let them alone, and the thing will work itself right in the end."

Mr. Rogers's corporation will hardly, however, be strong enough for dealing with the whole country, when the provinces, as the *Star* anticipates, follow the example of the metropolis. As we hate every sort of centralization, we shall be proud of this, not sorry for it. Other philanthropists will come forward, other aldermen will join them, other subscription lists will be opened, other councils will be constituted; and we shall have about the country several centres of volunteers, without much unity of plan or coherence of operation, working away to collect subscriptions, negotiate with trustees, peck at charities, and potter at middle-class education in general. And the question will be hung up for a great many years to come.

It is singular that Mr. Tite, who at the Mansion-House meeting quoted Erasmus's blame of the plan of entrusting the management of a school to a trading company, did not reflect that what was blamed by the clearest intelligence then in Europe was likely to be blamable, and that Dean Colet's piece of claptrap was really no answer. Sooner or later we shall all learn, even we English people, that there is an appointed sphere for public function as well as for private, and that this sphere is a good deal wider than we think. We are very proud of our hospitals. They are excellent, undoubtedly, but entirely insufficient. In other words, for adequately fulfilling a public service like that of hospitals, private effort has not, and cannot have, the necessary powers. Have the admirers of our voluntary system of hospitals ever heard what is the difference in the number of hospital beds here and in Paris? And how in London do we make up for the short supply of hospital beds that our voluntary system gives us? By the workhouse hospitals. The voluntary system is in the field; it does enough to keep up appearances, to prevent our being forced to organize a public system; and the horrors of that miserable makeshift, the workhouse hospital, are the price we pay. So it threatens to be with middle-class education. Schemes, excellent, benevolent schemes, like that of Mr. Rogers and his aldermen, will keep up appearances, and we shall be able to flatter ourselves that the work is being done. A few good schools will probably be established; so much is gain. But an adequate supply of good schools for the middle class, a proper distribution of them through the country, a thorough use of funds available for them, a right regulation of their studies, a due esteem of their importance, a due status for their teachers, a due security for those who use them, we shall never get in this way. We shall, in fact, be further off from it than ever; we shall be perpetuating all our present makeshifts. And this we have to set against the gain which a new school in Finsbury and half a dozen new schools elsewhere will bring us.—Your obedient servant,

A LOVER OF LIGHT.

Schools and Universities on the Continent

'The thing is not, *to let the schools and univer-sities go on in a drowsy and impotent routine; the thing is, to raise the culture of the nation ever higher and higher by their means.'*

WILHELM VON HUMBOLDT.

Preface

(1868)

I was in 1865 charged by the Schools Enquiry Commissioners with the task of investigating the system of education for the middle and upper classes which prevails in France, Italy, Germany, and Switzerland. In the discharge of this task I was on the Continent nearly seven months, and during that time I visited the four countries named, and made as careful a study as I could of the matters to which the Commissioners had directed my attention. The present volume contains the report which I made to them. I have here adapted it to the general reader's use, and divested it of some details which for his use were unnecessary.

It is the education of the poor, not the education of the middle and upper classes, which principally occupies public attention in this country at present. In Switzerland, more than in any other country with which I am acquainted, all classes use the same primary school; and in Switzerland, therefore, I had occasion to touch upon the primary school,—the school of the poor,—because there this school forms a link in the chain of schools in which the middle and upper classes are educated. Accordingly, the English reader will in the following pages find a full account of the primary school system in Canton Zurich,—a region free like England, industrial like England, Protestant like England. School attendance is obligatory there, and the schools are very good; both in their goodness and in all the important points of their system resembling the schools of Germany, of which, therefore, and of their system, the reader, after acquainting himself with the Zurich schools, will be able to form a clear notion.

I hope the growing interest in the subject of popular education will induce my countrymen to inform themselves accu-

rately what on the Continent the primary school, at any rate, is, and what a different sense words bear according as they are applied to popular education here, or on the Continent. At present, when in canvassing the subject of English popular edu-
5 cation the example of the Continent is adduced, the example is in general perfectly fallacious, because the terms which we employ are perfectly ambiguous, or our application of them perfectly inaccurate. It is constantly said,—no less a personage than the secretary to the National Society, Mr. Wilson, said it
10 at the Society's last general meeting,—that 'it appears that in 1858 the proportion of scholars to population was, in England and Wales, 1 to 7·7; in Holland, 1 to 8·11; in France, 1 to 9; and in Prussia, 1 to 6·27.' It is at once argued from thence, as Mr. Wilson argued, that 'our own country, therefore, is in
15 advance of Holland and France, and not far behind Prussia.' Mr. Pease, at the annual meeting of the British and Foreign School Society in May last, said: 'Prussia supplied an education superior to that of any country in the world, and he was glad that ours fell but little short of it.' To the same effect Mr.
20 Joseph Spencer, at the recent Congregationalist Meeting in Manchester, met the weighty and impressive speeches of Mr. Baines and Mr. Morley on our educational condition, by saying that 'he believed we did not stand behind any country except Prussia.' Still more recently, Lord John Manners has
25 declared that 'our primary education is ahead of all the countries in the world except Prussia;' and this, he added, 'is shown by figures which no one doubts and everybody admits.' No wonder, therefore, that anti-alarmists should, like Mr. Wilson, pronounce it 'highly satisfactory to find that, notwithstanding
30 many confident assertions to the contrary, the state of education in England and Wales will bear favourable comparison with the state of education in the most advanced of continental countries, even in Prussia, where attendance at school is compulsory.' No wonder that a sanguine man should even go a
35 little beyond this, and, like Mr. Joseph Spencer, pronounce that 'the system of education in Prussia being surrounded with so many things which are objected to in England, he believed we might be considered on an equality with Prussia.'

But when these gentlemen congratulate themselves because it appears that the proportion of scholars to population is in England and Wales 1 to 7, while in Holland it is only 1 to 8, in France only 1 to 9, and even in Prussia not more than 1 to 6, there is a fallacy in their use both of the word *appears* and of the word *scholars*, which requires notice. In the first place, that in England and Wales the proportion of scholars to population is 1 to 7, *appears* in a very different way, and on very different evidence, from the way and the evidence by which the proportion of scholars to population in France or Prussia is established. For France or Prussia such statistics are got from a series of administrative authorities, with machinery and power to collect them. For England, the statistics come from the Education Commissioners of 1859. These Commissioners have themselves told us how they procured their information. They had no series of administrative authorities through whom to collect it; such a series does not exist in England; it could not, as we are often told, be tolerated by a high-spirited and intelligent people like ourselves. The Commissioners sent enquirers, with no power to enforce an answer to their questions, through about one-eighth of England; and from the information thus obtained for about one-eighth of the country, they made a generalisation as to the remainder. The only information they could get of the same quality and trustworthiness as the information on which the continental returns are based, was for that minority of our schools which is in connection with the Committee of Council. It was not, of course, the Commissioners' fault that the returns, by which it appeared to them that the proportion of scholars to population was, for England and Wales, 1 to 7, were of this incomplete kind; they had no means of getting complete returns. But it is obvious how different a sort of appearing is this by which the English rate of scholars appears to be 1 in 7, from that by which the foreign rates appear to be 1 in 9 or 1 in 6. The English Commissioners *guess* their proportion; the foreign authorities *know* theirs. Therefore we ought not to say: 'It *appears* that in England 1 in 7 of the population is in school, in France 1 in 9, in Prussia 1 in 6;' but we should say: 'It is *thought likely* that in England 1 in 7

of the population is in school; it is *ascertained* that in France
1 in 9 is in school, in Prussia 1 in 6.' Perhaps this ought not
wholly to extinguish the high satisfaction with which, as Mr.
Spencer and Mr. Wilson say, the comparison of English educa-
5   tion with that of continental countries is calculated to fill us;
but at all events it must tend to somewhat abate it.

In the same way, a fallacy lurks under our use of the word
scholars. England, says the secretary to the National Society,
is in advance of Holland and France, and not far behind Prus-
10   sia, because our proportion of scholars to population is not
far behind Prussia's, and is in advance of that of Holland and
France. I feel that I ought to apologise, in passing, to that admirably educated people, the Dutch, for even quoting what
they must think such an impertinence as the assertion that
15   England is in popular education ahead of Holland; but the
impertinence comes, in truth, from those who utter it being
the victims of an ambiguous use of words. They do not know
what the continental nations mean by the word *scholar*. They
do not know that the continental nations and we mean some-
20   thing wholly different by it. Prussia means by a scholar a
child who has been subjected from his sixth year to his fifteenth
to obligatory instruction, either in public schools under certificated teachers who have had a three years' training in a normal
school, or in private schools under teachers who produce the
25   same, or higher, guarantees of competency. France means by
a scholar a child who is either in a public school under a certificated teacher, or in a private school under a certificated
teacher. Both public and private schools must, in France, be
under certificated teachers, and both are liable to State-inspec-
30   tion; the public schools alone, however, to complete inspection, the private schools to partial inspection only. But then,
of the children,—some four millions and a half in number,—
who are counted as scholars of the primary schools in France,
nearly three millions and a half are in public, completely in-
35   spected schools; there are no more than 922,000 in private,
partially inspected schools. In England, on the other hand, out
of some two millions and a quarter of children whom our
Education Commissioners count as scholars, there are only

920,000 in schools with certificated teachers, or under any public inspection, complete or incomplete, whatever; all the rest are in schools which give no tangible guarantees of any kind, which do not, therefore, in a foreigner's eyes, possess any real claim to style themselves schools, and their pupils scholars, at all. It is probable that some of these schools are schools coming up to the foreign standard of what a school is, and with scholars coming up to the foreign standard of what a scholar is. It is known that very many of them fall immeasurably below this standard. But how many come up to it, and how many fall below it, we have no certain means of knowing; no certain means, therefore, of ascertaining our proportion of scholars, in the continental sense of the word, to population. All that is certain is, that the proportion of 1 to 7 is not the true one, because it counts very many children as scholars who, on the Continent, would not be counted as such. It is true that Mr. John Flint, the registrar to the English Commissioners of 1859, says in a remarkable letter to the *Times,* that in reckoning scholars he regards quantity not quality, and that he has nothing to do with quality; and for English purposes this view of a scholar may perhaps serve very well; but it is obviously illusive when we are comparing school-returns with the foreigners, who do not regard quantity of scholars merely, but who regard quality also.

So far are the foreigners from accepting our estimate of what constitutes a scholar, or thinking, with the secretary of our National Society, that the state of education in England and Wales will bear favourable comparison with the state of education in the most advanced of continental countries,— so far, I say, are they from this, that a foreign Report on education, which I have now before me, goes on, after remarking that the number of our school children over ten years of age diminishes every year, to sum up our condition as follows:— *L'Angleterre proprement dite est le pays d'Europe où l'instruction est le moins répandue.*' The reporter does not consider that 1 in 7 of our population is a scholar, in the sense in which 1 in 8 of the population of Holland is a scholar, or he would not speak in this manner. Not finding any complete returns

of our school population, and not being disposed, even if they
found them, to accept Mr. John Flint's law of disregarding
quality, foreigners seek elsewhere for data enabling them to
compare our primary instruction with their own. They pro-
5   duce statistics showing that, in the Prussian army, the proportion of illiterate recruits is 2 per cent.; in the French army 27
per cent.; in the English army 57 per cent. Even allowing
these statistics to be trustworthy, it must be admitted that,
recruited as our army is, the comparative instruction of our
10 recruits is not a fair test by which to try our popular education as pitted against that of France or Germany. It is a
sounder test, perhaps, than the generalisation of the Education
Commissioners of 1859, applied in conformity with Mr. John
Flint's law; but it is not an accurate test. Probably, with the
15 sort of civil administration we possess, and are proud of possessing, we cannot obtain the means of accurately comparing
our popular education with that of the Continent. But then
Mr. Wilson and Mr. Spencer and others ought to beware of
building too much upon an inaccurate comparison of it.
20   In short, it is expedient for the satisfactory resolution of
these educational questions, which are at length beginning seriously to occupy us, both that we should attend to the experience of the Continent, and that we should know precisely what
it is which this experience says. Having long held that noth-
25 ing was to be learned by us from the foreigners, we are at
last beginning to see, that on a matter like the institution of
schools, for instance, much light is thrown by a comparative
study of their institution among other civilised states and nations. To treat this comparative study with proper respect,
30 not to wrest it to the requirements of our inclinations or
prejudices, but to try simply and seriously to find what it
teaches us, is perhaps the lesson which we have most need to
inculcate upon ourselves at present. No ability or experience
in the judge who pronounces on these matters can make up
35 for his not knowing the facts. Mr. Fraser and Canon Norris
both of them assert, that our inspected schools at present are
at least equal to the best primary schools of any other country, if not superior to them. Many others amongst us say the

same thing. Mr. Lowe, the author of the Revised Code, thinks
'our system, though partial, may compare favourably with any
system in the world;' and evidently, by what he says of America, he believes that our English schools must necessarily be
superior to those of less favoured countries, where, as he says, 5
'examination as practised under the Revised Code in England
is totally unknown.' Mr. Fraser, again, lays it down as certain, that our inspectors and inspection are better than those
of any other country. I have every interest in accrediting all
possible good report of our inspectors and our inspection; 10
but, having seen those of the Continent, I am not of Mr.
Fraser's opinion. Neither am I of his, and Canon Norris's, and
Mr. Lowe's opinion as to the equality, if not more than equality, of our inspected schools with the best primary schools of
the Continent. I have that high respect for the abilities and 15
judgment of these three gentlemen, that if I understood them
to have seen with their own eyes the best primary schools
of Holland, Switzerland, and North Germany, as well as our
own schools, and then to have arrived at this favourable judgment of the English schools, I should at once defer to their 20
opinion, and conclude that my own judgment, which is not
so favourable to the English schools, was mistaken. But now
I do not understand them to have seen the Dutch, and German, and Swiss schools and inspectors with their own eyes;
but they speak from report, or from the pleasant impressions 25
they have received from English inspectors with whom they
have come in contact, or from their warm admiration of the
Revised Code. This admiration goes so far with some people,
that Lord Hartington boldly says of Mr. Lowe, who produced
the Revised Code, that English education owes more to him 30
than to any other man living. And no doubt Lord Hartington
knows; but he does not tell us the grounds on which he has
built up his knowledge.

I have seen Dutch, German, and Swiss schools, I have seen
their inspection; and I think both them and their inspection, 35
in general, better than our schools and inspection at present.
I think, as a matter of fact, they are better; and I think, as a
matter of likelihood, it seems likely they should be better.

The working-class in Zurich or Saxony is, in general, less raw
and illiterate than ours; and every one knows that children
brought up with raw and illiterate parents are more stubborn
material as scholars, than children brought up in more civilised
5 homes. Then these Swiss and German children are obliged to
be under teaching from their sixth to their fifteenth year. Mr.
Fraser thinks it vain even to talk of keeping in school the
mass of our children after their tenth year. Then again, in
Prussia, the regular school-course for primary schools con-
10 sists of the following matters: religious instruction, reading,
writing, the mother-tongue, object lessons, geography, history, physics, natural history, arithmetic, drawing, needlework, gymnastics, singing. Prussian inspection extends to all
these matters, and the German nature abhors making instruc-
15 tion mechanical. In England, since the Revised Code, the
school-course is more and more confined to the three paying
matters, reading, writing, and arithmetic; the inspection tends
to concentrate itself on these matters; these matters are the
very part of school-teaching which is most mechanical, and
20 a natural danger of the English mind is to make instruction
mechanical. Finally, the Swiss or German schoolmaster has in
general had a three years' training in a normal school, is a
public servant, enjoys much consideration as discharging an
important function, and through bodies such as the School-
25 Synod described in a later part of this volume, makes his voice
heard in the school legislation and school regulation of his
country. With us he has an inferior training, has no sort of
representation by which to make his ideas and experience
reach the Education Department; while, as to his status, there
30 was no part of Mr. Lowe's reforms on which he valued himself more, and which more recommended itself to many people, than that by which he made the schoolmaster know his
place, and got rid of the danger and impropriety of seeming
to give him rank as a public official. For my own part, I have
35 always looked with some apprehension upon this check administered to the schoolmaster; because it seems to me of the
first importance, in dealing with any organism, not to do anything *to depress its powers of life;* and the powers of life in

our public education were undoubtedly the schoolmasters, animated by the hopes, advantages, and belief in their mission, which Sir James Shuttleworth had given to them. To have administered a check to a body of which some members were pragmatical, and to have escaped the danger, so grave in the eyes of the country gentlemen, of having in our schoolmasters a band of public servants, appear to me a doubtful compensation for having discouraged the whole body of schoolmasters, and thereby lowered for the present, and till some action other than ours comes in to repair what we have done, the powers of life of our whole public education. This way of thinking, however, seems contrary to that of many able people in this country, and, being so, is probably erroneous; only, as their way of thinking assumes that our schools under the Revised Code may compare favourably with any schools in the world, I should be glad if my countrymen would try to acquaint themselves with the best continental schools, and satisfy themselves by actual observation whether this is so. It is not so very rare for English people to find themselves at Basle, or Berlin, or Leipzig, and the primary schools on the Continent are in general thrown open readily enough to visitors. If Mr. Fraser, after bringing to bear on the best foreign schools the same keen eyes and shrewd judgment which he has brought to bear on English and American schools,* were then to assure us that he thought our schools and inspection better, I should be much staggered in the contrary opinion, and even inclined to surrender it to the authority of so much more capable a judge. But at present he and other good judges seem to lie under a sort of disadvantage in giving their judgment for the one of two things, without having seen the other.

Even where we have made up our minds as to the course which in this or that school matter we wish to adopt, it can do us no harm to see what is the course followed by the continental schools in this particular, and why they follow it. Take the matter of schoolmasters' certificates, for instance.

* As to the significance of the American schools, which Mr. Fraser, from personal observation, can compare with those of England, see the note at p. 277 of this work.

Certain influential people amongst us have schools with uncertificated teachers; they object to being forced to employ
certificated teachers; and yet they demand to be allowed to
try and earn the examination grants offered by the Revised
5   Code. They say that it is hard to oblige a small rural place to
maintain a teacher of the same class as a town. This sounds
plausible; yet it is interesting to know that, in Prussia, it is
just in the small rural places that the elementary school is made
of the most complete and effective kind, because in these
10   places the burgher or middle school of towns,—a second stage
of school, higher than any elementary school we have,—cannot be provided. But then people say, that the Revised Code
pays for results, and that when they offer results, they ought
to be paid for them without any more questions being asked.
15   Certainly they seem to have a case as against the eminent author of the Revised Code, who declared the other day at Edinburgh in plain words: 'It is the business of the State to ascertain
results, and to pay in proportion to them.' Many persons, accordingly, think their demand ought to be granted, and
20   granted, perhaps, it will be. But at least it is curious and interesting to know that on the Continent, these influential employers of uncertificated schoolmasters, instead of being allowed to earn public grants, would have their schools closed
by public authority. No doubt this is one of 'the many things,'
25   as Mr. Spencer says, 'surrounding foreign education which are
objected to in England;' but there is always some profit in
having these things in black and white. The foreigners defend
their arbitrary proceeding by saying, that the public has an
interest and a right to take securities of the schools which edu-
30   cate its children; and that, 'to ascertain results,'—that is, to
examine all school-children once a year for a few minutes in
reading, writing, and arithmetic,—is an unsound security, while
the employment of a teacher who has passed three years under
the best training for him the country can give, is a sound
35   security. It will be objected not only that this foreign doctrine
is at variance with Mr. Lowe's high authority, but also that
it is un-English to regard the mass of the public, the parents
of school-children, instead of regarding influential managers,

because in England we have reversed Sieyès's famous rule, and say: 'Nothing *for* the people, everything *by* the people.' And against such an objection I do not presume to contend; only I urge that we may as well know, in all its nakedness, the foreign practice and the foreign theory in this matter.   5

As to compulsory education, again, denominational education, secular education, the continental precedents are, I maintain, to be studied for the sake of seeing what they really mean, and not merely for the sake of furnishing ourselves with help from them for some thesis which we uphold. Most English   10 liberals seem persuaded that our elementary schools should be undenominational, and their teaching secular; and that with a public elementary school it cannot well be otherwise. Let them clearly understand, however, that on the Continent generally, everywhere except in Holland, the public elementary   15 school is denominational,* and its teaching religious as well as secular. Then as to compulsory education. It may be broadly said, that in all the civilised states of Continental Europe education is compulsory except in France and Holland. The opponents of compulsory education quote Mr. Pattison, to show   20 that in North Germany 'compulsory attendance is a matter which produces comparatively little practical result.' They quote a report of mine, to show that in French Switzerland 'the making popular education compulsory by law has not added one iota to its prosperity.' But yet the example of the   25 Continent proves, and nothing which Mr. Pattison or I have said disproves, that in general, where popular education is most prosperous, there it is also compulsory. The compulsoriness is, in general, found to go along with the prosperity, though it cannot be said to cause it; but the same high value among a   30 people for education which leads to its prospering among them, leads also in general to its being made compulsory. Where the value for it is not ardent enough to make it, as it is in Prussia and Zurich, compulsory, it is not, for the most part, ardent enough to give it the prosperity it has in Prussia   35 and Zurich. After seeing the schools of North Germany and of German Switzerland, I am strongly of this opinion. It is

* Of course with what we should call a conscience clause.

the same thing as in religion. The vitality of a man's religion
does not lie in his imposing on himself certain absolute rules
as to conduct; but, in general, if his religion is vital, it will
make him lay on himself absolute rules as to conduct. Above
5 all, it will make a newly awakened sinner do this; and England, in spite of what the secretary to the National Society
says, I must take leave to regard, in educational matters, as a
newly awakened sinner.

Therefore I do not think the example of Prussia and Switzer-
10 land will serve to show that compulsoriness of education is an
insignificant thing; and I believe that if ever our zeal for the
cause mounts high enough in England to make our popular
education 'bear favourable comparison,' except in the imagination of popular speakers, with the popular education of Prussia
15 and Switzerland, this same zeal will also make it compulsory.

But the English friends of compulsory education, in their
turn, will do well to inform themselves how far on the Continent compulsory education extends, and the conditions under
which alone the working classes, if they respect themselves,
20 can submit to its application. In the view of the English friends
of compulsory education, the educated and intelligent middle
and upper classes amongst us are to confer the boon of compulsory education upon the ignorant lower class, which needs
it while they do not. But, on the Continent, instruction is
25 obligatory for lower, middle, and upper class alike. I doubt
whether our educated and intelligent classes are at all prepared
for this. I have an acquaintance in easy circumstances, of distinguished connections, living in a fashionable part of London,
who, like many other people, deals rather easily with his son's
30 schooling. Sometimes the boy is at school, then for months
together he is away from school, and taught, so far as he is
taught, by his father and mother at home. He is not the least
an invalid, but it pleases his father and mother to bring him
up in this manner. Now I imagine no English friends of com-
35 pulsory education dream of dealing with such a defaulter as
this, and certainly his father, who perhaps is himself a friend
of compulsory education for the working classes, would be
astounded to find his education of his own son interfered with.
But if my worthy acquaintance lived in Switzerland or Ger-

many, he would be dealt with as follows. I speak with the school-law of Canton Neufchâtel immediately under my eyes, but the regulations on this matter are substantially the same in all the states of Germany and of German Switzerland. The Municipal Education Committee of the district where my acquaintance lived would address a summons to him, informing him that a comparison of the school-rolls of their district with the municipal list of children of school-age showed his son not to be at school; and requiring him, in consequence, to appear before the Municipal Committee at a place and time named, and there to satisfy them either that his son did attend some public school, or that, if privately taught, he was taught by duly trained and certificated teachers. On the back of the summons my acquaintance would find printed the penal articles of the school-law, sentencing him to a fine if he failed to satisfy the Municipal Committee; and, if he failed to pay the fine, or was found a second time offending, to imprisonment. In some continental states he would be liable, in case of repeated infraction of the school-law, to be deprived of his parental rights, and to have the care of his son transferred to guardians named by the State. It is indeed terrible to think of the consternation and wrath of our educated and intelligent classes under a discipline like this; and I should not like to be the man to try and impose it on them. But I assure them most emphatically,—and if they study the experience of the Continent they will convince themselves of the truth of what I say,—that only on these conditions of its equal and universal application is any law of compulsory education possible.

Of the education of the middle and upper classes, however, I have no need to speak at length here, for almost the whole of the following pages is devoted to that subject. It is not, like popular education, a subject which very keenly interests at present our educated and intelligent classes. It concerns their own education, and with their own education they are, it seems, tolerably well satisfied. Yet I hope that here again these classes,—above all I hope that the great middle class which has much the widest and the gravest interests concerned in the matter,—will not refuse their attention to the experience afforded by the Continent. Before concluding that they can have nothing to learn from it, let them at any rate know and weigh it.

To three points particularly let me invite their consideration. In the first place, let them consider in its length and breadth the facts, established in the following pages, that on the Continent the middle class in general may be said to be brought up *on the first plane*, while in England it is brought up *on the second plane*. In the public higher schools of Prussia or France 65,000 of the youth of the middle and upper classes are brought up; in the public higher schools of England,—even when we reckon as such many institutions which would not be entitled to such a rank on the Continent,—only some 15,000. Has this state of things no bad effect upon us? If the training of our working class, as compared with the working classes elsewhere, inspires apprehension, has the training of their employers, as compared with employers elsewhere, no matter of apprehension for us? There are people who say that the labour questions which embarrass us owe their gravity and danger at least as much to the inadequacy of our middle class for dealing with such questions, as to the inadequacy of our working class. 'English employers of labour,' these people say, 'are just now full of complaints of the ignorance and unreasonableness of the class they employ, and of suggestions, among other things, for its better instruction. It never occurs to them that their own bad instruction has much to do with the matter. Brought up in schools of inferior standing, they have no governing qualities, no aptitude, like that of the aristocratic class, for the ruling of men; brought up with hollow and unsound teaching, they have no science, no aptitude for finding their way out of a difficulty by thought and reason, and creating new relations between themselves and the working class when the old relations fail.' I do not say that this is certainly so, but I say that the bearings of our education on the matter,—our education both in itself and in comparison with that of the Continent,—are at least worth studying.

The second point is this. The study of continental education will show our educated and intelligent classes that many things which they wish for cannot be done as isolated operations, but must, if they are to be done at all, come in as parts of a regularly designed whole. Mr. Grant Duff, who directed his attention to educational matters long before they were in everybody's talk as at present, has pointed this out with great truth and clearness. Our educated and intelligent classes, in their solicitude for our backward working class, and their alarm for our industrial preëminence, are beginning to cry out for technical schools for our artisans. Well-informed and distinguished people seem to think it is only necessary to have special schools of arts and trades, as they have abroad, and then we may take a clever boy from our elementary schools, perfected by the Revised Code, and put him at once into a special school. A study of the best continental experience will show them that the special school is the crown of a long co-ordered series, designed and graduated by the best heads in the country. A clever boy in a Prussian elementary school passes first into a *Mittelschule,* or higher elementary school, then into a modern, or *real*, school of the second class, then into a *real* school of the first class, and finally, after all these, into the special school. A boy who has had this preparation is able to profit by a special school; to send him there straight from the elementary school, is like sending a boy from the shell at one of our public schools to hear Professor Ritschl lecture on Latin inscriptions.

I come, lastly, to the third point for our remark in Continental education. These foreign Governments, which we think so offensively arbitrary, do at least take, when they administer education, the best educational opinion of the country into their counsels, and we do not. This comes partly from our disbelief in government, partly from our belief in machinery. Our disbelief in government makes us slow to organise government perfectly for any matter; our belief in machinery makes us think that when we have organised a department, however imperfectly, it must prove efficacious and self-acting. The result is that while, on the Continent, through Boards and Councils, the best educational opinion of the country,—by which I mean the opinion of men like Sir James Shuttleworth, Mr. Mill, Dr. Temple, men who have established their right to be at least heard on these topics,—necessarily reaches the Government and influences its action, in this country there are no

organised means for its ever reaching our Government at all.
The most important questions of educational policy may be
settled without such men being even heard. A number of grave
matters enumerated in the following pages,*—our system of
5 competitive examinations, our regulation of studies, our whole
school legislation,—are at the present moment settled one
hardly knows how, certainly without any care for the best
counsel attainable being first taken on them. On the Continent
it is not so; and the more our Government is likely, in England,
10 to have to intervene in educational matters, the more does the
continental practice, in this particular, invite and require our
attention.

In conclusion. There are two chief obstacles, as it seems to
me, which oppose themselves to our consulting foreign experi-
15 ence with profit. One is, our notion of the State as an alien in-
trusive power in the community, not summing up and representing the action of individuals, but thwarting it. This notion
is not so strong as it once was, but still it is strong enough to
make it opportune to quote some words from a foreign Re-
20 port before me, which set this much obscured point in its true
light:—

'Le Gouvernement ne représente pas un intérêt particulier,
distinct, puisqu'il est au contraire la plus haute et la plus sincère
expression de tous les intérêts généraux du pays.'
25 This is undoubtedly what a government ought to be, and if it
is not this, it is the duty of its citizens to try and make it this,
not to try and get rid of so powerful and essential an agency as
much as possible.

The other obstacle is our high opinion of our own energy
30 and wealth. This opinion is just, but it is possible to rely on it
too long, and to strain our energy and our wealth too hard.
At any rate, our energy and our wealth will be more fruitful
and safer, the more we add intelligence to them; and here, if
anywhere, is an occasion for applying the words of the wise
35 man:—'If the iron be blunt, and a man do not whet the edge,
then must he put forth the more strength; but wisdom is
profitable to direct.'

* See pages 314–16 of the following work.

Preface

"It is expedient for the satisfactory resolution of those educational questions, which are at length beginning seriously to occupy us, both that we should attend to the experience of the Continent, and that we should know precisely what it is which this experience says."   5

So I said in the preface to the first edition of this work, published in 1868. The history of education on the Continent is now regarded in this country with a great and increasing interest, and I republish, therefore, my account of the schools and universities of Germany. I have abstained from attempt-   10
ing to bring the account down to the present time, either by the addition of chapters at the end, or by the insertion of notes and corrections in the body of the work. A book which, in its original state, was a whole, comes inevitably, by later additions and alterations of this kind, to be a whole no longer.   15
Nor are they requisite for the object of tracing the main lines of the development and character of intermediate and higher education in Germany. These main lines were already there in 1865; they have not come into being between that time and this. It is not probable that they will be changed. There is,   20
indeed, an increasing demand everywhere for modern or *real* studies, as they are called, and the school-course everywhere is being modified in compliance with this demand. But the need of those studies had been recognised by the organisers of German education before there arose a popular cry for them; and   25
now that the popular cry has arisen, it is in Germany that this cry is least likely, perhaps, to be suffered to destroy the true balance of education.

The cost of things has risen greatly in Germany since 1865, and the school-fees mentioned in the following account of German Schools are now, I am told, in many cases the double of what they then were. But the cheapness of good education in the German schools for the middle and upper classes still remains, relatively to its cost with us in England, as noteworthy now as it was then,—as noteworthy for us as the organisation of those schools, and as the universality of their provision.

February 1, 1882.

I

France

Chapter I

Development of Secondary Instruction in Europe

Origin of our Present Secondary Schools—Their Development Best Traced in France—Roman Period—Mediæval Period—University of Paris—Creation of Colleges—The Instruction in the Mediæval Schools—The University of Paris and the Renaissance—Schools of the Jesuits—The Old Schools Abolished at the Revolution—New Plans—Fourcroy's Law (1802).

Popular education has sprung out of the ideas and necessities of modern times, and the elementary school for the poor is an institution which has no remote history. With the secondary school it is otherwise. The secondary school has a long history; through a series of changes it goes back, in every European country, to the beginnings of civilised society in that country; from the time when this society had any sort of organisation, a certain sort of schools and schooling existed, and between that schooling and the schooling which the children of the richer class of society at this day receive there is an unbroken connection. In no country is this continuity of secondary instruction more visible than in France, notwithstanding her revolutions; and in some respects France, in that which concerns the historical development of secondary instruction, is a typical country. All the countries of western Europe had their early contact with Greek and Roman civilisation, a contact from which their actual books and schools and science begin; France had this more than any of them, except Italy. All the countries of western Europe had in the feudal and catholic Middle Age their universities, under whose wings were hatched the colleges and teachers that formed the germ of our actual secondary instruction; and the great Middle Age university was the University of Paris. Hither repaired the stu-

dents of other countries and other universities, as to the main centre of mediæval science, and the most authoritative school of mediæval teaching. It received names expressing the most enthusiastic devotion: the *fountain of knowledge*, the *tree of*
5 *life*, the *candlestick of the house of the Lord*. 'The most famous University of Paris, the place at this time and long before whither the English, and mostly the Oxonians, resorted,' says Wood. *Tandem fiat hic velut Parisiis ... ad instar Parisiensis studii ... quemadmodum in Parisiensi studio ...* say the rules of
10 the University of Vienna, founded in 1365. Here came Roger Bacon, Saint Thomas Aquinas, and Dante; here studied the founder of the first university of the Empire, Charles the Fourth, Emperor of Germany and King of Bohemia, founder of the University of Prague; * here Henry the Second in the
15 12th century proposed to refer his dispute with Becket; here, in the 14th, the schism in the papacy and the claims of the rival popes were brought for judgment. In Europe and Asia, in foreign cities and on battle fields, among statesmen, princes, priests, crusaders, scholars, passed in the middle ages this word
20 of recognition, *Nos fuimus simul in Galandia,*—the Rue de Galande, one of the streets of the old university quarter, the *quartier latin* of Paris.

  The countries of western Europe, leavened, all of them, by the one spirit of the feudal and catholic Middle Age, formed
25 in some sense one community, and were more associated than they have been since the feudal and catholic unity of the Middle Age has disappeared and given place to the divided and various life of modern Europe. In the mediæval community France held the first place. It is now well known that to place
30 in the 15th century the revival of intellectual life and the re-establishment of civilisation, and to treat the period between the 5th century, when ancient civilisation was ruined by the barbarians, and the 15th, when the life and intellect of this civilisation reappeared and transformed the world, as one
35 chaos, is a mistake. The chaos ends about the 10th century; in the 11th there truly comes the first re-establishment of civilisation, the first revival of intellectual life; the principal centre

* Founded 1348.

of this revival is France, its chief monuments of literature are in the French language, its chief monuments of art are the French cathedrals. This revival fills the 12th and 13th centuries with its activity and with its works; all this time France has the lead; in the 14th century the lead passes to Italy; but now comes the commencement of a wholly new period, the period of the Renaissance properly so called, the beginning of modern European life, the ceasing of the life of the feudal and catholic Middle Age. The anterior and less glorious Renaissance, the Renaissance within the limits of the Middle Age itself, a revival which came to a stop and could not successfully develope itself, but which has yet left profound traces in our spirit and our literature,—this revival belongs chiefly to France. France, then, may well serve as a typical country wherein to trace the mediæval growth of intellect and learning; above all she may so stand for us, whose connection with her in the Middle Age, owing to our Norman kings and the currency of her language among our cultivated class, was so peculiarly close; so close that the literary and intellectual development of the two countries at that time intermingles, and no important event can happen in that of the one without straightway affecting and interesting that of the other. As late as the year 1328 we find French an alternative language, at Oxford, with Latin; the students are to use *colloquio Latino vel saltem Gallico*. With the hostility of the long French Wars of Edward the Third comes the estrangement, never afterwards diminishing but always increasing. To this day it is impossible to read the French literature of the true Middle Age without feeling that here is the moment when the life of the French nation comes really closest to our own; thought and expression have both of them much which we recognise as akin to us, which we have in a great degree retained, while the French have gone away from it to a thought and expression more effective no doubt for many purposes, but more unlike ours. To show how this is the case with thought and style would need more space than I have here at command; one example out of a thousand,—the word *rescouer*, for instance, 'to rescue,' which the French had in the Middle Age, which we have still, but which

the French have no longer,—will show how it is the case with
language.

Roman civilisation in Gaul, as in other parts of the empire,
organised a system of schools. Before the ruin of that civilisation in the fourth century, there were great schools in important towns, Vienne, Lyons, Bordeaux, Arles, Agen, Clermont,
Périgueux; and at these schools, Christian children began to
appear. Then came the invasions of the barbarians, and the
break-up of the old order of things. For some time schooling
ceased to be a concern of lay society; it went on in the shelter
of the church and for the benefit of the ecclesiastical body.
The great schools from the 4th century to the 12th are the
monastery schools, such as the school of Saint Victor at Marseilles, of Lérins in the isles of Hyères, of Saint Claude in
Franche Comté, of Saint Médard at Soissons. There were 400
monks studying at the school of Saint Médard in the sixth century. A famous monastery school for women also, that of
Chelles near Paris, existed as early as the time of the Mero-
vingian kings. But as a new state of society gradually formed
itself and became solid, signs appeared of the lay class too
coming to school. A decree of Pope Eugene II., in 826, ordered that *in universis episcopiis subjectisque plebibus et aliis
locis in quibus necessitas occurrerit, omnino cura et diligentia
adhibeatur ut magistri et doctores constituantur, qui studia
literarum, liberaliumque artium dogmata, assidue doceant.* The
Council of Aix-la-Chapelle, in 816, had divided the school into
interior and exterior; the first for novices in training for the
Church, the second for lay boys. In 855 this arrangement
was carried into effect at Fleury sur Loire, one of the schools
which Theodulf, Bishop of Orleans, employed by Charlemagne
in his plans of social reconstruction, had founded. At Fleury
sur Loire was formed a school expressly for the sons of laymen, the youth of the upper class; it was called *Hospitale
Nobilium*. The Palace School of Charlemagne is well known.
Charlemagne's astonishing efforts at reconstruction were, however, premature; after his death followed another period of
confusion and slow formation. But about the 11th century
we see feudal society, with institutions naturally developed and

destined to endure for a long while, in possession of France, England, and Germany. From about the 11th century, date the beginnings of an instruction which has, with many changes of names, impulses, and objects, been going on uninterruptedly ever since.

Our Stephen Harding, the third abbot of Cîteaux, and the true founder of the great order of the Cistercians, was studying at the School of Paris in 1070. The name of Abelard recalls the European celebrity and immense intellectual ferment of this school in the 12th century. But it was in the first year of the following century, the 13th, that it received a charter from Philip Augustus, and thenceforth the name of University of Paris takes the place of that of School of Paris. Forty-nine years later was founded University College, Oxford, the oldest college of the oldest English University. Four nations composed the University of Paris,—the nation of France, the nation of Picardy, the nation of Normandy, and (signal mark of the close intercourse which then existed between France and us!) the nation of England.* The four nations united formed the faculty of arts. The faculty of theology was created in 1257, that of law in 1271, that of medicine in 1274. Theology, law, and medicine had each their Dean; arts had four Procurators, one for each of the four nations composing this faculty. Arts elected the rector of the University, and had possession of the University chest and archives.

The pre-eminence of the Faculty of Arts indicates, as indeed does the very development of the University, an idea, gradually strengthening itself, of a lay instruction to be no longer absorbed in theology, but separable from it. The growth of a lay and modern spirit in society, the preponderance of the crown over the papacy, of the civil over the ecclesiastical power, is

* Another mark of this close intercourse is the choice of a patron by the nation of France; this patron was Saint Thomas of Canterbury. That of the nation of England was Saint Edmund, the Saxon martyr-king. In the 15th century, when the Hundred Years' War had separated France and England, the nation of Germany took the place of ours, and Saint Charlemagne took that of Saint Edmund. In 1661 Charlemagne was made by statute the common patron of the University.

the great feature of French history in the 14th century, and to this century belongs the highest development of the University. But the ecclesiastical power never abandoned its claims to a control of education; it had numerous means of action on the University, and it waged a constant war for mastery, often with success. The Chancellor of the Cathedral of Notre Dame was the ecclesiastical chief, as the rector was the academical chief, of the University; the seal of the University, for the first twenty years of its existence, is the seal of its ecclesiastical chief, the Chancellor of Notre Dame. When, between 1221 and 1225, the University struck, for the first time, a seal of its own, the Chapter of Notre Dame complained to the papal legate at Paris of the usurpation, and the legate ordered the seal to be broken. The scholars rose in insurrection, assailed the legate's house, and compelled him to fly. The dispute was referred to the Pope, and at last Innocent IV., in 1244, granted to the University a seal of its own.

But the licence to teach, the crown of the University course, was conferred by the ecclesiastical power, the Chancellor of the Cathedral. Not till he was provided with this licence could the candidate appear before the masters of his faculty, and receive from them the bonnet of doctor in law, medicine, or theology, of master in arts. So far the University had to admit the intervention of the authority of the metropolitan church. Nor was it successful in freeing itself from the intrusion of the mendicant orders, who saw in the right of teaching a powerful means of influence. The Dominicans, on an occasion when the University had shut its schools, in 1229, offered themselves as teachers of theology; the University refused to them and the Franciscans the degree of master and the privilege of teaching; but on an appeal to the Pope the University had to give way, and in 1257 Saint Thomas Aquinas and Saint Bonaventura were made doctors in theology by the Chancellor, and admitted to teach in Paris. The admission of the other orders followed.

But the importance of the University in the 13th and 14th centuries was extraordinary. Men's minds were possessed with a wonderful zeal for knowledge, or what was then thought knowledge, and the University of Paris was the great fount from which this knowledge issued. The University and those depending on it made at this time, it is said, actually a third of the population of Paris; when the University went on a solemn occasion in procession to Saint Denis, the head of the 5 procession, it is said, had reached Saint Denis before the end of it had left its starting place in Paris. It had immunities from taxation, it had jurisdiction of its own, and its members claimed to be exempt from that of the provost of Paris; the kings of France strongly favoured the University, and leaned to its side 10 when the municipal and academical authorities were in conflict; if at any time the University thought itself seriously aggrieved, it had recourse to a measure which threw Paris into dismay,—it shut up its schools and suspended its lectures.

In a body of this kind the discipline could not be strict, and 15 the colleges were created to supply centres of discipline which the University in itself,—an apparatus merely of teachers and lecture-rooms,—did not provide. The 14th century is the time when, one after another, with wonderful rapidity, the French colleges appeared. Navarre, Montaigu, Harcourt, names so 20 familiar in the school annals of France, date from the first quarter of the 14th century. The College of Navarre was founded by the queen of Philip the Fair, in 1304; the College of Montaigu, where Erasmus, Rabelais, and Ignatius Loyola were in their time students, was founded in 1314 by two members of 25 the family of Montaigu, one of them Archbishop of Rouen. The majority of these colleges were founded by magnates of the church, and designed to maintain a certain number of bursars, or scholars, during their university course. Frequently the bursarships were for the benefit of the founder's native place, 30 and poverty, of which among the students of that age there was no lack, was specified as a title of admission.

Along with the University of Paris there existed in France, in the 14th century, the Universities of Orleans, Angers, Toulouse, and Montpellier. Orleans was the great French school 35 for the study of the civil law; Reuchlin and Theodore Beza studied it there. The civil law was studiously kept away from the University of Paris, for fear it should drive out other

studies, and especially the study of theology; so late as the year
1679 there was no chair of Roman or even of French law in
the University of Paris. The strength of this University was
concentrated on theology and arts, and its celebrity arose from
5   the multitude of students which in these branches of instruction it attracted.

One asks oneself with interest what was the mental food
to which this vast turbulent multitude pressed with such inconceivable hunger. Theology was the great matter; and there
10 is no doubt that this study was by no means always that barren
verbal trifling which an ill-informed modern contempt is
fond of representing it. When the Bishop of Paris publicly
condemned, as current in the University, such propositions as
these: *Quod sermones theologi sunt fundati in fabulis; Quod
15 nihil plus scitur propter scire theologiam; Quod fabulæ et falsa
sunt in lege christiana sicut et in aliis; Quod lex christiana im-
pedit addiscere; Quod sapientes mundi sunt philosophi tantum,*
it is evident that around the study of theology in the mediæval
University of Paris there worked a real ferment of thought,
20 and very free thought. But the University of Paris culminated
as the exclusive devotion to theological study declined, and
culminated by virtue of that declension. A teaching body with
a lay character could not have been created by the simple
impulse to theological study. The glory of the University of
25 Paris was its Faculty of Arts, its *artiens,* as they were called;
it was among the students in this faculty that the great ardour
showed itself, the great increase in numbers. The study of this
faculty was the seven arts * of the *trivium* and *quadrivium;*
the three arts of the *trivium* were grammar, rhetoric, and
30 dialectic; the four of the *quadrivium,* arithmetic, geometry,
astronomy, music. This was the liberal education of the middle
age, and it came direct from the schools of ancient Rome. In
the work, still extant, of Martianus Capella, an African grammarian established at Rome in the fifth century, the arts of
35 the *trivium* and *quadrivium* are set forth in order, in a mix-
ture of prose and verse; and this book was one of the chief

---

* Enumerated in this line of middle-age Latin verse:
   Lingua, tropus, ratio, numerus, tonus, angulus, astra.

text-books of the Middle Age, and its great guide to a liberal education. Such an education was apparently possible with the programme offered by the seven arts. Rhetoric included poetry, history, composition,—the humanities in general; dialectic took in the whole of philosophy. The mediæval teacher of grammar had for his text-books the grammars of Donatus and Priscian, grammars coming from fully competent authorities, and quite sufficient, if properly used, for the teacher's purpose. The great monastery schools of Cluny, Saint Victor, and the Bernardines, assigned three years to grammatical studies, and the University professed to admit to its teaching no student who was not already grounded in them; *qui nescit partes, in vanum tendit ad artes.* But a measure of the good sense of the grammatical studies of the time is supplied by *Donatus morali-zatus,* the grammar of Donatus *moralised,* as was then the fashion with all books used for instruction. 'What is the *pronomen?*' the learner is made to ask. 'Man is thy *nomen,*' the teacher answers, 'sinner is thy *pronomen.* Therefore, when thou makest thy prayer to God, use thy *pronomen* only, and say, "O heavenly Father, I call not upon thee as man, but I im-plore thee as sinner." ' Again: 'Why,' the learner asks, 'is the preposition the consideration of the joy of the elect?' The an-swer is: *'Quia illi præponuntur damnandis.'*

The scholastic philosophy remains a monument of what the Middle Age achieved in the favourite art, the art which starved all its six sisters,—Dialectic; but what was really the instruc-tion given and the proficiency acquired in the humanities and mathematics it is not so easy to determine. The word mathe-matics was at that time synonymous with magic, as is shown by a hexameter line in a poem for the use of the schools,—a line equally unpromising for their mathematics and for their scholarship: *Datque mathematicos comburi theologia.* The arithmetic most in esteem was that of the computers, which dealt with epacts, the golden number, the dominical letter, and all the calculations necessary for framing the ecclesiastical calendar. But a catalogue of the Sorbonne library, in 1290, shows that among the books was a treatise on geometry in French, *Practica Geometriæ in Gallico,* of which the first words are quoted in the catalogue. The catalogue of the same institution, in 1338, has several copies of a Latin version of Euclid's Geometry. There is no mention of any work on algebra or mechanics. In the Sorbonne catalogue of 1290 appears Ovid; in the catalogue of 1338 he is joined by Terence, Virgil, Horace, Lucan, Juvenal, Statius. Ovid was the favourite poet, and a special, though a curious, object of moralisation. Numerous translations of the Latin classics were made for John of France and Charles V., showing that much attention and interest was already drawn to these works; but the frequent mistakes show also how imperfect was the mastery of them by that age.

The Council of Vienne, in 1311, decreed that at the Court of Rome, and in the four Universities of Paris, Oxford, Bologna, and Salamanca, there should be classes of Hebrew, Arabic, and Chaldee. Pope Clement V. is said to have at the same time enjoined the study and teaching of Greek. It is certain that in the monasteries of the Dominicans, who for their missions in the East needed the Oriental languages, individuals acquired a knowledge of them; the Dominicans of Dijon in 1439 give themselves, in a document which has been preserved, the name of *Massorii*, as the inheritors of the tradition of the Jewish doctors. The same order, renowned for its devotion to learning, sent members of its body to learn Greek in Greece itself, and as early as the 13th century produced translations of Aristotle, Plato, and Proclus. But it is evident that the study of Greek and the Oriental languages was confined to a few individuals, and did not pass into the general school instruction of the time; for the project of founding the study of these languages, as something still lacking to the schools, appears again and again in the 15th century. In 1455, and again twenty-five years later, the schools of Paris propose the establishment of a chair of Hebrew, as still a desideratum; and an envoy of the Greek Emperor, Manuel Palæologus, found at Lyons, in 1395, no one who could understand his language.

The eminence of the University of Paris was in the scholastic philosophy; its culminating moment was the 14th century, its greatness was mediæval. It did not follow the growth

of the time, assimilate the new studies of the Renaissance and
the 16th century, make itself their organ, and animate with
them the French schools of which it was the head. Ramus, the
chief representative among French teachers of the new studies
and their spirit, who took as the subject of his thesis for the
degree of master of arts: *Quæcumque ab Aristotele dicta essent,
commentitia esse*—marking thereby the gulf which had begun
to separate men's spirit from the old learning—Ramus, though
he began his career as a servitor at the College of Navarre,
passed his life in bitter conflict with the University, by which
he was twice condemned, once for his anti-Aristotelian heresies,
once for his Calvinism. The languor of the retrograde spirit
took possession of the University, and, with the University,
of the colleges and schools of France, which depended on it.
The one learned institution which imbibed the spirit of the
Renaissance, which seriously established, for the first time in
France, instruction in Greek and Hebrew, which kept meeting
by the creation of successive chairs, chairs for mathematics,
philosophy, medicine and surgery, anatomy and botany, the
wants of the modern spirit, and which was spared by the Revolution when all the other public establishments for education
were swept away,—the College of France,—this institution was
a royal foundation of Francis the First's, and unconnected with
the University. A few names like that of Rollin stand out in
the annals of the University teaching of France, between the
Renaissance and the Revolution, and command respect; but in
general this teaching was without life and progress.

The Jesuits invaded the province long ruled by the University alone. By that adroit management of men for which they
have always been eminent, and by the more liberal spirit of
their methods, they outdid in popularity their superannuated
rival. Their first school at Paris was established in 1565, and
in 1762, two years before their dissolution, they had eighty-six
colleges in France. They were followed by the Port Royalists,
the Benedictines, the Oratorians. The Port Royal schools, from
which perhaps a powerful influence upon education might
have been looked for, restricted this influence by limiting very
closely the number of their pupils. Meanwhile the main funds

and endowments for public education in France were in the
University's hands, and its administration of these was as ineffective as its teaching. The only college whose pecuniary
state was solid was the College of Navarre, and Navarre was
5   administered not by the University, but by the *Cour des
Comptes*. The University had originally, as sources of revenue,
the Post Office and the *Messageries,* or Office of Public Con-
veyance; it had long since been obliged to abandon the Post
Office to Government, when in 1719 it gave up to the same au-
10   thority the privilege of the *Messageries,* receiving in return
from the State a yearly revenue of 150,000 livres. For this payment, moreover, it undertook the obligation of making the
instruction in all its principal colleges gratuitous. Paid or
gratuitous, however, its instruction was quite inadequate to the
15   wants of the time, and when the Jesuits were expelled from
France in 1764, their establishments closed, and their services
as teachers lost, the void that was left was strikingly apparent,
and public attention began to be drawn to it. It is well known
how Rousseau among writers, and Turgot among statesmen,
20   busied themselves with schemes of education; but the interest
in the subject must have reached the whole body of the community, for the instructions of all three orders of the States
General in 1789 are unanimous in demanding the reform of
education, and its establishment on a proper footing.
25   Then came the Revolution, and the work of reform soon
went swimmingly enough, so far as the abolition of the old
schools was concerned. In 1791 the colleges were all placed
under the control of the administrative authorities; in 1792
the jurisdiction of the University was abolished; in 1793 the
30   property of the colleges was ordered to be sold, the proceeds
to be taken by the State; in September of the same year the
suppression of all the great public schools and of all the University faculties was pronounced. For the work of reconstruction Condorcet's memorable plan had in 1792 been submitted
35   to the Committee of Public Instruction appointed by the Legislative Assembly. This plan proposed a secondary school for
every 4,000 inhabitants; for each department, a departmental
institute, or higher school; nine *lycées,* schools carrying their

studies yet higher than the departmental institute, for the whole of France; and to crown the edifice, a National Society of Sciences and Arts, corresponding in the main with the present Institute of France. The whole expense of national instruction was to be borne by the State, and this expense was estimated at 29,000,000 of francs.

But 1792 and 1793 were years of furious agitation, when it was easier to destroy than to build. Condorcet perished with the Girondists, and the reconstruction of public education did not begin till after the fall of Robespierre. The decrees of the Convention for establishing the Normal School, the Polytechnic, the School of Mines, and the *écoles centrales*, and then Daunou's law in 1795, bore, however, many traces of Condorcet's design. Daunou's law established primary schools, central schools, special schools, and at the head of all the Institute of France, this last a memorable and enduring creation, with which the old French Academy became incorporated. By Daunou's law, also, freedom was given to private persons to open schools. The new legislation had many defects. There was no provision for the reception of boarders in the central schools. There was no hierarchy of teachers; all the professors were of equal rank and independent one of another. The country, too, was not yet settled enough for its education to organise itself successfully. The Normal School speedily broke down; the central schools were established slowly and with difficulty; in the course of the four years of the Directory there were nominally instituted ninety-one of these schools, but they never really worked. More was accomplished by private schools, to which full freedom was given by the new legislation, at the same time that an ample and open field lay before them.

They could not, however, suffice for the work, and education was one of the matters for which Napoleon, when he became Consul, had to provide. Fourcroy's law, in 1802, took as the basis of its school-system secondary schools, whether established by the communes or by private individuals; the Government undertook to aid these schools by grants for buildings, for scholarships, and for gratuities to the masters; it prescribed Latin, French, geography, history, and mathematics

as the instruction to be given in them. They were placed under
the superintendence of the prefects. To continue and complete the secondary schools were instituted the lyceums; here
the instruction was to be Greek and Latin, rhetoric, logic,
literature, moral philosophy, and the elements of the mathematical and physical sciences. The pupils were to be of four
kinds: *boursiers nationaux*, scholars nominated to scholarships
by the State; pupils from the secondary schools, admitted as
free scholars by competition; paying boarders, and paying day-
scholars. Three Inspectors-General were appointed for these
schools, who were to be assisted by three Commissioners taken
from the Institute.

Chapter II

The French Secondary Schools from the Consulate to the Present Time

University of France. The Present Organisation of the French Secondary Schools is Founded under the First Empire—The French Secondary Schools under the Restoration and the Government of July 1830—Revolution of February, 1848—Change in Position of the University of France—Organic School Law of March 15, 1850 —The French Secondary Schools from 1850 to the Present Time.

The work now really began, and the present secondary instruction of France dates directly from the Consulate. The four greatest of the old schools of Paris were adopted, renamed,* and set to work. In the course of a year and a half 30 *lycées* and 250 secondary schools were started and in operation. More than 350 private schools received aid, while inspectors-general and members of the Institute traversed France to ascertain the educational condition of the country, and what were its more pressing requirements. The Normal School, the unique and best part of French secondary instruction, was launched at last; 'a boarding establishment for 300 pupils, for the purpose of training them in the art of teaching the letters and sciences.' In 1810 it was fairly at work. Meanwhile, from 1806 to 1808, Napoleon had established the centre in which all these schools, and all the schools of France, were to meet, the new University, the University of France. The freedom of teaching conceded by the Revolution was now withdrawn, for the control of the whole public instruction of France belonged henceforth to the University, no school being allowed to exist without the authorisation of its Grand-Master, no schoolmaster to give instruction unless he was a member of

* The *Lycée Impérial*, the *Lycée Napoléon*, the *Lycée Charlemagne*, and the *Lycée Bonaparte*.

the University and graduated in one of its faculties. These faculties were five,—theology, law, medicine, letters, mathematical
and physical sciences. The grades were three,—the baccalaureate, the licence, the doctorate. The licence answers to our
degree of master of arts. Twenty-seven *académies*, or University centres, each with its rector, council, and staff of inspectors,
were formed in the principal towns of France, and they carried
on, under the authority of the grand-master at Paris, the administration of the University.

The University was not a mere department of that State, it
was an endowed corporation. It had a revenue of about 2,500,-
000 of francs. Of this the fixed part proceeded from a permanent charge, granted to the University, of 400,000 francs a year
upon the public funds, and from the property, real and personal, of the old universities and colleges, so far as this property
was still unappropriated and at the State's disposal. This latter
source proved so inconsiderable that the average income ac-
cruing to the University from the whole of its landed estates
did not exceed 16,000 francs a year. The variable portion of
the University revenues was far the most important. This con-
sisted of dues paid for examinations and degrees, and of a contribution, one-twentieth of the fee paid for their schooling,
from all the scholars in the secondary schools of France. With
these revenues the University paid the expenses of its administration, the expenses of its faculties, and the charge of the Normal School. The public scholarships founded in the lyceums
and the insignificant contribution made at that time by the
State towards the expenses of primary instruction were paid
in the form of a subvention from the Minister of the Interior.

The legislation of the Empire accomplished little for the
primary instruction of France, but the secondary instruction it
established on a firm footing, and with the organisation which
in the main it still retains. In 1809 a statute restored to Greek
and Latin their old preponderance in this instruction, effacing
a mark which the Revolution, by the prominence given to
scientific and mathematical studies, had left upon it. It thus
resumed the mainly classical character common to it in the
corresponding institutions all through Europe. In 1813 the

Empire had thirty-six *lycées*, with 14,492 pupils, of whom 3,500 held public scholarships; in the private schools,—if private they can be called, when their teachers had to be members of the University, their studies and discipline to admit University inspection, and their students to pay the University   5 tax,—there were 30,000 pupils. The Restoration changed the title of the public schools from *lycée* to that of *collége royal*, and made an important division of the subvention paid by the State to secondary instruction, assuring part of it to the maintenance of the public scholarships, part of it to the payment   10 of the teaching staff. The whole of the subvention had hitherto gone to pay the scholarships endowed by the State, and the teaching staff had been paid out of the school-fees of the pupils. In the disasters of France the number of pupils in the schools fell off greatly, and their payments became irregular.   15 The Government of the Restoration wished to secure the position of the teaching staff, which had thus become very precarious. In order to effect this, it increased its subvention, but paid fewer scholarships than formerly, in order that it might pay teachers instead. The municipalities, as well as the State,   20 had by the legislation of the Empire been bound to provide a certain number of scholarships in the *lycées* with which they were locally connected. But the municipalities, and even that of Paris, had already, in the general pressure, resisted the obligation of providing their own share of scholarships; and when   25 the State, reducing its own number of scholarships, left that of the municipalities unaltered, and besides ordered the prefects to see that they were regularly paid, the resistance grew stronger still. The government had to yield to it, and the number of scholarships at the charge of the municipalities was   30 reduced by nearly one-half, while the reduction in the number of State scholarships was still maintained. The amount of free schooling in the French *lycées* was therefore seriously diminished. This diminution, however, was not ill-suited to the circumstances of the time, and soon began to be viewed with   35 favour. With the reviving prosperity of France families of the middle class became more and more capable of themselves meeting the moderate charge of their children's education; the

higher class, about whose ability to pay there could be no question, but who had hesitated to avail themselves of the new public schools, began more and more to use them; and a class whom
the prodigal supply of State scholarships had attracted to the
State schools, a class without the means of purchasing from their
own resources a liberal education, were, it was said, not proper
recipients of such an education, were rendered useless and
discontented citizens by it, and would be the better for being
excluded from it. So strong was the feeling in favour of this
exclusion, that at the very outset of the new and liberal Government of 1830, the report of a Commission recommended it
to the Chamber of Deputies in urgent and even harsh terms.
At the same time the better payment and the continued extension of the teaching staff in the public schools were desired
on all sides. Under this impulsion the State grant for scholarships steadily declined, that for the teaching staff steadily increased. Between 1815 and 1830 that for the former sank from
988,000 francs to 822,300; that for the latter rose from 812,-
000 francs to 927,500. The Government of Louis Philippe,
having undertaken the serious task of dealing with primary
education, was unable at first to give much attention to secondary; when, however, M. Guizot's memorable law of 1833
had founded primary instruction, a succession of ministers set
themselves to improve and develop the secondary schools.
The number of *lycées* had risen, under the Restoration, from
34 to 40; under the Government of July it rose to 54. The
contribution of the State to their support greatly increased.
But the increase was entirely for the fixed expenses, as they
are called, of the public schools, expenses in which the payment
of the teaching staff forms the grand item. These, from 920,000
francs, which was their amount in 1830, had risen, when the
Revolution of February overthrew the Government of July,
to 1,500,000 francs. The subvention for scholarships had fallen
in the same period from 822,300 francs to 710,950 francs.

The University had been made by Napoleon an endowed
corporation, and not a ministerial department, in order to
give it more stability and greater independence. The grand-
master was, however, to all intents and purposes, the Minister

of Public Instruction, and when in 1824 the head of the University, M. de Frayssinous, took this title of Minister, the change was one of name and not of substance. But the spirit of uniformity and method which the French bring to their system of public accounts is very strict, and gradually it began to be said that the University was in fact a public department with a special budget of its own, collecting and spending its revenues without supervision or responsibility, and that this was bad public economy. It was urged that the University ought to bring its estimates before the Chamber of Deputies, submit its accounts to the regular auditors of the national expenditure, and collect its revenues through the agency of the public collectors. The *Cour des Comptes* obtained an order to have the University accounts laid before it, and it found them irregular and unsatisfactory. In 1834, after a long discussion, the special budget of the University was suppressed, and the collection of its revenues and the control of its accounts assimilated to that of the other public departments. It was left in the possession of its endowment and property, an honour more nominal than real, since it no longer had the management of them; but it was thought that by retaining, as the possessor of an endowment and of property, the character of a *personne civile*, it might attract bequests and fresh endowments,* of which a department of State had no chance.

* So many questions arise, in England, about endowed schools, that I will take this opportunity of saying what is the state of the law, in France, about endowments for education.

These endowments are of far less importance in France than in England. In the first place the Revolution made a clean sweep of all old endowments; what exist date from a time since the Revolution. In the second place the French law sets limits to a man's power of disposing of his property, which in England do not exist. In France by the *Code Napoléon* (Art. 913, and the articles following) if a man leaves one legitimate child, he may dispose of one-half of his property, and no more, away from him; if he leaves two, he may dispose of one-third, and no more; if he leaves more than two, of one-fourth, and no more. If he has no children, a certain proportion of his property is similarly secured to his nearest representatives within certain limits. The amount of property free to be disposed of in benefactions is thus smaller in France than in England.

Its schools meanwhile continued to prosper, and had never been in so flourishing a condition as they were when the Rev-

---

In England a man names an individual to be trustee, or a number of individuals to be trustees, to carry into effect a charitable bequest, on
5 conditions assigned by him at pleasure. In France this cannot be done. A founder must entrust his bequest for charitable purposes to a *personne civile*, defined as an *être fictif, auquel la loi reconnaît une partie des droits qui appartiennent aux personnes ordinaires, et qui peuvent recevoir des libéralités.* Such a *personne civile* must be either a public establish-
10 ment (for instance, a public hospital, a parish church, a commune) or an establishment of public utility.

An establishment, not being a public establishment, can only be made an establishment of public utility, and capable therefore of receiving an endowment, by a decree of the Council of State, a body which prepares
15 Government bills, and is, besides, the highest administrative body in France, to which the most important matters of administration,—conflicts between the different departments of State, questions of jurisdiction between the administrative and the judicial authority, &c.,—are brought for final settlement.

20 The recipient, therefore, of an endowment must be a *personne civile;* but to enable even a *personne civile* to accept an endowment an express authorisation of the administrative authority is in each case required, and the natural heirs are heard on the other side. They are not heard on any point of law; if any such arises it goes to the ordinary legal tribunals;
25 they are heard on the question whether the bequest was a proper one for a man in the testator's condition of family and fortune to make. In some cases it is the prefect who gives this authorisation, with the advice of the *conseil de préfecture;* in general, and always when there is opposition on the heirs' part, it is the Council of State.

30 Illegal, immoral, or impossible conditions attached to a benefaction or bequest, are by the law of France null and void. The Council of State calls upon the living donor to rectify such conditions before his benefaction can take effect; in the case of a bequest, authorisation is given with reserve as to illegal conditions, which are set aside.

35 A bequest to an establishment for purposes not within the legal attributions of that establishment is thus set aside. For instance, if a bequest is left to a church for a school, it cannot take effect, because the law does not recognise school-keeping as an attribution of a church; so the Council of State authorises the commune, which is by law a school-keeping
40 establishment, to accept jointly with the church, and the commune manages the bequest.

Again, a bequest to an elementary communal school, saddled with the condition that the school shall be taught by the religious for ever, is set aside, because the school law of France gives to the communal and de-

olution of February broke out. Their pupils, 9,000 in 1809, 15,000 in 1830, numbered 20,000 in 1848. Their grant from Government at that time reached, as I have already mentioned, the sum of 1,500,000 francs; the sums received from scholars' fees for board and instruction exceeded 6,200,000 francs. The staff of professors and other school functionaries had never been so fully organised or so well paid. But the University had enemies whose attacks grew with time stronger and stronger; of these enemies the most persevering, passionate, and formidable were the clergy. Its lay character made it particularly obnoxious to them; they constantly assailed it with the charge that it instructed and did not educate; they attacked its constitution, its studies, the orthodoxy of its teachers, and even

———

partmental authority the right of deciding for themselves whether a communal school shall be under lay teaching or the teaching of the religious. A condition giving to an authority other than that named by the school law of France the nomination of a communal teacher, or the selection of the free scholars in a communal school, would be equally invalid. So would a condition forbidding a private school to be under Government inspection, or enabling it to be under an uncertificated teacher; because by the French law all schools, private as well as public, must admit inspection, and must have a certificated teacher. Private schools are at present not inspected as to their teaching; there is now before the Council of State a law for putting under inspection the teaching as well as the buildings, healthiness, morals, &c., of private schools which enjoy their endowment by virtue of an authorisation.

It is to be remembered that public establishments and recognised establishments of public utility, have their rules of management for institutions depending upon them, which cannot be set aside by the directions of a testator. A commune is a public establishment, and the school of a commune follows a certain order of management fixed for such institutions. The congregation of the Christian Brothers is a recognised establishment of public utility, and the order of management of the Christian Brothers' schools is fixed by the statutes of the congregation, statutes which have had to obtain the Government's sanction.

In general, therefore, the action of founders is greatly limited in France, as compared with England.

A proper *personne civile* having been properly authorised to enjoy an endowment, the administrative authority does not further interfere. A man's heirs, however, may, if the legal conditions of his endowment are not complied with, bring an action before the ordinary legal tribunals for a restitution of the property to them.

their morality. It is difficult perhaps to find a perfectly precise sense for the charge that an institution instructs and does not educate, but it is well known with what great and damaging effect this charge can be used. The monopoly of the University made the charge the more dangerous, at the same time that this monopoly recruited the ranks of the University's chief assailants, the priests, with auxiliaries from quarters the most opposite, whose interests or whose principles it wounded. With the fall of the Orleans dynasty fell the privilege of the University. In 1848 the government of General Cavaignac struck the first blow at its academical organisation, which had remained unchanged since the Emperor Napoleon's decree first founded it in 1808. The 27 academies, which had carried on the administration of the University for forty years, were reduced to 20. Then came the law of March 15, 1850, the organic law which now governs public instruction in France, and which transformed the regulation of this instruction completely. By this law persons not members of the University became free to open schools, and the exclusive privilege of the University ceased. The shadow of a corporate and endowed existence which had been left to it ceased also; its endowment no longer appeared as an item of the public debt, its estates were made part of the public domain. Eighty-six academies, one for each department of France, at first replaced the old academical organisation of 1808; but very soon * these 86 academies were reduced to 16, each academy including in its district several departments; and this is the organisation in force at the present moment.

Before I come to the schools as they now exist a few words must be given to the immediate effect produced upon them by the legislation of 1850. The unsettled state of the times, the derangement of many private fortunes, and the opening of a number of private schools, at first affected the *lycées* very unfavourably. The sums received from the pupils in them for board and lodging fell from 6,204,693 francs in 1848 to 5,191,-666 francs in 1851. This diminution in the receipts, as the State refused to make it good, necessitated a reduction in the pay-

* In 1854.

ments to teachers and functionaries. With all the economy that could be exercised the embarrassment was great and increasing, when the government, in 1853, hit on the simple expedient of raising the fees for board and schooling, which had remained nearly stationary since they were first fixed in 1802. The fee for board in a Paris *lycée* had been 600, 700, 800, or 900 francs, according to the pupil's place in the school. It was now fixed at 950, 1,050, 1,150, and 1,500 francs. The fee for schooling, which had at first been a uniform fee of 60 francs, and then had been raised to 100 francs, was made, according to the subjects taught, 120, 150, 200, or 250 francs. Proportionate additions were made to the school charges in the departments, where these charges are always lower than in Paris.

Far from emptying the public schools, this rise in their charges answered perfectly. The old charges had been very low, the new charges were not in themselves high, and were accompanied by an improved and developed programme of studies. The return of tranquillity and the growing wealth and prosperity of the country enabled families to support them the more easily. The *lycées* filled again, and the new scale of charges produced an addition of 800,000 francs in the yearly amount received from their scholars. In 1855 the number of *lycées*, which had been 54 before the February Revolution, had risen to 63; the number of pupils in them, which had fallen to 19,000 in 1851, had in 1855 increased to 21,219. The communal colleges at the charge of the towns where they are situated had been less successful. The law of 1850 required every town which wished to preserve its communal college to bind itself to pay for five years its teachers' salaries; several municipalities refused to saddle themselves with this obligation. Their colleges passed out of their hands into those of a private proprietor, generally an ecclesiastic; and thus out of the spoils of the communal colleges, though not out of those of the *lycées*, the new private schools which the law of 1850 admitted into existence did, to a certain extent, enrich themselves. In 1857 the communal colleges were only 244 in number, having been 306 in 1849; eight of the chief of them, however, had in the meanwhile been converted into *lycées*. The pupils in the communal colleges had numbered 31,706 in 1849; in 1855 they numbered only 28,219.

So the public secondary schools of France had, in 1855, in round numbers, 49,500 scholars. The total expenditure for these schools was (again in round numbers) 19,500,000 francs, or 780,000*l*. The expenditure for the *lycées* was 480,000*l*.; that for the communal colleges 300,000*l*. For the *lycées* the State contributed about 76,000*l*.;* for the communal colleges, which are municipal institutions, barely 4,000*l*. The State subvention for 1855 to French secondary instruction may be put, therefore, at about 80,000*l*.; the municipal subvention to the communal colleges amounted to nearly the same sum. There remained 620,000*l*. (216,000*l*. for the communal colleges, 404,-000*l*. for the *lycées*) to be raised by the schools themselves. The State subvention, exclusive of the grant for scholarships, gave, in 1847,† an average of 28,900 francs for each of the 54 *lycées* then existing; in 1855, when the *lycées* numbered 63, the State subvention of the year gave an average of but 20,665 fr. for each *lycée*. The aid was insufficient even with the increased fees charged, and the total expenditure for 1855 on the *lycées* outran the total receipts by 354,052 francs, about 14,160*l*.

At the present moment France has 74 *lycées*, 20 more than she had in 1847, and 11 more than she had in 1855. She has 247 communal colleges, 59 less than she had in 1849, but three more than she had in 1857. In these schools she has 65,832 scholars; 32,794 in the *lycées*, 33,038 in the communal colleges. Thus the 74 *lycées* have very nearly as many pupils as all the 247 communal colleges together. And while the number of pupils in the *lycées* tends to increase, and is about 1,000 more this year than last, in the communal colleges it tends slightly to diminish, and is about 100 less. The state schools have altogether 15,000 more scholars than in 1855, a sign of the advance of the country in prosperity. The amount of state aid received by them is much higher than in 1855, a time of re-

---

* 1,301,908 fr. for the *dépenses fixes*, and 635,237 fr. for scholarships.
† In this year the subvention was 1,560,750 fr.

duction and distress; it reaches, including the grant for state scholarships, 3,000,000 of francs in round numbers, a third more than in 1855, 120,000*l*. now to 80,000*l*. then. Of this sum the *lycées* receive 1,900,000 fr. for their fixed expenses, and 868,000 for bursarships; * the communal colleges receive 223,000 fr., having received less than 100,000 fr. in 1855. The mean rate of grant to each *lycée* is still, however, slightly below what it was in 1847, though nearly one-third greater than the rate of 1855. It is intended to place a *lycée* in every department of France, and five new ones are at the present time in progress.

* The actual number of bursarships in the French *lycées* is now 1,057, divided among 1,588 holders. It is worthy of note that the ten colleges of Paris alone, before the Revolution, had 1,046 bursars, almost the number of the bursarships for the whole of France at present.

Chapter III

Government, Administration, and Teaching Staff of the French Secondary Schools at Present

Government, Administration, and Organisation of the French Secondary Schools—Ministry of Public Instruction—Imperial Council of Public Instruction—Academic Councils—Departmental Councils —Inspectors-General—Administration of the French Lycées— Regulations as to their Functionaries and Professors—Aggregation —The Normal School—Position and Payment of Teachers in the French Lycées.

He who has seen one *lycée* or communal college in France, I will not say has seen all, but at any rate may consider that he can form for himself a pretty accurate notion of all. In all, the course of studies is very nearly the same, following pro-
5   grammes drawn up by authority. In all, the books used are very nearly the same, specified in a list drawn up by authority. In all, the professors and principal functionaries of every kind are appointed by the Minister of Public Instruction, and can be dismissed by him. In all, the arrangement and training of
10   classes, the arrangements for boarding, the hours of work and recreation, the means of recreation, the mode of government, and the whole system of discipline, are the same.

The Minister of Public Instruction is the head of this vast organisation. His office, in Paris, has six divisions, under him-
15   self and his secretary-general. Each of these six divisions has its chief, and is divided into two bureaux, each, again, with its head. First come the three divisions for superior instruc-tion, secondary instruction, primary instruction. The first bureau of each of these is for the *personnel* of the branch of
20   public instruction administered by the division,—treats, that is, all matters relating to persons, appointments, and studies;

the second bureau is for the *matériel* and *comptabilité,—* whatever relates to buildings, finance, or accounts. The three remaining divisions have charge, one, of the department's business with the Institute and with the public libraries; another, of its business with the scientific and literary establishments (such as the Museum of Natural History, the French school at Athens, the observatories of Paris and Marseilles, &c.) in connection with it; the third, of the expense of the central office, and of the general revision of the whole finance and accounts of the department. Under the Minister's presidency is the Imperial Council of Public Instruction, which in concert with him fixes the programmes of study in the state schools and the books to be used in them. It is also consulted as to the formation of new state schools, and as to the whole legislation and regulation of French public instruction. The important measures which have lately been introduced and passed for the furtherance of professional instruction, as it is called,—measures of which I shall have to speak presently, —were all of them thus brought by M. Duruy, the present minister, before the Council, and there discussed. Certain members of the Council formerly proceeded from election; in 1852, under the pressure which then caused, in France, the strengthening of the hand of government everywhere, proposal by the Minister of Public Instruction and nomination by the President of the Republic was substituted for election in these cases. The Emperor still nominates on the Minister's proposal; but M. Duruy's disposition has certainly been rather to enlarge the part of action for others than to keep all action for himself; thus he has lately given to the functionaries of public instruction, whom the law of 1852 gave him the power to dismiss off-hand, the security of a committee of five, chosen out of the Council of Public Instruction, by whom the case of the functionary whose conduct may be in question is to be examined, his defence heard, and the merits of the case reported on.

But the names of the actual members of the Council guarantee its fitness for its functions, whether it comes from election or from nomination. The Minister is the President, and

M. de Royer, the Chief President of the *Cour des Comptes,*
is Vice-President. The great bodies of State are represented,
so is the Church, so are the Protestants, so are the Jews, so
is the law, so is the Institute, so are the schools, public and
5   private. There are thirty-two members, with a secretary; and
among the thirty-two, not to speak of the great official personages, are M. Franck, M. Silvestre de Sacy, M. Guigniaut, M.
Milne-Edwards, M. Michel Chevalier, M. Ravaisson, M. Dumas
the chemist, M. Le Verrier, and M. Nisard. It will not be dis-
10 puted that these are men whose opinion on matters of instruction may with propriety and advantage be asked.

After the Imperial Council come the Academic Councils.
By the law of 1854, as I have said, the number of the academies,
or University centres, was fixed at 16. They are now, by the
15 addition of academies for Savoy and Algiers, 18. The Minister
of Public Instruction is the titular Rector of the Academy of
Paris, and the ordinary functions of the rectorate are in this
academy discharged by the Vice-Rector. In the other academies they are discharged by the Rector, who must have the
20 degree of doctor in one of the faculties, and who is the head
of the superior and secondary instruction of the departments
which form the district of his academy, and the president of
the academic council. The main control of primary instruction,
including the right of nominating the schoolmasters, was in
25 1854, by a change made from political reasons, but which
nearly all friends of education condemn, taken away from the
rectors and given to the prefects. The rectors are assisted by
academy inspectors, of whom there must be one at least (at
Paris by a special rule there are eight) for each department
30 comprised in the academy. As there are only 17 academies for
France, most of them, of course, have a district of several
departments; the academic centre, the residence of the rector
and the seat of the faculties, is in general placed in the most
important chief town of their departments. In the other depart-
35 ments of the district the academy inspectors exercise in fact
the functions of rector, having their offices in the several chief
towns, entering the names of candidates for degrees in the different faculties, and inspecting the public schools. All their

reports on these schools converge, however, to the centre of the academy, to the rector's office; and from these reports, from the reports of the immediate authorities of the schools, and from his own inspections, the rector makes up the monthly report which he is bound to transmit to the Minister in Paris. With the rector is placed, to form his council, not only the academy inspectors of his district, but also the deans of faculties, and seven other members chosen every three years by the Minister. These seven are an archbishop or bishop from the district, two ministers of the Catholic, Protestant, or Jewish worship, two members of the magistrature, and two public functionaries or other notables of the district. The well-known M. Coquerel is thus a member of the academic council of Paris, and M. Devienne, the First President of the *Cour Impériale*, is another. This council consists of some 30 members in the academy of Paris, where the academy inspectors are very numerous; in the other academies it consists of from 15 to 20 members. It holds two sessions a year, lasting about a fortnight each, when it receives reports from the academy inspectors and deans of faculties on the whole instruction of the district, and deals with all questions which come before it respecting the administration, finance, discipline, or teaching of the public schools.

There is also, for each department of France, a Departmental Council, of which the prefect is president, and the academy inspector, a primary inspector, the bishop and an ecclesiastic named by him, a representative of the Protestant and of the Jewish communions, the chief law-officer of government in the department, a judge, and three or four members of the Council General,* are members. The primary inspector, the Protestant and Jewish representatives, the judge, and the members of the Council General, are named by the Minister of Public Instruction. This departmental council has to do with primary rather than secondary instruction; with the public secondary schools it does not meddle, but certain matters affecting the private secondary schools come before it from the

* The Council General is an elective body consisting of the notables of the department.

academic authority, with appeal to the Imperial Council of
Public Instruction in Paris. Of these matters I shall speak by-
and-by. The departmental council meets twice a month.

Besides the Minister, the Imperial Council, and the academic authorities, six inspectors-general have special superintendence of secondary instruction. Three of these inspectors
are for letters, three for sciences; every year they are sent by
the Minister on tours of inspection, and they visit the *lycées,*
the more important communal colleges, and a certain number
of private secondary schools.

Now I come to the *lycées* themselves. Their administration,
properly so called, is in the hands of a provisor, a censor, and
a steward, who themselves take no part in the teaching, but
who admit the scholars, correspond with the parents, keep the
accounts, manage all the household economy, superintend the
discharge of his duties by each member of the establishment,
and maintain the discipline. There are also two or more chaplains, and the great *lycées* of Paris, which receive a very large
number of boarders, have also a certain number of officers,
with the title of General Superintendents, attached to the governing body. To all French *lycées* is attached a Council of
Administration, revising the conduct of their business affairs,
and each academy has a Commission of Health, charged with
the care of the sanitary interests of the establishments of public
instruction in the academic district. A Central Commission of
Health exists for the special benefit of the Paris *lycées.* But,
in the first instance, the governing and administering body in
a French *lycée* consists of these three functionaries,—the *proviseur,* who is the chief of all, the *censeur,* and the *économe*
or steward. Then come the teachers, professors of different
degrees of rank. Then the *maîtres répétiteurs,* on whom falls
the task of that constant supervision of the boys out of class
hours, for which French schools have with us in England such
a notoriety. The professors give their lessons and are then free
to depart. They have nothing whatever to do with the boys
out of school hours. The *maîtres répétiteurs,* or *maîtres d'étude,*
as they are more generally called,—the ushers, as we should
call them,—are with the boys when they are preparing their

lessons, and at their meals, and at their recreation, and in their dormitories. The highest class of these ushers assists the boys in the preparation of their lessons; a lower and far larger class is inadequate for this task of tutor, and is simply charged with the duty of superintending and reporting.

All these functionaries, from the *proviseur* to the *maître d'étude*, are nominated by the minister. The *proviseur* and the rector, indeed, present for the minister's acceptance candidates for the post of *maître d'étude* and of teacher of the lower classes in the communal colleges; and the rector has to keep a record of service and seniority among the professors in the *lycées* of his academy, which record, no doubt, guides the minister in making his nomination. Still the mass of patronage vested in the minister must appear to our eyes extraordinary. But it is right to say that the law in France has imposed conditions on the minister's exercise of his patronage which inevitably keep it within strict bounds. As the rector must be a doctor in some faculty, and the academy-inspector must be a licentiate (intermediate between a bachelor and a doctor, and answering to our master), so each functionary of the *lycée*, from the *proviseur* to the *maître d'étude*, must present some guarantee of intellectual capacity. The *proviseur* must be a licentiate. The *maître d'étude* must be a bachelor of letters or sciences. But it is for the professor's office that the most stringent security is required. To be a full professor (*professeur titulaire*) the title of *agrégé de lycée* is necessary. We have nothing corresponding to this in England. It is not a university grade but a special certificate or diploma. The examination for it requires the possession of a university grade, and covers the whole ground of the intended professor's teaching. The title exists for superior instruction also; there are *agrégés de faculté* as well as *agrégés de lycée;* to be full professor in a faculty, indeed, guarantees beyond the *agrégation* (for example, the rank of doctor or of member of the Institute) are demanded; but even to be acting professor (*professeur suppléant*) in a faculty, the title of *agrégé* in that faculty must be obtained; and to obtain it the candidate has to pass a strict examination in the matters which he will have to teach.

The *agrégés de lycée* are of seven orders, corresponding to
the kinds of instruction given in the *lycées*. There are *agrégés*
for the classes of mathematics, of natural sciences, of philosophy, of higher classics, of lower classics, of history and geog-
5   raphy, of modern languages. To be an *agrégé* for any one of
them the candidate must be twenty-five years old, and must
have had five years' practice of teaching in a public or private
school. A certain maturity and experience are thus ensured
at the outset. Then the intending *agrégé* for the classes of math-
10 ematics must possess the degree of licentiate of mathematics,
and that of licentiate either of physics or of natural sciences;
for the classes of natural sciences the same; for the classes of
philosophy, the degree of licentiate of letters (master of arts),
and that of bachelor of sciences; for the higher classical divi-
15 sion, the degree of licentiate of letters; for the lower, the same;
for the classes of geography and history, the same; for those of
modern languages, a certificate of fitness (obtained only after
examination) to teach them.

These preliminary securities being taken, the candidates un-
20 dergo a written examination. If they fail in the written examination they are rejected. If they pass in it, they proceed
to a *viva voce* one. In every case the examination is based on
the programme of the classes for which the candidate wishes
to become *agrégé*, and the oral examination includes one or
25 more lessons delivered as if to a class. The programmes of the
different classes are, as I have already said, fixed by authority.
I will just mention in passing what the candidate for the
classes supérieures de lettres (higher classical division) has
to do. His paper-work consists of a piece of Latin verse, a
30 piece of translation from French into Greek and Latin, a piece
of translation from Greek into French, a Latin essay and a
French essay, one on a philosophical the other on a literary
subject, and a piece of translation into French from a modern
language, English or German. In his *viva voce* he has to correct
35 aloud two exercises of boys in the higher classical division
of a *lycée*, to translate with full comments and explanations
a passage from a Latin and Greek author read in the *lycées*,
and to comment on a passage from one of the French classics

read there. He has also to translate a passage from an English or German book. Finally, he has to give, as if to a class, a lesson on either grammar, classical literature, philosophy, history, or modern languages, at his own choice.

Having proved his fitness by his examination, the candidate 5 is then nominated professor in a class of the order for which he has obtained the title of *agrégé*. But he cannot be employed in a class of another order without obtaining by examination the title of *agrégé* for that class; thus an *agrégé* for the higher classical division cannot be employed in a mathematical class 10 or a class for natural sciences, nor can an *agrégé* for the lower classical division be employed in the higher. The spectacle so often seen in English schools of a classical master teaching, without any real acquaintance with his subject, mathematics, or modern languages, or history, is not to be seen in France. 15

The pupils of the Normal School (*École Normale Supé-rieure*) can hold the place of professor without being *agrégés;* but they cannot hold the more important and better paid post of *professeur titulaire* without this test, they can only be divisional,* acting, or assistant professors (*professeurs division-* 20 *naires, suppléants,* or *adjoints*). And the examinations of the Normal School are in themselves a test, and a very strict one, of the fitness of its pupils for their business. I have already mentioned this admirable institution; it enjoys a deserved celebrity out of France as well as at home, and nowhere else does there 25 exist anything quite like it. Decreed by the revolutionary Government, and set to work by that of the first Napoleon, it had two periods of difficulty,—one under the Restoration, when it attracted hostility as a nest of liberalism, and it was proposed to abate its importance by substituting for one central 30 Normal School several local ones; another after the revolution of February, when the grant to it was greatly reduced, and the number of its pupils fell off. But it has now recovered its grants and its numbers, and few institutions in France are so rooted in the public esteem. Its main function is to form teachers for 35

* The full professor (*professeur titulaire*) has the *class;* the class, if large, is divided, and the divisional professor has charge of a division, as contradistinguished from a class.

the public schools. It has two divisions; one literary, the other scientific. Its pupils at present number 110; they are all bursars, holding a scholarship of 40*l.* a year, which entirely provides for the cost of their maintenance. The course is a three years'
5 one; but a certain number of the best pupils are retained for a fourth and fifth year; these, however, are lost to the secondary schools, being prepared for the doctorate and for the posts of superior instruction, such as the professorships in the faculties.

Every Englishman who has been at Oxford or Cambridge
10 must in France remark with surprise that institutions like these universities of ours, taking a young man at the age of eighteen or nineteen, and continuing his education, with the shelter of a considerable, though modified, control and discipline till the age of twenty-three or twenty-four, seem to be
15 there, for laymen, quite wanting. It is true that in France, as in Germany, there is a superior instruction, a faculty instruction, much more complete than ours, and that our Oxford and Cambridge are, in fact, as Signor Matteucci, who had studied them well, said to me at Turin, not establishments of superior
20 instruction at all, but simply *hauts lycées*. This is true, and it is to be regretted that we have not a better organised superior instruction; still Oxford and Cambridge, in prolonging a young man's term of tuition and prolonging it under discipline, instead of his being thrown at large on the life of a great city,
25 Paris or London, where he follows lectures, are invaluable, and it is in this direction that foreigners may find most to envy in English education. But it must be remarked that there are great government schools in France which in some measure perform the part of Oxford and Cambridge, and supply yearly
30 a body of laymen whose intellectual training has been prolonged, under stringent discipline, for several years beyond boyhood; a body sufficient, even in itself, to keep society fed in the several departments of practice and knowledge with a number of intellectually trained men of a high order, and to
35 preserve the intellectual level from sinking. The Polytechnic School, which trains civil as well as military engineers for the State, the *École Forestière* (School of Woodcraft), the *École Impériale des Chartes*, the *École Française d'Athènes*, are

all of them establishments discharging this function. But the chief of the establishments which discharge it is the *École Normale Supérieure*. This school is in the Rue d'Ulm, in the old school quarter of Paris on the left bank of the Seine, where the Sorbonne, and by far the greater part of the *lycées* and centres of instruction, secondary and superior, are still to be found. The building is large and handsome, something like one of the more modern colleges at Oxford or Cambridge; it has chapel, library, and garden; the tricolour flag waves over the entrance to it. Everything is beautifully neat and well kept; the life in common which economy compels these great public establishments, in France, severely to practise, has,—when its details are precisely and perfectly attended to, and when, as at the *École Normale*, the resources allow a certain finish and comfort much beyond the strict necessary of the barrack or hospital,—a more imposing effect for the eye than the arrangements of college rooms, though I am far from saying the life in college rooms is not preferable. The pupils, even here, sleep in large dormitories, but the beds are screened from one another by partitions stopping short of the ceiling, in the fashion adopted in some of the more recent Normal Schools for our primary teachers here in England; each student has thus a small chamber to himself.

Last year 344 candidates presented themselves for 35 vacancies, and these candidates were all picked men. To compete, a youth must in the first place be over 18 years of age and under 24, must produce a medical certificate that he has no bodily infirmity unfitting him for the function of teacher, and a good-conduct certificate from his school. He must enter into an engagement to devote himself, if admitted, for 10 years to the service of public instruction, and he must hold the degree of bachelor of arts if he is a candidate in the literary section of the school, of bachelor of sciences if in the scientific. He then undergoes a preliminary examination, which is held at the same time at the centre of each academy throughout France. This examination weeds the candidates; those who pass through it come up to Paris for a final examination at the *École Normale*, and those who do best in this final examination

are admitted to the vacant scholarships. A bare list of subjects
of examination is never very instructive; the reader will better
understand what the final examination is, if I say that the candidates are the very *élite* of the *lycées*, who in the highest classes

5   of these *lycées* have gone through the course of instruction,
literary or scientific, there prescribed. In the scientific section
of the Normal School, the first year's course comprehends the
differential and integral calculus, and it will at once be seen
what advanced progress in the pupil such a course implies.

10 By a favour which has been very rarely accorded even to authorised inquirers, and for which I am very grateful, I was
permitted to be present at several of the lessons of the school,
and I can answer for the preparation and attention of the
pupils, and for the excellence of the teaching. Better lessons

15 than those which I heard on Lucretius's account of the plague
at Athens, on some chapters of Thucydides, and on the
Femmes Savantes of Molière, better, whether as respects the
lecturer's performance or the students', I really cannot imagine.
I also heard a mathematical lesson; on the merits of such a les-

20 son I am unfortunately,—and it is a misfortune I had continually to regret while discharging my errand,—most incompetent
to give an opinion; but here too I could see and admire the
evident easy mastery of the lecturer over his subject, the rapidity with which he went, his constant and dexterous use of the

25 black board; while his hearers seemed all to be held in hand,
and to follow with a quickness and adroitness answering to
his own. In the third year there is a division in the scientific
section, some pupils giving their chief study to pure mathematics and astronomy, others to physics and natural sciences.

30 I found, as I have said, 110 pupils in the Normal School, all
bursars; commoners, to use our expression, are not received.
For these 110 students there are, besides the director-general
and a director of scientific studies and another of literary
studies, 23 professors, or *maîtres de conférences*, as in this

35 institution they are called. The professors are pretty equally
divided between letters and sciences. One of the most distinguished professors of the scientific section told me that in
this section they were a little under-officered, and that it would

be better if certain of the scientific lectures, which the students now have to go to the Sorbonne to hear, where the wants of the audience are not the same as theirs, could be given at the school itself, and by professors of the school. This really was the only drawback I could hear of to the complete efficiency of the school, and this, of course, was due to the common cause of such drawbacks, want of funds. The cost of the school last year was 307,610 fr.; in round numbers, 12,300*l*. The library, laboratory, and collections seemed to me excellent.

The pupils have half-yearly examinations, and they are practised to some extent, and, under the present Minister, M. Duruy, more than ever before, in the *lycées* of Paris. The teaching of the professors keeps always in view the scholastic destination of their hearers. At the end of the third year's course the student who has passed through it with distinction is authorised to present himself at once for aggregation. Five years' school practice, it will be remembered, is required of other candidates. The less distinguished student is at once nominated to a *lycée*, but to the post of assistant professor only, not of full professor; after one year's service in the capacity of assistant professor he may present himself for aggregation.

I have been somewhat minute in describing how the body of professors in the French public schools is formed, because the best feature of these schools seems to me to be their thoroughly trained and tested staff of professors. They are far better paid than the corresponding body of teachers in Italy; they have a far more recognised and satisfactory position than the corresponding body of teachers in England. The latter are, no doubt, better paid; but, with the exception of the head masters of the great schools, who hold a position apart, who need eminent aptitudes for other things besides teaching, and who are very few in number, they form no hierarchy, have no position, are saddled, to balance their being better paid, with boarding-house cares, have little or no time for study, and no career before them. A French professor has his three, four, or five hours' work a day in lessons and conferences, and then he is free; he has nothing to do with the discipline or religious

teaching of the *lycée*, he has not to live in its precincts; he finishes his teaching and then he leaves the *lycée* and its cares behind him altogether. The provisor, the censor, the chaplains, the superintendents, have the business of government and di-
5 rection, and they are chosen on the ground of their aptitude for it. A young man wishing to follow a profession which keeps him in contact with intellectual studies and enables him to continue them, but who has no call and no talent for the trying post of teacher, governor, pastor, and man of business
10 all in one, will hesitate before he becomes a master in an English public school, but he may very well become a professor in a French one. Accordingly the service of public instruction in France attracts a far greater proportion of the intellectual force of the country than in England. At the head of the Nor-
15 mal School which I have just been describing is M. Nisard, a member of the French Academy, and the author of a well-known history of French literature; the director of the scientific studies is M. Pasteur, a member of the Institute, and one of the first chemists in Europe. Among the *maîtres de con-*
20 *férences* is M. Gaston Boissier, whose name English readers of the *Revue des Deux Mondes* will recall as the author of some excellent articles on Roman history which lately appeared there; M. Boissier is also one of the professors at the *Lycée Charlemagne*. In the scientific section is M. Hermite, whose
25 name every mathematician knows; M. Hermite is a member of the Institute. But besides names thus widely known, the professorate of the Normal School and *lycées* abounds in names honourably known in their own country as those of men of mark and honourable performance or honourable prom-
30 ise in their several departments of sciences or literature; such are the names (I quote almost at random) of MM. Briot, Berger, Bénard, Jules Girard, Étienne. Two of the most eminent of modern Frenchmen, M. Cousin and M. Villemain, were originally professors in the French public schools; they
35 were both, also, Ministers of Public Instruction. M. Duruy, the present Minister, was a professor, an author of a very good school-book, and an inspector. M. Taine and M. Prévost-Paradol, personages so important in the French literature of the

present day, were both of them distinguished pupils of the Normal School. It is clear that this abundance of eminent names gives dignity and consideration to the profession of public teaching in France; it tends to keep it fully supplied, and with men who carry weight with the pupils they teach, and command their intellectual respect. And this is a very important advantage.

The salary of a professor is composed of two parts, the fixed part and the eventual part, as they are called. The fixed salary of a full professor is, at Paris, 4,500, 4,000, and 3,500 fr., according to the division in which the professor is placed; in the departments, 2,400, 2,200, and 2,000 fr.* The fixed salary of a divisional professor is in Paris 1,800 fr. or 1,200 fr.; in the departments it is 1,200 fr. The eventual salary used to be formed by taking nine hundredths of the fee for board and schooling paid by each boarder, and five-tenths of the fee paid for schooling by each day boy. The sum obtained by taking these fractions was in every *lycée* divided between the censor and the professors, and the share received by each was the eventual part of his salary.† But since 1862 the *traitement éventuel* has been fixed at a uniform sum of 3,000 fr. for professors in Paris; for those in the departments it is more than one half less. A professor also receives certain fees for examinations and conferences, and often he gives a certain number of private lectures. I was informed that from all these sources the income of an able Paris professor of the first rank in his calling reached very nearly 10,000 fr. (400*l.*) a year. For my own part I would sooner have this, with the freedom and leisure a French professor has with it, than 800*l.* a year as one of the under masters of a public school in England.

The divisional professors are poorly paid, especially those in the departments, but it is to be said that their condition is,

* There may be in Paris 30 professors at the first-named rate at a time, 35 at the second, any number at the third. In the departments, 133 at the first rate, the same number at the second, any number at the third.

† Formerly the divisional professors had no share in the *traitement éventuel,* but they are now admitted to a share in it.

or ought to be, one of passage only; they are on their road to the aggregation and the post of full professor. Meanwhile they, too, may turn their spare hours to account for the benefit of their income.

5   The position of the great body of the *maîtres d'étude* or *maîtres répétiteurs* is more discouraging. They are extremely numerous; the system of supervision practised in the French schools makes it necessary that they should be so, and their number of course renders it impossible that they should be
10   well paid, or that many of them should rise to the higher posts of the profession. Some of them rise; and distinguished men have begun their career in the post of usher. While superintending the *études*, or workrooms in which the boys prepare their lessons, the usher may be carrying on his own studies
15   for the aggregation, for which a five years' practice in teaching is one of the preliminary conditions, and service as an usher, even of the humblest grade, counts. To rise in this way through the aggregation to the professorate is of course in theory the true career of the usher; the majority of them, however, fail
20   to achieve it, and their regular line of promotion is to become *régents* in a communal college. There are three classes of them, —aspirants, second-class ushers, first-class ushers. An aspirant must be 18 years old, and must have the degree of bachelor of arts or sciences; a second-class usher must have served for
25   a year as aspirant; a first-class one must have served a year in the second class, and that, if he has the degree of master of arts or sciences, is sufficient; if he has not this degree, he must have served in the second class five years, three of them in the same *lycée*. The higher order of ushers may hold the post of
30   master in the lowest or elementary division of the school, or may be employed to supply the place of an absent professor; they also may act the part of tutor by explaining to the boys in their *étude* any difficulty in their lessons, and by helping them forward with them. Of course in the higher part of the
35   school an ordinary *maître d'étude* has not the attainments necessary for such a task as this. An usher acting as master receives in Paris about 60*l.* a year, in the departments from 40*l.* to 50*l.*; the three grades of ushers not in charge of forms receive from

30*l.* to 50*l.* in Paris, from 25*l.* to 40*l.* in the departments. It is to be remembered that they have in the *lycée* their board and lodging free, and those of them who, being masters of the lower forms, are not required to live in the *lycée*, have an allowance of about 20*l.* a year towards their board and lodging.

The Paris *lycées* no doubt get the best of the *maîtres répétiteurs*, and employ those of the highest grade; I was struck with the generally decent address and appearance of those whom I saw there, and everywhere I was inclined to wonder that for such a post at such a stipend the schools could supply themselves as well as they did. Of course it is not easy to induce the authorities to own that the *maître d'étude*, who is such an indispensable ingredient in that system of constant supervision which they think necessary, is and must be a weak part in it, and a stranger has few means of penetrating in such a matter below the surface; but I am inclined to think, chiefly, I own, from what I have heard from English boys brought up in French schools, that among these many *maîtres d'étude* there is a large stagnating mass in which there is much corruption and much mischief, and that from this mass a great deal that is noxious distils among the boys they are set to overlook, though perhaps the contempt with which the boys are apt to regard the usher makes his influence for harm somewhat less than it might otherwise be. The boys who spoke with disgust and contempt of the body of *maîtres d'étude* spoke, I must add, with great respect of that of professors.

To conclude this account of the governing and teaching staff in a French public school, I must add that their nomenclature in a communal college is somewhat different from that in a *lycée*. The director of a communal college is called the *principal*, not the *provisor;* the masters are called *regents*, not *professors*. The principal must have the degree of bachelor, and so must the regents; in those colleges which give the full course of secondary instruction, the regents charged with the higher parts of this course must be licentiates.

Chapter IV

Matters Taught in the French Secondary Schools

Divisions and Classes in a French Lycée—Matters Taught in Each Class.

After the teachers I come to the matters taught. The programme of the French public schools is, as I have said, fixed by authority; the arrangement of classes and studies is the same in all. A *lycée* has three divisions,—an elementary division, a
5 grammar division, and a superior division called often *division for humanities*. The classes, unlike those in our great public schools, have for their highest class not a *sixth* but a *first*. The lowest class is the *classe de huitième;* boys are admitted to it very young, as young as seven years of age, if they can read
10 and write; but even before this class the *lycées* are authorised to place a preparatory class, not numbered, in which the instruction given is mainly that of primary schools,* and does not include Latin. Here children of six years of age are admitted. The very good exercise of learning by heart from the
15 classics of the mother tongue begins even in this preparatory class, and is continued to the top of the school. Latin begins in the *classe de huitième*, and is carried further in *septième*. After *septième* begins another division, that of grammar. It is obvious that when boys are admitted at six or seven years old
20 a serious examination at entrance is out of place; but after the elementary division a boy's access to each division is guarded by an examination, which turns, of course, on the matters taught him in the division he is leaving. The lowest class in the division of grammar is *sixième*, the sixth form in the school,

25 * Primary instruction may be given by a primary schoolmaster, but he must hold, unless he has the degree of bachelor, the full certificate of a primary teacher.

according to the French way of reckoning. Here begins Greek, and also the study of the modern languages. These may be English, German, Spanish, or Italian, according to the wants of the localities and the wishes of the parents, France having a frontier either in contact or in close proximity with all these languages. It may wound an Englishman's vanity to find that the pre-eminence given in the schools of his own country to French is not given in France to English; in the *lycées* of Paris, German and English pretty nearly divide the pupils, the advantage resting, however, with German; partly because this is the native language of important provinces of France; partly because it is of more use to military students, which many boys in the *lycées* are going to be; and partly, no doubt, because in the scientific and intellectual movement of Europe at present England counts for so little and Germany for so much. In Germany, where French is obligatory, as with us, in the schools, and where English is optional, one cannot hear without a little mortification the two languages classified as, the one, the *Handel-Sprache*, the other, the *Cultur-Sprache;* English is the *Handel-Sprache*, learnt for mere material and business purposes; the *Cultur-Sprache*, learnt for the purposes of the mind and spirit, is French.

Drawing and singing are likewise obligatory matters of instruction in the French *lycées*, and are not paid for as extras. Two hours a week are, on an average, given to each. Drawing is taught as a matter of science, not of amusement, and the pupil is carried through a strict course from outline up to ornament and model drawing.

The fifth class (*classe de cinquième*) reads our old friend Cornelius Nepos, but it reads also authors not much, I think, in use in our schools,—Justin, Ælian, and Lucian. The division of lessons is the same here and in the sixth class; ten *classes*, as they are called, a week, and two hours of singing, one of drawing, and two of gymnastics.* A class lasts two hours; so this gives (not counting gymnastics) 23 hours of lessons in the week. The classes are thus divided: seven classes and a

* Gymnastics form part of the regular course in the *lycées*, and are not charged for as extras.

half (15 hours) for classics; one class (two hours) for history and geography; two half classes (two hours) for modern languages; one half class (one hour) for arithmetic. The weekly number of classes remains the same all through the school; but the proportion of time given to classics and to other subjects varies, and so does the amount of additional lessons.

In *quatrième*, the head form of the grammar division, Latin prosody in the classical instruction, geometry in the scientific, appear as new subjects. An hour less is in this form given to classics, an hour more to mathematics. An hour more than in the two forms below is here given to drawing.

Another divisional examination, and the boy passes into humanities. Of the *division supérieure* (humanities), the lowest class is *troisième*. Here Latin verse begins, and here, for the first time in the school, Homer appears. Among the books read in extracts by this form, and not commonly read, so far as I know, in our schools, I noticed Terence, Isocrates, Plutarch's *Morals*, and the Greek Fathers. Mathematics now get four hours a week; history, which we have just seen dividing its class with geography, gets the whole two hours; geography and modern languages become additional lessons, the first with one hour a week, the second with two. Music is reduced to one hour. The number of lesson-hours in the week (still not counting gymnastics) has thus risen from 24 to 26.

In *seconde*, the same proportion between sciences and letters; but in sciences the programme is now algebra, geometry, and natural history, instead of arithmetic and geometry. The distribution of additional lessons remains the same. The *Agricola* of Tacitus, the easier dialogues of Plato, the easier orations of Demosthenes, appear among the books read.

Then the boy rises into our sixth form, called with the French from old time not first class, but *Classe de rhétorique*. The classics read are much what would be read in our sixth form; but in the mother-tongue the pupil studies the *Pensées* of Pascal, the *Oraisons funèbres* of Bossuet, La Bruyère, Fénelon's *Lettre à l'Académie Française*, Buffon's *Discours sur le Style*, Voltaire's *Siècle de Louis XIV.*, Boileau's *Art Poétique*, and La Fontaine's *Fables*. Even the selection of a body of English classics like this, excellent in themselves and excellently adapted for the purposes to which they are destined, is a progress which English public instruction has yet to make. Letters have eight out of the ten classes in *rhétorique*, which is the great classical form of the school. Sciences have only one class, divided between geometry and cosmography; but with an object which I shall notice presently, an additional lesson of an hour in the week has been established for the benefit of those pupils who desire to refresh their knowledge of the scientific instruction given in *seconde* and *troisième*. Otherwise the lessons occupy the same number of hours as in those two classes.

But now, after the great classical form of *rhétorique*, comes a crowning of the edifice which we have not, and which in some degree, perhaps, represents that part of education which with us the student gets later, at the University. This is the class of *logique*, or, as it is now officially called, of *philosophie*. The design of this class is thus summed up by the present minister, M. Duruy: General revision of the classical and scientific studies of the three previous forms; instruction in physics; and, above all, as the two characterising studies of this class, philosophy,—making the pupil busy himself with the substance of ideas as in rhetoric he busied himself with their form, and developing his reflection as rhetoric developed his imagination and taste,—and contemporary history. The programme of the course of philosophy divides the subject thus: Introduction, psychology, logic, moral philosophy, theology, history of philosophy. That of the course of contemporary history goes from 1815 to the present time; the professor has to introduce it with a 'rapid summary of the general facts which have modified, from the 15th century onwards, the ideas, interests, and constitution of European society.' He concludes it with 'France's share in the general work of civilisation.' The programme is a skilfully constructed framework, capable of being by a good teacher so filled up as to make the course very interesting and useful. In *philosophie*, the design of this class being such as I have stated, Greek and Latin of course lose their preponderant share in the lessons. In the ten lessons they have now, indeed, only so much share as the language of four out of the nine authors read,—Xenophon (*Memorabilia*), Plato (*Gorgias*), Cicero (*De Republica, Tusculans* and *Offices*), and Seneca (select letters),—gives them; the remaining five authors read are French, and the books are: the Port Royal Logic; the *Discours de la Méthode* of Descartes; Pascal's *De l'Autorité en matière de Philosophie*, his *Réflexions sur la Géométrie en général*, and his *De l'Art de Persuader*; Bossuet's *Traité de la Connaissance de Dieu et de Soi-même*; and Fénelon's *Traité de l'Existence de Dieu*. But two hours of additional lessons in the week are given to going over the pupil's former classical work, and to Latin composition. The essay, Latin and French, appears for the first time in this form. Sciences now get the large share of five classes a week (ten hours). To algebra, geometry, and cosmography, are added physics and chemistry.

To pass through a form takes a year; the programme of studies for each form covers a year, and the pupil has to go through it. A boy therefore who came at eight years old and began in *huitième*, is seventeen years old when he has finished *philosophie*. Sixteen years is the age at which a candidate is allowed to present himself for the degree of bachelor in arts or science. The degree of bachelor of arts is the natural termination of the literary studies of the *lycée*, and the examination for this degree now turns, by express regulation,* upon the matters taught in the classes of *rhetoric* and *philosophy* in the *lycées*. A youth who has gone through these classes with success has no difficulty in obtaining the degree, and one sees on the benches of the *lycées* pupils who, having completed the age of sixteen, have gone in for their degree, and already got it. Examinations are held twice a year in each of the 16 seats of faculties of letters in France, and in 13 other towns whither the faculties of their respective academies send examiners. The examining jury is composed of three members of the faculty of letters and one of that of sciences. The examinations are public, partly on paper and partly oral, and they last two days.

* *Décret impérial du 27 novembre, 1864, relatif au Baccalauréat ès Lettres.*

Candidates who fail in the paper-work examination are not admitted to the oral one. The paper-work consists of Latin and French composition, and of translation from Latin into French; the *viva voce* work, of construing a passage from a Greek or Latin author and explaining a passage from a French one, and of answering questions in philosophy, history and geography, and mathematical and natural sciences. The paper-work counts for three marks, the construing and explaining for two, philosophy for one, history and geography for one, the sciences for two. Failure in any one of these five sections causes the candidate's rejection. If he loses three out of the nine marks distributed between the sections he is equally rejected. The part given to mathematics and natural sciences in an examination for the degree of bachelor of letters, is what will most strike us in going through this programme. A candidate who holds already the degree of bachelor of sciences is of course exempted from the scientific part of the examination. A candidate who has got, in the class of rhetoric or philosophy, one of the chief prizes for classics in the grand annual competition of the *lycées*, is exempted from the literary part of the examination, but the scientific part he must still go through. The dues for the degree of bachelor amount to 100 fr. (4*l.*)

But many of the best pupils of the *lycées* have in view not the arts degree, but a degree in sciences and admission to the *écoles spéciales*, as they are called,—schools like the Polytechnic, St. Cyr, the *École Navale*, the *École Forestière*, the *École Centrale des Arts et Manufactures*. Admission to these schools is a favourite object of ambition in France; it at once places a young man in a career; but it is guarded by a strict and competitive examination in mathematics and natural sciences. It is said that a clever boy who has gone through the *lycée* to the end of *philosophie*, and who has followed with diligence the scientific as well as the literary instruction of the different classes through which he has passed, is, at the same time that he has secured a thorough literary education, strong enough in sciences to obtain, with a little previous aid from private tuition, the degree of bachelor of sciences, and to present himself with this indispensable credential at one of the

special schools. To encourage boys destined for these schools
to complete their course of literary training first, the additional
lesson in sciences of which I spoke when I was describing
the rhetoric class has been added to the programme of that
5   class. The boy is thus enabled to keep his mathematics fresh
at the same time that he goes on with his classics. However,
it is admitted that in general a much stricter scientific training than this is necessary for a boy who wants to get into the
special schools. Two scientific classes are therefore placed
10 as appendages to the *lycée* system,—the class of elementary
mathematics and the class of special mathematics. The class of
elementary mathematics puts Greek altogether aside, and of its
ten weekly classes gives only one to Latin and French; one is
given to history; of the remaining eight, three are given to
15 natural sciences, five to mathematics. Modern languages, geography, and philosophy are provided for by additional lessons
of one hour in the week each. In special mathematics, the
mathematical and natural sciences have the same share of
classes, eight out of ten; but natural sciences get only two of
20 them, mathematics the other six. Latin and history disappear,
French literature has one of the two classes left, a modern language the other. An additional lesson of an hour in the week
is assigned to work in the laboratory.

After a year in elementary mathematics the pupil is ready
25 for the examination of the degree of bachelor of sciences or
that of the Military School of St. Cyr. The class of special
mathematics conducts to the more difficult examination of
the Polytechnic School, or to that of the scientific section of
the Normal School. It sometimes happens that the same student
30 passes for both the Polytechnic and the scientific section of
the Normal School; M. Duruy in a recent report notices with
pleasure that several students who had thus won the double
nomination elected for the Normal School. Nothing could
better show the credit with which this excellent institution has
35 succeeded in investing the somewhat unattractive profession
of schoolmaster.

But the Polytechnic and St. Cyr have fixed twenty as the
highest limit of age for their candidates; the competition, at

the Polytechnic especially, is very severe (some people say, too severe), and it is not easy to succeed the first time; a candidate wishes to have time for more trials than one. But a youth who goes through his literary course to the end of *philosophie*, and then takes his two years of mathematics, elementary and special, to fit him for the Polytechnic examination, finds himself with no margin of age to spare, and must succeed the first time or give up his object. Add to this that a boy with a strong aptitude for scientific studies often feels very little disposed for a nine years' conversation with Latin and Greek. Add again, that the parents of a promising boy often feel very little disposed for an eleven years' expense for his schooling, when he might be off their hands in eight or nine. To meet cases of this kind the well-known *bifurcation* had been established. On issuing from the division of grammar, and passing the examination which guards the issue from that division, a boy, instead of entering humanities, was allowed to choose whether his training should be henceforth literary or scientific. The *lycée* offered him his choice between a scientific section, supposed to prepare him for business, for the special schools, for degrees in science and medicine; or a literary section, conducting to degrees in letters and law, and, in general, giving what the world has agreed to call the education of a gentleman. A boy may be admitted at once to the grammar division; three years of classics, therefore, there, and then the *bifurcation*. But even after the *bifurcation* letters kept a strong hold on the follower of sciences; one-half of the school-time was in the scientific section given to literature, modern languages, and history, while in the literary section only one-fifth of the school-time was given to sciences. But neither the friends of letters nor those of sciences were satisfied with the *bifurcation*. It was said that it took the boys too young, before their vocation was sufficiently clear; that it damaged both scientific and literary studies, producing good students in neither. The present minister, M. Duruy, abolished it. The abolition, however, turns out, when one looks closely at it, to be more apparent than real. It is true that a scientific section of the *lycée* no longer exists in name, and that a boy who after he has done with the grammar division remains on at school, must enter *troisième*, the lowest class of the division of humanities, and pass his year there. It is desired, no doubt, by the framers of the new regulations that he should have the benefit of *seconde* and *rhétorique*, if not of *philosophie*, as well; but in these cases, where there is a current of interests which conflicts with the regulations, it is not what is desired, but what is enforced, that is important. The pupil is not obliged to proceed, after *troisième*, to *seconde*, or else leave the *lycée*; a lower division of the class of *mathématiques élémentaires*, under the title of *cours préparatoire*, receives the pupil whose parents wish the direction of his studies to be henceforth scientific rather than literary. He has first to pass an examination in what he has been taught in *troisième*; but once admitted to the *cours préparatoire* his literary classes are reduced to five, and his scientific classes are as numerous as those of *troisième*, *seconde*, and *rhétorique* altogether, and throw into one year the scientific instruction which those classes spread over three. From the *cours préparatoire* he issues into the regular class of *mathématiques élémentaires*, at the end of which follows naturally the examination for the degree of bachelor of sciences, this examination turning on the matters, scientific and literary, taught in the class of *mathématiques élémentaires* in the *lycées*. Afterwards, if, for the Polytechnic or the Normal School, or for any other object, he needs higher mathematical instruction, he goes on into *mathématiques spéciales*.

The changes introduced by M. Duruy have, therefore, made one year of humanities obligatory on the school-boy proceeding to the scientific classes. To this extent they are in favour of classics. M. Duruy urges also, though he does not enforce, a still longer course of humanities before the pupil gives himself to sciences. On the other hand, in his new programme he has strengthened the scientific instruction by introducing more of it into the higher classical forms than was formerly taught there. He has also, in general, simplified, compressed, and reduced the old programme of instruction in the *lycées*. Still more has he done this with that of the bachelor's degrees, both in arts and science. This programme, which was before a very wide one, he has now made identical, as I have said, with that of the *lycée*'s two highest classes in humanities, and with that of its class of elementary mathematics. This simplification, the degree in question being for youths of seventeen or eighteen, seems clearly judicious.   5

Chapter V

The *Lycées*

With the provision I have described for the supply of professors, they are a body, all through France, of one stamp and training; the pick of them no doubt comes, in the long run, to the Paris *lycées*, but the ablest of young professors may expect to find himself, at some moment in the beginning of his career, at a school in the provinces. The field for him in Paris, however, is large. Paris has seven great classical schools *de plein exercice*, as it is called; that is, in which the full course of instruction which I have detailed above is given. All *lycées* are *de plein exercice*, while of the 247 communal colleges only 152 are so. The rest have only the elementary division and the division of grammar; they do not add to grammar the division of humanities. The seven great classical schools of Paris are the *lycées* Louis le Grand, Napoléon, Saint Louis, Charlemagne, Bonaparte, Bourbon, and the Colleges Stanislas and Rollin. Of these the *lycées* Louis le Grand, Napoléon, and Saint Louis, and the two colleges, take boarders; Charlemagne and Bonaparte take day-scholars only. Most of them retain the site, at least, of an old pre-revolutionary school; Saint Louis is the *Collége d'Harcourt*, founded in that great school-movement of the 14th century which I have already mentioned, by two brothers, members of Philip the Fair's Council, Raoul d'Harcourt, canon of Paris, and Robert d'Harcourt, bishop of Coutances. Napoléon was the old *Collége Henri IV.*, and as, from the neighbourhood of the Panthéon, one sees its long pile, flanked by the Church of St. Étienne du Mont, where Pascal lies buried, one must own that a venerable look of old France it still retains. Bonaparte was the *Collége Bourbon*. Louis le

Grand was the famous Jesuit school of Clermont, which Louis the Fourteenth one day visited, and the performance of the scholars being admired by one of his suite: 'What would you expect?' said the king, '*c'est mon collége.*' That night the Jesuits erased the name of *Clermont*, fixed in large letters on the front of their building, and the next morning saw *Louis le Grand* in its stead. Louis le Grand is the only one of these Paris *lycées* which managed to live on through the Revolution, notwithstanding the decree suppressing the ancient colleges. The Jesuits had long been expelled, but it had an adroit director at its head; and though straitened by the trials of the time, it was never actually closed.

These seven establishments have a total of 5,968 scholars. Louis le Grand, the largest, has 1,330; Bonaparte has 1,220; Charlemagne 930; Saint Louis 800; Napoléon 688; Stanislas 620; Rollin 380. The *lycée* of Vanves, a mile or two out of Paris, formed to relieve Louis le Grand of its little boys and to give them country air, has 700 scholars; but without counting Vanves, the seven great schools of Paris contain very nearly 6,000 scholars. The nine English public schools which were the object of a Royal Commission's inquiry, have 3,027 scholars. Only six of the nine have really, in public estimation, the rank of great public schools, the rank which the seven great Paris schools hold; still, let them all be counted in, and yet the public classical schools of Paris alone have nearly twice as many scholars as the public classical schools of all England. Nay, of all Scotland and Ireland besides; for these two countries have no public classical schools of the rank of the great English schools or of the Paris *lycées*, and Scotch or Irish parents who desire, and can afford, schools of this rank for their children, must send them to the English schools.

I visited all the *lycées* of Paris, and I believe there is no part of a *lycée*'s organism, from the elementary division up to *mathématiques spéciales*, which I have not seen at work, and no part of the instruction which I have not heard given. The internal management and the working aspect of all these institutions are similar, though the exterior of the buildings is often strikingly different. The modern, handsome, and wealthy

appearance of the *lycée Bonaparte* suits its position in the
newer and more luxurious quarter of Paris,—the quarter most
frequented by visitors,—with the Rue de la Paix, the Grand
Hôtel, the Opéra, and the Madeleine for neighbours. On the
5   other side of the Seine, in the old quarter of the schools and
the religious, in the neighbourhood of the Sorbonne and Sainte
Geneviève, the somewhat dilapidated front of Louis le Grand
or Napoléon suits the antiquity and associations of the region.
Many of the public school buildings in France, the old school
10 sites and fabrics having been, as I have already said, restored
after the Revolution, as far as possible, to their former destination, are in fact very old, and the rebuilding and repairing
of the *lycées* and those sanitary works in connection with
them which earlier ages neglected, but which are now thought,
15 and rightly, to be of such great importance, are a cause of constant and heavy expense to the government. In this way the
whole front of Saint Louis, which stands on the new continuation, upon the left bank of the Seine, of the Boulevard Sébasto-
pol, has just been re-built, and a very handsome building this
20 *lycée* now is. You ring at the decorated entrance in the boulevard, and the porter admits you to the open and spacious vestibule, looking on the school's first great court, surrounded by
high white walls with uniform tiers of windows, and com-
municating directly with the *parloir*, where at all the French
25 public schools a boarder's parents, or those authorised by
them, can come and see him between twelve and one, or between half-past four and five. Ascending a staircase, one reaches
the *cabinet* of the censor and that of the provisor. The room
of the provisor communicates with the apartment where he
30 is lodged (for the provisor lives at the *lycée*), and the provisor's lodging at Saint Louis is most enviable. Its occupant
when I was there was M. Legrand, but he has since left it to
become provisor at Bonaparte, a much easier post, because at
Bonaparte there are no boarders. Every one who has had
35 opportunities of observing must have been struck to see how
much work Frenchmen seem able to do, and to do with spirit
and energy; the provisor of a great *lycée* certainly needs to
have ability of this sort, with the business and responsibility

of a boarding house of some 500 boys pressing upon him. M. Legrand had it to perfection; constantly appealed to, with a rain of letters, messages, meetings, applicants, visitors, perpetually beating upon him, he seemed to suffice to all claims, and to suffice not only industriously but smoothly; but he 5
began his work, he told me, at four in the morning. On several occasions he took me through the different departments of the *lycée*; the internal economy of such an institution could not be better seen than at Saint Louis and with such a cicerone as M. Legrand. The series of large courts for a school of 800 10
boys, courts generally quiet, but at the breaking up of a lesson or in the short time allotted to recreation noisy enough; spacious and airy, sometimes shaded with trees, but looking, to an ex-schoolboy from any of the great English schools, hopelessly prison-like; on the ground floor round the courts the 15
school-rooms, *salles de classe*, with their professor, and their 30 or 40 boys seated at desks rising one behind the other; or the work-rooms, *salles d'étude*, rooms of much the same aspect and dimensions as the *salles de classe*, but with a *maître répétiteur* presiding in them instead of a professor, and with the 20
boys learning their lessons instead of saying them; above, the refectories with their show of table napkins and silver cups, and the large dormitories scrupulously neat and clean, at one end the curtained bed of the usher in charge, in the door at the other end a window by which to overlook the room from 25
without, and, near it, ingenious mechanical devices by which the visits of the functionary whose business it is to see, so often in the night, that all is well in each bedroom, are recorded, and the controller is himself controlled; then the dispensary and infirmaries, the service done by sisters of charity, with 30
rooms for all stages of illness and the eternal usher overlooking those invalids who are up and together; the linen stores and clothes-rooms, everything beautifully kept, each boy's things ticketed and numbered with the greatest exactness; the bathrooms, offices, kitchens, the supplies of bread and wine, the 35
soup, meat, vegetables, pastry, all in preparation on a grand scale and all of them which I tasted excellent,—this is what may be seen in every great *lycée* in France; but at Saint Louis,

from the newness and freshness of the buildings, and the perfection of finish and order which is reached, it may be seen
to special advantage. Finish and order are, however, in the
great majority of cases, rules of French administration; and as
I have already remarked, the march of a great public service,
such as is the service of one of these establishments, has inevitably something imposing in it if regularly and well conducted, which the arrangements of private establishments, in
which the individual has, very likely, his tastes more consulted
and a life more to his mind, cannot well equal. But when we
come to consulting the individual's taste and giving him a life
to his mind, we generally come at the same time to expense;
a cheap private establishment, without the regularity and economy of a great machine, and without the costly luxury of independent comfort, is a slipshod thing, full of meanness and
misery. It is to be remembered that in one of the Paris *lycées*
a boy is to have board, instruction, books, writing materials,
clothes, washing, medical attendance, and medicine, for 50*l.* a
year. The question is, how these may be given best for that
money.

The medical service is excellent; the general rate of sickness
in the *lycées* is certainly surprisingly low, and probably to the
excellence of the medical service,—for ability, completeness,
and attention, far exceeding, like that of a great hospital,
anything the inmates of the establishment could command at
home,—this is in great measure owing. The meals are four in
number; breakfast, dinner at noon, the *goûter*, as it is called,
at half-past four, and supper in the evening. The breakfast is
a slight, and the *goûter* a very slight affair; this latter is in fact
a roll of bread and nothing more; the dinner and supper are
the substantial meals. The dinner is in general soup, then two
dishes and a vegetable, then dessert; there is an allowance of
wine. It will be seen how different is the system of meals from
ours, or at least from what ours was; but it is in great measure
climate and differences of physical organisation which determine the varieties in these things. I have heard some complaints
of the way the boys are fed in the *lycées*; not as to the quality
of the food, but the quantity, I have heard several people com-

plain, is apt to be insufficient. I give these complaints, on a matter which, with boys, very easily gives rise to them, and where
it is not very easy to test their exact justice, for what they are
worth.

The boys in a *lycée* have, it must be said, to our notions a
long and exhausting day; they rise earlier than our boys, later
than boys in Italy (this again is an affair mainly of climate);
the boarders in a French *lycée* rise between five and six, and
their allowance of school hours is more than ours, their allowance of air and exercise less. The hours of class are but four a
day, from eight to ten in the morning, and from two to four
in the afternoon; but this is only a small part of the work-day
of the French schoolboy, his hours passed at *conférences*, at
examinations, and above all at preparing his lessons in the *salle
d'étude*, under the eye of the *maître répétiteur*, have to be
added to it. It seems to me that the French schoolboy is at
lessons, on an average, ten or eleven hours a day, and that his
time for meals and recreation is not, on an average, more than
two hours. Thursday is a half-holiday, and the only one. Certainly, the boys, at their quarter-hours or half-hours of recreation, seem to enjoy themselves with great spirit, and their
gymnastics are probably a better physical training for the short
time they have to give to exercise than our boys' amusements
would be; but they did not, in general, to my thinking, look
so fresh, happy, and healthy as our public-school boys. The
master of a well-known *pension*, who had English boys as well
as French, assured me that the French boys were not to be
judged by their complexions, that they had more endurance
and a tougher fibre than our boys, and that when he took
them out together on long excursions his English boys, vigorous at first, knocked up sooner than his French boys. This is
the old reproach of the Latin races against the northern bar-
barian, that he is lusty, and melts and gives way in the sun;
there may be some truth in it, and the spirit and gaiety of an
English boy do not go with him into his exercise,—he flags
in it,—if he does not feel he is at play and free in it; thus it
has been observed that gymnastics do not flourish in our
schools, they are too much of a drill or a lesson; and for the

same reason the volunteer company has not so many or such ardent recruits as cricket or boating. And no doubt the physical energy of the young English *pensionnaire* would show to more advantage if he was matched in cricket or boating with his French comrades, than in gymnastics or a walking excursion, where he is a little damped by the sense of constraint and rule. Still it is hard to believe, and I do not believe, that the confinement, the scanty recreation, and the long school-hours of a French schoolboy are without some unfavourable effect on his health and development; the long school-hours, however, are an almost inevitable result of placing large boarding schools in the heart of large cities, where space for exercise and freedom of range must be limited, and the boys therefore must be kept more at work to save them from the mischief of being penned up together in idleness with few or no resources of amusement. The placing large boarding schools in large cities is itself, again, an almost inevitable result of having large day-schools attached to the boarding schools; for the supply to large day-schools can only be found, of course, in large cities, and indeed the need for them only exists there. It must be added, besides, that a body of professors such as the *lycées* of Paris are proud, and justly proud, of possessing, is hardly to be obtained out of a large city. Many of these professors have pursuits, independent of their work at the *lycées*, which tie them to Paris; and the *lycées*, if they were planted in the country, amidst better conditions of physical development for their boys, might have some loss in professors to set against the gain in other respects.

The French *lycées*, however, are guiltless of one preposterous violation of the laws of life and health committed by our own great schools, which have of late years thrown open to competitive examination all the places on their foundations. The French have plenty of examinations; but they put them almost entirely at the right age for examinations, between the years of fifteen and twenty-five, when the candidate is neither too old nor too young to be examined with advantage. To put upon little boys of nine or ten the pressure of a competitive examination for an object of the greatest value to their parents, is to offer a premium for the violation of nature's

elementary laws, and to sacrifice, as in the poor geese fatted
for Strasbourg pies, the due development of all the organs of life
to the premature hypertrophy of one. It is well known that the
cramming of the little human victims for their ordeal of competition tends more and more to become an industry with a   5
certain class of small schoolmasters, who know the secrets of
the process, and who are led by self-interest to select in the
first instance their own children for it. The foundations are
no gainers, and nervous exhaustion at fifteen is the price which
many a clever boy pays for over-stimulation at ten; and the   10
nervous exhaustion of a number of our clever boys tends to
create a broad reign of intellectual deadness in the mass of
youths from fifteen to twenty, whom the clever boys, had they
been rightly developed and not unnaturally forced, ought to
have leavened. You can hardly put too great a pressure on a   15
healthy youth to make him work between fifteen and twenty-
five; healthy or unhealthy, you can hardly put on him too light
a pressure of this kind before twelve.

The bursarships in the *lycées* are, therefore, not given away
by competitive examination among children from eight to   20
twelve; they are given on the ground of poverty, either to the
children of persons having some public claim, or to the most
promising subjects from the primary schools. This seems to
me quite right, and I wish the English reader to remark how
here, as elsewhere, we suffer from our dread of effective ad-   25
ministration and from the feudal and incoherent organisation
of our society. In the hands of individuals and small local bodies
patronage like that of our foundation schools becomes out-
rageously jobbed; at last the public attention gets directed to
this, and the patronage has to be otherwise dealt with; but   30
there is no body of trained and competent persons with authority to decide deliberately how it may be best dealt with;
so it ends by the local people through whose laches the difficulty has arisen throwing a sop to Cerberus, and gratifying an
ignorant public's love of claptrap by throwing everything   35
open to competitive examination. On the Continent, there is
an Education Minister and a Council of Public Instruction to
weigh matters of this kind; so far from jobbing being promoted
by this, the examination test is much more strictly applied in

France than with us, but there is a competent authority to decide when it is rational to apply it and when absurd. Neither are there any complaints of the way the *lycée* bursarships,—it being judged best not to give these by competitive examina-
5 tion,—are distributed; because here again all that is done is done with the safeguards of joint action between several competent agencies, of publicity, and of responsibility. It is a mistake to suppose that a government bureau, in an administrative organisation like that of France, has no checks; it has far more checks
10 than a government bureau here, which has been extemporised to meet some urgent want, and is not part of a well-devised whole. The secretary of our Education Department is almost invited to settle of his own authority education-questions which M. Duruy, though a minister, would not settle without refer-
15 ring them to a Council composed as we have seen. Nay, and even supposing our secretary refers them to his chiefs and they refer them to the Committee of Council,—how is this Committee of Council composed? Of three or four Cabinet Ministers, with no special acquaintance with educational matters.
20   The want of more air and exercise for their schoolboys is a matter which is occupying the attention of the authorities of public secondary instruction in France; they are beginning with the greatest sufferers by the old system, the little boys, and the *lycée du Prince Impérial*, at Vanves, is a fruit of their
25 awakened solicitude for these children. Vanves is charming. It lies a mile or two out of Paris on the Vaugirard road. It was a summer villa of the Prince of Condé; when the then holder of this title emigrated at the Revolution, Vanves was sold as emigrant's property, and was bought very cheap by
30 the *lycée* Louis le Grand, which managed, as I have said, to subsist through the storms of the revolution. It is now, like every other *lycée*, the property of the State, and after having for some time served as a juvenile department for Louis le Grand only, it is now an independent establishment for little
35 boys, beginning with primary instruction and carrying them no further than *cinquième*, when they are passed on, not necessarily to Louis le Grand only,—though the old connection of Vanves with this *lycée* is felt as a strong tie,—but to whatever school the pupil chooses. Seven hundred little boarders

(for Vanves takes no day-scholars) of from five to ten or
eleven may be seen here, and a pretty sight they are. The
park and garden are quite delightful, and the ground beautifully thrown about; the high hill on which stand the school
buildings commands a magnificent view of Paris on the one   5
side, and of the country towards La Celle St. Cloud and St.
Germain on the other. The buildings have been of late greatly
enlarged, and every improvement in school construction and
arrangements, according to the French notions, introduced;
and whoever wishes to see French school construction and   10
arrangements at their very best should go and see Vanves. The
school is popular, and no wonder; at the lodge at the foot of
the hill one sees carriages waiting, and in the glades of the park
the mammas whom they have brought may be descried walking with their little boys. Being so young the pupils pay the   15
lower rate (40*l.* to 45*l.* a year) fixed by authority for the
younger divisions in the Paris *lycées;* but it is on little boys,
they say, not yet come to the terrible appetite of fifteen, that
the great profits are made; and while many *lycées* can hardly
make both ends meet, Vanves is in the highest prosperity. It   20
is self-supporting, and after paying all its expenses has a profit
of 4,000*l.* a year. Its progenitor, Louis le Grand, clears a profit
of more than 3,000*l.* Profits of this kind go to the State, the
proprietor of the *lycées*, and are available for the general expenses of secondary instruction. In this way a prosperous   25
lycée helps to pull a struggling *lycée* through; but a *lycée*
which brings in plenty of money will always be liberally
treated for its own improvements and extensions.

Vanves has no day-scholars; its boarders are all housed on
the premises, and all pay about 40*l.* a year. In the ordinary 30
lycées it is not so. These, with scarcely an exception,* take
day-scholars, and do not themselves lodge all their pupils who
are boarders. They all charge a rate fixed by authority,† rang-

* At the *Collége Rollin* they are all boarders.

† *Décret du 5 août* 1862. In the elementary division boarders pay   35
40*l.*, in the grammar division 44*l.*, in the superior division 48*l.*, in special
mathematics (where they have, perhaps, the best scientific and mathematical teaching to be got anywhere) 60*l.* Day-scholars pay, in the
elementary division 6*l.*, in grammar 8*l.*, in humanities and special mathematics 10*l.*   40

ing, for their boarders, from 40*l* to 60*l*. a year; for their day-
scholars, from 6*l*. to 10*l*. For the boarder this includes everything; his *tutor*, as we should say,—that is, the professor who
gives him the benefit, out of class hours, of certain *conférences*
5 and examinations, and the *répétiteur*, who helps him with his
lesson,—as well as his class instruction and his board; for the
day scholar, it only includes his class instruction, and he pays
from 3*l*. to 5*l*. a year extra, according to his place in the school,
for *tutor*. This makes a day scholar's expense come to from
10 9*l*. to 15*l*. a year. Some boys are half-boarders, passing the
twelve hours from 8 a.m. to 8 p.m. at the *lycée*, getting their
dinner and their *goûter* there, but not breakfasting, supping,
or sleeping; these have the full instruction, and they pay from
22*l*. to 34*l*. a year. The *externe surveillé* is a day-scholar who
15 learns his lessons in the *salle d'étude* under the usher's eye, and
is thus off his parents' hands the whole day except an hour in
the middle of it, but has no meals at the school; he pays, as an
ordinary day-scholar with the full instruction, from 9*l*. to 15*l*.
a year, and 80 francs (about 3 guineas) a year besides for super-
20 intendence.

But all the boarding-scholars of a *lycée* which takes boarders
are not boarders of the *lycée* itself; and many of the day-
scholars of a *lycée* which takes no boarders are boarders,
though not in the *lycée*. At Louis le Grand, for instance, the
25 greatest of the *lycées*, there are 800 boarders (*internes*) and
500 day-scholars (*externes*); but all these *externes* do not live
at home. Charlemagne and Bonaparte have no *internat*, they are
day-schools; but the population of Bonaparte is thus divided:
day-scholars who live at home (of these, 151 are *externes sur-*
30 *veillés*), 707; day-scholars who are at a boarding-house, 493;
total, 1,200. And that of Charlemagne thus: day-scholars who
live at home, 200 (70 of them *externes surveillés*); day scholars
who are at a boarding-house, 790; total, 990. A boarding-house
of this kind is called in France *pension, institution;* its director
35 is called *chef de pension, chef d'institution*.

These establishments are private, or, as the French prefer to
call them, free (*école libre, institution libre*).

Chapter VI

Private or Free Schools, and Communal Colleges

Pensions or Institutions Libres—The Communal Colleges—Private Schools—The Seminaries.

Private or free schools in France are not free in the sense that any man may keep one who likes. To keep one a man must be twenty-five years old, must have had five years' practice in a school, and must hold either the degree of bachelor, or a certificate which is given after an examination of the same na- 5 ture as the examination he would have to pass for the degree of bachelor. Thus he cannot, as in England, be perfectly igno- rant and inexperienced in his business; neither can he, as in England, be a ticket-of-leave-man, for the French law declares every man who has undergone a criminal condemnation in- 10 capable of keeping a school. Neither can he have his school- room in ruins or under conditions dangerous to his pupils' health or morality; for if it is a new school he is establishing, he has to signify his intention beforehand to the academic au- thority of his department, and if this authority makes objec- 15 tion, the Council of Public Instruction in Paris, in the last re- sort, decides. If within a month the academic authority makes no objection, he is then free to open his school; but it is at all times liable to inspection by the academic authority or the inspectors-general of secondary instruction, to ascertain that 20 nothing contrary to health, morality, or the law, is suffered to go on there. The inspector of a school of this kind does not meddle with its instruction.

Much the most famous of these institutions is Sainte Barbe, near the Panthéon; it is in the neighbourhood of Louis le 25 Grand, and boards a great number of boys who follow the classes of that *lycée*. Sainte Barbe answers more than anything

97

else I saw in France to a public school with us; I do not mean
at all in the mode of management and teaching, which is that
of all French schools; but it is not a State establishment, and
yet has antiquity, important buildings, a great connection,
5   a *genius loci*, and general consideration. Its head, M. Labrouste,
is a member of the Imperial Council of Public Instruction.
Many families which frequent the great classical *lycée*, Louis
le Grand, have used Sainte Barbe as their boarding-house for
generations; the *Collége Rollin* was once held here; and the
10   prosperity of the establishment is now so great that it has recently founded a Vanves of its own for its little boys at Fontenay aux Roses, near Paris; and Fontenay, like Vanves, is well
worth seeing. But just because it has this exceptional character,
Sainte Barbe, of course, is not a good sample of the French
15   *pensions;* neither is it a good example of the French private
schools, because its chief function, though it has classes of its
own, is to serve as a great hereditary boarding-house to the fre-
quenters of Louis le Grand. So I will go elsewhere for specimens of the *pension*, which now occupies us.
20   These institutions abound in Paris, and the files of uniform-
wearing schoolboys whom one meets in the streets are generally *pensionnaires* going under the care of the master of the
pension or one of his ushers to or from the *lycée* whose classes
they follow. The Commissioners will ask, as I did, why, if a
25   boy is not to live at home, but to be a boarder somewhere, he
does not go and board at the *lycée* whose classes he follows.
The answer in the case of Sainte Barbe to the question why
the *institution* has the preference over the *lycée* is, as I have
said, old hereditary connection. But generally the answer is this:
30   parents seek a somewhat less vast assemblage of boys, a somewhat more domestic management, and a somewhat more attentive supervision of studies out of class hours than they find, or
think they find, at the *lycée*. At the same time they like the
name of the *lycée*, its guarantees, and its professors. So they
35   send their boy to a *pension* where he is with fifty, a hundred,
two hundred boys, not with four or five hundred; where the
master's wife imports the feminine element into the direction
of household affairs, and where their boy gets more looked

after in learning his lessons, and better tutored; and then he is to add to this the benefit of the *lycée* professors and the *status* of a public school boy.

Two of these *pensions* I visited, besides Sainte Barbe; M. Cousin's in the Rue du Rocher, and the *Institution Massin* in the Marais. A German would hardly think of visiting M. Cousin's *pension*, but it has an interest for an Englishman in being one of the very few boarding-houses which approach in expensiveness our Eton and Harrow. It is in connection with the *lycée Bonaparte*, and is fed, like that *lycée*, from the wealthy and luxurious quarter of Paris. A certain number of great personages send their sons to the classes of Bonaparte, and have a tutor for him at home. This, however, gives the paternal house the benefit of the boy's residence, which, unless the paternal house is very large, is not always convenient; besides, a tutor at all equal to the tutors of a good *pension* is a costly luxury if one has him all to oneself. So many of the great people of the rich quarter send their boys to M. Cousin. His expensiveness has been exaggerated; about 120*l.* a year is the cost for an elder boy there, and the cost for a younger boy is less. M. Cousin's house is a good one, and he has a garden, which, for Paris, is delightful; the meals are said to be very good; the older boys have excellent rooms to themselves; the younger ones are not more than two or three in a room; the time given to recreation is something more than in the *internats* of the *lycées*, and the whole establishment has a more domestic character than they have, and not their rigid, formal, and military air. As to lessons and sports, however, the difference between M. Cousin's and the *lycée* is, to an Englishman's notions, slight; the system is in the main much the same, and necessarily so; but there is no doubt that the preparation of the boys for their classes, and the individual help given them out of *lycée* hours, is much more considerable at M. Cousin's; indeed, one may say roundly that he employs professors where the *internat* only employs ushers. The *conférences* and *répétitions* of the *lycée* are, indeed, by professors, and are designed to meet the want of tutoring; but the amount of these which falls to the *interne's* share is not to be compared with the

amount he gets of *salle d'étude* work under an usher, who is
as different from a professor as chalk from cheese; and it is the
object of establishments like M. Cousin's to make the *maître
répétiteur*, as tutor, disappear, and come in only as watchman,
5 and, as tutor, to put the professor in his place. This M. Cousin
does, and it is the best ground for his high charges.

I must add that M. Cousin himself is an ex-functionary of
public instruction, and that the success he enjoys seemed to me
thoroughly well earned.

10 As M. Cousin feeds Bonaparte, so the *Institution Massin* feeds
Charlemagne. As Bonaparte is a somewhat fashionable *lycée*,
so Charlemagne is a somewhat democratic *lycée;* selected, in
general, by poor but clever school-boys from the provinces
whose parents wish to give them the advantage of one of the
15 great *lycées* of Paris. It is on the right bank of the Seine, but
beyond the wealthy quarter. Charlemagne has no *internat*, yet
four-fifths of its pupils are boarders. They board in *pensions*
not like that of M. Cousin; and the *Institution Massin* in the
Marais close by,—a quarter which has long ceased to be aris-
20 tocratic and fashionable,—is a good sample of them. It was
founded in 1810, at the revival of secondary instruction in
France, by M. Massin, from whom it takes its name; its present
head is M. Lesage, who has the grade of licentiate, the title
of *agrégé*, and was for twelve years a professor at Charle-
25 magne. He too, then, is no adventurer, and may be supposed
to know his business. An Englishman can at once see the difference between the domestic arrangements at M. Cousin's and
those of a *lycée*, though the general course of study and play
will seem to him to be pretty much alike at the two places.
30 At the *Institution Massin* the march of the domestic arrangements and the aspect of the premises seem to me not to differ
much from those of the *lycée*. The expense at M. Lesage's differs very little from that at a *lycée;* in France it is a very small
body of parents which will exceed this rate, and the *pensions*,
35 therefore,—the immense majority of them,—keep their charges
very near the rate of the public schools. At M. Lesage's the
charges for boys in special mathematics are slightly lower than
those in the *internat* of a *lycée;* for other boys they are from

five to ten pounds a year higher. That is to say, a boy in humanities at Charlemagne who boards with M. Lesage, pays
M. Lesage for his board and tuition 1,200 fr. a year, and pays
the class-fees of Charlemagne, 250 fr., besides; in all, 58*l.* a year.
As an *interne* in humanities at Saint Louis, his board, tuition,   5
and class-fees would all be covered by 1,200 fr. (48*l.*). The
same in the lower divisions; M. Lesage's boarders pay the same
as the *internes* of a *lycée*, with the class-fees of the *lycée* in
addition. The pupils in special mathematics spring at once, if
internes of a Paris *lycée*, from 1,200 fr. to 1,500 fr., a great   10
leap; the class-fees, however, are the same in humanities as in
special mathematics. The increase of 300 fr., then, is for board
and private tuition alone; and this increase M. Lesage does not
think it needful to make, but charges a boy in special mathematics, like a boy in humanities, 1,200 fr. a year for his board,   15
and 250 fr. a year for his *lycée* class-fees.

A certain number of M. Lesage's pupils are boys who are too
backward for the *lycées*, or who, from their age, have not
time to follow the *lycée* course; these have their whole instruction at the *pension*, an instruction in the main identical with   20
that of the *lycée*. These pay the same as the other boarders,
minus the *lycée* class-fees. Their education, therefore, costs
them from 5*l.* to 10*l.* a year less; but it says much in favour
of the *lycée* classes that the boys fit for them almost invariably
pay the fees and follow them.   25

The aspect of things at M. Lesage's, the internal arrangements, the large dormitories, the *salles d'étude*, the courts, the
chapel, are all to an English eye hardly distinguishable from
those of a *lycée*. The meals are the same; a sister is to be seen
in the infirmary; there are the two *aumôniers* to give religious   30
instruction to the Catholics, and the Protestant ministers to
pick out their sheep and conduct them to the *temple*. There is
the same preparation for the degree of bachelor as at the *lycées*,
even the same special preparation for the great Government
schools as at Saint Louis.* Only there is, or is believed to be,   35

---

* At Saint Louis the special and elementary mathematics of the ordinary *lycées* are organised with peculiar and minute reference to the
examinations of the several Government schools, and take the title of

a more effective and sustained tutoring; there is Madame Lesage to give an eye to the younger boys or to invalids; the
movement of the whole establishment does not seem so entirely mechanical, and the numbers, though large, are not, as
5   in the *internats* of the great *lycées* of Paris, so vast that a boy
feels lost in them. Charlemagne having no *internat*, it is obvious that a boy who does not live in Paris, and wants to go to
Charlemagne, must board elsewhere than at Charlemagne. But
the notion that a *pension* is more homelike and less barrack-
10 like than the *internat* of a *lycée*, that there is more individual
care, and that the tutoring is better done, tells in some degree,
no doubt, in favour of an establishment like M. Lesage's, as well
as in favour of one like M. Cousin's, though in the case of
M. Lesage's, as I have said, the difference from a *lycée* is not
15 very perceptible.

There are *pensions* formed on some special principle of
grouping, such as nationality or religion; for instance, for Pol-
ish boys frequenting the *lycées*, for Protestant boys frequenting the *lycées*; of course, with this further tie between the
20 inmates, the principle of association becomes still less mechanical. The march of the institution, however, its scale of expense, and the reasons for preferring it, will be found, I think,
in nearly all cases pretty much what I have described them.

But the Commissioners will desire to hear of humbler public
25 schools than the great *lycées* of Paris. Let us then take the
Collége Communal at Boulogne, close at our own door, which
almost any of us may have an opportunity of seeing. Again
a large, imposing building; it stands in one of the principal
streets of the town, and it gives its name, *Rue du Collége*, to
30 one of the side streets. Again the University of France, with
its guarantees and inspection; *Collége Communal de Boulogne-
sur-Mer; Instruction Publique; Académie de Douai*, is the full
style of the institution. 'The public establishments for secondary instruction,' says the organic law,* 'are the lyceums
35 and the communal colleges. Boarding-houses may form part of

_____

'École Préparatoire aux École Spéciales du Gouvernement.' There is
a two-year course of special mathematics.

* *Loi du 15 mars 1850 sur l'Enseignement*, art. 71, 72, 74, 75.

them. The lyceums are founded and maintained by the State, with the co-operation * of the departments and towns. The communal colleges are founded and maintained by the communes. In order to establish a communal college, every town must fulfil the following conditions: it must furnish premises suitable for the purpose, and undertake to keep them up; in these premises it must place and keep up the necessary fittings for the classes, and for the boarding-house too, if the school is to take boarders; it must guarantee, for five years at least, the fixed salary of the principal and the professors, which shall be held to be an obligatory charge upon the commune in case the resources of the college itself, the school-fees paid by day scholars and the proceeds of the boarding-house, are insufficient. The object and extent of the instruction in each communal college shall be determined, regard being had to the wants of the locality, by the Minister of Public Instruction, in Council,† on hearing the proposition of the Municipal Council and the opinion of the Academic Council thereon.'

The Communal College of Boulogne exists in conformity with these provisions of the law. Its inspectors are the rector of the Academy of Douai, the academy-inspector for the department of the Pas de Calais, and any one of the eight inspectors-general for secondary instruction whose tour of inspection brings him that way. It is a communal college *de plein exercice;* that is, it has not only the elementary division and the division of grammar, but that of humanities also. And it is the college of the municipality, kept in its own hands, and entrusted *en régie* only (as it is called) to the principal as their functionary. Sometimes the communal college is made entirely over to the principal, with a subvention from the municipality, and the condition annexed that he shall take a certain number of scholars on certain terms. Beyond this, he may make what he can out of the school, and he conducts it at his own risk. The principal of the Boulogne College, M. Blaringhem, told me that he had held a municipal college in this manner, but that he preferred to hold it as at present,

* This co-operation consists in the foundation of scholarships (*bourses*).
† This is the Imperial Council of Public Instruction.

en régie, with a fixed salary. I asked him if it was not more lucrative to be able to charge for one's boarders what one liked, instead of having the tariff settled by authority; he said, no, because the public school tariff fixed, with the most rare 5 exceptions, the tariff for all the schools in the country. And this is what I have again and again been told.

So the Boulogne College has its council of administration, like a *lycée,* to overlook its business affairs, and to go through its accounts in concert with the principal, as the council of a 10 *lycée* goes through them in concert with the provisor. Only as the college is a municipal institution, while the *lycée* is a State institution, and it is the French rule that the administration of a public establishment shall mainly belong to that public authority,—whether the State, the department, or the 15 commune,—with which it is in immediate connection, the council of administration of the Boulogne college is a municipal body. It consists of the mayor, the ex-mayor, a judge of the civil tribunal at Boulogne, the president of the Boulogne tribunal of commerce, and two lawyers, one of them a mem- 20 ber of the Boulogne municipal council, the other the mayor's adjoint. The scale of school-charges is fixed by this body in concert with the principal, and with the sanction of the rector of the Academy of Douai, to which Boulogne belongs. The charges are much lower for French boys than at Paris. A 25 boarder under 12 pays but 23*l.* a year; over 12 but under 15 he pays 25*l.;* above 15, 28*l.* The day scholar's fee is the old Paris school fee before 1853, 100 fr. (4*l.*) For English boys (of whom there are several) the rate is higher, because they have to be taught the French language; but for them the rate 30 is not in itself high; for boarders under 12 years of age, 39*l.* a year, from 12 to 15, 42*l.,* above 15, 48*l.* English day scholars pay 4*l.,* 5*l.,* or 8*l.*

The school arrangements, hours, and lessons are just the same as in a *lycée;* there is primary instruction for the little boys, 35 then an elementary and a grammar division with their regular classes; then humanities conducting to the degree of bachelor of letters, and a scientific training conducting to a degree in sciences, and to the great Government Schools. The college staff consists,—besides the chaplain, the teachers of modern languages and drawing, and a primary schoolmaster,—of the principal, and twelve regents, one for philosophy, one for history, three for science and mathematics, seven for classics. The principal must hold at least the degree of bachelor; eight of the twelve regents (all above the division of grammar) must hold the degree of licentiate, the other four must hold that of bachelor. The degrees of licentiate and bachelor are obtained, as I have said, only by examination. The degree of licentiate means more than an Oxford or Cambridge degree of master of arts, for which there is no examination. But I should like to see in any one of our considerable towns over against Boulogne,—Dover, Ramsgate, Canterbury,—a public school with a staff of 13 functionaries holding degrees, literary or scientific, from the universities of Oxford, Cambridge, or London. And the four other principal towns of the *Pas de Calais* have each, as well as Boulogne, their public school; Saint Omer * has a *lycée*, Arras, Béthune, and Saint Pol have communal colleges.

It is obvious that when the public schools of a country educate 66,000 of its boys of the upper and middle classes, the work left for private schools to do cannot be nearly so considerable as with us. I have remarked already that the population of the nine schools on which a Royal Commission reported barely exceeds the half of that of the great classical schools of Paris alone. But the *Public Schools Calendar* gives a list, after the nine schools, of all the chief endowed grammar schools of this country, and of the chief schools of modern foundation, such as Cheltenham and Marlborough. Certainly a good many of the endowed schools in the list do not at present rank as high as even a communal college; but giving all of them, and all of the schools of modern foundation enumerated in the calendar, the rank of public schools, and adding their population to that of the nine schools, I find that our public school boys

* Arras is the chief town of the Pas de Calais, but the *lycée* is not always in the chief town.

in England number (in round figures) 16,000, to match the
66,000 public school boys of France. I think the English reader
will be startled, as I was, by this comparison. If a public school
education is an advantage, then this advantage is enjoyed by
5   50,000 more boys in France than with us.

Therefore private education is by its volume a much less
important affair in France than with us. I cannot pretend to
give any accurate statistics of it. There are said to be 1,395
institutions of secondary instruction in France conducted by
10 laymen or by the secular clergy; the clerical seminaries, therefore,—223 in number,—are included in this body of schools.
The 1,395 schools have a total of 112,628 scholars. There are,
besides, 33 institutions of secondary instruction belonging to
religious corporations; these 33 have a total of 5,285 scholars.
15 This gives, in round numbers, 52,000 boys in private secondary
schools, clerical and lay, against 66,000 in the secondary schools
of the State. The French Government are intending to bring
out a great statistical work on secondary instruction, and this
will contain interesting information on the number and popu-
20 lation of the private schools; but this work is still only in prospect. I find that Paris contains 131 private secondary schools
(*établissements libres d'instruction publique*), but in this number are included establishments like M. Cousin's and the *Institution Massin*, acting mainly as feeders to the public schools;
25 and a very large number of the 131 are places of this kind. If
we take the departments, where the private secondary schools
are almost universally independent of the *lycées*, we shall be
struck with their insignificant number compared with what
we are used to in England. Let us take the Academy of Paris.
30 The district of this Academy includes nine departments:
Seine, Cher, Eure et Loir, Loir et Cher, Loiret, Marne, Oise,
Seine et Marne, Seine et Oise. Setting aside the metropolitan
department, the number of the private secondary schools is as
follows: in Cher, four; in Eure et Loir, four; in Loir et Cher,
35 four; in Loiret, four; in Marne, six; in Oise, five; in Seine et
Marne, eleven; and in Seine et Oise (a department *quasi* metropolitan, of which Versailles is the capital), nineteen; 57 in

all. These same eight departments contain four *lycées* * and twenty-one communal colleges.

Two private establishments which I visited I will mention, because they both enjoy a high reputation. One is the school of Sainte Geneviève in the Rue des Postes, the other is the Jesuits' school at Vaugirard. Like the school at Vaugirard, the school in the Rue des Postes is in the hands of the religious. Both are considerably more expensive than the public schools, keep up a brisk competition with them, and make them very jealous. This is particularly the case with the school in the Rue des Postes, which is a special preparatory school for the Polytechnic, Saint Cyr, the Naval School, and other Government establishments of the kind; the charge is 1,800 fr. a year (72*l*.), and certain matters are extras which are not extras in the *lycées;* a boy here does not cost less than 80*l*. But the course is for not more than two or three years; a boy comes here at the age when he would be entering *mathématiques élémentaires* at the *lycée;* here, too, he gets a thorough mathematical training, but this school aims at uniting this training with a truly religious education (*unir de fortes études mathématiques à une éducation vraiement religieuse* †). I found 300 boys here, with 35 masters, half for superintendence and half for teaching. It is, of course, to its superintendence that an establishment of this kind aims at giving a character entirely different to that of the superintendence in the establishments of the State. For the special scientific training of their pupils these religious are free to use, and do use, along with duly qualified teachers of their own order, the best lay instructors of the capital, the same as the *lycées* themselves employ. Their charges are high, and they can afford to provide thoroughly good teaching. Private tuition is an extra, and their pupils are the sons of wealthy people and can afford this extra. They admit their pupils with careful tests as to character and capacity, and they

---

* The easy access to the great *lycées* of the metropolitan department explains the fewness of the *lycées* in the other departments of this academy district.

† The words of the prospectus of the school.

keep them for the first three months on probation; the seclu-
sion is greater than in the *lycées;* the boys have 'leave out' but
once a month instead of once a fortnight; visits in the *parloir*
are permitted only twice a week instead of every day. No
5   wonder, then, that this abundance of care, concentration, and
appliances bears fruit, and that the candidates from the Rue
des Postes are remarkably successful in the examinations for
the Government schools.

    I was particularly struck with the good appearance of the
10 boys here. In the *lycées* I had been struck with their good manners, and the natural politeness they showed, down quite to
the little boys, when tried by the unusual incident of the entrance of a stranger and a foreigner into their school-room; I
am sure in England there would have been much less rising
15 and bowing, and much more staring and giggling; but here,
besides having good manners, the boys certainly looked, I
thought, fresher and better than in the *lycées.* They are a
great many of them the sons of the old noble families of France,
amongst which, as is well known, Catholic sentiment is strong.
20 They have probably had more advantages for their health and
growth and good looks than the mass of the *lycée* boys, and
the grounds and recreation of the school itself, though not
without a general resemblance to those of a *lycée*, had something much more attractive in them. The great religious house,
25 with its large cool galleries looking on the convents and gardens of that old quarter of Paris, and the figures of the religious
moving about, had certainly a repose and refreshment for the
spirits which in the great barrack-like machine of a *lycée* is
wanting.

30   The same may be said of the Jesuits' school at Vaugirard.
This school is even more interesting than that of the Rue des
Postes, being a complete school, while that is only a set of scientific classes. At Vaugirard they go through the whole course,
as in the *lycées,* from primary instruction to *philosophie* and
35 *mathématiques spéciales.* Here, too, as in the Rue des Postes,
they are very successful in the examinations for the great Government Schools; and for the same reasons. The boys are all
boarders; the fees are high (about the same rate as in the Rue

des Postes); no expense need be spared, and the tutoring as well as the class-lesson is very careful and good. The instruction is given by the religious, and as they work for love and for the good of their order, of course one great cause of expense in lay schools,—the payment of teachers,—is cut off. I heard the teaching in *philosophie, rhétorique, quatrième,* and the elementary division. The Jesuits seemed to me quite to merit their reputation as teachers. The superior is in every respect a remarkable man. He was a distinguished pupil of the *École Normale;* then he became a Jesuit, and, of course, quitted the service of the State; but his experience in the *École Normale* is no bad thing for his school. The good appearance of the boys struck me here as in the Rue des Postes, and the number of well-known names one heard among the boys was curious, and showed from what class this school is fed. Among the little ones I found a Maronite, and a young American from Mobile who could hardly speak French yet, and was glad, poor child, to be addressed in his own language. The cosmopolitan character of France is well shown by the number of boys from different parts of the world whom one finds getting their education in her schools. At Saint Louis I noticed a boy whose face was evidently that of an Oriental, and found on inquiry that he was the son of a Persian of rank, and had been sent there all the way from Persia.

The instruction at Vaugirard, having the degree of bachelor or the Government Schools in view, cannot but follow, in general, the same line as that of the *lycées;* the tutoring is the great difference. The house, class-room, and recreation arrangements have also a general similarity with those of the public schools, but the sense of a more agreeable, happier, and milder life than that of the *lycée* is felt at Vaugirard, and more at Vaugirard than in the Rue des Postes; for Vaugirard, though still Paris, is the very outskirts of Paris, and of the convent quarter of Paris,—a region full of trees and gardens. The Jesuit school is at the extremity of Vaugirard and gets the air of the country. In the Rue des Postes, too, the boys are older, and it is for the little boys that the cast-iron movement of the *lycée* appears most dismal, and the guidance of the ecclesiastical hand in

bringing them up seems most protecting and natural. Something of this ecclesiastical shelter we are used to in the great
schools and universities in England; and perhaps it is on this account that in spite of all which is to be said against the Jesuits
5   and their training, I could not help feeling that the Vaugirard
school was of all the schools I saw in France the one in which
I would soonest have been a schoolboy.

Sorèze, Lacordaire's school, which I have elsewhere * described, was a first-class private school under the Dominicans,
10   as Vaugirard under the Jesuits. The law forbids the title of
lycée or *collége* to be taken by any private establishments, but
the Minister of Public Instruction can authorise certain old
established schools of this kind to keep the name of *collége*
if they have been used to bear it. It is in this way that two out
15   of the seven great classical schools of Paris, *Rollin* and *Stanislas*,
get the title of *collége*. They, however, though not state establishments, not only follow the same course of teaching as the
lycées, but employ professors of the same stamp. Private establishments are bound, as I have already said, to have for
20   their head the holder of the degree of bachelor at least, or else
of a certificate of capacity; but for their assistant teachers they
may employ whom they will. But they are bound to keep a
register with the full name, age, and birthplace of each assistant
whom they employ, and to produce it whenever the inspector
25   requires. And the authorities of public instruction have the
power,† in a case of misconduct or immorality, to reprimand,
suspend, or altogether interdict from teaching, either the head
of a private school or any of his assistants, with the right of
appeal, when the penalty goes so far as suspension or interdic-
30   tion, to the Imperial Council in Paris. A teacher interdicted
cannot be employed thenceforth in any school public or private. These powers seem extensive; but I am bound to say
that all the private teachers whom I asked informed me that
they were exercised in a way to cause no complaint; and that
35   neither as to authorising the establishment of a private second-

---

* See *A French Eton, or Middle-Class Education and the State.*
(Macmillan.)

† *Loi du* 15 *mars* 1850 *sur l'Enseignement,* art. 67, 68.

ary school in the first place, nor as to inspecting or interfering with it afterwards, was the action of Government in the least degree unfair or vexatious.

The *séminaires*, where the clergy are educated, are under ecclesiastical management. They are nominally subject to state superintendence; * but so far as I could learn this superintendence comes to nothing, and no inspector ever enters them.

* *Loi du* 15 *mars* 1850, art. 70.

Chapter VII

Character of Discipline and Instruction in the French Secondary Schools

Discipline in the French Schools—Instruction—Greek—Latin—Versions Dictées—School-Books—The Mother-Tongue—Modern Languages—Geography—History—Mathematics and the Natural Sciences—Foreign Judgment of English Mathematical Teaching—Religious Instruction—Realschule Instruction—Recent Attempts to Develope it in France—M. Duruy's Enseignement Secondaire Spécial.

The long school-hours and the constant supervision in the French schools are favourable to discipline, and the Frenchman is born with a turn for military precision and exactitude which makes the teacher fall easily into the habit of command, and the pupil into that of obedience. French teachers who have seen our schools are struck with the greater looseness of order and discipline in them, even during class hours; and I have seen large classes in France worked and moved with a perfection of drill that one sometimes finds in the best elementary schools in England, but rarely, I think, in our classical schools. Our government through prepositors or prefects, and our fagging, are unknown in the French schools; for the former, the continual presence and supervision of the *maître d'étude* leaves no place; the latter is abhorrent to French ideas. The set of modern opinion is undoubtedly against fagging, and perhaps also against government through the sixth form; one may doubt, however, whether the force of old and cherished custom, the removal of excess and abuses in the exercise of these two powers, and certain undeniable benefits attending that of, at any rate, the latter of the two, may not yet long preserve them in the great English schools. The same can hardly be said of flogging, which, without entering into long discussions about it, one may say the modern spirit has irrevocably condemned as a school punishment, so that it will more and more come to appear half disgusting, half ridiculous, and a teacher will find it more and more difficult to inflict it without a loss of self-respect. The feeling on the Continent is very strong on this point. The punishments in the French schools are impositions and confinement; at Vanves I saw a kind of *punishment-parade*, the culprits being marched round and round a court. The employment of punishments, however, is certainly less than with us, and here, too, the great number of school hours saves the French schoolmaster from a difficulty. It is a part of the censor's business to collect, and to give at the end of every week to the provisor, a report from the usher on the behaviour, and from the professor on the progress, of each boy in the school; at the end of every quarter the provisor forwards the summary of these reports to the parents.

Comparing the instruction with that of our own great classical schools, one is at once struck by the fact that the French schools carry Greek by no means so far as we do. Their Greek composition is next to nothing; there is no Greek verse, and even the Greek exercise has lately been abolished in *troisième* and *seconde*, on the ground that it was the merest grammatical exercise, not carried far enough to give the pupil the least power of really writing Greek, and that an exercise of this sort was out of place after *troisième* began. Different *lycées* have a special reputation for different branches of instruction; thus Saint Louis is famous for mathematics, Louis le Grand for the humanities generally, Charlemagne for Greek. But even at Charlemagne the upper boys, whom I heard at lesson under a distinguished professor, M. Boissier, had certainly nothing like the mastery of Greek of the upper boys in our best public schools; one might almost say that in the iambics of Sophocles they could get along pretty well, but that any chorus was decidedly too much for them. The Greek lessons are much fewer in number than with us. The grounding seemed to me good enough. The little boys in *sixième* whom I heard at Bonaparte saying their Greek grammar left nothing to be desired.

In Latin the French schools seem to me quite equal with ours; perhaps it is from the affinity of the language with their own, but they seem, if there is a difference between our best schools and theirs, to be more at home with Latin, and to take to it more kindly than we do. They do not, however, get through nearly so much of the Latin authors, but their Latin composition, prose and verse, is very good. From the specimens I saw I should say they had a Ciceronian and Virgilian tradition just like some of our famous schools, and produced work very much the same as the best of them. In this respect both we and they, I think, beat Germany, though a German boy has a fuller command of a Latin of a certain kind than either our boys or the French.

Both in Latin and Greek the quantity of writing work done by the French boys strikes an Englishman with astonishment; the professors seem to be extraordinarily fond of *versions dictées,* as they are called; a passage from a classic is dictated, the boy takes it away with him, translates it out of class hours, and a good deal of time in a subsequent class hour is given to the revision of this translation of his. A day boy sometimes makes strange work of the passage dictated, and then, as he has not the *étude* to do his translation in, gets no opportunity of setting himself straight, and is altogether bewildered. I cannot but think that the French might with advantage write a good deal less, and adopt our plan of making the boys learn and say their lesson out of a book a good deal more. In our elementary schools I have often regretted that the master teaches the lessons so much, instead of making the boys, as in our classical schools, learn it beforehand; the French professors proceed more like our elementary teachers in this respect, and then, when the master *teaches* the lesson, of course there has to be a great deal of going over it again afterwards, in the *étude* or the *conférence.* The *lycées* have much more of this than our schools, and I am inclined to prefer, at least for teaching classics, our plan, which makes the boy depend more on himself, and, above all, takes him through a great deal more of an author.

The French use books of selections a great deal, and I believe Rugby was rather an exception to the common rule of the English public schools in using them in the higher forms so very little. I suppose no one who has been used to the Rugby practice can much like the other. About their school books in general the French are conservative, and amusing stories are told of German scholars at Paris pointing out errors in the received school books, and getting a fine, instead of thanks, for their pains. It is a just instinct, however, which makes the French university cling to fixity in its elementary school books, and their boys learn grammar better than ours in consequence. A boy does not enter into the *rationale* of grammar; what he wants is a system of clear categories to re-fer the cases in his reading to. What is that infinitive?—It comes under the *hinc spargere voces* category.—Why is it *patientiâ* after *abutêre?*—By the rule that *utor* and its compounds take an ablative. This is a good mental exercise for a boy, and he is capable of it; but that he may practise it with advantage, his categories should be as plain and few as possible, and should be firmly fixed in his own mind and in his questioner's. When he is capable of comprehending the *rationale* of grammar (quite another affair), he is of an age to *consult* a grammar, not learn it, and his grammar can then hardly be too philosophi-cal and full. Half a dozen grammars of this kind are sufficient for the needs of a whole school. But we, and the Germans too, keep trying to put the *rationale* of grammar into the first grammar, the grammar that is learnt, not consulted; the boy's mental digestion rejects the *rationale*, and meanwhile the fixity needed for categories to which he is promptly and precisely to refer all his cases,—an effort of which his mind is perfectly capable,—is sacrificed. Thus, with all the faults of the old Latin grammar, twenty years ago boys of twelve and thirteen did their grammar work a thousand times better than they do it now, because the substance of fixity of categories had not then been abandoned for the shadow of *rationale*. Up to a certain point, therefore, I think the French authorities wise in their zeal for fixity of text-book.

From the bottom of the French schools to the top one finds recitation, reading, and exercises, in the mother tongue. Writing French is as considerable a part of a boy's work as writing

Latin. So far is this pushed that there are to be found in France
hostile critics of the *lycées* who say that to judge by their teaching you would suppose every boy in them was meant to be
afterwards by profession a man of letters. It is probable too
5 much stress may be laid on teaching matters of literary work-
manship and style, graces which, after all, *nascuntur non fiunt;*
but the reading and reciting from the classics of the mother
tongue and the getting some knowledge of its literary history,
is clear gain; and if the French attempt to teach too much, and
10 of what cannot be taught, in style and the art of writing, we do
not, or at least did not when I knew our schools, attempt to
teach enough, and of what can.

M. Duruy is very anxious to promote the teaching of modern
languages in the schools, and that the boys should learn to speak
15 them, not to read them only. From the beginning of the grammar division to the top of the school modern languages form
a regular and seriously taught part of the school work, and I
have heard the little boys in *sixième* patiently practised at
speaking sentences in English or German. This attempt, of
20 course, necessitates the employment of foreign teachers, and
then comes the well-known difficulty as to discipline, which
the French experience just as we do. Perhaps, from the many
other fields open to Englishmen, the supply of good English
teachers abroad is particularly limited; that of Germans seemed
25 to be considerably better. I mean, it is much more common,
I think, to find an educated, competent German, a man in
whom his employers have a good bargain, teaching in a French
school, than to find an Englishman of like stamp there. With
these drawbacks much is not at present effected; but more, I
30 think (still speaking from my own remembrance of our great
schools), than is done with us; partly because the conditions
of the problem are better understood, partly because its solution is more seriously attempted.

Geography forms the object of distinct lessons of which the
35 graduated course is traced in the ministerial programme.
Neither the German classical schools nor ours teach it, in
general, in this manner; and after the elementary classes it is
surely best taught in connection with other lessons, which af-

ford plenty of occasions for teaching it, and give a better chance, by attaching it to interesting events, of making it likely to be remembered and more than a dry and soon lost nomenclature. The professor in France uses the blackboard and traces outline maps with an adroitness and accuracy which may often be seen in our elementary schools, but not often, I think, in our classical.

History, too, is taught according to a graduated programme, which begins in the lowest class of the grammar division with the East,—Egypt and Asia,—and proceeds through Greece and Rome to the history of the modern nations, finishing, as I have already said, in the philosophy class with contemporary history. The programme system,—the programme being drawn, as it is, by a competent hand and with great care,—seems to me of service here. It gives the teacher himself a valuable clue, serves to guide his reading, and leads him to group his ideas and methodise his teaching. I do not think any educated man could read the programme of Middle-Age and modern history for the French *lycées* without profit,—without being reminded of gaps in his knowledge, and stimulated to fill them. The history lessons I heard given to the higher classes were evidence in favour of the system, for they were well-arranged and very interesting.

Modern languages, geography, and history have an *agrégation* of their own; that for modern languages having been introduced by the present minister. They have thus, of course, special professors, and are not taught, as I remember them taught in our schools, by each classical master to his own form.

As often as I approach mathematics and natural sciences, I am confronted by my own ignorance of them, and warned not to say much. Something, however, of what I heard and saw I must report as well as I can. The French have a reputation for their teaching of these matters; their language is excellent for it, and their text-books are clear and good. But what strikes one most, is the prominence of oral teaching here; and oral teaching seems here in its right place. The text-book is merely the basis of the professor's instruction, and by itself can give no idea of what the French mathematical teaching is. In these

studies, again, the programmes seem to be of advantage, and the system of revision and repetition of lessons, which in classics I thought pushed too far, is so serviceable in mathematics and natural sciences that it may well have got its currency from its
5 usefulness in these branches. I never shall forget the impression made upon me by teacher and pupils in the class of *mathématiques spéciales* at Saint Louis, under a young and distinguished professor, M. Vacquant. Teaching so vivid, and a class of fifty so borne along, I should hardly have thought possible.
10 No pupil is allowed to enter the class of *mathématiques spéciales* without being first examined to test his ability to profit by it. But down to the arithmetic of the lower classes the teaching, in this branch, seemed to me always searching and good. A distinguished Swiss, well known to many persons in this coun-
15 try, M. William de la Rive, told me he could trace in the educated class of Frenchmen a precision of mind distinctly due to the sound and close mathematical training of their schools. I heard, too, several lessons in the natural sciences; M. Duruy has sought to strengthen the whole of the scientific teaching at the
20 same time that he did away with the *bifurcation*. The mathematical lessons, however, seemed to me better than the lessons in physics; partly, no doubt, because the latter need an apparatus for illustration and experiment which the former do not, and which a school cannot always procure in due abun-
25 dance and efficiency. But the French lay the greatest stress on the importance of teaching the natural sciences, and regard mathematics as subsidiary to this object; they severely criticise our Cambridge teaching for devoting itself so exclusively to pure mathematics, and making the instrument into an end. The
30 barrenness in great men and great results which has since Newton's time attended the Cambridge mathematical teaching is mainly due, they say, to this false tendency. Comte's judgment on the study of sidereal astronomy is well known, and the leaning of practice and opinion among French mathematical
35 teachers at present tends in the same direction as that judgment.

In general, the respect professed in France for the mathematical and scientific teaching of our secondary schools is as low as that professed for our classical teaching is high. A French schoolmaster who had seen a number of our schools said to me: 'Your boys do not learn arithmetic, the science of numbers; they learn to reckon (*le calcul*).' And every one who has watched a French teacher employing with his pupils the simple process called *réduction à l'unité*, and has also watched an English boy's bewildered dealing with a rule of three sum, and heard his questions about its 'statement,' which to him is a mere trick, learnt mechanically, not understood, and easily misapplied, has a good notion of the difference between the arithmetic of French and of English schools. I must not forget to add that our geometry teaching was in foreign eyes sufficiently condemned when it was said that we still used *Euclid*. One of the great sins of Cambridge was her retention of *Euclid*. I am bound to say that the Germans and the Swiss entirely agree with the French on this point. *Euclid*, they all said, was quite out of date, and was a thoroughly unfit text-book to teach geometry from. I was, of course, astounded; and when I asked why *Euclid* was an unfit text-book to teach geometry from, I was told that Euclid's propositions were drawn out with a view to meet all possible cavils, and not with a view of developing geometrical ideas in the most lucid and natural manner. This to me, in my ignorance, sounded plausible; but at any rate the foreign *consensus* against the use of *Euclid* is something striking, and I cannot but call the English reader's attention to it.

I have several times mentioned the *aumôniers*, or chaplains, attached to the French public schools. None of these schools, secondary or primary, are secular schools; in all of them religious instruction is given. It is given, too, in the vast majority of private schools. An hour's lesson in the week, certain exercises and prizes in connection with this lesson, and service on Sundays, are what this instruction amounts to in the secondary schools. The provisor and the chaplain regulate it between them; that of Catholic boys is under the inspection of the bishop of the diocese or his delegate, in concert with the provisor. Protestant and Jewish boys receive the religious instruction of their own communion, regulated, *mutatis mutandis*, precisely like that of Catholic boys. The great *lycées*

of Paris have Protestant and Jewish chaplains attached to them,
just as they have Catholic chaplains. Where Protestants or Jews
are not numerous enough for the school to have a special chaplain for them, boys of those persuasions still receive their religious instruction from ministers of their own creed appointed
to visit them, and are entirely exempted from the religious instruction of the Catholics. I cannot myself see that the religious
lessons (I do not, of course, speak of the services and ordinances of religion) come to very much in secondary instruction, though I must think, differing in this respect from many
liberals, that they have an important and indispensable part
in primary. But it is indisputable that they give rise neither in
France nor Germany to any religious difficulty, as we say,
whatever; they are regulated with absolute fairness, and there
are no complaints at all of improper interference and prose-
lytism. This, I say, is indisputable; and Protestants and Jews
would testify to it as much as Catholics.

Hitherto all the schools spoken of have been classical schools,
with Latin and Greek for the staple of instruction, and a greater
or less admixture of mathematics and natural sciences with
these. But in France, as elsewhere, an important sign of the times
is the dissatisfaction with the predominance and omnipresence
of Latin and Greek in secondary instruction. The greatest
lover of the classics must admit that the modern spirit shows a
certain hostility to them; and it is remarkable that in the secondary schools * of that great manifestation of the modern
spirit, the French Revolution, only two professors out of fourteen were assigned to classics and *belles-lettres*. Napoleon, as
I have already mentioned, did away with the central schools,
and restored Latin and Greek to their old supremacy, but the
bifurcation, which began as early as 1821, showed the tendency
to elude, when it was impossible to gainsay, that supremacy.
The upper primary schools, which were instituted by M.
Guizot's school legislation in 1833, were another attempt to get
rid of difficulties caused by that supremacy. The two great
municipal schools of Paris, the *Collége Chaptal* and the *École*

* The central schools instituted by the Convention in 1795.

Turgot, were another. The *Collége Chaptal* has 1,000 scholars, 600 of them boarders paying 40*l.* a year. The *École Turgot* takes day scholars only, paying from 6*l.* to 7*l.* a year. The director of this latter school, which I visited, is M. Marguerin, a gentleman who was sent by the Prefect of the Seine to see our secondary schools in London, and whose report on what he saw there is well worth reading. In both these establishments Latin and Greek are wholly excluded from the school course, which is filled by French, modern languages, mathematics, natural sciences, and the other parts of what is called a modern education. The Christian Brothers have a successful school of the same kind at Passy. The friends of this new instruction were strong enough to insert in the organic school law of 1850 a paragraph binding the minister to appoint special juries to give certificates to the imparters of the *enseignement professionnel,* as it was then called.* Commissions were set to organise it, but while they proceeded slowly with their task, it so far organised itself that 64 *lycées* out of 74, and nearly all the communal colleges, made some provision for giving it; and last year, of the 66,000 boys in the schools of the State, 20,000 were receiving this modern instruction, while in private schools of one sort and another 40,000 boys were receiving it.

M. Duruy is entitled to speak for his own 20,000 boys at any rate, and he declares that, in their case, with hardly any exceptions, this instruction proved a failure.† The commissions appointed to study the subject reported that this instruction was a failure, too, in the majority of private schools. Its teachers were proceeding at random, without any distinct and well-digested plans; they were ill-paid, and their position was uncertain; they were, in general, without the requisite collections and apparatus. A *grande inutilité,* M. Duruy says, has to be transformed into an effective institution.

The law of the 21st of June of last year [1865] is designed so to transform it. On the one hand, say the authors of that law, to

* 'Le ministre, sur l'avis du Conseil supérieur de l'instruction publique, instituera des jurys spéciaux pour l'enseignement professionnel.'—*Loi du 15 mars 1850 sur l'Enseignement,* art. 62.
† *Circulaire du 2 octobre 1863 relative à l'enseignement professionnel.*

balance the old so-called liberal professions, for which a classical education was supposed to be the best preparation, there have arisen in modern society a number of industrial, commercial, and agricultural professions, which did not exist a hundred
5 years ago, and which require a different preparation from that for the old professions. On the other hand, the superior primary instruction of 1833, with a course of study not ill adapted to the requirements of these new claimants, did not take, because it had an air of inferiority about it from its connection
10 with the primary schools, and 'on veut rarement,' says the reporter to one of the commissions which examined the new law, 'avoir l'air d'être au niveau des humbles.' So out of social vanity boys flocked into the Latin and Greek classes for whom these classes were not suitable; but the vanity, as M. Duruy
15 shrewdly enough says, which sets people against non-classical studies, does not carry them so far as to make them pursue classical studies with any success.

It was required, for the sons of a new class of professional men not socially inferior to the members of the liberal profes-
20 sions, to provide schools of equal rank with the classical schools. To effect this, two parallel courses of secondary instruction have been formed; a secondary instruction in arts and sciences, for boys destined to agriculture, commerce, or manufactures; a secondary instruction in classics for boys des-
25 tined to the so-called liberal professions. The two courses are to be of equal rank, held in the same institutions, and furnished with the same encouragements. The teachers of the one are to enjoy an equal position and to offer equal guarantees with those of the other.

30 The new legislation, therefore, unites in the public schools the classical and non-classical pupils in the same buildings, under the same government, but gives the non-classical pupils separate lessons, and separate professors. It establishes a normal school, occupying the old Benedictine abbey of Cluny, for the
35 training of the latter. It provides a distinct aggregation for them, as the professors of classics, mathematics, and modern languages have a distinct aggregation. It fixes for them a scale of payment. It provides a separate supply of scholarships for

their pupils, and it draws out a separate set of programmes for the new instruction. It institutes a local body, with the title of *conseil de perfectionnement,* in connection with each establishment where the new instruction is given, and a *conseil supérieur de perfectionnement* to advise the minister in Paris. Finally, 5 it extends to private schools giving the new instruction that power of obtaining, if judged worthy, from the communes, departments, or state, a building and a subvention, which the law of 1850 bestowed on the private secondary schools.

It is the French theory that the State's duty is to establish 10 models and so improve private institutions. M. Duruy has certainly taken great pains to adapt his model to the purpose for which it is wanted. The pupils of the new instruction are likely to have time for only a three or four years' course, instead of the seven or eight years' course of the classical school; and the 15 new instruction, therefore, is arranged for four years, and for boys from about the age of 12 to 16. Even this shorter course is more likely than the classical course to be abridged by the boy's sudden withdrawal; it has been attempted, therefore, to make as far as possible each year's plan of study complete in 20 itself. Neither for the professor, nor for the pupil, has the culture to be carried so far as in the classical school; for both, therefore, the highest class of payments is cut off. In Paris the rate of payment to the professors of the new instruction is about the rate of payment to classical professors in the prov- 25 inces; out of Paris, something below this; but then these new teachers will often come from the class where only primary instruction at present goes recruiting for teachers, and to this class the rate of salary will appear good. The boys, whether boarders or day scholars, pay as in the elementary division and 30 the grammar division of the classical school; the higher rates of *philosophie* and *mathématiques spéciales* are cut off. Provision is made for drafting into the classical school boys who show aptitudes which make the prolonged training, classical or mathematical, of that school, desirable for them. 35

The name of the new instruction was rather a matter of difficulty. It had got that of 'professional,' but this word gives the idea of a school where particular trades and businesses are

learnt, and this is not the design of the new schools. 'We do
not,' say their promoters, 'put the workshop in the school;
in these new establishments the teaching is still a means, not
an end, and when the pupil leaves them, the knowledge he
possesses will be general knowledge. The true professional
school comes later; it is such a school as the School of Commerce, or the School of Agriculture, or the School of Woodcraft.' Others proposed the name 'French;' we in England have
inclined to that of 'modern;' but the name actually adopted is
that of 'special,' not a very good one as it seems to me. *Enseignement secondaire spécial* is the authorised description of
the new instruction.

Leaving out Latin and Greek altogether, it comprehends the
mother tongue and its literature, history, geography, mathematics, natural sciences, modern languages, information of common use about the government, laws, administration, commerce, industry, and agriculture of France; accounts, book-
keeping, drawing, music, and gymnastics. Mathematics and
physics are taught with a direct view to application; the three
great classes of professions, industrial, commercial, and agricultural,—for one or other of which every pupil is supposed
to be destined,—being had in mind. Instruction in morals and
religion forms, as in all the public schools, part of the course.
The new and elaborate programmes for the whole course are
drawn with great care, and are well worth studying. They are
contained in a volume which has recently issued from the
department of public instruction at Paris.* Taking the boy on
his leaving the primary school at 11 or 12, when he is supposed (and this is worth remarking) besides his religious instruction, reading, and writing, to possess the elements of grammar, the four rules of arithmetic both in whole numbers and
in vulgar and decimal fractions, and the metric system, it gives
him, first, a preparatory year, in which what he possesses is
perfected, his slight smattering of history and geography ex-
changed for a methodical foundation of those studies, a modern

* *Enseignement secondaire spécial; décrets, arrêts, programmes et documents relatifs à l'exécution de la loi du 21 juin 1865.* Paris: Imprimerie
Impériale, 1866.

language, geometry, and natural history begun. Then, by a regular gradation, which yet leaves the instruction of each year as far as possible a complete whole in itself, it carries him through a four years' course in the matters named by the law. The attention paid to teaching the mother tongue, and not only its history and literature but how to write it, is as remarkable in this course as in that of the classical schools. But perhaps the greatest novelty is the information on common subjects, as it may in brief be called. The choice and arrangement of this information, simple matter as it seems when it stands in the programme, must have cost much thought and pains, there being such a lack of models to follow; and it seems to me most successful. The programme headed *législation usuelle*, giving the outline of a course on the public and private law and the administrative organisation of France,—how the government is composed, what are the functions of its different departments, how the municipalities are constituted, how the army is recruited, how taxes are raised, what is the legal and judicial system of the country, how in the most important relations of civil life, marriage, inheritance, holding property, buying, selling, lending, borrowing, partnership, the laws affect the citizen,—this programme in particular seems to me quite admirably composed, both for what it inserts and what it omits. The programmes on the legislation of commerce and industry, and on rural, industrial, and commercial economy, are also very interesting; but each of these is more particularly designed for a single division of pupils, according to the class of profession to which they are destined; whereas the programme for *législation usuelle* is designed for all, containing what it is important for all alike to know; and therefore this latter programme is not so easy a programme to prepare, and has a more general interest when prepared.

It is as yet too soon to judge of the success of this important addition of M. Duruy's to the public secondary instruction of France, but the correspondent of the *Museum*,—an English educational periodical deserving to be more widely known than it is,—seems to me not far from the truth, when he says that to find a population for these new schools is the difficulty,

as the rich class of people wanting to use them is small, and
the large class of people wanting to use them is poor. The loud
demand for them comes chiefly from a certain number of
rich industrialists, with views about education, and opposed to
5 the tyranny of Latin and Greek, who yet wish their sons' school
to be a school of as high social rank as the classical school.
This has been done by giving the new instruction the title and
apparatus of secondary instruction, and its cost, of course,
along with them. A boarder in one of the new schools pays
10 from 40*l*. to 45*l*. a year; a day scholar pays from 8*l*. to 10*l*.
The rich industrialist with views about education is of course
enchanted to pay this, and give his boy the prestige of a
lycée at the same time that he gets rid of what he thinks its
rubbish of Latin and Greek; but these rich industrialists are
15 not very numerous. An immense class of well-to-do parents,
whom M. Duruy would gladly see relieving the classical school
of what he calls its *non-valeurs*, boys *sans aptitude pour les
belles-lettres*, and sending them to the modern school, have
still, and for some time are likely to have, the notion that a
20 social stamp is put upon a youth by a classical education, and
they continue sending their boys to the classical school to obtain this stamp. On the other hand, the instruction of the modern school is the very thing which the artisan class, the higher
portion of it at any rate, desires; it is the supreme object, in
25 the way of education, of the ambition of this class, which is
quite free from any genteel weakness for Latin and Greek;
but here the rates of payment form an insuperable obstacle.

Nevertheless, as one may say of flogging, that the set of the
modern spirit is so decisively against it that it is doomed, what-
30 ever plausible arguments may be urged on its behalf, so is the
set of the modern spirit so decisively in favour of the new instruction, that M. Duruy's creation, whatever reasons may be
given why it should not succeed, will probably in the end
succeed in some shape or other. This current of opinion is,
35 indeed, on the Continent, so wide and strong as to be fast
growing irresistible; and it is not the work of authority. Authority does all that can be done in favour of the old classical
training; ministers of state sing its praises; the reporter of the

commission charged to examine the new law is careful to pay
to the old training and its pre-eminence a homage amusingly
French.* Men of the world envy us a House of Commons
where Latin quotations are still made, school authorities are
full of stories to show how boys trained in Latin and Greek   5
beat the pupils of the new instruction even in their own field.
Still in the body of society there spreads a growing disbelief
in Greek and Latin, at any rate as at present taught; a growing
disposition to make modern languages and the natural sciences take their place. I remark this in Germany as well as   10
in France; and in Germany too, as in France, the movement
is in no wise due to the school authorities, but is rather in their
despite, and against their advice and testimony. I shall have
an opportunity, by-and-by, to say a few words respecting
what appears to me the real import of this movement, and the   15
part of truth and of error in the ideas which favour it. All I
wish now to lay stress upon is its volume and irresistibility.

* 'On ne saurait trop exalter l'importance sociale des lettres classiques.
*Ce sont elles qui ont assuré depuis des siècles la suprématie intellectuelle
de la France.'*—Enseignement secondaire spécial, p. 438.   20

Chapter VIII

Superior or University Instruction in France

Superior Instruction—Faculties—Letters and Sciences—Theology —Law—Medicine—Other Institutions in France for Superior Instruction—Use of Such Institutions—Conclusion.

I have incidentally said something of the superior instruction of France as I went along, and at the outset I disclaimed all pretension to treat it fully; but a very short notice of it as a whole ought to be given before I pass elsewhere. The superior
5 instruction of France consists of the faculties, and of certain other institutions,—such as, for instance, the College of France, the Museum of Natural History, the School of Living Oriental Languages,—where the studies and lectures are of a pitch which presupposes that the student's secondary instruction is
10 completed. The students of French superior instruction are not, like our undergraduates at Oxford or Cambridge, boarded in colleges, they only attend lectures. There were in 1862 no less than 23,371 students in the French faculties; 14,364 of this number were in those of Paris. There are five faculties: the-
15 ology, law, medicine, sciences, and letters. The faculties are attached to the academies, of which by the law of 1854 there are, as I have more than once said, sixteen.* It is only sciences and letters which are represented in every academy. For each of these, therefore, there are 16 seats of faculties in France,
20 with a total of 97 chairs for sciences, 86 for letters. Large towns, not the seat of a faculty of sciences or letters, have the power of establishing auxiliary schools † of superior instruc-

---

* Two more, Chambéry and Algiers, have been added, but neither of them is as yet the seat of any faculty.
25 † *Écoles préparatoires à l'enseignement supérieur des sciences et des lettres.*

tion, attendance at the lectures of which is allowed to count, within certain limits, as attendance at faculty lectures. To pass beyond the degree of bachelor it is necessary to have attended certain courses of professors' lectures. Of course the chairs of a faculty in Paris are almost always much more numerous than in the provincial academies, and in the more important of these they are more numerous than in the less important. The faculty of sciences has in the academy of Paris, for example, 18 chairs; in the academies of Clermont, Nancy, and Poitiers it has but four. These four, which may be taken as representing the absolute necessary for a faculty of sciences, are the following: physics, chemistry, pure and applied mathematics, natural history. In letters the Paris faculty has eleven chairs, the provincial faculties have five each, which in all of them, except that of Toulouse, are the same: ancient literature, French literature, foreign literature, philosophy, history. Toulouse substitutes for chairs of ancient and of foreign literature chairs of Greek and of Latin literature.

Theology has seven seats of faculties, five for the Catholics and two for the Protestants. The seats of the two Protestant faculties are Montauban and Strasbourg. The chairs of these faculties are nowhere more than seven or fewer than five. The subjects common to them all are dogmatic theology, ecclesiastical history, and (here I use the French titles) *éloquence sacrée*, and *morale évangélique*. The faculty of theology, which has in all 42 chairs, is the least important of all the faculties in France, because the Church of Rome does not recognise its degrees, and they have no canonical validity. Of course, for those who aspire to be professors in this faculty, its degrees and attendance at its lectures are indispensable; and by an ordinance of the Government of 1830 its degrees are required for all ecclesiastical preferment down to the post of *curé de chef-lieu de canton* inclusive; but as a certain number of years' pastoral service was to be accepted as an equivalent for these degrees, and they were not to be required of anybody who when the ordinance appeared was more than twenty-one years old, they have not come to much. The French church is not eminent at present for theological learn-

ing, and what theological learning it has does not come to it
from the University.

Law has eleven seats of faculties, with 98 chairs. The great
chairs in this faculty are those for the *Code Napoléon*, Roman
law, civil procedure, commercial law, administrative law. The
Code Napoléon has to itself six chairs at Paris and three in
each of the other ten seats of faculties. Two of these ten,
Nancy and Douai, have been recently added, and the reader
may like to know how an additional faculty, when wanted,
is provided. The town of Nancy, already the seat of an academy, of a faculty of sciences, and of a faculty of letters, desired a faculty of law also, Lorraine having formerly, under
its old sovereigns, possessed one. The State agreed to establish one there, the municipality of Nancy undertaking on its
part to raise every year and pay to the treasury a sum re-
imbursing the State for its outlay on the new faculty, its professors, *agrégés*, and courses of lectures. Douai got its faculty
of law on the same terms. The State gives the character of a
national institution, the guarantee of publicly appointed teachers, and the privilege of conferring degrees; and the town is
abundantly willing to pay for this.

No one in France can practise as a barrister (*avocat*) without the degree of licentiate of law. No one can practise as a
solicitor (*avoué*) without the *certificat de capacité en droit*.
Let us see what the possession of these two diplomas implies.

A licentiate of law must first have got the degree of bachelor
of law. To get this he must have the degree of bachelor of
letters, have then attended two years' lectures in a faculty of
law and undergone two examinations, one in Justinian's *Institutes*, the other in the *Code Napoléon*, the Penal Code, and
the Codes of Civil Procedure and Criminal Instruction. Dues
for lectures, examinations, and the diploma, make the diploma
of bachelor of law cost, when the candidate has obtained it,
nearly 25*l*.* The new bachelor must then, in order to become
licentiate, follow a third year's lectures in a faculty of law,
undergo two more examinations, the first on the *Institutes* of

* To be exact, 620 fr.

Justinian again, the second on the *Code Napoléon,* the Code of Commerce, and Administrative Law, and must support theses on questions of Roman and French Law. The degree of licentiate costs 24*l.*

A solicitor, to obtain the 'certificate of capacity in law,' must for one year have attended lectures in a faculty of law, embracing in this one year both the first and the second year's course of lectures on the *Code Napoléon,* and on Civil and Criminal Procedure, and undergoing an examination on the subject of each course. The cost of this certificate, all fees for lectures, &c., included, is from 11*l.* to 12*l.**

The professors in the faculty of law are men eminent in the knowledge of their several branches. English readers will do well to compare this regular and educative course of legal instruction with the way in which a barrister is left, with us, to pick up the trick of his trade as he likes; and they may bear in mind at the same time the resources of our universities and Inns of Court for legal education, and how our universities and Inns of Court apply them.

Medicine has three great seats of faculties, with 61 chairs. The faculties are at Paris, Montpellier, and Strasbourg. To be a physician or surgeon in France, a man must have the diploma of doctor either in medicine or in surgery. To obtain this, he must have attended four years' lectures in a faculty of medicine, and had two years' practice in a hospital. When he presents himself for the first year's lectures, he must produce the diploma of bachelor of letters; when for the third, that of bachelor of sciences, a certain portion of the mathematics generally required for this degree being in his case cut away. He must pass eight examinations, and at the end of his course he must support a thesis before his faculty. His diploma, by the time he gets it, has cost him a little over 50*l.*†

A medical man with a doctor's degree may practise throughout France. To practise without it, a man must have the diploma of *officier de santé.* To practise without the diploma either of doctor or of *officier de santé* is penal. The *officier de*

* The exact sum is 285 fr.   † 1,260 fr. is the exact sum.

santé must have attended three years' lectures in a faculty
and had two years' practice in a hospital, and he must pass five
examinations and write a paper bearing on one of the subjects of his instruction. Before he can be admitted to attend
lectures in a faculty of medicine he must produce a *certificat
d'examen de grammaire*, a sort of minor bachelor of arts degree, turning on the matters taught in *quatrième*, the highest
class in the grammar division of the *lycées*. Thus his having
learnt some Latin and Greek is, our British Association will
be shocked to hear, rendered necessary. His diploma costs him
altogether about 32*l.*, but it only authorises him to practise in
the department where he has been received *officier de santé*,
and he may not perform any great operation except in the presence of a doctor.

A kind of branch of the faculties of medicine is formed by
the *Écoles supérieures de Pharmacie*, three in number, with
nineteen chairs. These schools, too, are at Paris, Montpellier,
and Strasbourg. Chemistry, toxicology, pharmacy, and natural
history are the main matters of instruction. For medicine and
pharmacy there are, as for sciences and letters, auxiliary
schools * in a number of the large towns of France, with professors only a grade below the faculty professors, with lectures
allowed to count, to a certain extent,† as faculty lectures, and
with the right of examining for some of the lower diplomas
and granting them. No one can practise as a druggist or apothecary in France without getting either a first or a second class
diploma. A first class diploma necessitates three years' study
in an *École supérieure de Pharmacie*, three years' practice
with a regularly authorised apothecary, and the passing eight
examinations, the last of which cannot be passed before the
age of twenty-five. The cost of obtaining this diploma comes

* *Écoles préparatoires de médecine et de pharmacie.* There are twenty-
two of them.

† For instance; for a doctor of medicine's diploma, three years' and
a half attendance on lectures in an *école préparatoire*, and one year's
in a faculty, is accepted in lieu of four years' attendance on faculty
lectures. For a druggist's second class diploma, a year and a half's instruction in an *école préparatoire* is accepted in lieu of a year's instruction in one of the three *écoles supérieures de pharmacie*.

to nearly 56*l.* A *pharmacien* with this first class diploma may practise anywhere in France. A second class diploma only entitles its holder to practise in the department chosen by him when he entered his name for lectures. But to hold this second class diploma he must have attended faculty lectures for one or two years, have practised six or four * years with a regular *pharmacien,* and passed four or five examinations, for the last of which he must be twenty-five years old. The candidate for the first class diploma must have the degree of bachelor of sciences before he can enter himself to follow the lectures of the pharmacy school; the candidate for the second class diploma must have the *certificat d'examen de grammaire* mentioned above.

I must add that our whole regulation, or rather non-regulation, of the teaching and practice of pharmacy strikes the best judges on the Continent with perfect astonishment, and is condemned there with one voice. I see that an eminent English physician declared last year, at the meeting of the British Association, that while the practitioner whom in England, where he knows less of chemistry than anywhere else, we are pleased to call a chemist, can in France or Germany perform any analysis which the physician may require of him, in this country he is in nine cases out of ten quite incompetent for such a task. This exactly corresponds with what I have heard on the Continent. Here, at any rate, we can trace a clear practical inconvenience from our educational shortcomings. Signor Matteucci, whom I have already quoted, a most favourable judge of England, who, though he says Oxford and Cambridge are but *hauts lycées,* hopes we shall long keep them, told me that he considered the strengthening of our superior instruction, especially in the direction of the sciences, our most pressing need of all in the matter of public education.

In Paris the seat of the faculties of theology, sciences, and letters is at the Sorbonne; of the faculty of medicine, at the *École de Médecine;* † of that of law, at the *École de Droit.*‡

---

* A second year's attendance on lectures is accepted in lieu of two years' practice.

† In the *Place de l'École de Médecine.*   ‡ In the *Place du Panthéon.*

There are eight inspectors of superior instruction,—three for letters, three for sciences, one for medicine, and one for law. Six of the eight are members of the Institute, and their names will probably be familiar to many English readers: M. Ravais-
5   son, M. Nisard, M. Dumas (the chemist), M. Le Verrier, M. Brongniart, and M. Charles Giraud. Their salary, like that of the faculty professors in Paris, is 12,000 fr. a year, a high salary for France; and the posts of inspector-general and pro-fessor of superior instruction form a valuable body of prizes
10 for science and literature. Each faculty has an aggregation, similar in plan to that which exists for the professors of sec-ondary instruction, and which I have described; but, for ag-gregation in a faculty, very high and complete studies are necessary. In general, the course of promotion is this: the in-
15 tending *agrégé* first obtains the degree of doctor in his faculty; after being admitted *agrégé* he becomes assistant professor, and finally full professor. A full faculty professor must be thirty years old. The Dean of Faculty is chosen by the Min-ister of Public Instruction from among the professors of his
20 faculty. While the minister has power to dismiss of his own authority the functionaries of secondary instruction, those of superior instruction can only be dismissed by imperial decree.*
The faculties have also the right of proposing candidates for their vacant chairs, though the Emperor, who nominates, is
25 not bound to adopt their proposal.

Free or private courses on the matters of superior instruc-tion cannot be publicly given, in France, without the authori-sation of the Minister of Public Instruction, who, before grant-ing it, takes the advice of the prefect and the academic rector
30 for the locality where it is proposed to open them.

Outside the faculties are a number of important State-estab-lishments, all of them contributing to what may be called the higher instruction of the country. The most remarkable of these is the College of France, founded at the Renaissance, to
35 make up, one may say, for the short-comings of the mediæval universities, and which has grown in scale, value, and con-

* *Décret organique du 9 mars 1852 sur l'instruction publique*, art. 3.

sideration till it now has thirty-one professors, covering with
their instruction all the most important provinces of human
culture, and many of them among the most distinguished
men * in France. The *École des Chartes*, the pupils of which
have laboured so fruitfully among the archives of France   5
and the early documents of her history, has seven professors.
The Museum of Natural History has sixteen. The School of
Living Oriental Languages has nine. The School of Athens is
designed to give to the most promising of the young professors, from the age of about twenty-five to thirty, of French   10
public instruction, the opportunity of for two years studying
on the spot the language and antiquities of Greece. All who
have made these a special object of study know what sound
and useful memoirs have proceeded from pupils of the French
School of Athens. I may mention, as a specimen, the memoir   15
on the Island of Eubœa, by M. Jules Girard. All these establishments, with the *Bureau des Longitudes,* and the public
libraries of the capital,—the great library in the Rue Richelieu,
the Mazarine Library, the Sainte Geneviève Library, the Ar-
senal Library, and the Sorbonne Library,—are under the Min-   20
ister of Public Instruction. Other ministers have special schools,
some of which I have already mentioned, attached to their
department. The Minister of War has thus the Polytechnic,
Saint Cyr, and the Cavalry School of Saumur; the Minister
of Marine has the Naval School and the Schools of Hydrog-   25
raphy; the Minister of Finance has the School of Woodcraft
(*École forestière*); the Minister of the Household has the
School of Fine Arts; the Minister of Agriculture, Commerce,
and Public Works has the Schools of Agriculture, the Veterinary Schools, the Schools of Arts and Trades, the Central   30
School of Arts and Manufactures, the School of Commerce,
the Schools of Mines and Miners, and the *École Impériale des
Ponts et Chaussées.* The grants to the Institute and to the

---

* Among them at the present moment are MM. Élie de Beaumont,
Flourens, Coste, Franck, Laboulaye, Michel Chevalier, Alfred Maury,   35
Munk, Caussin de Perceval, Jules Mohl, Stanislas Julien, Sainte Beuve, and
Paulin Paris. The salary of a professor at the College of France is
7,500 fr. a year.

Academy of Medicine (a sort of medical institute) come into the estimates of the Minister of Public Instruction. Into his estimates come also all grants, whether for pensions, gratuities, missions,* publications, or subscriptions, which fall under the head of grants for literature, science, and art. For 1865 these grants amounted to 680,000 fr. (27,200*l.*). The grants to the Institute and Academy of Medicine, grants which really come under the same category as the preceding, amounted to above 26,000*l.* more. These figures have an eloquence which I will leave the English reader, acquainted with our national expenditure for the advancement of literature, science, and art, to appreciate for himself.

Public establishments such as these which I have enumerated serve a twofold purpose. They fix a standard of serious preparation and special fitness for every branch of employment; a standard which acts on the whole intellectual habit of the country. To fix a standard of serious preparation is a very different thing, and a far more real homage to intelligence and study, than to demand,—as we have done since the scandal of our old mode of appointment to public functions grew too evident,—a single examination, by a single board with a staff of examiners, as the sole preliminary to all kinds of civil employment. Examinations preceded by preparation in a first-rate superior school, with first-rate professors, give you a formed man; examinations preceded by preparation under a crammer give you a crammed man, but not a formed one. I once bore part in the examinations for the Indian Civil Service, and I can truly say that the candidates to whom I gave the highest marks were almost without exception the candidates whom I would not have appointed. They were crammed men, not formed men; the formed men were the public school men,

* It may be worth mentioning how, in France, a public department usually proceeds with a report like mine to the Schools' Enquiry Commission, for instance. It sends its reporter and receives his report, but it does not print and publish it in an official volume. It leaves its author to publish it as an ordinary book, the department, however, subscribing for 200 or 300 copies, which it distributes among institutions or individuals that it wishes to inform on the matter to which the book relates.

but they were ignorant on the special matter of examination,
—English literature. A superior school forms a man at the
same time that it gives him special knowledge. The reader
may have seen, probably, a correspondence published last year
respecting some appointments to the British Museum. What-   5
ever we may think of the points in dispute between Mr. Panizzi
and the Civil Service examiners, it will hardly be maintained
that the certificate of these examiners is an adequate guarantee
for the fitness of an archivist or librarian for his functions. In
France a public archivist or librarian does not go before one   10
or two gentlemen of general education, and satisfy them on
their general questions; he must have the diploma of *archiviste
paléographe*. To possess this he must have for three years attended lectures at the *École des Chartes*,—free lectures, by men
masters of their subject. At the end of each year he is ex-   15
amined, and if he cannot pass, is set aside; success in the third
year's examination, and a thesis publicly supported on some
matter of palæography, bring him his diploma and his appointment.

Again: we have Eastern possessions and interests compared   20
with which those of all other European nations are insignificant,
but France has a public school of living Oriental languages and
we have none. Professors, among whom are M. Stanislas Julien,
M. Garcin de Tassy, and M. Caussin de Perceval, teach there
Arabic, Persian, Turkish, Armenian, Hindustani, modern   25
Greek, Chinese, Malay, and Japanese. And pupils from all parts
of Europe come to their instruction.

A second purpose which such public establishments serve is
this. They represent the State, the country, the collective community, in a striking visible shape, which is at the same time   30
a noble and civilising one; giving the people something to be
proud of and which it does them good to be proud of. The
State is in England singularly without means of civilisation
of this kind. But a modern state cannot afford to do without
them, and the action of individuals and corporations cannot   35
fully compensate for them; the want of them has told severely
on the intelligence and refinement of our middle and lower
class. It makes a difference to the civilisation of these classes

whether it is the Louvre which represents their country to them, or the National Gallery; and whether the State consecrates in the eyes of the people the great lines of intellectual culture by national institutions for them, or leaves them to take care of themselves. What the State, the collective permanent nation, honours, the passing people honour; what the State neglects, they think of no great consequence.

It is in this point of view that the national institution, on the Continent, of all that interests human culture seems to me especially important. In France, in her superior and still more in her secondary instruction, there is undoubtedly too much regulation by the central government, too much prescribing to teachers the precise course they shall follow, too much requiring of authorisations before a man may stir. If the professors were left free to arrange their programmes by concert among themselves, if any one, not ἄτιμος, and with proper guarantees of capacity (for to a rigorous demand for these there ought to be no objection) were free to open a school or to deliver public lectures without any further check whatever, thought and learning in France would in my opinion be great gainers. This change, however, would but remove what is an excrescence upon the public establishment of education, a noxious excrescence due to political causes, and to their predominance in France as with us (only with us they have operated in another way by preventing the public establishment of education altogether) over intellectual interests. All the salutary and civilising effects of the public establishment of education are to be had without this excrescence. When I come to Germany I will show them so existing.

II

Italy

Chapter IX

Development and History of the Italian Secondary Schools

Mediæval Schools of Italy—The Renaissance and the Italian Universities—The Catholic Reaction—Long Torpor of the Italian Schools—Efforts at Improvement—Piedmontese Administration—The French in Italy; Their Improvements—Reaction After 1815.

I have said that the early history of secondary and superior instruction might be traced in France as in a kind of representative country, because France was the main centre of that great movement of the eleventh and twelfth centuries, in which the seats of this instruction,—seats where it took the char-   5
acter which it everywhere still keeps more or less, and in England keeps to a remarkable degree,—had their origin. These seats were the universities, and the University of Paris was in early times the most important of them. But Italy has universities which for antiquity and early importance run the   10
University of Paris very hard. Tradition attributes the first beginnings of the University of Pavia to Charlemagne, and our Lanfranc, William the Conqueror's Archbishop of Canterbury, studied in the school of law there. But in the twelfth century the law school of the University of Bologna eclipsed   15
all others in Europe. The two great branches of legal study in the middle ages, the Roman law and the canon law, began in the teaching of Irnerius and Gratian at Bologna in the first half of the twelfth century. At the beginning of this century the name of university first replaces that of school; and   20
it is said that the great university degree, that of doctor, was first instituted at Bologna, and that the ceremony for conferring it was devised there. From Bologna the degree and its ceremonial travelled to Paris. A bull of Pope Honorius, in 1220, says that the study of *bonæ literæ* had at that time made the   25

141

city of Bologna famous throughout the world. Twelve thousand students from all parts of Europe are said to have been congregated there at once. The different nations had their colleges, and of colleges at Bologna there were fourteen. These were founded and endowed by the liberality of private persons; the university professors, the source of attraction to this multitude of students, were paid by the municipality, who found their reward in the fame, business, and importance brought to their town by the university. The municipalities of the great cities of northern and central Italy were not slow in following the example of Bologna; in the thirteenth century Padua, Modena, Piacenza, Parma, Ferrara, had each its university. Frederick II. founded that of Naples in 1224; in the fourteenth century were added those of Pavia, Perugia, Pisa, and Turin. Colleges of examiners, or, as we should say, *boards*, were created by Papal bull to examine in theology, and by imperial decree to examine in law and medicine.

It was in these studies of law and medicine that the Italian universities were chiefly distinguished. The medical school of Salerno carries back its origin to the most remote antiquity, and boasts the same priority for its teaching of medicine which Bologna boasts for its teaching of law. The statutes of foreign universities regulate their studies *ad instar studii Bononiensis,* just as they so often regulate them by the example of Paris. But Paris had the pre-eminence in theology and philosophy, and as these were the great studies of the mediæval universities, the university which took the lead in them surpassed all others in importance. So complete was the lead of Paris in the study which swallowed up all others,—the so-called philosophy of the schoolmen,—that the technical style of this philosophy was called by the humanists of the Renaissance, who inveighed against it: 'the style of Paris.'

To Italy we owe the Renaissance, and in the fourteenth century she took the intellectual lead which in the twelfth century belonged to France. But the movement of the Renaissance did not in Italy any more than in France possess itself of the universities and schools, and make these its grand channels. The Renaissance was a literary movement, and the great men of the Renaissance were the humanists. The grand business of the universities was the scholastic philosophy, and this governed all the rest of their teaching, even their teaching of letters. The humanists were men, like Petrarch, outside of the established school-teaching of their day, and hostile to it; but this teaching went on in spite of them. There were isolated efforts by men of genius to bring education too into the movement of the Renaissance, and to give the guiding of education to humanists and the humanities; such an effort was that of Vittorino da Feltre with his school at Mantua, and very interesting the history of such efforts is. But they did not succeed. The organised official teaching of Italy remained mediæval and barbarous long after her great writers and artists had launched their country, and Europe along with her, on the line of modern ideas and modern civilisation.

The last phase of the scholastic philosophy was Averroism,—Aristotle interpreted through the *Great Commentary* of Averroes. What this second or third hand Aristotle was,—an Aristotle that had passed through Syriac, Arabic, Hebrew, and Latin translation, with blunders in each, and was then studied by the light of his Arabian commentator, and with the uncritical spirit of the Middle Age, with a view to find in him a philosophy of the universe,—is now well known. Averroism ruled in the Italian universities down to the seventeenth century, long after it had disappeared from the French schools, its earlier stronghold, and when the humanities, which Italy herself had had so large a share in introducing, and the new philosophy of Descartes, had extinguished it everywhere else. The extraordinary number of copies of certain Averroist professors' lectures, still preserved in manuscript in the libraries of northern Italy, shows the popularity of this teaching, and enables us to trace its duration.* Cremonini, who is called the last schoolman, was professor at Padua in 1631. This countryman of Galileo, after the discovery of Jupiter's satellites, judging that this discovery contradicted Aristotle, would never consent to look through a telescope again. One could not have

* See *Averroès et l'Averroïsme,* par M. Renan, p. 324.

a better incident to end the career of the scholastic philosophy.

The Averroist doctrines, in this later phase in which the Italian universities received them, were at wide variance with Catholic orthodoxy, and the Lateran Council of 1512 condemned them. Still the theologians were, at bottom, not ill-disposed to the routine, the respect for authority, the clinging to established texts, which the Averroist teaching shared with their own, and which both of them had learned in the same uncritical school of the Middle Age. The Averroist professors, on their part, made connivance easy by drawing the distinction, so often drawn since, between philosophy and religion. According to philosophy, they always said, according to Aristotle and Averroes, this is so and so; if the Church says otherwise, we are obedient sons of the Church, and we submit our opinion to hers. On the other hand, it was not the arid jargon and barren formulas of the Averroist schoolman, it was his free canvassing of problems such as the unity of the intellect and the immortality of the soul, which drew the Italian students, full of the scepticism and intellectual agitation of that time, to their lectures. 'Tell us about the soul,' was the cry with which, at Padua and Bologna, the crowd of students is said to have received a new professor. By this side Averroism might also win some indulgence from the school of positive and experimental science which was rising beside it, the creation of that scientific intellect of Italy, which is one of her chief glories, and, perhaps, her chief force; and which, through the worst times of the last three centuries, has never failed her.

Nothing, indeed, could be more surely fatal to scholasticism, in all its forms, than the growth of positive and experimental science, and nothing could seem a more certain means to have swept it, in the end, out of the Italian universities. But Averroism and all the philosophical and literary movement, both of the Italian universities and of the Italian nation, fell by another cause. It fell by the Catholic reaction which followed the abortive attempts to bring about a reform of religion in Italy. The intellectual development which the England of Elizabeth seemed to promise was in like manner checked by the triumph of Puritanism; but the triumph of Catholicism in Italy was far more complete, was the triumph of a far more unprogressive and anti-intellectual influence, and far more fatal. Boards of reform, as they were called, were instituted for the supervision of studies; religious orders, like the Jesuits, the Barnabites, and the *Padri Scolopi*, took to school-keeping, and many pious foundations for education date from this period; but education was by the promoters of this movement not valued for its own sake, as the liberal culture of the human spirit, but was applied as an auxiliary to promote the authority of the old religion, and as a preventive against heresy.

Thus the soul was taken out of it, and with education and government well matching each other, the brilliant Italy of the Renaissance settled down into the frivolity and torpor of its eighteenth century. The number of professors' chairs at Bologna, which in the seventeenth century had been 166, had in 1737 fallen to 72. The communes which had disputed eagerly the possession of a distinguished professor, and bidden against one another for his services, sunk into apathy. The boards of examiners, distinct from the regular teachers of the students, which in the earlier and flourishing times of the universities had made examinations independent, honest, and searching, fell into disuse. Universities came to be regarded not as seats of learning, but as mere instruments for conferring degrees, and their examinations were a farce. At Naples, the noble family of Avellino had the privilege assigned to it of giving, after a pretence of examination, the diploma of doctor in law and medicine, and of exacting the fees for it. It is remarkable, however, that through all this period of apathy and decline, the scientific tradition of Italy was never broken; a continuous chain of great names carries on this tradition uninterrupted from the sixteenth century to our own: Falloppio, Galileo, Torricelli, Malpighi, Vallisnieri, Spallanzani, Galvani, Volta, Scarpa. In letters and philosophy, on the other hand, Italy has, perhaps, from the seventeenth century to the nineteenth, only one truly great name to set against this illustrious list,—the name of Vico. It shows how insufficient are the natural sciences alone to keep up in a people culture and life, that the Italians, at the end of a period with the natural sciences alone

thriving in it, and letters and philosophy moribund, found themselves, by their own confession, with 'a poverty of general culture, and in an atmosphere unpropitious to knowledge,' which they sorrowfully contrast with the condition of other
5   and happier nations.

Two efforts after life and improvement break this long period of deadness in the education of Italy. The first is the endeavour of the princes of the House of Savoy to make the organisation of public instruction in their own states more
10   efficient. The Royal Constitutions of 1729 and 1772 were the fruit of such an endeavour. By these constitutions the control of secondary instruction was taken away from the religious orders, and the *Collegio delle Province*, with 100 free studentships, was established with the aim of preparing, in con-
15   nection with the University, teachers qualified to give this instruction. Schools of method were established to prepare teachers for primary schools, and with the title of *Magistrato della Riforma* the germ of a well-composed Council of Public Instruction appeared. The regulations of this Council gave
20   strictness to the lax university examinations, and thus braced the University studies. Inspired by a political interest rather than by a love for culture and science, these reforms of the Turin Government had, probably, for their main design to give the State the control of so powerful an instrument as
25   public education; but in certain circumstances such a design may prove to be patriotic and useful. The Turin Government imported into education the ideas which the Italy of that time so greatly needed, and which have made Piedmont's fortune in Italy; the ideas of public spirit, effective administration, honest
30   work, and rigid discipline. These alone are not enough to form what the Italians well call an *atmosfera intellettuale propizia agli studi*, but they form character, and prepare the indispensable foundations for a people's greatness: and even in that sub-alpine soil where, as Peyron, the celebrated Piedmontese
35   hellenist, contemptuously said: 'The thyme of Attica refuses to strike root,' their application produced a system of schools the best worked and managed, on the whole, in Italy.

The second effort was due to the French occupation. We

in England, impressed with their faults because it was our lot to meet them as enemies, do not in general know the true merits either of the French Revolution or of the first Napoleon. Their faults are palpable and undeniable; their merits are equally undeniable, but it needs some knowledge of the Continent, and some reflection, to make them palpable to an Englishman. The great merit of the French Revolution, the great service it rendered to Europe, was *to get rid of the Middle Age;* very few Englishmen yet perceive even that. The great merit of the first Napoleon, the great service he rendered to Europe, was *to found a civil organisation for modern society.* With all his faults, his reason was so clear and strong that he saw, in its general outline at least, the just and rational type of civil organisation which modern society needs, and wherever his armies went, he instituted it.

That the French Revolution's merit and service was a real one is shown by all the world, as it improves, getting rid more and more of the Middle Age. That Napoleon's merit and service was a real one is shown by the bad governments which succeeded him having always got rid, when they could, of his work, and by the progress of improvement, when these governments become intolerable and are themselves got rid of, always bringing it back. Where governments were not wholly bad and did not get rid of Napoleon's good work, this work turns out to have the future on its side, and to be more likely to assimilate the institutions round it to its pattern than to be itself assimilated by them. The Rhine province of Prussia has the *Code Napoléon* and Westphalia has not; but there is far more likelihood of Westphalia's having one day the *Code Napoléon* than of the Rhine province having the law of Westphalia.

The absurdities and abuses of which the old education of Europe was full, and nowhere so full as in Italy, the French reformed with unsparing vigour. Convents were turned into schools, and in the half-barbarous district of Southern Italy Joseph Bonaparte's government planted *licei* in the towns, while it extirpated brigandage in the country. The now existing public schools at Bari and Lecce were then established.

Medical study in the kingdom of Naples having declined from the diplomas of the school of Salerno to those of the Princes of Avellino, the French restored it by founding the *Collegio Medico-chirurgico Napolitano,* in which medical students

5 were boarded, lodged, and taught by special professors of their own; to this day, I am told, one of the best institutions in Europe for its purpose. Faculties and universities, of which it is easy to have,—and Italy had and has,—too many, were suppressed, and the expenditure on them turned to better ac-

10 count for the interests of public instruction. Thus at Ferrara the feeble and unneeded university was closed, and a *liceo,* which the city up to that time did not possess, and a school of hydraulics, for which Ferrara by its situation offers special advantages, substituted for it. Other universities, like Pavia,

15 strong already, were strengthened still more; indeed, such a constellation of famous names as is seldom seen was to be found at Pavia under Napoleon's rule: Volta, Spallanzani, Frank, Scarpa, Foscolo, and Monti, were all professors there at the same time. The exact sciences, which stir the whole man less

20 than letters and philosophy, are better suited than letters and philosophy to a political system like the first Napoleon's; and his own special turn, too, was for the exact sciences; so in Italy, as in France, these throve and shone far more than letters. Yet for letters, too, and general culture, Napoleon did the very best

25 thing, perhaps, that any government could do for them, by founding the Normal School of Pisa, on the model of, and in connection with, the Normal School of Paris, of which I have said so much. At the present moment the Pisa school is the sheet anchor of Italian secondary instruction.

30   With the fall of the first French Empire all this improvement stopped. The Normal School of Pisa was closed. I have mentioned the French reforms in medical study at Naples. Besides reforming this, the French Government had reorganised the whole University, established new chairs, museums, a botanic

35 garden, &c. But 'the Bourbon restoration,' says Signor Matteucci, 'struck particularly at the University, reducing the number of students as much as possible by creating in the provinces university faculties, which had often only a nominal existence,

and by confiding all instruction to the Jesuits and to the clergy.'
As it was at Pisa and Naples, so it was everywhere. At Turin
itself, the early seat of reform of a certain kind, the University
was in 1821 closed. The attempts of the better Italian governments to do something for education were but half-hearted   5
attempts, made without light and faith. In Tuscany the Grand-
Ducal Government reopened in 1846 the Normal School of
Pisa; but so languid was this effort at revival, and so unfavourable were the circumstances for it, that in 1862 there was not
a single pupil left.   10

Chapter X

The Italian Secondary Schools Since 1859

The New Kingdom of Italy—The Legge Casati—The Italian Secondary Schools at the Present Time—Laxity in Working the Legge Casati.

Meanwhile those events happened which consolidated Italy and placed the Piedmontese Government at its head. Count Cavour well knew how necessary an agent in the regeneration of Italy was a good system of public instruction. He knew
5 too that in modern times the State cannot remain a stranger to this instruction. The first Piedmontese Minister of Public Instruction had been appointed in 1847. The first Council of Public Instruction was nominated at the same time. Piedmont was at that time only Piedmont. It began at once to organise
10 and improve instruction within its own borders, and the Piedmontese habits of discipline, regular work, and honest administration, produced, as I have said, excellent results in the Piedmontese schools, though the literary and scientific genius of Italy, and her love for all humane culture, do not come
15 to her from Piedmont. The moment the first annexation had taken place, the Turin Government hastened to provide for the now enlarged requirements of its public instruction by a new law. This law was the education law of the 13th of November, 1859,—the *Legge Casati*, as, from the name of the
20 Minister of Public Instruction who introduced it, it is generally called. As fresh portions of Italy came under King Victor Emmanuel's rule, this law was extended to them also,* with some slight modifications. From that time to this, min-

* To Tuscany by the Tuscan Government's law of March 10th, 1860;
25 to the Neapolitan provinces by the law of the Government of the Lieutenancy, February 10th, 1861; to Sicily by the decree of the Prodictatorial Government, October 17th, 1860.

istries have rapidly succeeded one another in Italy; no Minister of Public Instruction has held his post long, and from each, while he held it, numerous regulations and rearrangements have proceeded. There is, therefore, a certain want of unity in what has been hitherto done. But the law of 1859 imposed on the Council of Public Instruction the duty of making a report to the Minister at the end of every five years on the state of all parts of public instruction in the Italian Kingdom. The first quinquennial period expired in November, 1864, and in May, 1865, the Council, through their Vice-President, Signor Matteucci,—himself at that time an Ex-Minister of Public Instruction,—addressed to the Minister, Baron Natoli, a report full of interest on the actual condition of superior, secondary, and primary education in the kingdom of Italy, with recommendations for dealing with them. The Council had prepared itself for its task by sending inspectors through the kingdom, by addressing questions to the university and school authorities, and by collecting statistics. To ascertain the progress made since 1859 was of course the immediate object of the Council's inquiry; but in elucidating this, they threw clear light on the condition of studies which the law of 1859 found existing. I begin with secondary instruction; and my notice of superior instruction, except at its point of contact with secondary, will, as before when I was speaking of France, be very brief.

In 1865 there were in the northern provinces of the Italian kingdom 40 *licei*, in the central provinces 19, in the southern provinces 14, in Sardinia 2, in Sicily 7; 82 in all. The *licei* are established in the principal towns; the State has one, at the least, in each province, and there are 59 provinces. Sixty-two of the 82 *licei* are State establishments. The course in a *liceo* is of three years only, and they correspond with the superior division of the French *lycées*. With the grammar division and elementary division correspond the *ginnasi*, or gymnasiums, with a five years' course, answering to the two classes of the French elementary division and the three of the grammar division. Only in the Neapolitan provinces is the *ginnasio* a part of the *liceo;* the united institution there takes

the name of *liceo-ginnasiale*. In other provinces they are separate schools under separate management and often in separate
premises. A certain number of *ginnasi* are, like the *licei*, at
the State's charge; * one, at least, in each province is so; but
in every chief town of a province, or district of a province
(*circondario*, the French *arrondissement*) where the State has
not a *ginnasio*, the municipality is bound by the law of 1859
to provide and superintend one. Many municipalities prefer
to provide the requisite funds and to hand over the task of
superintendence to the State; and this is permitted by the law.
There were, in 1865, 117 *ginnasi* in the northern provinces, 43
in the central, 17 in the southern, 12 in Sardinia, and 29 in
Sicily; 218 in all. Ninety-five of these are State establishments. After the *licei* and the *ginnasi* come the *scuole tecniche*.
These are a creation of that modern desire for schools not
exclusively classical which has founded the *Realschulen* in
Germany, and is founding the *enseignement secondaire spécial*
of France. In Piedmont the first attempt to satisfy this desire
was made in 1840, when Latin was struck out of the programme
of the primary schools, and arithmetic, geography, and history,
introduced into that of the secondary. A step further was
taken in 1848, when there was instituted ('by way of experiment,' as the law said †) a special course in the public schools
for boys whose studies were not to be classical. This special
course embraced the usual matters,—the mother-tongue and
modern languages, modern history, mathematics and natural
sciences, drawing, account-keeping, &c.,—which we have seen
it embrace elsewhere. A bifurcation was thus established, not,
as in France, in the middle of secondary instruction, but at
its outset, and immediately after primary instruction; and the
technical course, like the gymnasial, was of five years. Sub-
ventions were offered by the State to provinces and communes which would establish special courses of this kind, and

---

* Of the *liceo*, however, the material as well as the personal expenses
(as they are called) are at the State's charge; that is, the State pays for
buildings, repairs, fittings, &c., as well as for teachers; of its *ginnasi* and
scuole tecniche only the personal expenses, the teachers' salaries, are
defrayed by the State.

† *Legge del* 4 *Ottobre* 1848, *sui collegi nazionali*, art. 25.

the law of 1859 allowed the municipalities which were under the obligation of providing a *ginnasio* to provide a *scuola tecnica* instead of it. The same law entirely separated the technical from the classical schools, and divided the technical or special course into two grades: the first of three years in   5
the *scuola tecnica;* the second of two years in the *istituto tecnico.* The *scuola tecnica* remained in connection with the department of Public Instruction, and its teaching was made gratuitous. The *istituto tecnico* was attached to the department of Agriculture and Commerce, and became a special or   10
trade school, rather than a school of general secondary instruction, classical or non-classical.

Of *scuole tecniche* there were, in 1865, 85 in the northern provinces, 44 in the central, 7 in the southern, 3 in Sardinia, and 18 in Sicily; 157 in all. A certain number of these schools,*   15
too, are State establishments, having been originally founded by the State, or transferred to its care by the municipalities. Every State school takes the prefix of 'royal' (*regia*).

The schools which are not State institutions are divided into *pareggiate* and *non-pareggiate. Pareggiate* means assimilated.   20
In the assimilated schools the course is the same as in the State schools; the pupils are classified in the same way, and the programmes which the Minister of Public Instruction, as in France, issues, and which differ little from the French programmes which I have already described, are followed. The non-assimi-   25
lated schools regulate their course, classify their scholars, and fix their studies, as they please.

The vast majority of the boys frequenting these schools are day-scholars. Italy, however, has a great many foundations for the free board and lodging of a certain number of scholars in   30
connection with the schools of the place where the foundation exists. An establishment where scholars are boarded and lodged is in Italy called a *convitto.* It may happen that pupils who pay for their board and lodging are received there as well as scholars proper, or bursars, but the *convitto* exists for the   35
sake of the latter. Many of these foundations are in the hands of the religious, many in those of the municipalities; the State

* 45 out of the 157.

has nine of them, and these State foundations are called *convitti nazionali.*

The expenditure of the State on these nine *convitti,* and on the 62 lyceums, 95 gymnasiums, and 45 technical schools, with which it has charged itself, was, in the school-year 1863–64, 2,194,634 fr.; in round numbers, 88,000*l.* The rest of the public secondary schools are maintained by local expenditure on the part of the provinces and communes, of which no complete accounts have yet been collected and published.

The population of the public secondary schools of the Italian kingdom * is 24,492.† It is divided as follows. The *licei* have 3,362 scholars; the *ginnasi,* 12,862; the *scuole tecniche,* 8,268. To divide it in another way: the classical public schools have 16,224 pupils, the non-classical, 8,268. For the body of 24,492 scholars there are 2,342 teachers, of whom 905 are ecclesiastics.

This is extravagant work on the face of it, for we have here a teacher to every ten scholars and a fraction. The more we examine the school statistics the more clearly does the extravagance of the present order of things come out. The best frequented schools by far are those of the northern provinces, the old dominions of the throne of Sardinia; but even in these schools the supply of pupils reaches on an average only 19 and a fraction per class for the *licei,* 15 and a fraction per class for the *ginnasi,* and 24 pupils and a fraction per class for the *scuole tecniche.*‡ But in the new provinces of the Italian kingdom the proportion is very much lower. In central Italy the

---

* The kingdom of Italy contained, by the census of 1861, 21,747,334 inhabitants.

† These numbers are taken from the recent report of the Superior Council of Public Instruction to the Minister. The statistics, however, collected with so much pains for that most valuable document, are not absolutely complete; the returns from some places either could not be procured, or arrived too late to be used. See *Sulle Condizioni della pubblica Istruzione nel Regno d'Italia; Relazione generale presentata al Ministro dal Consiglio Superiore di Torino* (Milan, 1865), p. 245.

‡ As in France, the *class,* in Italy, represents a year of the school course, and the school has as many classes as it has years of course. The *licei* and *scuole tecniche* have thus a three-year course and three classes; the *ginnasi,* a five-year course and five classes.

licei have on the average only 9 pupils per class, the *ginnasi* 10, and the *scuole tecniche* only 8. As we go farther south the proportion becomes lower still. It is calculated by the Council of Public Instruction that in northern Italy and Sardinia there are at present twice as many *licei* as are wanted, in central Italy 5 four times as many as are wanted, in southern Italy and Sicily more than four times. The pupils are wanting to the schools, they say, not the schools to the pupils; and it is in the classical schools that the deficiency of pupils is greatest and increases, while the non-classical schools are continually getting fuller. 10

The Council do not recommend the suppression, at present, of any of the existing *licei*, but, to diminish a source of needless expense, they propose to put the literary and mathematical instruction of the *licei* into the two first years of the course there, and the instruction in natural sciences into the third year, 15 and that in all those *licei* which are unprovided with the proper outfit for giving the latter instruction, the course shall be restricted to two years, and the third year's course suppressed.

A more efficacious retrenchment is proposed in the case of the lower secondary schools. It is proposed to strike Latin and 20 Greek out of the first three years of the gymnasial course, to fill these three years with the modern and practical studies of the technical school, to make the first three years' course gratuitous, and to amalgamate the technical school with the lower part of the gymnasium. Latin and Greek are not to come 25 till the two last years of the gymnasial course. This seems a very sensible proposal. The separation established by the law of 1859 between the technical school and the gymnasium was costly and unnecessary. It had more inconveniences than the old French bifurcation, because it separated the boys younger. 30 It is in general premature to decide for a boy, the moment his primary instruction is finished, whether his secondary instruction shall be classical or non-classical. In any case, whether it is to be classical or non-classical, much of his instruction,— arithmetic, geography, history, and so on,—must be the same; 35 and to have two schools and two sets of teachers for the same thing, is to double your expenses needlessly. Communes and municipalities, with funds and population really but for one

secondary school, were obliged, by the law of 1859, to make
their school either altogether classical or non-classical; they
were pulled different ways between an influential minority
of their inhabitants who wanted a classical school, and the bulk
5   of their middle class who wanted a non-classical; and they
often ended by establishing two schools, a *ginnasio* and a *scuola
tecnica,* both of which could not be maintained properly,
though one might have been. The practical studies, as they are
called, of the earlier years of the *ginnasio,* were besides in-
10 sufficient, especially if it be considered how few boys, comparatively, pass on from the *ginnasio* to the *liceo;* for how
many, therefore, the five gymnasial years of Latin and Greek,
and nothing else, are time misused. Nor are even Latin and
Greek properly learned in the *ginnasio* during these five years,
15 as the examinations at the end of the course show; they might
be better learned in two years, a good substratum of modern
instruction having preceded them. So the Council propose,
as I have said, 'the unification of the first triennium of the
ginnasio with the first grade of the *scuola tecnica.*' If the united
20 pupils exceed 40 or 50 per class, a second teacher is to be provided. But with the present school population the unification,
if adopted, will, in a very great number of cases, enable three
teachers to do what six are now employed for, and effect an
important saving. The two last years of the *ginnasio* will re-
25 main devoted, as before, to classical instruction and to preparation for the *liceo.* The boy who does not want this will go, after
his three years of modern instruction, either straight into business, or to one of the *istituti tecnici,* the special schools under
the Minister of Agriculture and Commerce.
30   The Council foresee that this recommendation may expose
them to the charge of discouraging Latin and Greek, and they
meet this anticipated accusation by drawing a picture of the
study of Latin and Greek, as this study exists at present in the
Italian schools. Everything that I myself observed entirely con-
35 firms the faithfulness of the Council's picture; but the testimony of Italians is more weighty in this case than that of any
foreigner. 'What fruits,' the Council ask, 'do we obtain from
our classical studies at present? After a youth has spent seven

or eight years in the study of Latin, five or six in that of Greek, is he in a condition to read with pleasure and without effort a Latin author, to write correctly a short piece of Latin prose, to make out by himself one of the easiest Greek authors? The Latin compositions which the Council have had before them, the entrance examinations at the University,* in which one or more members of this Council have since 1860 constantly borne part, the competitive examinations for the studentships in the *Collegio delle Province*, the accounts we have received from the inspectors, and for the southern provinces the detailed reports of the Visiting Commission of 1862, afford convincing proof that Latin is neither studied nor liked by our youth, and that there is a notable going back in the knowledge of it in the last twenty-five years. What shall we say of Greek? The study of Greek in our schools leads to such scanty result, our young men, the moment they leave school, forget so utterly all the little Greek they have ever learned, that it is impossible not to consider as lost the time and labour which pupils and masters have spent on it.'

And elsewhere the Council speak of the inferiority of Italy to other countries in secondary instruction, and above all in the literary and classical part of it,† as a matter too clear for doubt or concealment.‡ This inferiority is indeed patent. It is often said, and with truth, that in English classical schools there is a great disproportion between the amount of time and labour spent in teaching Latin and Greek, and the result obtained; the same might be said everywhere; still no one who knew the work in the highest forms of the great public schools of England, Germany, or France, would draw such a picture of classical instruction in those three countries as the Italian reporter draws of it in Italy.

The state in which the law of 1859 found it, accounts for its present deficiencies. The relative superiority of the schools in the north of Italy I have already mentioned. Elsewhere

* Of Turin, where the candidates come from schools which, compared with those of other parts of Italy are, as I have said, well worked.
  † *Sulle Condizioni della pubblica Istruzione nel Regno d'Italia*, p. 258.
  ‡ *Sulle Condizioni*, &c., p. 236.

(I quote again the Italian reporter) 'secondary instruction had lost the organisation given to it under the French empire, and was reduced to Latin, a little Italian, and, in the last years of the school course, elementary mathematics, physics, and the reading of certain treatises of philosophy.' As the proper means of teaching physics were in general wanting, this bill of fare may certainly be pronounced scanty. With this instruction the scholars managed, however, nearly always to pass the University examinations; 'but' (says the reporter again) 'the Government delegates who inquired into their examinations, and had not only the registers but the candidates' papers before them, could not but come to the conclusion that the examinations were nothing but a pure form, so great was the laxity used in passing one and all of the candidates.' The attendance in the secondary schools was irregular to an inconceivable degree. In many of the new provinces from one-third to one-half of the pupils absented themselves daily.

The law of 1859 introduced programmes, mainly after the French model; a staff of inspectors-general at head-quarters, and, in each province, a *provveditore* to represent the State, and a Provincial School Council to represent the local authority. It required guarantees of capacity from teachers. It exacted for admission to the *liceo* the production of the *licenza ginnasiale*, a certificate showing that the candidate had passed with success an examination in the studies of the *ginnasio;* for admission to the University, the production of the *licenza liceale*, showing the same thing with respect to the studies of the *liceo*. It introduced greater strictness into the university examinations, providing that they should be given by boards of examiners named by the universities or by the Minister of Public Instruction.

But many causes combined to impair the effectual operation of this law. It was extended to other parts of the kingdom as they were annexed. Having been made for one part of the kingdom, it could not be extended to others without some modification; the principle of modification having been once admitted, relaxations and exceptions were conceded to importunity, and by these the sound provisions of the original law were in many cases made a dead letter. The programmes were pitched too high; for instance, geometry and algebra were in the programme of the *ginnasio*, and these were so evidently beyond the pupils' state of preparation, that they had to be struck out and arithmetic by itself substituted for them. For arithmetic the law had provided that there should be separate teachers, but it had omitted to impose any test of fitness on them. Unqualified persons were therefore appointed, and arithmetic was ill taught. The degree of bachelor, obtainable after three years of university study, was made the condition of admission to the higher masterships of secondary schools, and a certificate of capacity, obtainable by examination (*esame d'abilitazione*), was required for the lower; but by admitting *equipollent titles*, as they are called, that is, titles of admission allowed to count instead of the degree or the certificate, a door was opened to great abuse, and the law was continually evaded. The school authorities were out of humour with changes which interrupted the easy life they had hitherto led, and which gave them a great deal of fresh work and trouble. In the *ginnasi*, arithmetic having been assigned to a special master, one master was to be charged with all the other work,— Latin, Italian, history, and geography,—of his class; it having been found that when there was a master for each subject, the pupil learnt next to nothing from any one of them, as they had no firm hold on him. When, however, one master had the four subjects, it soon appeared that he taught none of these subjects but Latin. In the *licei*, the pupils, accustomed to lax discipline, without thorough grounding in classical studies, and borne, by what inclination for knowledge they had, anywhere rather than in the direction of these studies, showed themselves entirely averse to the Latin and Greek lessons, and it needed vigorous measures to prevent their absenting themselves from them. The *licenza ginnasiale* is indispensable for a number of Government employments, the *licenza liceale* is indispensable for admission to the university, the degrees of which are required for the exercise of law and medicine; so through the school the pupil must go; but he manifests, it is said, a febrile impatience to get through as

fast as possible, he is nearly always pushed into a class above his real attainments, cannot profit by its teaching, and passes out of it by an examination which is illusory. With this pressure on the part of pupils and parents, and the general low
5 standard of studies, the school authorities are apt to be slack and indulgent; two-thirds of those presented for the *licenza ginnasiale* and the *licenza liceale* now pass, but it is calculated by the Council that hardly one-third of them ought to pass. The same reasons make the provincial school councils also,—
10 coming, as they do, within the influence of local feelings, —slack and indulgent. The *provveditore* and the one or two central inspectors representing the State, have had no staff through which to exercise an efficient inspection or control; for the law of 1859, while providing that the inspection of
15 the secondary schools should be entrusted to two inspectors-general *and their representatives*, had omitted to say who or what these representatives should be. Nor did the university examinations, as remodelled by the legislation of 1859, suffice to raise the standard of instruction throughout the country.
20 In the first place, the most important articles of that legislation were, as regards many universities, withdrawn or suspended. The change they introduced was too sweeping, the opposition they provoked too strong. Thus, in the great University of Naples, a university with some 5,000 students, there
25 still continues to be no obligatory matriculation, and therefore no obligatory examination of the student at entrance. In the second place, high pitched examinations are the result, not the cause, of a high condition of general culture, and examinations tend, in fact, to adjust themselves to studies. So long,
30 therefore, as the Italian secondary schools are what they are, the standard of university examinations in Italy, even when they are enforced, is irresistibly dragged down below the point at which the reformers of education try to fix it. The prescribed strictness is not maintained; in the university year
35 1862–63 the rejected candidates for degrees in the Italian universities were not more than six for every hundred who passed; in similar trials in France, Belgium, Germany, and England, the proportion rejected is far larger, though no one will say

that the candidates in these countries present themselves worse prepared than in Italy. The admission examinations show the same over-indulgence, nearly every candidate being admitted in some Italian universities, while for the corresponding examinations in France,—those for the degree of bachelor,—the number of rejections is on an average 20 per cent. at least, and sometimes rises as high as 50 per cent.

Chapter XI

The Italian Universities

*Paucity of Students in Arts—Great
Number of Universities in Italy.*

From 1858 to the present time there has been in Italy a slight
but steady falling off in the attendance at the universities. From
the want of admission registers at Naples it is impossible to
determine with accuracy the total number of students in the
5   Italian Universities in a given year; 10,000, however, is not
far from the mark. In the French faculties, in 1862, 23,371
students were entered; 14,364 of them in Paris alone. In the
nineteen universities of Germany, exclusive of Austria, there
are about 30,000 students.* It is calculated that France has
10 about one university student for every 1,900 inhabitants, Germany one for every 1,500, Italy one for every 2,200. But the
great difference between Italy and these countries is in the
character of studies followed by the university students.
While a fourth of the German students study letters and phi-
15 losophy, the proportion of Italian students who study these is
utterly insignificant. The prevalence of the study of letters
is a good test of a country's general condition of culture and
civilisation; and that it is so is strikingly confirmed by Turin,
—the centre not, certainly, of the most gifted part of Italy,
20 but of the best governed, trained, and civilised part,—having
in its university incomparably more students in letters than

* So says Signor Matteucci, and I leave his numbers for the sake of
the remarks he founds on them; but in 1864 there were only (in round
numbers) 20,000 *matriculated* students in all the German universities,
25 including those of Austria. It is possible Signor Matteucci reckons un-
matriculated attendants at lectures, and so gets his high number of students, but I have been able to find no statistics corroborating the high
number he assigns.

any other university town of the kingdom. The greater part of the universities have next to none. Pavia, out of 1,200 students in the year 1864, had only eight of them in the faculty of letters. The principal of the Normal School at Pisa reports that his pupils are often the sole attendants at the lectures in the faculty of letters at Pisa, and he adds that in several universities, and notably in that of Naples, there are years in which not a single degree in letters, or, as we should say, *arts*, is given. Nor is this because of the greater popularity of the natural sciences. It is not the faculty of mathematical and natural sciences,—a faculty which, like that of letters and philosophy, the student in general follows simply for purposes of education,—it is not this faculty that is frequented at the expense of the faculty of letters. The throng of students is in the faculties where *Brodstudien*, as the Germans say, are prosecuted,—in medicine and laws. This is especially the case at Naples, where I have seen in the lecture-rooms of these faculties a concourse of students said, and I can well believe it, to number not less than 400.

The Italian universities had, in 1862–63, 714 professors, of whom 542 are full or regular professors (*ordinarii*). It is the abundance of supplementary professors which shows intellectual life and movement in a university; through means of their lectures a subject gets treated on all its sides, the regular professors are kept up to the mark by a competition which stimulates them, and men fitted to be, when their turn comes, regular professors, are enabled to show themselves. The extra-professors and the *Privat-docenten* are thus the life of the German universities. The smaller universities there have nearly as many regular professors as the greater; what distinguishes Berlin or Heidelberg is the multitude of able men, who, as extra-professors or as *Privat-docenten*, are swelling the volume of university instruction there, and developing their own powers at the same time. The University of Freyburg in the Duchy of Baden has only seven regular professors less than Heidelberg; one has 34, the other 27; but Heidelberg has 53 extra-professors and *Privat-docenten*, while Freyburg has only 14. Berlin, in like manner, has 111 extra-professors and *Privat-*

docenten to its 55 regular professors. In this way not only is
the teaching augmented and stimulated, but the State, which
pays the regular professors, is saved expense by having to
provide fewer of them, and is enabled to pay them better and
to make their chairs, as they should be, valuable prizes. Neither
the stimulus nor the economy are to be found in the Italian
university system. The university professors are,—for Italy,
where officials are in general paid miserably, and none more
miserably than those of secondary instruction,—not ill paid.
A law passed in 1862 fixes the salaries of professors in the
principal universities at 200*l.* and 240*l.* a year; of those in
the less important ones at 120*l.* and 144*l.* But the burden of
all these salaries has to be borne by the State. Nor does it get
full work out of this host of regular professors. The same
laxity and want of discipline which astonish us in the secondary schools prevail generally in the universities. The students
are in the habit of departing when they think term (as we
should say) has lasted long enough; as vacation time ap-
proaches, which is when the students please, and not when the
Regolamento pleases, 'the whole body of students with one ac-
cord,' says the official report, 'sometimes leave the schools
deserted.' * Here again Turin forms an exception to the other
Italian universities, and is exempt from their irregularity. Again,
in France and Germany there are from thirty-two to thirty-
seven weeks of lectures in the university year, with four lectures a week from all lecturers charged with the principal
matters of study; a professor's yearly course, therefore, contains from 90 to 120 lectures. From 60 to 70 lectures, or even
less, is all that the Italian professors give a year. Finally, the
students are in the habit of migrating from the university
where they have studied to take their degree in some other university where the examinations are reported to be easier.

Italy has 15 universities,† which, with the *Istituto Superiore*
of Florence, an establishment with a part of the teaching and

* *Sulle Condizioni, &c.*, p. 197.
† They are the following: Bologna, Pisa, Pavia, Turin, Naples, Palermo,
Modena, Parma, Genoa, Catania, Siena, Cagliari, Messina, Sassari, Macer-
ata. To these will now be added the universities of Venetia.

of the degrees of a university, are all of them State institutions.
She has also four free universities,* as they are called; municipal
institutions supported by their own funds, and, when these fall
short, by the municipality. Thus, for instance, the free university of Camerino has property of the value of 35,469 francs
a year; like several of the other universities, it has not the complete number of faculties, it has only two,—law and medicine.
The municipality is bound, in return for the privilege of possessing a body which gives instruction and degrees in law and
medicine, to make good to the two faculties their expenses,
so far as they are not covered by what their property and their
fees bring them in.

The fifteen universities of the State are a heavy burden to
it. The State has taken their property, but their property and
their fees together represent an annual sum not approaching
that which the State spends upon them. Bologna had property
which now lets at 15,000 francs a year, but the State spends
490,000 francs on Bologna. Naples had a charge on the *Gran
Libro* of 19,591 francs a year; this is now handed over to the
Clinical Institute, and the State spends 670,000 francs a year
on the University of Naples. Palermo had nearly 145,000 francs
a year, which is now received by the Treasury; but the Treasury pays back to Palermo more than 420,000 francs. The University of Turin is still the nominal possessor of its own property; but this property is administered by the State, and what
it brings in is treated as ordinary State revenue, not as revenue to be specially applied to the university, which, however,
gets from the State nearly 620,000 francs a year. In short, the
fourteen or fifteen millions of francs which is what the total
property of the Italian universities, when they became State
establishments, was worth, represent in annual value less than
an eighth part of the annual sum which the State now spends
on the universities. Italy is spending yearly on her faculty-
instruction the prodigious sum of 5,500,000 of francs; France
spends 3,500,000; Prussia 3,000,000. But of the 3,500,000 of
francs which the French Treasury spends on faculty-instruc-

* Urbino, Perugia, Camerino, and Ferrara.

tion, it gets back in fees, which are high and collected with regularity, more than 2,500,000; so that the real cost of this instruction to the State does not exceed 800,000 francs. In Prussia the fees are low, but the State outlay on faculty-in-
5 struction is in the first instance £100,000 less than that of Italy; and the State has for low fees this compensation, that what the student thus saves he spends on extra instruction, and at least the culture of the nation is a gainer. In Italy the fees are so low and so irregularly collected that they produce
10 to the State less than 500,000 francs. Nor has the State the consolation of seeing its students, as in Germany, by paying extra-teachers who supplement the regular instruction, turn the cheapness of this to the best account.

As the municipal liberality, the vigorous organisation, the
15 intellectual stir, of which in the Middle Age the Italian univer- sities had the benefit, have died out, so has the college system of the Middle Age. Only a few years ago there were still left at Bologna one or two foreign colleges for free students; 're- mains,' says Signor Matteucci, 'of the so many and famous col-
20 leges of the various nations which individuals and govern- ments had founded in this celebrated university.' They are gone; and the college system of the mediæval university is no doubt unsuited to meet the general requirements of those who seek university instruction in our own time. The *Collegio delle*
25 *Province*, which I have already mentioned, a foundation of comparatively modern date, still exists at Turin; and in con- nection with the university of this city there are not less, in all, than 170 free maintenances for students. Pavia has still the *Collegio Ghislieri*, with 66; some of the holders of these enjoy
30 them at the University of Pavia, others at the Normal School of Pisa, others at the special schools of Turin and Milan. Pavia has also the *Collegio Borromeo*, with 28 free studentships. But the whole yearly sum which the State now disposes of for bur- sarships and exhibitions at the universities amounts to no more
35 than 153,063 francs.*

* *Sulle Condizioni, &c.*, p. 161.

Chapter XII

Private Schools and Ecclesiastical Schools

State Universities and Schools Better than any Others in Italy—Religious Congregations and Their Schools—The Secular Clergy and Their Seminaries—Trenchant Reforms in the Schools of the Religious.

There seems no doubt that the free universities are the laxest in passing candidates; as Turin, with its traditions of a strict public service, and Naples, with the life and competition created by its 5,000 students, are the strictest. There seems no doubt, too, that the secondary schools of the State are in general better than the private schools; that the laxity, too great in the public schools, is yet greater in the private, which have also remained untouched by what improvement and progress have, since 1859, appeared in the public schools. 'The great danger of our private teaching,' say the Italian reports, 'consists in this: that blind and ignorant parents suffer themselves to be misled by the usurped reputation of a master who, knowing nothing, takes upon himself to teach everything, from *a, b, c,* to philosophy.' The same danger attends unregulated private schools in all countries; only in England we always console ourselves with our favourite maxim that the parents who send their children to these schools are 'acting in the spirit of self-respect and independence.' * In the same independent spirit, parents and boys like to cut as short as they can the period given to schooling. 'We find a febrile impatience' (say the Italian reports again) 'to shorten the term of study; and to gratify this impatience a number of private schools have sprung up, in which the getting through the work well is sacrificed to the getting through it quick.' These

---

* See in the *Times,* of October 30th, 1866, the letter of Mr. Flint, Registrar to the Royal Commission on Popular Education.

schools profess to do in two years what the public schools do in three; and as examinations have hitherto been very lax in Italy, and as in the assimilated or semi-private schools, which have been allowed to examine all comers, and which for the
5   sake of the fees were glad to attract as many examinees as possible, they have been laxest of all, the half-prepared private school boy presented himself at an *istituto pareggiato* to pass the examination for the gymnasial licence or the lyceal licence, and generally managed to scramble through. This abuse be-
10   came so flagrant that the minister has been obliged to take away from the *istituti pareggiati* the right of examining for the licence any pupils but their own.

In Upper Italy rather less than a fifth of the candidates for the gymnasial licence, and rather more than a fourth of the
15   candidates for the lyceal licence, come from private schools. In Central Italy private school teaching, if estimated by the number of candidates it presents for these examinations, would appear next to nothing; its candidates are not six per cent. of the whole number presented. In Southern Italy, where edu-
20   cation of all kinds is wanting, the whole number of candidates is, to be sure, insignificant; but of what there are the private schools send a better proportion; they send about a third of the candidates for the gymnasial licence, about a sixth of those for the lyceal.

25   As regards lay private schools, anything like complete statistics and information is not at present to be had. As regards ecclesiastical private schools it is different. These are of two kinds, the schools of the religious corporations and the seminaries or schools under episcopal control. In the report of
30   the Superior Council of Public Instruction, from which I have quoted so much, no account is given of these schools. But at the end of 1865 the Minister of Public Instruction, Baron Natoli, having first instituted the necessary inquiries, drew up two reports * on them, which have since been printed, and
35   which are full of curious and interesting matter.

* *Statistica del Regno d'Italia: Istruzione data da Corporazioni religiose;* and *Statistica del Regno d'Italia: Istruzione data nei Seminari.* Florence, 1865.

All through Italy, in the Catholic reaction which followed the stoppage of the Reformation there, religious congregations were formed which took the management of education. The Jesuits have a world-wide celebrity, but the names at least of other congregations are not wholly unfamiliar to most of us; the Barnabites (authorised in 1533), the *Scolopi*, or *Scuole Pie* (1621), the Theatines (1524), the Redemptorists (1732), the Christian Brothers, of French origin, but extended to Italy (1600). Pious persons left money to build and endow schools in connection with these societies. There were societies of each sex, with schools for each sex, for primary instruction and for secondary, for boarders and for day scholars. Anti-civil and anti-modern tendencies are generally imputed by the friends of progress to these corporations, and at the end of the last century they had fallen into disfavour. The reforms of the Emperor Joseph II. were hostile to them in his Italian dominions. The French rule, with its resolute maxims of lay and civil organisation, was more hostile still; but the governments which were restored in 1815 made alliance with them. Austria persisted for some time in the Josephine traditions, but after 1848 events forced her into the policy which led to the Concordat of 1855, and to the religious corporations this policy was, of course, favourable. Piedmont began the decisive change in this as in other things. The Piedmontese law of the 29th of May, 1855, suppressed a number of religious corporations. Then came 1859 and the annexation of the new provinces. These provinces, the moment they expelled their old governments, adopted the Piedmontese law, carrying it a little further. The Piedmontese law assigned for the benefit of the poorer and underpaid clergy the property of the corporations which were suppressed. The new provinces assigned a certain proportion to lay instruction and to charitable institutions. The Piedmontese law, however, had suffered the teaching corporations to subsist, while it abolished other religious corporations; and this exemption was maintained in the new provinces in order to keep their legislation at one with that of Piedmont. The party of progress regarded this as a mere temporary compromise, and demanded a far more radical reform. The government brought before the Italian Parliament a bill for the dissolution of all religious corporations. Baron Natoli says that the majority in the country desired such a measure. But the time was, at all events, not fully ripe for it, and the bill was, as we all remember, withdrawn.

Regarding, however, the respited corporations as certainly doomed, and their dissolution as only adjourned for a little while, the minister has taken the inventory of his victims' effects. It appears that there are 63 institutions in which secondary instruction is given by religious corporations. These institutions have 462 teachers and 5,752 boys. The girls are much more numerous. Of the boys 30 per cent. are boarders. Primary instruction, with which I am not now concerned, is given by the religious corporations to a far larger body of pupils, and among these, again, the girls far outnumber the boys.*

The minister speaks unfavourably of the instruction given by the religious. Attentively read, however, his criticisms point rather to disaffection in these teachers than to ignorance and incompetence. He says that their teaching tends to make bad citizens, and to keep up a spirit of resistance to the new order of things in Italy. He relates that when a royal inspector asked a girl in a school of the Ursuline nuns at Benevento who was the king of Italy, the girl, to avoid acknowledging the lawful sovereign, answered: *Il nostro re è Gesù Cristo.* He maintains that letters and sciences get a peculiar and illiberal tinge when taught in the cloister. He adds, going to more indisputable ground, that the management of their property by the religious corporations is in the highest degree wasteful and injudicious, and that in many cases funds once ample have by this management been rendered insufficient for the proper maintenance of the schools. In other cases funds still ample are abused; and he cites the instance of a college for girls at Milan, where with a revenue of 8,000*l.* a year a band of 37 governesses and lay sisters maintain and teach 30 pupils.

* The numbers are as follows: total number of pupils of the religious corporations, 97,440; 62,901 girls and 18,712 boys. Of the latter, 12,960 are receiving primary instruction; 5,752 (as I have said) secondary.

The minister has been able to deal with the seminaries more effectually than with the schools of the religious corporations. The seminaries were instituted by the Council of Trent to train young men for holy orders without exposing them to the influence of the universities. These schools were placed in every diocese; they were governed by a rector whom the bishop nominated; they were subsidised out of the bishop's revenues, and entirely under his control. At first they confined themselves to their original design of solely training for the priesthood, and even exacted repayment from those who after benefiting by their endowments did not proceed into orders. Soon, however, their character changed. It was according to the notions of those days that education should be under clerical direction; persons desirous to found an endowment for the instruction of the lay youth in their locality founded it in connection with the seminaries. Municipalities, too poor to establish schools of their own, assigned grants to the seminaries on condition of their undertaking the instruction of those children who required it. The governments of the old time, looking upon the clergy as their natural and useful allies, not only did their best to get lay schools attached to the seminaries,—augmenting their property from the State domains, or diverting lay and communal foundations for their benefit, —but they also tried to put under the bishops' rule the schools of the religious corporations. The bishops were glad of the additional influence which an extended control over education placed in their hands. So it comes to pass that the kingdom of Italy, which has the prodigious number of 231 dioceses, has 260 seminaries or episcopal schools, one for each diocese and 29 to spare. These schools have 13,174 scholars, of whom 9,726 are boarders. There are 1,208 of their pupils under 12 years of age; the vocation of these, therefore, cannot be supposed to be yet very strongly declared. As many as 1,297 boys wear the lay costume and make no profession of any intention to go into orders; 8,429 wear the clerical habit, but numbers of these wear it for a time only, for the sake of a host of small exhibitions given by the seminaries to youths professing to prepare for orders, and for the sake of exemption from military service.

When their object has been gained, when they have enjoyed their exhibition and escaped the conscription, they renounce their intention of going into orders. The recruitment for the clergy is becoming difficult in Italy, and this with 260 seminaries to serve as a field for it.

In fact not more than 52 of these institutions are real theological colleges. The mass of them are very indifferent secondary schools, too numerous to be well off either in good teachers or in pupils. They have on an average but 57 pupils to each institution, and 12 pupils to each class. The inquiries made by the minister convinced him of the general weakness of seminary instruction. The theological studies themselves are in a very depressed condition; with these, however, the State assumes no right to meddle. It leaves the care of these to the bishops, to whom the Council of Trent gave it. But the legislation of 1859 gives to the government in Italy the right of inspecting all establishments of secondary instruction, of exacting certain guarantees of capacity from those who conduct them, and of satisfying itself that nothing in their teaching or management violates morality or the laws. It was notorious that the seminaries openly preached disaffection. Two of them had become a public scandal from proved immorality. In most of them the teaching, consisting of Latin, a little Italian,—not the Italian of the classics of Italy, but an Italian false in taste and false in style,—very little arithmetic or mathematics, still less geography and history, and no study of the natural sciences at all, was quite unsuited to the wants of the present day. The schools of the religious associations had at least admitted inspection and satisfied the law by providing their teachers with the requisite certificates (*patenti d'idoneità*). But the ordinaries of the Italian dioceses maintained that State inspection of the seminaries was contrary to the laws of the church, which gives to the bishops the sole superintendence of the instruction and education in the seminaries. Employing a line of argument familiar to the clergy everywhere, they asked who but the bishops ought to exercise this superintendence, since they were to answer before God for the learning and virtue of those on whom they at ordination laid their hands. The

government replied that of the learning and virtue of those whom they were going to ordain it left them the sole guardians, but that it had to satisfy itself about the learning and virtue of that great majority of their pupils who were destined to lay callings. A very few bishops accepted inspection with a good 5
grace; many submitted reluctantly; some broke up their seminaries sooner than admit it; others shut their school-doors against it. The government persisted, and ordered the closing of all seminaries which would not admit the State inspector.

Eighty-two were closed by the middle of the year 1865. 10
Then, by a decree dated the 1st of September in that year, the government ordered the reopening of all the seminaries which had been closed. But they were to reopen far other than they had closed. The State sequestrated their whole revenues. One-third it gave back, in each seminary, to the 15
ordinary for a strictly theological college; the other two-thirds it assigned to the municipality for the purposes of public and lay secondary instruction. The task of seeing the work of partition and transformation carried into effect was committed to a gentleman who has many friends in this country, Signor 20
Fusco. He accomplished his commission during the spring of 1866.

Chapter XIII

Reforms Proposed for Schools and Universities in Italy

The Executive Supported in Its Reforms by Public Opinion—Extensive Reforms Proposed for the Universities and Lay Schools—Need of the Reforms Proposed—Intelligence of Italian Statesmen.

The Italian reformers of public instruction consider, however, that they have thus made only a beginning in what needs to be done with the seminaries. The minister announces a plan for reducing the 231 dioceses of the Italian kingdom at one blow
5   to 59, a diocese for each province. Each diocese is to have one real theological college, *alto istituto seminaristico*, for training its clergy. This institution is alone to enjoy that exemption from State inspection which the seminaries claim. Schools for the laity are to be under laymen; or, if ecclesiastics wish
10   to conduct such schools, they must conduct them on the same conditions as laymen, by providing themselves with the legal guarantees of capacity, and by admitting State inspection.

The English jealousy of the executive, and reverence for vested interests, would probably incline us to designate these
15   proceedings (at least it would if they were not employed against Papists) as tyrannical. I will only observe that in every single instance where a seminary has been closed, the local municipality has declared its satisfaction with the measure; in every single instance where endeavours have been made to get
20   a closed seminary reopened, the local municipality has petitioned the government not to reopen it. The executive in Italy is in fact at this moment much stronger than even in France. It represents the lay and civil elements in society; and the Italians, or that part of them which really determines the national
25   policy, know that to make this element triumph is the necessity of the present moment for them. Thus the right of inspec-

tion of private schools, which in France is construed not to
extend to their instruction, and, therefore, except in the case
of some signal offence against health, morality, or the law of
the land (the three matters which the inspection of private
schools is defined as regarding), remains practically unexer- 5
cised,* and could not be exercised without exciting discontent
and opposition, is in Italy construed, and with acquiescence
and applause on the part of the public, to extend to the instruction, and to authorise the same examination as is practised by
the State in the public schools. Unless we see what the lessons 10
are, say the government authorities, how are we to satisfy ourselves that they do not contravene morality or the laws? A
similar argument might be used in France; but in truth it is
public opinion, and the national sense of what the wants of
the nation are, that determines, for such a State right as the 15
right of school inspection, the exact limits of its exercise. Only,
if this right itself is not written in the laws, abuses of the
gravest kind may prevail in the education of a country, and
things may even come to a dead-lock, whatever the wants of
the nation may meanwhile be, without the possibility of apply- 20
ing a remedy.

The Superior Council recommends, for the universities and
lay schools, reforms hardly less thorough than those which
the minister recommends for the seminaries. The Council in-
sists, in the first place, on the necessity of one organic educa- 25
tion law for the kingdom,—*una legge universalmente accettata,
e non derogata con provvedimenti transitori o particolari.*
Recognising the expediency of interesting the provinces and
communes in the secondary and primary schools by giving
them a share in the supervision and management of them, it 30
yet maintains that with the State, represented by the Minister
of Public Instruction, rests the supreme duty of seeing that
the whole concern of national education is properly and effi-
ciently worked. It proposes to reduce the 59 *provveditori* to
10 or 14, to make the 59 provinces into 10 or 14 school dis- 35
tricts by grouping several provinces together for each district,

---

* It must be remembered, however, that the preliminary guarantee is
taken of requiring titles of his capacity from every head of such schools.

and to put at the disposal of each *provveditore* two or more visitors, or, as we should say, inspectors. These *provveditori* are the delegates of the State in the provinces, and, with their inspectors, answer in the main to the rectors and academy in-spectors of France. As in France, there is to be at head-quarters a body of inspectors general, who are to make annual tours of inspection and annual reports. Their reports are to be published. It is calculated that this organisation, while it will enable the government to have for its ten or fourteen provin-cial delegates men of real weight and reputation, and while it will provide what is wanting at present, an effective inspection, will cost only half as much as the present system. The dele-gates who exercise inspection on behalf of the local powers, the Provincial School Council and the communes, are to be appointed by them and unpaid.

The Council further proposes that all teachers in the second-ary schools shall be required to hold a diploma from a normal school. The only exceptions are teachers of arithmetic, who are to undergo an *esame d'abilitazione* before appointment. No equipollent titles are in future to be admitted, except works of approved merit published by the candidate on the subjects he is to teach, and recognised as of approved merit by the Superior Council of Public Instruction.

New programmes are to be drawn up by different commis-sions for the different branches of instruction, and after being adjusted to one another, and revised by a single commission formed by representatives from all the separate commissions, are to replace the present programmes, thrown together piece-meal, from different quarters and different hands, and without unity of aim.

For text-books used in the public schools approval by the Superior Council is to be strictly required. Only one grammar is to be used; for other matters more than one text-book may be used, but no text-book which has not had the Council's sanction.

The leaving examination at the *ginnasio* * is to have for a

---

* *Licenza ginnasiale.*

counterpart and check to it an entrance examination at the *liceo* turning on exactly the same matters * and of exactly the same degree of difficulty. In like manner, the sincerity of the leaving examination at the *liceo* † is to be tested by an exactly corresponding entrance examination at the university.‡ The candidate must get seven-tenths of the allotted number of marks in each matter on which he proposes to follow lectures at the university. An attentive study of German schools and universities is visible in this and other parts of the Italian report.

Finally, to check cram for single examinations, and to check, in general, the scamped and hurried work which is laid to the charge of private schools, the Council proposes that the boy who comes from a private school or a private tutor to try for the *licenza liceale* shall undergo, besides the leaving examination for the license itself, the two examinations which the public school boy has had to undergo at the end of his first and second school years.

Abroad far more than in England, where university instruction is the privilege of comparatively few, secondary instruction leads to superior or university instruction. For good superior instruction, says Signor Matteucci most truly, the two great requisites are, first, good secondary schools; secondly, first-rate men in the university chairs. It is the professor and not the charter which really makes the university,—*il successo di siffatti istituzioni riposa interamente sulla celebrità degli insegnanti.* Only the presence of such men can create that interest, that glow of intellectual life, which constitutes what the Italians, with their love of fine culture, happily call an *atmosfera intellettuale propizia agli studi.* To have their chairs filled by first-rate professors the Italian universities are at present far too numerous. The Council proposes to retain but three facul-

---

* These are, on paper, translation from Latin, and composition in Italian; *viva voce*, Latin, Greek, and Italian grammar, elementary mathematics, history, and geography.

† *Licenza liceale.*

‡ These are, on paper, translation from Greek into Latin, and an Italian essay; *viva voce*, Greek, Latin, and Italian authors, philosophy, mathematics, physics, and natural history.

ties of letters for all Italy. These faculties are at the same time
to be normal schools to form schoolmasters for secondary instruction; their degrees are to be the schoolmaster's certificate,
and the special examination for *agrégation* and the title of
agrégé, of which I have spoken at length in my account of
France, are to be introduced, and are to form, in Italy as in
France, the schoolmaster's *honours*, and his title to the higher
posts in his profession. The universities of Turin, Pisa, and
Naples are to be the seats of these faculties. Pisa already possesses a normal school, which now in fact comprises, one may
say, the whole body of students following the faculty of letters
at Pisa. Turin has in its *Collegio delle Province* an institution
just suitable to be amalgamated, for normal school purposes,
with the faculty of letters at the university. Naples is so great
a university that the literary normal school for southern Italy
must clearly be placed there; and the new institution may probably awaken some of that zeal for the study of letters which
at present is wanting in the Neapolitan university.

Similarly there are to be but three high faculties or superior
normal schools for the mathematical and natural sciences.
These are to be in connection with the universities of Naples
and Turin and the Museum of Florence. These three schools
will alone examine and give degrees in mathematics and natural
sciences, as the three schools or faculties of Turin, Pisa, and
Naples will alone examine and give degrees in letters.

The remaining universities will only preserve two faculties,
those of law and medicine. The government will maintain
eleven of each; it will maintain faculties both of law and medicine at Naples, Turin, Bologna, Pisa, Pavia, Palermo, Genoa,
Catania, Parma, and Modena; a faculty of law at Sassari, and
one of medicine at Cagliari.

The reorganisation of theological study is left for a future
occasion. At present the seminaries have possession of this
study. It will be desirable, say the authorities, to connect it,
in part at least, with the universities, the dogmatic part being
still left to the seminary, the auxiliary parts of a theological
training being committed to the university, and university degrees being required in them. But this connection of the clergy

with the universities,—from the point of view of a nation's civil interests, at any rate, so desirable,—has not yet been accomplished even in France.

Provinces, communes, and private associations are still to be at liberty to maintain free universities; and the Council recommends that the government should cede to them, on application, the buildings, collections, and scientific apparatus of the faculties which it abandons. These free universities, however, are only to admit students who pass the entrance examination to be fixed by an organic law for the whole kingdom, which examination is henceforth to be required of every university student; and they are not to confer degrees, which will only be conferred by examining commissions in connection with the faculties maintained by the State.

These examining commissions are to be named by the Minister of Public Instruction, and to consist of university professors and members of the principal literary and scientific bodies of the kingdom. The programmes of examination are to be approved by the Superior Council of Public Instruction.

English university men will be astonished at hearing that an Italian student's average yearly cost for maintaining himself at the university is calculated at 800 fr. (32*l.*) It is proposed that the State should found a certain number of scholarships of this value, and of half this value, to be obtained by competitive examination. These scholarships are to be in connection with free universities, as well as with those of government. The fees for university lectures are to be raised. These fees have been reduced very low, without any corresponding increase in the number of students frequenting the lectures. The duration of the university courses, the number of lectures in them, the periods at which the preparatory examination and the final degree examination for the *laurea,* or doctorate, shall occur, are all to be fixed by the organic law. All university examinations are to be *per materia,* and not, like ours at Oxford and the old examinations in Italy, in several matters lumped together.

The Council proposes, in order to complete the organisation of superior instruction for the kingdom, certain high schools for practical and professional instruction also. The present *scuole d'applicazione* at Turin, Milan, and Naples, are to form three high schools of engineering, civil and military. Six clinical institutes, to receive pupils who have completed

5 their studies in a faculty of medicine, are to be established in connection with the great hospitals of Bologna, Florence, Milan, Naples, Palermo, and Turin. The seven or eight observatories of the kingdom, following the plan of strengthening by suppression and amalgamation which the establishments of

10 Italy so generally need, are to be reduced to three or four. It is even recommended that in this country of local academies and municipal spirit one representative academy should be formed, to take the lead as embodying the science and culture of Italy. There are at present, in the kingdom of Italy, 54

15 literary or scientific institutions with the name or nature of an academy.

These are sweeping reforms to propose,* but then education in Italy needs to be reconstructed from the very bottom. We must remember from what a state of neglect, laxity, and bad

20 government the start has to be made. Nearly three quarters of the population of Italy, over five years of age, are *analfabeti*,† as the Italians call it,—unable to read and write. The old government of Naples opposed the establishment of even infant schools; there were actually but four of them in the city

25 of Naples before the revolution. Primary schools hardly existed; the municipality of Palermo has set on foot 140 of them since 1859. There were hardly any public secondary schools; bad schools kept by the monks and Jesuits, in which some Latin was taught, but scarcely anything else,—no Greek, no

30 modern languages or modern history, and no natural history, —were the substitute. Since 1859 there has been a great movement of school opening and school organising; but this movement has to work with the instruments it finds ready to its hand, and these instruments have the slack and easy-going

35   * They have not yet (at the end of 1867) been carried into effect.
     † The exact rate is 746·82 of *analfabeti* for each 1,000 of population. The proportion is greater for the female sex than the male: 812·66 for the former to 680·98 for the latter.

habits which so many Italians seem to have contracted from
the conditions of their national life during the last two centuries. One or two men of genius in important posts work
themselves nearly to death, but to get day after day a fair
day's work out of every one of her citizens who has an employ-   5
ment, public or private, to discharge, seems at present, to a
stranger, the great want for Italy. Her school system is very
much modelled on that of the French; and this makes the slack
habits of so many of the Italian schools, those in the south
particularly, the more conspicuous, because one is reminded of   10
France, where a similar school organisation has all done for
it that hard work, discipline, and exactitude can do. The professors in the Italian secondary schools are underpaid; 2,000
fr. (80*l.*) a year is at present their highest salary; but they are
also in general underworked, some of them not having more   15
than three hours' work a week, and most of them giving you
the impression that what they really require is an iron system
which shall get five or six hours of steady work every day out
of them. I find in my notes this entry respecting a great Italian public school which I will not name: 'Good building, bad   20
smells, unsatisfactory *proviseur,* weak professors, and inaccurate
Latin and Greek.' The same entry would more or less apply
to far too large a number of the public schools in Italy.

The schools under ecclesiastical management were in some
respects the best of those I saw in Italy. Nowhere on the   25
Continent have I seen such good accommodation, according
to our English notions, for boarders, as at the *Collegio Nazareno*
in Rome and at the Barnabites' School at Moncalieri. The
boys have rooms to themselves, and excellent rooms. Nowhere
in Italy did I find the Greek so good (but a lesson was not   30
more than three or four lines of Homer) as at Moncalieri.
Nowhere in Italy did I find such good Latin as that which the
Collegio Romano at Rome, in its *Virgil* lesson and its boys
questioning one another in prosody, showed me. Very likely
he who has been reared in an English public school has in   35
general a certain prepossession for schools conducted by ecclesiastics, and has, from his own training, a stronger satisfaction at finding Latin and Greek properly learnt than at find-

ing anything else. But there is no doubt that the current which
is bearing the Italians away from clerical schools, and carrying
them towards public and lay schools, is the main current of
modern civilisation. Perhaps even in the aversion of her students for the old classical studies, in their strong preference
for studies which are scientific, modern, and positive, Italy is
again showing that quick instinct of a change in the forms and
conditions of the higher culture, that tact for a new phase of
intellectual life, which she has so decisively shown before.
The most animated and effective lessons, as regards both teachers and pupils, that I saw given in Italy, were lessons to a large
class in the *liceo Parini* at Milan, on the sense of hearing and
on magnetism.

The Italian schools may, possibly, flourish without the Latin
or Greek of the great German or English or French schools,
but without their steadiness and genuine work they cannot.
They are themselves beginning to see this, and at the Normal
School of Pisa,—where, in 1862, at the first competitive examination, out of 31 candidates who presented themselves, 20
were admitted,—at last year's examination only 7 candidates
were admitted out of 27, the diminution being due, not to a
falling off in the candidates' attainments, but to a rise in the
examiners' standard. If the distinguished statesmen who now
direct public instruction in Italy can but get this bracing and
stringent treatment resolutely applied and strictly followed,
their direction will soon show excellent fruits. Intelligent this
direction is sure to be; for no statesmen can perceive more
clearly than the statesmen of this *terre des sentiments humains*,
that a government's duty in education is not to fear and flatter
ignorance, prejudice, and obstructiveness, but *comprendere, ed
insinuare nello spirito pubblico, che una buona organizzazione
degli studi, e la grandezza intellettuale di una nazione, sono i
più saldi fondamenti della potenza degli stati e della vera e
ordinata libertà dei popoli.*

III

Germany

Chapter XIV

Development of the German Secondary Schools

The Renaissance and the Reformation—The German Schools and the Reformation—Decline of the German Schools and Their Recovery—The Prussian Schools Representative of Those of Germany.

The schools of France and Italy owed little to the great modern movement of the Renaissance. In both these countries that movement operated, in both it produced mighty results; but of the official establishments for instruction it did not get hold. In Italy the mediæval routine in those establishments at first   5
opposed a passive resistance to it; presently came the Catholic reaction, and sedulously shut it out from them. In France the Renaissance did not become a power in the State, and the routine of the schools sufficed to exclude the new influence till it took for itself other channels than the schools. But in Germany   10
the Renaissance became a power in the State; allied with the Reformation, where the Reformation triumphed in German countries the Renaissance triumphed with it, and entered with it into the public schools. Melanchthon and Erasmus were not merely enemies and subverters of the dominion of the Church   15
of Rome, they were eminent humanists; and with the great but single exception of Luther, the chief German reformers were all of them distinguished friends of the new classical learning, as well as of Protestantism. The Romish party was in German countries the ignorant party also, the party un-   20
touched by the humanities and by culture.

Perhaps one reason why in England our schools have not had the life and growth of the schools of Germany and Holland is to be found in the separation, with us, of the power of the Reformation and the power of the Renaissance. With us, too,   25
the Reformation triumphed and got possession of our schools;

but our leading reformers were not at the same time, like those
of Germany, the nation's leading spirits in intellect and culture.
In Germany the best spirits of the nation were then the reformers; in England our best spirits,—Shakspeare, Bacon, Spenser,
5 —were men of the Renaissance, not men of the Reformation,
and our reformers were men of the second order. The Reformation, therefore, getting hold of the schools in England was
a very different force, a force far inferior in light, resources,
and prospects, to the Reformation getting hold of the schools
10 in Germany.

But in Germany, nevertheless, as Protestant orthodoxy grew
petrified like Catholic orthodoxy, and as, in consequence,
Protestantism flagged and lost the powerful impulse with which
it started, the school flagged also, and in the middle of the
15 last century the classical teaching of Germany, in spite of a
few honourable names like Gesner's, Ernesti's, and Heyne's,
seems to have lost all the spirit and power of the 16th century
humanists, to have been sinking into a mere church appendage,
and fast becoming torpid. A theological student, making his
20 livelihood by teaching till he could get appointed to a parish,
was the usual schoolmaster. 'The schools will never be better,'
said their great renovator, Friedrich August Wolf, the well-
known critic of Homer, 'so long as the schoolmasters are theologians by profession. A theological course in a university, with
25 its smattering of classics, is about as good a preparation for a
classical master as a course of feudal law would be.' * Wolf's
coming to Halle in 1783, invited by Von Zedlitz, the minister
for public worship under Frederick the Great, a sovereign
whose civil projects and labours were not less active and re-
30 markable than his military, marks an era from which the classical schools of Germany, reviving the dormant spark planted

---

* See a most interesting article on Wolf in the *North British Review*
for June 1865. Not only for its account of Wolf, but for its sketch of
the movement in the higher education of Germany at a very critical
35 time, this article well deserves studying; and having been obliged to
make myself acquainted with many of the matters which its writer
touches, I may perhaps be allowed, without appearing guilty of pre-
sumption, to add that it seems to me as trustworthy as it is interesting.

in them by the Renaissance, awoke to a new life, which, since the beginning of this century, has drawn the eyes of all students of intellectual progress upon them. Prussia was the scene of Wolf's labours, and the Prussian schools, both from their own excellence and from the preponderating importance of Prussia at the present time, are naturally the first in Germany to attract the observer's attention. Having begun with France, and then proceeded to Italy, which it was desirable to visit before the full heats of summer set in, I could not reach Germany till the beginning of July, when it wanted but a fortnight of the annual school vacation. This fortnight I spent in Berlin, and before the schools closed I visited all the more important of them, and attended their classes as I had attended those of the schools in France and Italy. Then came the holidays, longer than ours because the foreign schools have in their school year only this one break of any importance; at Christmas and Easter they have only a few days' vacation. The holidays not beginning at the same time in North and South Germany, I was enabled, after leaving Berlin, to see some schools at work in the Rhine Province, and later I visited the famous establishment of Schulpforta, and other establishments both in Prussian and in non-Prussian parts of Germany. In general, however, though everywhere I was obligingly received and furnished with all possible information, the holidays, either in prospect, actual, or just ended, interfered so much with my seeing the schools in full operation, that the fortnight I passed at Berlin remained the most valuable part, by far, of my experience in German schools. This being so, and it being evidently convenient to select the school system of some one country of Germany for particular description, and for a representative of that of others where the schools follow, in general, the same course, I will choose that of Prussia for this purpose. As a rule, the secondary schools of Northern and Central Germany are better than those of Southern, and those of Protestant Germany better than those of Catholic. This will hardly be disputed; yet the school system all through Germany is in its main features much the same, and is, in its completeness and carefulness, such as to excite a foreigner's admiration. In Aus-

tria this excellent school system is not wanting; what is wanting there is the life, power, and faith in its own operations
which animate it in other parts of Germany. Nowhere has it
this life and faith more than in Prussia. It has them, indeed, in
5   other and smaller German territories as well; a Prussian will
himself readily admit that the schools of Frankfort,* or of the
kingdom of Württemberg, are as good as his own. But it is in
countries of the scale and size of Prussia that a living and
powerful school system bears the most noteworthy fruits; and
10   it is in Prussia, therefore, that I now proceed to trace them.

* This was written before Frankfort became Prussian.

Chapter XV

Present Organisation of the Secondary or Higher Schools in Prussia

Higher Schools of Prussia—Gymnasien—Progymnasien—Real-schulen—Höhere Bürgerschulen—Vorschulen, or Preparatory Schools—Numbers of Teachers and Scholars.

The schools with which we are concerned, the secondary schools as the French call them, the higher schools (*höhere Schulen*) as the Germans call them, are in Prussia thus classed: Gymnasiums, Progymnasiums, Real Schools, Upper Burgher Schools (*Gymnasien, Progymnasien, Realschulen, höhere* 5 *Bürgerschulen*). Above these are the universities, below them the primary or elementary schools.*

At the head of these secondary schools, and directly leading to the universities, are the *Gymnasien*. The uniform employment of this term *Gymnasium* to designate them, dates from 10 a government instruction of 1812. Before this they were variously called by the names of Gymnasium, Lyceum, Pædagogium, College, Latin School, and others.

A gymnasium has properly six classes, counted upwards from the sixth, the lowest, to the first (*prima*), the highest. But, in 15 fact, in all large schools the classes have an upper part and a lower part, and each part has, if necessary, two parallel groups (*cœtus*). The sixth and fifth classes form the lower division of the school, the fourth and third the middle division, the second and first the upper division. In former times the *Fach-* 20

---

* The middle school (*Mittelschule*), variously called *Stadtschule, Bürgerschule, Rectoratschule,* is in truth only an elementary school of a higher grade, and in France is called *école élémentaire supérieure,* in Switzerland, *höhere Volksschule, Secundarschule.* A description of a school of this kind will be found in my account of the schools of 25 Canton Zurich.

system, or system by which the pupil was in different classes for the different branches of his instruction, was prevalent; since 1820 this system has been gradually superseded by the *Classensystem,* which keeps the pupil in the same class for all his work. The course in each of the three lower classes is of one year, in each of the three higher of two years, making nine in all; it being calculated that a boy should enter the gymnasium when he is nine or ten years old, and leave it for the university when he is eighteen or nineteen.

The *Lehrplan,* or plan of work, is fixed for all *Gymnasien* by ministerial authority, as in France and Italy. It is far, however, from being a series of detailed programmes as in those countries. What it does is to fix the matters of instruction, the number of hours to be allotted to them, the gradual development of them from the bottom of the school to the top. Within the limits of the general organisation of study thus established, great freedom is left to the teacher, and great variety is to be found in practice.

Some years ago the hours of work were 32 in the week. This was found too much, and since 1856, in the lowest class of a gymnasium there are 28 hours of regular school work in the week, in the five higher classes there are 30 hours. The school hours are in the morning from 7 to about 11 in summer, from 8 to about 12 in winter; in the afternoon they are from 2 to 4 all the year round. As in France, there is but one half-holiday in the week, and it is in the middle of the week.

Latin has ten hours a week given to it in all five classes below *prima,* and eight in *prima.* Greek begins in *quarta,* and thenceforward has six hours a week in each class, by which the reader will at once see that we are no longer in France or Italy, but in a country whose schools treat the study of Greek as seriously as the best schools among ourselves. The mother tongue (and here we quit the practice of English schools) has two hours a week in all classes below *prima,* and three in *prima.* But in the two lowest classes it is always taught in connection with Latin and by the same teacher, and time may, if necessary, be taken from Latin to give to it. Arithmetic or mathematics have four hours a week in *secunda* and *prima*, three in *quinta*, *quarta*, and *tertia*, and four again in the lowest class. French begins in *quinta*, and is the only modern language except their own which the boys learn as part of the regular school work; it has three hours a week in *quinta*, and two in all the classes above. Many gymnasiums offer their pupils the opportunity of learning English or Italian, but as an extra matter. Geography and history have two hours a week in *sexta* and *quinta*, and thenceforward three hours. The natural sciences get two hours in *prima* and one in *secunda*, in the rest of the school they are the most movable part of the work, the school authorities having it in their power to take time from them to give to arithmetic, geography, and history, or to add time to them in places where there is no *Realschule* and the boys in the middle of the gymnasium wish to study the natural sciences in preference to Greek. Drawing is a part of the regular school work in the three lower classes of the school, and has two hours a week. *Sexta* and *quinta* have three hours a week of the writing master.

Every class has religious instruction; *sexta* and *quinta* for three hours a week, the four higher classes for two. All the boys learn singing and gymnastics, and all who are destined for the theological faculty at the university learn in *secunda* and *prima* Hebrew; but these three matters do not come into the regular school hours.

I have said that in places where there is no *Realschule* boys in the middle division of a gymnasium may substitute other studies for that of Greek. Where there is a *Realschule* accessible, this is not permitted; and in the upper division of a gymnasium it is nowhere permitted. In general, the gymnasium is steadily to regard the *allgemeine wissenschaftliche Bildung* of the pupil, the formation of his mind and of his powers of knowledge, without prematurely taking thought for the practical applicability of what he studies. It is expressly forbidden to give this practical or professional turn to the studies of a pupil in the highest forms of a gymnasium, even when he is destined for the army.

Progymnasiums are merely gymnasiums without their higher

classes. Most progymnasiums have the lower and middle divisions of a gymnasium, four classes; some have only the lower
division and half of the middle, three classes; some, again, have
all the classes except *prima*. The progymnasium follows, so far
as it has the same classes, the *Lehrplan* of the gymnasium. In
the small towns, where it is not possible to maintain at once
a progymnasium and a *Realschule*, the progymnasium has often
parallel classes for classical and for non-classical studies. But
in general the tendency within the last five years has been for
the progymnasium to develope itself into the full gymnasium,
and when I was at Berlin Dr. Wiese, a member of the Council
of Education there, to whom I am indebted for much valuable
assistance,* pointed out to me on the map a number of places,
scattered all about the Prussian dominions, where this process
was either just completed or still going on.

To reform the old methods of teaching the classics, to reduce
their preponderance, to make school studies bear more directly
upon the wants of practical life, and to aim at imparting what
is called 'useful knowledge,' were projects not unknown to the
seventeenth and eighteenth century as well as to ours. Comenius, a Moravian by birth, who in 1641 was invited to England
in order to remodel the schools here, and in the following century Rousseau in France and Basedow in Germany, promulgated, with various degrees of notoriety and success, various
schemes with one or other of these objects. The Philanthropinum of Dessau, an institution established in pursuance of
them, was an experiment which made much noise in its day.
It was broken up about 1780, but its impulse and the ideas
which set this impulse in motion, continued, and bear fruit in
the *Realschulen*. The name *Realschule* was first used at Halle;
a school with that title was established there by Christoph
Semler, in 1738. This *Realschule* did not last long, but it was
followed by others in different parts of the country. They

* Dr. Wiese has written an interesting work on the English public
schools, but his book on those of Prussia, *Das höhere Schulwesen in
Preussen*, Berlin, 1864 (pp. 740), is a mine of the fullest, most authentic
information on the subject of which it treats, and is indispensable for
all who have to study this closely.

took a long time to hit their right line and to succeed; it is said to be only from 1822 that the first really good specimen dates. This one was at Berlin, and though it did not begin to work thoroughly well till 1822, it had been founded in 1747, and had been in existence ever since that time. Its founder's 5 name was Johann Hecker, who was a Berlin parish-clergyman. The Government began to occupy itself with the *Realschulen* in 1832, and as the growth of industry and the spread of the modern spirit gave them more and more importance, a definite plan and course had to be framed for them, as for the *Gym-* 10 *nasien*. This was done in 1859.* *Realschulen* were distinguished as of three kinds; *Realschulen* of the first rank, *Realschulen* of the second rank, and higher Burgher Schools. For *Real-schulen* of the first rank the number and system of classes was the same as that for the *Gymnasien;* the full course was of nine 15 years. The *Lehrplan* fixes a rather greater number of hours of school work for them than the *Gymnasien* have; 30 for the lowest class, 31 for the class next above, 32 for each of the four others.

All three kinds of *Realschulen* are for boys destined to call- 20 ings for which university studies are not required. But Latin is still obligatory in *Realschulen* of the first rank, and in the three lower classes of these schools it has more time allotted to it than any other subject. In the highest class it comes to its minimum of time, three hours; and in this class, and in 25 *secunda*, the time given to mathematics and the natural sciences amounts altogether to eleven hours a week. As the *Real-schule* leads, not to the university, but to business, English becomes obligatory in it as well as French. French, however, has most time allotted to it. Religious instruction has the same num- 30 ber of hours here as in the *Gymnasien*. Drawing, which in the *Gymnasien* ceases after *quarta* to be a part of the regular school work, has in the *Realschule* two hours a week in each of the five classes below *prima*, and three in *prima*.

It is found that after *quarta*, that is, after three years of 35 school, many of the *Realschule* boys leave; and an attempt

* By the *Unterrichts- und Prüfungsordnung für die Realschulen und die höheren Bürgerschulen*, of the 6th of October in that year.

is therefore made to render the first three years' course as substantial and as complete in itself as possible.

The *Realschulen* of the second rank have the six classes of those of the first; but they are distinguished from them by not having Latin made obligatory, by being free to make their course a seven years' course instead of a nine, and, in general, by being allowed a considerable latitude in varying their arrangements to meet special local wants. A *general*, not professional, mental training, is still the aim of the *Realschule* of the first rank, in spite of its not preparing for the university. A lower grade of this training, with an admixture of directly practical and professional aims, satisfies the *Realschule* of the second rank.

Where a gymnasium and a *Realschule* are united in a single establishment, under one direction, the classes *sexta* and *quinta* may be common to both, but above *quinta* the classes must be separate.

The term *Bürgerschule* was long used interchangeably with that of *Realschule*. The regulations of 1859 have assigned the name of higher Burgher School to that third class of *Realschulen*, which has not the complete system of six forms that the *Gymnasien* and the other two kinds of *Realschulen* have. The higher Burgher School stands, therefore, to the *Realschule* in the same relation in which the *Progymnasium* stands to the *Gymnasium*. Some Burgher Schools have as many as five classes, only lacking *prima*. The very name of the *Bürgerschulen* indicates that in the predominance of a local and municipal character, and in the smaller share given to classics, they follow the line of the *Realschulen* of the second order. Still Latin has three or four hours a week in all the best of these schools. They are, however, the least classical of all the higher schools; but several of them, in small places where there cannot be two schools, have gymnasial classes parallel with the *real* classes, just as certain *Gymnasien*, in like circumstances, have *real* classes parallel with their classical classes.

As the elementary schools pursue a course of teaching which is not specially designed as a preparation for the higher schools, it has become a common practice to establish *Vorschulen*, or preparatory schools, as in France, to be appendages of the several higher schools, to receive little boys without the previous examination in reading, writing, arithmetic, grammar and Scripture history, which the higher school imposes, and to pass them on in their tenth year, duly prepared, into the higher school. These *Vorschulen* have in general two classes.

These are the higher or secondary schools of Prussia. Before the recent war, the population of Prussia was 18,476,500. The latest complete school returns are those for the year 1863. In 1863, Prussia possessed 255 higher schools, with 3,349 teachers in them, and 66,135 scholars. She had 84 *Vorschulen*, or public preparatory schools, with 188 teachers, and 8,027 scholars. Of the 255 higher schools, 172 were classical schools, gymnasiums or progymnasiums, with 45,403 scholars; 83 were non-classical schools, belonging to one or other of the three orders of *Realschulen*, with 20,732 scholars.

All these schools have a public character, are subject to State inspection, must bring their accounts to be audited by a public functionary, and can have no masters whose qualifications have not been strictly and publicly tried. The reader will recollect that we found in the public schools of France 65,832 scholars in the year 1865. He will recollect also that we found, I will not say in the public schools of England, but in all the schools which by any straining or indulgence can possibly be made to bear that title, 15,880 scholars. In the public higher schools and preparatory schools of Prussia we find 74,162 scholars.

I will not now press this comparison, but will pass on to show in what way the higher schools of Prussia have a public character.

Chapter XVI

Government and Patronage of the Prussian Public Schools

Common Law of Prussia—State-Action and Regulation—Origin and History of the Central Education Department—Origin and History of the Provincial School Authorities—Provincial School Boards and District School Boards—Examining Commissions— Local and Municipal School Authorities—Endowments and Charities; Their Management—Patronage of Schools.

There is no organic school-law in Prussia like the organic school-law of France, though sketches and projects of such a law have more than once been prepared. But at present the public control of the higher schools is exercised through ad-
5 ministrative orders and instructions, like the minutes of our Committee of Council on Education. But the administrative authority has in Prussia a very different basis for its operations from that which it has in England, and a much firmer one. It has for its basis these articles of the *Allgemeine Landrecht*,
10 or common law of Prussia, which was drawn up in writing in Frederick the Great's reign, and promulgated in 1794, in the reign of his successor:—

'Schools and universities are State institutions, having for their object the instruction of youth in useful information and
15 scientific knowledge.

'Such establishments are to be instituted only with the State's previous knowledge and consent.

'All public schools and public establishments of education are under the State's supervision, and must at all times submit
20 themselves to its examinations and inspections.

'Whenever the appointment of teachers is not by virtue of the foundation or of a special privilege vested in certain persons or corporations, it belongs to the State.

'Even where the immediate supervision of such schools and the appointment of their teachers is committed to certain private persons or corporations, new teachers cannot be appointed, and important changes in the constitution and teaching of the school cannot be adopted, without the previous knowledge or consent of the provincial school authorities.

'The teachers in the gymnasiums and other higher schools have the character of State functionaries.'

To the same effect the Prussian Deed of Constitution (*Verfassungs-Urkunde*) of 1850 has the following:—

'For the education of the young sufficient provision is to be made by means of public schools.

'Every one is free to impart instruction, and to found and conduct establishments for instruction, when he has proved to the satisfaction of the proper State authorities that he has the moral, scientific, and technical qualifications requisite.

'All public and private establishments are under the supervision of authorities named by the State.'

With these principles to serve as a basis, administrative control can be exercised without much difficulty. These principles, however, may with real truth be said to form part of the common law of Prussia, for they form part of almost every Prussian citizen's notions of what is right and fitting in school concerns. It would be a mistake to suppose that the State in Prussia shows a grasping and centralising spirit in dealing with education; on the contrary, it makes the administration of it as local as it possibly can; but it takes care that education shall not be left to the chapter of accidents.

Up to the middle of the last century, however, the higher schools were so far left to this chapter of accidents, that the State practised little or no interference with the free action of patrons. But it is important to observe that the State was always, in Prussia, an important school patron itself, and exercised its rights of patronage, while in England these rights slipped from its hands. Royal foundations for schools are in Prussia very numerous, and in all Prussian schools of royal foundation the patronage remains vested in the Crown till this day. Schools like Eton and Westminster, like King Edward's School at Bir-

mingham, like the grammar schools of Sherborne, of Bury St. Edmunds, and so many others, would have been in Prussia 'Crown patronage schools,' with a public, responsible, disinterested authority nominating their masters. So far, therefore, even without any assertion of the right of the State to control private patrons, the higher schools of Prussia have a security which ours have not. The assertion of such a State right, beyond the mere rights of the Crown as a patron, appears in the reign of Friedrich Wilhelm I., and gains definiteness and purpose from that time forth. The *General-Directorium* created by this sovereign, in 1722, was a ministerial body with a department for spiritualities (*Geistliches Departement*) to which the exercise of the Crown rights of control over churches and schools was entrusted. This department was in a few years attached to that of the Minister of Justice, and as such it was held by an able minister, formed in Frederick the Great's school, Von Zedlitz, who in 1787 separated the church and school affairs of the *Geistliches Departement*, and committed the school affairs to a High Board of Schools (*Ober-Schulcollegium*). In the great movement of reconstruction which between 1806 and 1812 renewed the civil and military organisation of Prussia, the Board of Schools was abolished, and the Education Department was made, in 1808, a section of the Home Office. Wilhelm von Humboldt was placed at its head.*
Finally, in 1817, this Education section became an independent ministerial department, and its chief took the title of Minister for Spiritualities and Education (*Minister der geistlichen und Unterrichtsangelegenheiten*). The first minister was Freiherr von Altenstein. Medicine having been added to the affairs over which this department has supervision, the minister's full style now is *Minister der geistlichen, Unterrichts- und Medicinalangelegenheiten*. The present minister is Dr. von Mühler.

When the Education Department was made a section of the Home Office, Wilhelm von Humboldt had two functionaries

* In June 1810, Wilhelm von Humboldt went as Prussian envoy to Vienna, and the rest of his public life was chiefly passed, as is well known, in the diplomatic service of his country.

with the title of *technische Räthe*, technical counsellors, placed
with him. These *technische Räthe* have now grown into eight,
and they, with the Minister and the under Secretary of State
for the department, constitute the central authority for the
affairs of education.   5

But in Prussia it is not the central minister who has the most
direct and important action on the schools, it is the authorities
representing the State in the several parts of the country. It
is from Wilhelm von Humboldt's accession to office in 1808
that the establishment of a fruitful relation between these two   10
authorities, the schools and the central power, really dates. Before that time, in accordance with the notions which closely
connected the School with the Church, the provincial authorities with an action upon the schools were the consistories.
These were, indeed, State authorities, for their members are   15
named by the Crown, or head of the State; the head of the
State being in Prussia far more practically than in England the
head of the Church also, inasmuch as in Prussia the Crown is
actually *summus episcopus*, the powers of supervision and discipline vested of old in the bishops, and in England, where   20
we have kept our bishops, still vested in them, having gone,
in Protestant Germany, straight to the Crown. The Crown as
summus episcopus exercises its rights through consistories, and
the members of the consistories are in consequence nominees
of the State. The consistories therefore supplied a provincial   25
State authority for dealing with schools. But the employment
of them for this purpose had two evident administrative inconveniences, to say nothing of other objections to it. In the first
place, the consistories were in relation at the centre of Government not with the Education Department but with the High   30
Consistory. In the second place, it is only as a Protestant sovereign that the King of Prussia is head of the Church and represented throughout the country by consistories. As a Catholic
sovereign he is not head of the Church, and has in the provinces no consistory or ecclesiastical authority which is also a   35
State authority. But Prussia has nearly seven millions of Catholic subjects. For Catholic schools, therefore, as well as for

Protestant, a provincial State authority was required, and this authority the consistory could not supply.

The administration of 1808 established in each of the *Regierungen*, or governmental districts, into which Prussia was divided, a deputation for worship and public instruction (*Deputation für Cultus und öffentlichen Unterricht*). These deputations were in immediate connexion with the Education Department at Berlin; they represented, in the supervision of the schools in the provinces, the State authority, and exercised for the most part the Crown patronage. In 1810 were added three Scientific Deputations (*Wissenschaftliche Deputationen*), one at Berlin, one at Königsberg, one at Breslau, to examine teachers for the secondary schools and to advise the Government on all important matters relating to these. The Berlin deputation had for its members the two *technische Räthe* of the Education Department, Süvern and Nicolovius, and besides these, Ancillon, Friedrich August Wolf, and Schleiermacher. The English reader will observe the sort of persons who in Prussia were chosen for the management, at a critical moment, of the State's relations with education.

The higher schools of Prussia feel to this day the benefits of that management. Variations took place in the organisation of the provincial authority, as the different divisions of the Prussian monarchy were constituted afresh, but its general character remained the same, and has remained so till this day. Prussia is now divided into eight provinces,* and these eight provinces are again divided into twenty-six governmental districts, or *Regierungen*. There is a Provincial School Board (*Provinzial-Schulcollegium*) in the chief town of each of the eight provinces, and a Governmental District Board in that of each of the twenty-six *Regierungen*. In general, the State's relations with the higher class of secondary schools are exercised through the Provincial Board, its relations with the lower class of them, and with the primary schools, through the District Board. In Berlin, the relations with these also are managed by the Provincial Board. A *Provinzial-Schulcollegium* has for

* I speak throughout of Prussia as she was before her late war with Austria.

its president the High President of the province, for its director the vice-president of that governmental district which happens to have for its centre the provincial capital. The Board has two or three other members, of whom, in general, one is a Catholic and one is a Protestant; and one is always a man practically 5
conversant with school matters. The District Board has in the provincial capitals the same president and director as the Provincial Board; in the other centres of *Regierungen* it has for its president the President of the *Regierung,* and three or four members selected on the same principle as the members 10
of the Provincial Board.

The provincial State authority, therefore, is, in general, for gymnasiums, the larger progymnasiums, and *Realschulen* of the first rank, the Provincial School Board; for the smaller progymnasiums, *Realschulen* of the second rank, the higher 15
Burgher Schools, and the primary schools of all kinds, the Governmental District Board. Both boards are in continual communication with the Education Minister at Berlin, and every two or three years they have to draw up for him a general report on the school affairs of their province or district. 20

The Scientific Deputations are now replaced by seven Examination Commissions (*Wissenschaftliche Prüfungscommissionen*).* The most important business of these Commissions being to examine teachers for the secondary schools, they have seven members, one for each of the main subjects in which 25
teachers are examined,—philology, history, mathematics, pædagogy, theology, and the natural sciences. These Commissions report to the Minister every year.

Besides the central and provincial administration there is a local or municipal administration for schools that are not 30
Crown patronage schools. Matters of teaching and discipline, —*interna* as they are called,—do not in any public schools, even when their patrons are municipalities or private persons, come within the jurisdiction of the local authority; they are referred to the provincial and district boards. The local au- 35

* The seats of these seven Commissions are the towns of Berlin, Königsberg, Breslau, Halle, Münster, Bonn, and Greifswald. These towns are also the seats of the Prussian universities.

thority administers *externa*,—that is, it manages the school
property, fixes the school fees, gives free admissions to poor
scholars, and the like; and it nominates, when the patronage
is private or municipal, the teacher; but for his confirmation
5   recourse must be had to the State authority, provincial or
central. Thus, if local or municipal patrons chose to appoint
a master who had not got his certificate from one of the Examination Commissions, the appointment would be quashed.
In most towns the local authority for schools of municipal
10 patronage is the town magistracy, assisted by a *Stadtschulrath;*
sometimes the local authority is a *Curatorium* or *Schulcommission.* To take one case as a specimen. The two town gymnasiums at Breslau are under a *Curatorium*, of which the composition is as follows: a member of the magistracy (who must
15 be a lawyer), president; two members chosen by the representative body of the commune, and the rectors of the two
gymnasiums. This body draws up the school estimate, of which
presently; looks after the administration of the school property, sees that the school premises are kept in order and prop-
20 erly supplied with what they want, represents the town at
the leaving examinations, or other public solemnities in which
the gymnasiums are concerned, has a consultative voice as to
any change in the mode of regulating the free admissions,
receives from the rector, when he and the majority of the
25 masters are agreed on a boy's expulsion, notice that a boy has
been expelled, with the grounds for it; if the rector and a
majority of his *Lehrercollegium* differ as to the propriety of
expelling, the *Curatorium* decides. It is not the *Curatorium*
that nominates the masters, but the town magistracy, subject
30 to approval by the proper State authority. The teaching and
all that relates to it are in each gymnasium under the rector's
control, who is responsible on this head to the Provincial
Board and not to the *Curatorium.*

In cases where the Crown has had a share in endowing a
35 school, or has made a grant to it, it acquires joint rights of
patronage with the local patrons, and for the exercise of these
rights it is represented by a commissioner, who is always, as
such, a member of the *Curatorium.*

Only a few Prussian schools, such as those of Schulpforta and Rossleben, or the Joachimsthal School at Berlin, have so large an endowment that it can fully support them. But a very large number have endowments of some sort, or else grants from some school charity or other, such as the *Marienstift* at 5 Stettin for schools in Pomerania, the *Sacksche Stiftung* in Silesia for schools in the principalities of Glogau, Wohlau, and Liegnitz, and many other such foundations. The Provincial or District Boards supervise the *externa*, the property concerns, as well as the *interna*, the teaching concerns, of all 10 schools of Crown patronage; but by the Prussian law, wherever there is an endowment there is a public right to see that this endowment is properly employed; so that there is a public control for the management of all endowments of private as well as of Crown patronage. The school appoints a man 15 of business (*Rendant, Rechnungsführer*) charged with the financial administration (*Cassenführung*) of the school; the authority in whom the patronage of the school is vested (*Patronatsbehörde*) draws out a school estimate (*Schul-Etat*) every three years, showing in detail the school's income, actual and 20 estimated, for the three years about to commence, and its estimated expenditure. In every government district, or *Regierung*, there is a public functionary whose business it is to review these estimates, and who addresses to the *Rendant* his remarks and requirements (*Revisionserinnerungen, Revisions-* 25 *forschungen*), which the *Rendant* has to lay before the *Patronatsbehörde*, whatever this may be, *Curatorium, Schulcommission*, &c., and to which this authority must pay attention. An abusive application of trust funds, or of grants from a charity, is thus checked: all expenses not in the estimate have to be ac- 30 counted for, and all improper expenses are disallowed. The local patrons can only resist by applying to the administrative authority next above that which has dealt with them (*vorgesetzte Instanz*), and this appeal they will never make when they know they have a bad case. 35

The State has part in the patronage of more than half of the secondary schools in Prussia; in 72 of them as absolute patron, in 74 of them as part patron. The immense majority of the schools of which it is absolute patron belong to the category of *Gymnasien*, the highest and most expensive class of secondary schools. There were, in 1864,* 145 *Gymnasien* in Prussia; of 65 of these the Crown had the exclusive patronage. At the same date there were 28 *Progymnasien*, 49 *Realschulen* of the first rank, 16 of the second, and 21 higher Burgher Schools. Of only seven of these had the Crown the exclusive patronage; of three progymnasiums, two *Realschulen* of the first rank, one of the second, and one higher Burgher School. Under municipal patronage were 26 gymnasiums, 11 progymnasiums, 35 *Realschulen* of the first rank, 10 of the second, and 13 higher Burgher Schools. The municipalities thus show that leaning towards *real* instruction which might be expected from them; of the 49 *Realschulen* of the first rank they have 35. What is most striking to an Englishman is the small number of public schools under patronage neither royal nor municipal, but under the patronage of some church, or corporation, or private person; there are but 12 of them altogether, five *Gymnasien*, two *Progymnasien*, one *Realschule* of the first order, and four higher Burgher Schools. The question therefore as to the rights and interests of private patrons of public schools does not take, so far as the number of their schools goes, very important dimensions. The total expenditure on the higher schools and their *Vorschulen* was, in 1864, 2,580,684 thalers (in round figures, about 387,100*l.*). Of this sum the scholars' fees contributed 1,193,055 thalers; the State 526,722 thalers, the municipalities 401,046 thalers; school property produced 384,224 thalers, and benefactions not under public administration, 75,637 thalers. The State is therefore, after the scholars themselves, the great supporter of the public schools, as well as the principal patron of them.

But the reader will ask, in what sense are the schools with private patrons to be called public schools? They are public schools because they fulfil the requirements, adopt the title and constitution, and follow the *Lehrplan*, fixed by public au-

* A year later than the year for which there are complete returns, and for which I gave, as the total of Prussian higher schools open in that year, 255. In 1864 there were 259.

thority for the five classes of public secondary schools, and
by so doing obtain the *status* and privilege of such schools.
Are there not a great many important establishments, then,
the reader may next ask, which do not care to get this status,
but prefer to be independent? I answer: No school in Prussia 5
can be *independent*, in the sense of owing no account to any
one for the teacher it employs, or the way in which it is conducted; for every school there is a *verordnete Aufsichtsge-
walt*, an ordained authority of supervision. But private persons are no doubt free to open establishments of their own, 10
give them a constitution of their own, and follow a *Lehrplan*
of their own. There are ten large private schools in Berlin
for the class of boys who go to secondary schools; these private
schools, however, have the public schools in view, and take
boys whose parents do not like to send them very young to the 15
great public schools, classical or non-classical; but when these
boys are ready for the middle division of the public Gymnasium or *Realschule*, they pass on there. These private schools
are merely preparatory schools for the public schools, and
accordingly they are organised as progymnasiums and as higher 20
Burgher Schools. They represent no anti-public-school feeling,
no rival line in education. Two remarkable institutions which
did not prepare for the public schools, which gave a complete
course of secondary instruction of their own arranging, and
which were private schools, *écoles libres*, in the full sense of 25
the term,—the *Plamannsche Anstalt* and the *Cauersche Anstalt*,
—existed at Berlin not long ago, but they exist there no longer.
Experiments of the same kind are being tried elsewhere. The
Victoria Institut, at Falkenberg, is a prominent specimen of
them; it is a regular private boarding school, charging 400 tha- 30
lers (60*l.*) a year, and it professes to give the training either of
the gymnasiums or of the *Realschulen*, whichever the pupil
prefers. The English generally know more of schools of this
kind than of the public schools in Germany, because this kind
of private school has a boarding establishment and the public 35
schools have not, and a foreign parent generally looks out for
a school with a boarding establishment. For the most part he
is no judge at all of schools on their real merits; he sends his son

to a foreign school that he may learn the modern languages, and the boy will learn these at a private school just as much as at a public one. But the Germans themselves undoubtedly prefer their public schools. An attendance in the public secondary schools of 74,000 pupils, in a population of 18,500,000, which is Prussia's population, shows that the Prussians prefer them. And it is the same in other German countries.

Chapter XVII

Preponderance of Public Schools. The *Abiturientenexamen*

Preference for Public Schools—The Leaving Examination (Abiturientenexamen); Its History—Present Plan of the Leaving Examination in Gymnasien—Object Proposed by the Founders of the Leaving Examination—Leaving Examination in Realschulen—Examinations of Passage.

I believe that the public schools are preferred, in Prussia, on their merits. The Prussians are satisfied with them, and are proud of them, and with good reason; the schools have been intelligently planned to meet their intelligent wants. But the preponderance of the public schools is further secured by the establishment in connexion with them of the 'leaving examinations' (*Abiturientenprüfungen, Maturitätsprüfungen, Entlassungsprüfungen, Abgangsprüfungen*), on which depends admission to the universities, to special schools (*Fachschulen*) like the *Gewerbe-Institut* or the *Bauakademie*, and to the civil and military service of the State. The learned professions can only be reached through the universities, so the access to these professions depends on the leaving examination. The pupils of private tutors or private schools can present themselves for this examination, but it is held at the public schools, it turns upon the studies of the upper forms of the public schools, and it is conducted in great part by their teachers. A public schoolboy undoubtedly presents himself for it with an advantage; and its object undoubtedly is, not the illusory one of an examination-test as in our public service it is employed, but the sound one of ensuring as far as possible that a youth shall pass a certain number of years under the best school-teaching of his country. This really trains him, which the mere application of an examination-test does not; but an

examination-test is wisely used in conjunction with this training, to take care that a youth has really profited by it. No
nation that did not honestly feel it had made its public secondary schools the best places of training for its middle and
5   upper classes, could institute the leaving examination I am
going to describe; but Prussia has a right to feel that she has
made hers this, and therefore she had a right to institute this
examination. It forms an all-important part of the secondary
instruction of that country, and I hope the reader will give me
10 his attention while I describe it.

Before 1788 admission to the Prussian universities was a very
easy affair. You went to the dean of the faculty in which you
wished to study; you generally brought with you a letter of
recommendation from the school you left; the dean asked you
15 a few questions and ascertained that you knew Latin; then
you were matriculated. The *Ober-Schulcollegium*, which was
in 1788 the authority at the head of Prussian public instruction, perceiving that from the insufficiency of the entrance
examination the universities were cumbered with unprepared
20 and idle students, determined to try and cure this state of
things. In December of that year a royal edict was issued to
the public schools and universities directing that the public
schools should make their boys undergo an examination before
they proceeded to the university; and that the universities
25 should make the boys who came up to them from private
schools undergo an examination corresponding to that of the
public schoolboys. Every one who underwent the examination was to receive a certificate of his ripeness or unripeness
for university studies (*Zeugnis der Reife, Zeugnis der Un-
30 reife*). The candidates declared to be unripe might still enter
the university if their parents chose; but it was hoped that,
guided by this test, their parents would keep them at school
till they were properly prepared, or else send them into some
other line. No plan of examination was prescribed, but the cer-
35 tificate was to record, under the two heads of *languages* and
sciences, the candidate's proficiency in each of these matters.

The *Allgemeine Landrecht*, promulgated in 1794, after complaints had been rife that the universities had still a number

of unprofitable students, and that young men went there merely to escape military service, made yet stricter regulations. It ordered the examination held at the university for boys coming from private schools to be conducted by a Commission; and it forbade the matriculation of any one who did not obtain a certificate of his ripeness.

But the omitting to prescribe a definite plan for the examination, and the entrusting them to two different bodies, the schools and the universities, caused the intentions of the Government to be in great measure frustrated. There was no uniform standard of examination. The schools made the standard high, the universities made it low; and numbers of young men, leaving the public schools without undergoing the *Abiturientenexamen* there, waited a little while, and then presented themselves to be examined at the university, where the examination was notoriously much laxer than at the school.

The great epoch of reform for the higher schools of Prussia is Wilhelm von Humboldt's year and a half at the head of the Education Department. The first words of a memorandum of this date on a proposal not to require Greek except of students for orders: *Es ist nicht darum zu thun, dass Schulen und Universitäten in einem trägen und kraftlosen Gewohnheitsgange blieben, sondern darum, dass durch sie die Bildung der Nation auf eine immer höhere Stufe gebracht werde,**—might be taken as a motto for his whole administration of public instruction. It was Wilhelm von Humboldt who took the most important step towards making the *Abiturientenprüfung* what it now is. He was the originator of a uniform plan of examination obligatory on all who examined candidates for entrance to the university. Schleiermacher, who, as I have said, was a member of the Education Council, wished to take away this examination from the universities, and to give it entirely to the schools. This was not done, but the course of examination was strictly defined, and a form of certificate, fully indicating its results, was prescribed. The certificate was of three grades; No. 1 de-

---

* 'The thing is *not*, to let the schools and universities go on in a drowsy and impotent routine; the thing is, to raise the culture of the nation ever higher and higher by their means.'

clared its possessor to be thoroughly qualified for the university, No. 2 declared him to be partially qualified, No. 3 to be unqualified (*untüchtig*). But this plan of reform, which was brought into operation in 1812, could not produce its due
5   fruits so long as the double examination was maintained. After the peace of 1815 there was a great flow of students to the universities; many of them were very ill prepared; but the universities, with the natural desire to get as many students as possible, eased the examinations to them as much as they could,
10 and admitted the holders of any certificate at all, even of No. 3, to matriculation. At Bonn, in 1822, out of 139 certificates for that year, 122 were of No. 3, declaring the holder unqualified for the University; 16 were of No. 2, declaring him partially qualified; only one was of No. 1, declaring him thor-
15 oughly qualified. The Provincial School Boards reported to the minister that the efforts of the schools were frustrated by the laxity of the university commissions, which got more and more candidates. The schools in their turn were inclined to make the first grade of certificate a reward of severe competitive
20 examination, which was by no means what those who instituted it intended. The admission to the universities of young men declared to be unqualified, the two kinds of examining bodies with differing views and standards, and the threefold grade of certificate, were found fatal obstacles to the successful
25 working of the reform of 1812.

All three obstacles have been removed. The regulations at present in force date from 1834 and 1856.* The leaving examination is now held at the *Gymnasien* only. The threefold grade of certificate is abolished, and the candidate is, as in old
30 times, certified to be either *reif* or *unreif*. No one, as a general rule, can without a certificate attend university lectures at all; and no one without a certificate of ripeness can be regularly matriculated in any faculty. The examining body is thus composed: the director of the gymnasium and the professors
35 who teach in *prima*; a representative of the *Schul-Curatorium*, where the gymnasium has a *Curatorium*; the Crown's *Compa-*

---

* *Reglement vom 4. Juni 1834*, completed by *Verfügung vom 12. Jan.* 1856.

tronats-Commissarius (joint patronage commissary) where there is one; and a member or delegate of the Provincial School Board. The representative of the Provincial School Board is always president of the examining commission. The *Abiturient*, or leaving boy, must have been two years in *prima*. The examination work is to be of the same pitch as the regular work of this class, though it must not contain passages that have been actually done in school. But neither, on the other hand, must it be such as to require any *specielle Vorstudien*. It embraces the mother tongue, Latin, Greek, and French; mathematics and physics, geography, history, and divinity. An *Abiturient* who is going to enter the theological faculty at the University is examined in Hebrew. The examination is both by writing and *viva voce*. The paper work lasts a week,* and the candidate who fails in it is not tried *viva voce*. The examination papers are prepared by the director and teachers, but several sets have to be in readiness, and the president of the examining commission, who represents the Provincial School Board and the State, chooses each paper as it is to be given out. He also, at the *viva voce* examination, chooses the passages if he likes, and himself puts any question he may think proper. The Provincial School Board have at any time the power to direct that the same examination papers shall be used for all the gymnasiums of the province. Each performance is marked *insufficient, sufficient, good,* or *excellent,* and no other terms, and no qualifications of these, are admitted. A candidate who is fully up to the mark in the mother tongue and in Latin, and considerably above it either in classics or mathematics, is declared *reif,*—passes,—though he may fall below it in other things. If the commission are not unanimous about passing a candidate, they vote; the youngest member voting first and the

---

* Specimens of the subjects set for the German and Latin essay at these examinations are the following. For the German essay:—'How did Athens come to be the centre of the intellectual life of Greece?' —'From Goethe's *Götz von Berlichingen* draw out a picture of the social state of Germany at the time in which the action of the play is is laid.' For the Latin essay:—*P. Clodio, cum, ut Ciceronem in exilium ejiceret, in animum induxisset, quæ res fuerint adjumento?—Hannibal quibus de causis, quod sibi proposuerat, Italiam subigere, non potuit?*

president last. If the votes are equal the president has a casting vote. But the president may refuse to pass a candidate though the majority have voted for him. In this case, however, the candidate's papers must go to the highest examining authority, the *Wissenschaftliche Prüfungscommission* in whose district the province is, for their decision upon them. To this same High Commission all the papers of half the gymnasiums of each province are each half year referred for their remarks; their remarks, if they have any to make, are addressed by them to the Provincial School Board, and by the Provincial School Board transmitted to the gymnasiums concerned.

The examination takes place about six weeks before the end of the half. The certificates are given out to the successful candidates at the solemnity * which takes place in the *Aula* of a German public school at the end of a half year, or *Semester*. Each member of the examining commission signs the certificate, which, besides defining the candidate's proficiency in each of the matters of examination, has three additional rubrics for *conduct, diligence,* and *attainments,* which are filled up by the school authorities as he deserves.

The candidate who is considered *unreif,* and not passed, is recommended, according to his examination and his previous school career, either to stay another half-year at school and then try again, or to give up his intention of going to the university. If he still persists in going there at once he may; but he must carry with him a certificate of his present unfitness (*Zeugnis der Nichtreife*), a certificate with the same rubrics as the other, and signed in the same way. With this certificate he holds an exceptional, incomplete position at the university; he cannot enter himself in any faculty except that of philosophy, and then he is entered in a special register, and not regu-

---

* At this solemnity a dissertation is read by the director or one of the professors, and every European student knows how much valuable matter has appeared in these dissertations. I have before me the dissertations held in the last year or two at several of the schools I visited. The following are specimens of their subjects:—*De Sallustii dicendi genere commentatio.—Criticarum scriptionum specimen.—Der Prediger Salomo.—Die Erziehung für den Staatsdienst bei den Athenern.— Untersuchungen über die Cissoide (mathematische Abhandlung).*

larly matriculated. He can, therefore, attend lectures; but his time does not count for a degree, and he can hold no public benefice or exhibition. He may be examined once more, and only once, going to a gymnasium for that purpose; the three or four years' course required in the faculty which he follows only begins to count from the time when he passes.

The reader will recollect that for the learned professions,— the church, the law, and medicine,—and for the post of teachers in the high schools and universities, it is necessary to have gone regularly through the university course and to have graduated.

Candidates who have not been at a public school, but who wish to enter the university, must apply to the Provincial School Board of their province for leave to attend a certificate examination. They have to bring testimonials, and a *curriculum vitæ* written by themselves in German, and are then directed by the school board to a gymnasium where they may be examined. They have to pay an examination fee of 10 thalers. If they fail, the examining commission of the gymnasium is empowered to fix a time within which they may not try again, and they may only try twice. They may, however, if they fail to pass, go up to the university on the same condition as the public school boys who fail. These *externi*, as they are called, are not examined along with the *Abiturienten* of the gymnasium, though they are examined by the same examining commission; but the boys who come from private instruction are by the minister's directions to have allowance made for their not being examined by their own teachers, and, so far, to be more leniently treated in the examination than the *Abiturienten*. On the other hand, boys who have been at a gymnasium and who have left it in order to prepare themselves with a private tutor, are not entitled to any special indulgence. Indeed a public school boy, who to evade the rule requiring two years in *prima*, leaves the gymnasium from *secunda*, goes to a private school or private tutor, and offers himself for examination within two years, needs a special permission from the minister in order to be examined. So well do the Prussian authorities know how insufficient an instrument for their object,—that of promoting the national culture and filling the professions with fit men,—is the bare examination-test; so averse are they to cram; so clearly do they perceive that what forms a youth, and what he should in all ways be induced to acquire, is the orderly development of his faculties under good and trained teaching.

With this view all the instructions for the examination are drawn up. It is to tempt candidates to no special preparation and effort, but to be such as 'a scholar of fair ability and proper diligence, may at the end of his school course come to with a quiet mind and without a painful preparatory effort tending to relaxation and torpor as soon as the effort is over.' The total cultivation (*Gesammtbildung*) of the candidate is the great matter, and this is why the two years of *prima* are prescribed, 'that the instruction in this highest class may not degenerate into a preparation for the examination, that the pupil may have the requisite time to come steadily and without overhurrying to the fulness of the measure of his powers and character, that he may be securely and thoroughly formed, instead of being bewildered and oppressed by a mass of information hastily heaped together.' All *tumultuarische Vorbereitung* and all stimulation of vanity and emulation is to be discouraged, and the examination, like the school, is to regard *das Wesentliche und Dauernde*—the substantial and enduring.*

Accordingly, the composition and the passages for translation are the great matters in German examinations, not those papers of questions by which the examiner is so led to show his want of sense, and the examinee his stores of cram.

That a boy shall have been for a certain number of years under good training is what, in Prussia, the State wants to secure; and it uses the examination test to help it to secure this. We leave his training to take its chance, and we put the examination test to a use for which it is quite inadequate, to try and make up for our neglect.

The same course is followed with the *Realschulen* and with the higher Burgher Schools. For entrance to the different

* *Perverse studet qui examinibus studet,* was a favourite saying of Wolf's.

branches of the public service, the leaving certificate of the classical school had up to 1832 been required. For certain of these branches it was determined in 1832 to accept henceforth the certificate of the *Realschule* or the higher Burgher School instead of that of the gymnasium. Different departments made their own stipulations; the Minister of Public Works, for instance, stipulated that the certificate of the candidate for the *Bauakademie* (School of Architecture) should be valid only when the candidate's *Realschule* or higher Burgher School had been one of the first class, or with the full number of six classes, and when he had passed two years in each of the two highest classes. I mention a detail of this kind to show the English reader how entirely it is the boy's school and training which the Prussian Government thinks the great matter, and not his examination. Since 1832 the tendency has been to withdraw again from the *Realschule* certificate its validity for the higher posts in the scientific departments of the public service; for these posts, the gymnasial leaving certificate is now again required. But for a very great number of posts in the public service the certificate of the *Realschule* is still valid, and for a still greater number of posts in the pursuits of commerce and industry employers now require it. The Education Department issued in 1859 the rules by which the examination for this certificate is at present governed. They are the same, *mutatis mutandis*, with those for the *Maturitätsprüfung* at the gymnasium. The examining commission is composed in precisely the same way; the examination and the issue of the certificates follow the same course. The subjects are: divinity, the mother tongue and its literature, the translation of easy passages from Latin authors, but, in general, no Latin writing; French and English, in translation, writing, and speaking; ancient history; the history of Germany, England, and France, for the last three centuries; geography; physics and chemistry; pure and applied mathematics, and drawing. Excellence in one subject may counterbalance shortcomings in another, but no candidate can pass who absolutely fails in any. *Externi* who want the certificate are admitted to examination on the same terms, and at the same fee, as in the *Gymnasien*. In *Realschulen* of the second rank the examination is easier than in those of the first, but the certificate has not the same value. The *Abgangsprüfung* and *Abgangszeugnis* of a higher Burgher School, again, are still more easily passed and won, but still less valuable. The *Abgangszeugnis* of a higher Burgher School entitles the holder to enter the *prima* of a first-rate *Realschule;* often a very important opening to a clever boy in a small country place, who for one year can afford to go to a school away from home, but could not have afforded to get all his schooling there.

To the passage from the *tertia* and *secunda* of the gymnasium or of the *Realschule,* examinations are also attached, for which certificates, if the boy leaves after passing one of them, are given, declaring his ripeness at that stage. For many subordinate employments in the civil service these certificates are accepted. To be a teacher of drawing in a public school, for instance, a certificate of ripeness for *secunda* of a gymnasium or of a first rank *Realschule* or higher Burgher School is required; this if the candidate has not been at a public school and has to be examined as an *externus;* * if he has been at a public school, the certificate of his having passed the examination out of *secunda* at a second rank *Realschule* is sufficient. One important employment of school certificates is to entitle the holder to shorter military service (*Zulassung zum einjährigen freiwilligen Militairdienst*). Young men who volunteer to serve for one year, arming and clothing themselves, the term of military service to be then at an end, must, to be accepted, produce a certificate of a certain value, either from a gymnasium or a *Realschule.*

It shows how many more gymnasium boys there are who go through the full school course than *Realschule* boys, that whereas from the *Gymnasien* in 1863 there were 1,765 *Abiturienten* from *prima*, from the *Realschulen* in the same year there were but 214. Adding to the 1,765 *Abiturienten* 40 *Externen* who passed at the same time, we have 1,805 boys who got the classical certificate of ripeness in 1863. Of this number 1,563 went in that year to the Prussian universities. Of the 214 *Abitu-*

* For the examination of *externi* for this lower kind of certificate, the fee is four thalers.

rienten from the *Realschulen* (to whom are to be added three
Externen, making 217), 124 went into the public service, 92
into the pursuits of commerce or industry; one went to prepare for the gymnasial leaving examination, that he might go
into a learned profession. Evidently the mass of those who go   5
into business leave the *Realschule* before *prima*, and the majority of those who stay for *prima* stay with the hope of public
employment. But the minor certificates accessible to those who
leave *secunda* and *tertia* promote an attendance at school longer
than that which boys going into business would without the   10
attraction of these certificates be willing to give; and they
promote, too, a wholesome return upon the school work done,
and a mastering of it as a whole, which tend, the school work
having in the first instance been sound and well given, to make
culture take a permanent hold upon the future tradesman or   15
farmer. Accordingly, it is common to meet in Germany with
people of the tradesman class who even read (in translations,
of course) any important or interesting book that comes out
in another country, a book like Macaulay's *History of England*,
for instance; and how unlike this state of culture is to that of   20
the English tradesman, the English reader himself knows very
well.

Chapter XVIII

The Prussian Schoolmasters; Their Training, Examination, Appointment, and Payment

Examination for Schoolmasters—Its History—Present Plan of Examination for Schoolmasters—Normal Seminaries for Schoolmasters—Probation and Practising Lessons of Schoolmasters—Appointment of Schoolmasters, and Jurisdiction over Them—Intervention of the Education Minister—Religious Instruction—Denominational Character of the Prussian Schools—Wide Acceptation of the Denomination Evangelisch—Exclusion from School Posts of Certain Dissenters and of Jews—Rank and Title of Schoolmasters—Payment of Schoolmasters.

To insure that the school work, which so much is done to encourage, shall indeed be sound and well given, it is not in Prussia thought sufficient to test the schoolboy and the candidate for matriculation; the candidate for the office of teacher is

5   tested too. This test is the famous *Staatsprüfung* for schoolmasters (*Prüfung der Candidaten des höheren Schulamts*), and is the third great educational reform I have enumerated (the *Lehrplan* and the *Maturitätsprüfung* being the other two) which owes its institution to Wilhelm von Humboldt. Before

10   1810 a certificate of having proved his fitness was not required of a candidate for the post of schoolmaster. Municipal and private school patrons in particular made their nomination with little regard to any test of the kind. There was generally in their school a practice of promoting the teachers by sen-

15   iority to the higher classes, and this practice had very mischievous results. A project was canvassed for giving to the authorities of public instruction the direct appointment to the more important posts in schools even of municipal or private patronage. This project was abandoned. 'But,' said Wilhelm

20   von Humboldt, 'the one defence we can raise against the mis-

use of their rights by patrons, is the test of a trial of the intending schoolmaster's qualifications.'

This test was established in 1810. An examination and a trial lesson were appointed for all candidates for the office of teacher. It was made illegal for school patrons to nominate as teachers any persons who were not *geprüfte Subjecte*. As time went on, the security thus taken was gradually made stronger. The trial lesson was found to be an inutility, as any one who has heard trial lessons in our primary Normal Schools can readily believe, and a trial year in a school (*Probejahr*) was in 1826 substituted for it. In the following year it was ruled that the *pädagogische Prüfung*, which forms part of the examination of candidates for orders, and which had hitherto been accepted in lieu of the new test, was insufficient; and that persons in orders, as well as others, must go through the special examination for schoolmasters. This regulation gave full development to a policy which had been contained in the reform of 1810, a policy which Wolf had long before done his best to prepare and had declared to be indispensable if the higher schools of Prussia were to be made thoroughly good,— the policy of making the schoolmaster's business a profession by itself, and separating it altogether from theology.

The rules now in force for this examination date in the main from 1831. It is held by the High Examining Commissions (*Königliche Wissenschaftliche Prüfungscommissionen*) of which I have already described the composition, and which are seven in number. The candidate sends in his school-certificate of fitness for university studies, and his certificate of a three years' attendance at university lectures. With these certificates he forwards to the commission a *curriculum vitæ*, such as used to be required from candidates for the Oriel fellowships. The candidate for the gymnasium writes this in Latin; the candidate for the *Realschule* may write it in French. The certificate given takes the form of a *facultas docendi*, or leave to teach; and this is *bedingte* or *unbedingte*,—conditional or unconditional. The matters for examinations are grouped under four main heads (*Hauptfächer*): first, Greek, Latin, and the mother tongue; secondly, mathematics and the natural sciences;

thirdly, history and geography; fourthly, theology and Hebrew. This last *Hauptfach* concerns especially those who are
to give the religious instruction in the public schools; if they
have been examined for orders before a theological board and
have passed well, an oral examination is all the divinity examination they have to undergo before the Commission. Those
who are to give the secular instruction have likewise only an
oral examination in divinity, and are not examined in Hebrew;
but they must satisfy the Commission as to their acquaintance
with Scripture and with the dogmatic and moral tenets of
Christianity. Candidates weak in their divinity have this weakness noted in their certificate, and the Provincial School Boards
are directed not to appoint any teacher weak in this particular
till he has been re-examined and has passed satisfactorily; and
the *curriculum vitæ* of every candidate has in the first instance
to state what he has done at the university to keep up and increase his knowledge of divinity (*seine religionswissenschaft-
lichen Kenntnisse zu erweitern und tiefer zu begründen*).
These latter regulations date from within the last twenty years.

The unconditional *facultas docendi* is only given to that
candidate who in his *Hauptfach* shows himself fit to teach
one of the two highest forms, and sufficiently acquainted with
the matters of the other *Hauptfächer* to be useful to his class
in them. The candidate who in one *Hauptfach* is strong enough
for any class up to *secunda* inclusive, but falls altogether below
the mark in other sciences, receives a *bedingte* 'facultas docendi,' for the middle or the lower forms, according as his
capacity and the extent of his performance and of his failure
seem to merit.

All candidates are required to be able to translate French
with ease, and they must know its grammar. All must show
some acquaintance with philosophy and pædagogic,* candi-

---

* The Germans, as is well known, attach much importance to the
science of pædagogic. That science is as yet far from being matured,
and much nonsense is talked on the subject of it; still, the total un-
acquaintance with it, and with all which has been written about it, in
which the intending schoolmaster is, in England, suffered to remain,
has, I am convinced, injurious effects both on our schoolmasters and
on our schools.

dates for the unconditional *facultas docendi* a very considerable acquaintance; and all must satisfy the examiners that they have some knowledge of the natural sciences.

The candidate for a *Realschule* or a higher Burgher School need not take Greek, but he must pass in Latin. His *Hauptfächer* are: mathematics, natural sciences, history and geography, the mother tongue, modern languages. His examination in all the non-classical matters is even more stringent than that of candidates for the gymnasium, because of his comparative exemption from classics.

The trials *pro loco* and *pro ascensione* are examinations imposed when the nominee to a place has not yet proved his qualifications for that place. For instance, the holder of a conditional *facultas docendi* cannot be appointed to a class in the highest division without being re-examined, and the holder of an unconditional *facultas docendi* cannot teach another matter than the *Hauptfach* in which he has proved his first-class qualification, without being re-examined.

A special *facultas docendi* is given to the foreign teacher of modern languages; but even he, besides the modern language he is to teach, must know as much Latin, history, geography and philosophy as is required of candidates who are to teach in the middle division of a gymnasium. This provision guards against the employment of subjects so unfit by their training and general attainments to rule a class, as those whom we too often see chosen as teachers of modern languages.

The High Commissioners send yearly to the Provincial School Board of each province a report of these examinations for that province, with the necessary remarks. The candidates for masterships present themselves, with their certificates, to the School Board of the province in which they wish to be employed. In certain exceptional cases candidates may be employed two half-years running without a certificate; but at the end of that time, if they have not passed the examination, they must be dismissed.

Those who at the university have taken, after examination, the degree of doctor, and have published the Latin dissertation required for that degree, are excused from the written part of the schoolmaster's examination. When this examination was first

instituted, both Schleiermacher and Wolf, being then members
of the Education section, declared themselves strongly against
allowing any university title to exempt candidates for the *höhere Schulamt* from going through the special examination.
Probably they were right, for the seriousness of the degree
examination, and the value of the degree, is not the same in
every German university. They were over-ruled, however;
but little or no inconvenience does in fact arise from the allowance, in this case, of an equipollent title; because if a candidate brings the degree of doctor from a university whose
degrees are not respected, and if he inspires any suspicion, the
patrons who are to nominate him, or the Provincial Board
which is to confirm him, invite him to go through the special
examination first; and if he refuses, or if he cannot pass, his
appointment is not proceeded with.

The *Probejahr*, or year of probation, must, as a general
rule, be passed at a gymnasium or a *Realschule*, not at a progymnasium or a higher Burgher School. In this way the
schoolmaster of the lower class of secondary schools is a man
who has known the working and standards of the higher. The
probationer is commonly unpaid, but if he is used in the place
of an assistant master the school which so uses him must pay
him. The schools are, however, expressly directed not to treat
the probationer as a means of relieving an overtasked staff, but
to give him an opportunity of learning, in the best way for
himself, the practice of his business, and to let him therefore
work with several different classes in the course of his year.
At the end of his year he receives a certificate from the school
authorities as to the efficiency which he shows.

The time passed in a Normal seminary counts instead of
the *Probejahr;* but these seminaries have not in Prussia, any
of them, the importance of the *École Normale* in France.
There is not the same need of the institution in Germany as
in France, and no German professor is obliged to pass through
it. The *École Normale* is of much more use in giving its student
the thorough possession of what he knows and the power of
independent application of it, than in teaching him to teach;
and these more valuable functions of a Normal school are

performed in Germany by the *Gymnasien* and the universities, to an extent to which the *lycées* and faculties in France by no means perform them. Hence in France the need and utility of the *École Normale*. The normal seminaries in Germany are connected with the different universities, and designed, in general, to give the future schoolmaster a more firm and thorough grasp on the matters he studies there. The pædagogical seminaries have not been so important or so fruitful to him as the philological seminaries, where this design has been applied to what has hitherto been the grand matter of his studies,—*Alterthumswissenschaft*, the systematic knowledge of classical antiquity. It was as the head of the philological seminary at Halle that Wolf gave that impulse to the formation of a body of learned and lay schoolmasters of which Germany has ever since felt the good effects. This seminary was opened in 1787, and Wolf was its director for nearly twenty years, till the University of Halle was closed by Napoleon after the battle of Jena, and Wolf went to Berlin to be a member of the Department of Education there. During the latter part of Wolf's time at Halle, he was assisted in the seminary by Immanuel Bekker. There were 12 seminarists, with a small exhibition of 40 thalers (6*l.*) a year each; the exhibition was tenable for two years. No one was admitted to an exhibition who had not already completed his first year's course in the university, but students from any of the faculties might attend the seminary lectures. They attended in great numbers, and for the exhibitions themselves there were at the first examination 60 candidates. The seminary lessons were interpretation lessons and disputation lessons, the former being, as the name implies, the interpretation of a given author; the latter being the discussion, between two or more of the seminarists, either of a thesis set long beforehand and treated by them in written exercises, or of a thesis set by Wolf at the moment and then and there treated orally, in Latin, by his pupils. Wolf's great rule in all these lessons was that rule which all masters in the art of teaching have followed,—to take as little part as possible in the lesson himself; merely to start it, guide it, and sum it up, and to let quite the main part in it be borne by the learners.

The more advanced seminarists had some practice in the Latin
school of the Orphan House at Halle. The more recent statutes
of this philological seminary have set forth in express words,
as the object of the institution, the design which Wolf always
had in his mind in directing it;—the design to form effective
classical masters for the higher schools. Every Prussian university has a philological seminary, or group of exhibitioners much
like that which I have described at Halle, not more than 12
in number, with a two years' course following one year's academical study, and *Alterthumswissenschaft* being the object
pursued. There are generally two professors specially attached
to the seminary, one for Greek, the other for Latin. Besides
the ordinary members or seminarists, a good number of extraordinary members, and a yet much larger number of *Aus-
cultanten*, attend the lessons. The staff of the philological
seminary at Berlin has this constellation of names, from 1812,
when this seminary was founded, to the present time:—Boeckh,
Buttmann, Bernhardy, Lachmann, Haupt. The philological
seminary of the University of Bonn was founded in 1819, and
has had on its staff Professors Näke, Welcker, Ritschl, Otto
Jahn. The mouth of the student of *Alterthumswissenschaft*
in other countries may indeed water, when he reads two such
lists as these.

At the University of Bonn there is also a *Naturwissenschaft-
liches Seminar*, founded in 1825, on the express ground that
qualified teachers of the natural sciences in the secondary
schools were so much wanting. Bonn has, too, a *historisches
Seminar* founded in 1861 for the promotion of historical
studies, and also to provide good history-teachers for the secondary schools. Dr. von Sybel, the well-known historian, is
at present one of its professors. The Universities of Breslau,
Greifswald, Königsberg, have likewise historical seminaries,
serving either by statute or in practice the same end, of preparing specially qualified teachers of history for the public
schools. Berlin, Königsberg, and Halle have also seminaries
either for mathematics, or for mathematics and the natural
sciences together; these, too, serve, in their line of study, the
same end as the philological and historical seminaries serve in

theirs. Berlin has also travelling fellowships of a year's duration, to enable Germans, who are to teach French in the
public schools, to study the French language and literature
in France itself. Two exhibitions of 45*l.* a year each are attached to the Royal French School in Berlin, with the like   5
object of enabling the future teacher of French to learn French
practically and thoroughly. These are Crown foundations; the
Crown, associations, and private individuals, are all founders
of seminaries. The estimate of none of those which I have
named exceeds 1,000 thalers (150*l.*) a year. It is astonishing   10
how much is done in Prussia with small supplies of money.

Special pædagogic seminaries (*pädagogische Seminarien*)
exist at Berlin, Königsberg, Breslau, Stettin, and Halle. Of these
the assigned business with their seminarist is 'to introduce him
to the practical requirements of the profession of school-   15
master;' but this introduction is still to be carefully accompanied by a continuance of his general intellectual culture. In
general, the seminarist here must have passed the examination
pro facultate docendi, and instead of the *Probejahr* in a school
he spends two or three years in the pædagogic seminary. Each   20
seminarist has a certain number of hours' practice (six hours
a week at Berlin) in a secondary school; he is present at the
conferences, or teachers' meetings, of the school to which he
is attached, and he lives with one of its older masters. The
Berlin *pädagogische Seminar* was founded in 1787, at first   25
with a single gymnasium (the *Friedrich-Werdersche*) assigned
as its practising school; since 1812 all the gymnasiums of Berlin have served in common for this purpose. There are now
ten regular exhibitioners, but the exhibitions here are good,
and the estimate for the seminary is much larger than that for   30
any other seminary I have named; it is 2,390 thalers a year.
Dr. Boeckh is the director of this seminary as well as of the
philological one, and this joint direction well illustrates the
close relation at present, in Germany as elsewhere, of the
schoolmaster with philology. At Stettin the seminary has only   35
four regular exhibitioners; they have good exhibitions, lasting
for two or three years. This seminary is for the benefit in the
first instance of the province of Pomerania, and the semi-

narists have to engage themselves to take, when their exhibition expires, any mastership the Provincial School Board offers them, and to keep it three years.

It is evident from what I have said that these exhibitions do not exist in sufficient number to provide seminary training for anything like the whole of that large body of teachers which the secondary schools of Prussia employ. It is found too that the directors and masters of great schools in large towns, who have a great deal to do and constant claims upon their attention, do not like being saddled with the care of seminarists either at their homes or in their classes. The same difficulties tell against their giving to probationers in their trial year due supervision. But it is the living for a time with an experienced teacher and the making the first start in teaching under his eye, that is found to be so especially valuable for promising novices. It is proposed therefore, instead of founding fresh pædagogic seminaries, to make arrangements for selecting a certain number of good schoolmasters, who will take charge, for payment, of a batch of novices (not more than three) for a two years' probationary course before launching them independently; and a *stipendium*, or exhibition, such as is given in the seminaries, is to be bestowed on those probationers whose circumstances require it. It is hoped in this way to provide a preliminary training of two years for all the most deserving subjects who go into the profession.

At the end of his term of probation the probationer gets his appointment. I have said before that for all appointments to masterships in the secondary schools the intervention of the State authority is necessary. In schools of Crown patronage the appointment is called *Bestallung;* in schools not of Crown patronage it is called *Vocation;* the State can give *installation,* absolute occupation; other patrons can only nominate, and their nominee, if an improper person, is rejected, with reasons assigned, by the State authorities. The Crown, exercising its patronage through the Education Minister, appoints, in all Crown patronage gymnasiums and *Realschulen,* the director. The Provincial Boards, in the minister's name and by commission from him, appoint the upper masters (*Oberlehrer*) in

these schools, and the rector in all Crown patronage progymnasiums and higher Burgher Schools. The other masters in
Crown patronage schools the Provincial Board appoints by
its own authority. The nomination of a director in schools
of municipal or private patronage requires the Crown's assent   5
and the minister's confirmation. The nomination of an *Oberlehrer* in such schools requires the minister's assent and the
Provincial Board's confirmation. The nomination of other
masters in such schools the Provincial Board is empowered to
confirm without the assent of the minister. All directors and   10
masters, whether appointed by the State or only confirmed by
it, take an *Amtseid*, or oath of office, by which they swear
obedience to the Crown. In schools of Crown patronage,
when the minister directs, on special grounds, the appointment, promotion, or transference, of a master, the Provincial   15
Board must comply.

The minister, however, has in Prussia a far less immediate
and absolute action upon the secondary schools than the
minister has in France. In France the minister can dismiss any
functionary of secondary instruction; in Prussia he can repri-   20
mand him and stop his salary for a month, but he cannot of his
own authority dismiss him. Directors and upper masters are
under the jurisdiction of the Court of Discipline for the Civil
Service (*Disciplinarhof*) at Berlin; this court is a judicial body,
four of its members belonging to the Supreme Court of Berlin;   25
and any complaint requiring the dismissal of a director or upper
master must be tried before it. From the sentence of this court
there is an appeal to the minister; but he is bound to appoint,
for hearing the appeal, two referees, one of whom must be
a member of the Department of Justice; and their decision is   30
final. Complaints of like gravity against other masters (*ordentliche Lehrer*) are tried by the Provincial Board, which like the
Court of Discipline hears counsel, and examines witnesses on
oath; from the sentence of the board there is also an appeal to
the minister, who appoints in this case one referee only, but   35
the referee, before deciding the appeal, has to take the opinion
of the Court of Discipline. Everywhere in Prussia and in all
German countries we shall find a disposition to take security

against that immediate and arbitrary action of the executive
which we remark in France; and though the Germans give
effect in a very different way from ours to this innate disposition of the Teutonic race, yet they give such effect to it as
to establish a notable difference,—the more manifest the more
one examines the institutions of the two countries,—between
the habit and course of administration in Germany and in
France.

I cannot but think an Education Minister a necessity for
modern States, yet I know that in the employment of such
an agency there are inconveniences, and I do not wish to hide
any of them from the English reader. I have said that in France
political considerations are in my opinion too much suffered to
influence the whole working of the system of public education.
In Prussia the minister is armed with powers, and issues instructions showing how he interprets those powers, which in
England would excite very great jealousy. He tells the provincial authorities that no reproach must attach to the private and
public life, any more than to the knowledge or ability, of a
candidate for school employment; he tells them that they are to
take into consideration the whole previous career, extra-
professional as well as professional (*das gesammte bisherige
amtliche und ausseramtliche Verhalten*), of such a candidate;
and that schoolmasters should be men who will train up their
scholars in notions of obedience towards the sovereign and the
State.

I know the use likely to be made, in England, of the admission that a Prussian Education Minister uses language of this
kind; and I will be candid enough to make bad worse by saying
that the present minister, Dr. von Mühler, is what we should
call in England a strong Tory and a strong Evangelical. It
is not, indeed, at all likely that in England, with the forces
watching and controlling him here, a minister would use language such as I have quoted; and even if it were, I am not at
all sure that to have a minister using such language, though it
is language which I cordially dislike, is in itself so much more
lamentable and baneful a thing than that anarchy and ignorance
in education matters, under which we contentedly suffer.

However, what I wish now to say is, that in spite of this language, the political influence which has such real effect upon the public education of France, has no effect, or next to none, upon that of Prussia. I do not believe that it has more on that of Prussia than it has on that of this country. I took great pains to inform myself on this head. The last few years have been a time of great political pressure in Prussia; I arrived there when this pressure was at its height, and I conversed mainly with persons opposed, some of them bitterly opposed, to the Government. They all told me that the State administration of the schools and universities was in practice fair and right; that public opinion would not suffer it to be governed by political regards, or by any but literary and scientific regards; and that public opinion would always, in this particular, find strong sympathies among the ministers themselves. I heard of one director to whom Dr. von Mühler had refused confirmation because his politics, which had been very strongly declared, were unacceptable. This director I had the pleasure of seeing; he told me himself, what I heard also from others, that his case was an isolated one; and that it had caused such strong dissatisfaction, not only among the public, but to the school authorities who represent the State in the provinces and consider themselves responsible for the march and efficiency of secondary instruction, that the minister had found himself obliged to appoint him, within a very few months, to a Crown patronage school of greater importance than the municipal school for which he had refused him confirmation. The director added, and this too was confirmed by others, that such an intrusion of political feeling as had prevented his confirmation, was in the case of a *Lehrer* or teacher,—either an upper teacher or an ordinary teacher,—absolutely unknown.

The truth is, that when a nation has got the belief in culture which the Prussian nation has got, and when its schools are worthy of this belief, it will not suffer them to be sacrificed to any other interest; and however greatly political considerations may be paramount in other departments of administration, in this they are not. In France neither the national belief in culture nor the schools themselves are sufficiently developed

to awaken this enthusiasm; and politics are too strong for the
schools, and give them their own bias.

I have spoken several times of the religious instruction as
forming part of school work and of examinations. The two
legally established forms of religion in Prussia are the Protestant (*evangelisch*) and the Catholic. All public schools must
be either Protestant, Catholic, or mixed (*Simultananstalten*).
But the constitution of a mixed school has not been authori-
tatively defined, and though the practice has grown up, especially in *Realschulen*, of appointing teachers of the two confessions indifferently, yet these *Simultananstalten* retain the
fundamental character of Christian schools, and indeed usually
follow the rule either that the director and the majority of the
masters shall be Catholic or that they shall be Protestant. In
general, the deed of foundation or established custom determines to what confession a school shall belong. The religious
instruction and the services follow the confession of the school.
The ecclesiastical authorities,—the consistories for Protestant
schools, the bishops for Catholic schools,—must concur with
the school authorities in the appointment of those who give
the religious instruction in the schools. The consistories and
the bishops have likewise the right of inspecting, by themselves
or by their delegates, this instruction, and of addressing to the
Provincial Boards any remarks they may have to make on it.
The *ordinarius*, or class-master who has general charge of the
class, as distinguished from the teachers who give the different
parts of the instruction in it, is generally, if possible, the religious instructor. In Protestant schools the religious instructor
is usually a layman; in Catholic, an ecclesiastic. The public
schools are open to scholars of all creeds; in general, one of the
two confessions, evangelical or Catholic, greatly preponderates,
and the Catholics, in especial, prefer schools of their own confession. But the State holds the balance quite fairly between
them; where the scholars of that confession which is not the
established confession of the school are in considerable numbers, a special religious instructor is paid out of the school
funds to come and give them this religious instruction at the
school. Thus in the gymnasium at Bonn, which is Catholic, I

heard a lesson on the Epistle to the Galatians (in the Greek) given to the Protestant boys of one of the higher forms by a young Protestant minister of the town, engaged by the gymnasium for that purpose. When the scholars whose confession is in the minority are very few in number, their parents have to provide by private arrangements of their own for their children's religious instruction.

Prussia has 11,289,655 Protestant inhabitants, 6,901,023 Catholic inhabitants. She has nearly 300,000 inhabitants who are classed neither as *evangelisch* nor as Catholic, and these are principally Jews. In her public higher schools, out of 66,135 boys, 46,396 are Protestant (*evangelisch*), 14,919 are Catholic. The rest, 4,820, are Jews.

The wide acceptation which the denomination *evangelical* takes in the official language of Prussia prevents a host of difficulties which occur with us in England. Under the term *evangelisch* are included Lutherans, Calvinists, and the United Church formed on the basis of what is common to Lutherans and Calvinists; Baptists also, Independents, Wesleyans (for there are Wesleyans in Prussia) are included by it, and, in short, all Protestants who are Christians, in the common acceptation of that word. The State, however, in Prussia, not only declares itself Christian (*der preussische Staat ist ein christlicher*, says the *Unterrichtsverfassung* of 1816) but it expressly disclaims the neutral, colourless, formless Christianity of the Dutch schools and of our British schools (*der Religionsunterricht darf durchaus nicht in einen allgemeinen Religionsunterricht hinübergespielt werden*). So the Protestant schools as well as the Catholic employ a dogmatic religious teaching. In all schools of the evangelical confession Luther's Catechism is used, and all Protestant boys of whatever denomination learn it. Not the slightest objection is made by their parents to this. It is true that Luther's Catechism is perhaps the very happiest part of Lutheranism, and therefore recommends itself for this common adoption, while our Catechism can hardly be said to be the happiest part of Anglicanism.

The various denominations of Protestant Christians are thus harmoniously united in a common religious teaching. But

the State, keeping in view the *christlichen Grundcharakter*
of itself and its public schools, refuses to employ any masters
who are not either Catholics, or, in the wide sense assigned to
the term *evangelisch*, Protestants. Dissenters who are not Christians, and specially the *Lichtfreunde*, as they call themselves
(they would with us generally go by the name of Unitarians
or Socinians), are thus excluded from the office of public
teacher, and so are Jews. In a country where the Jews are so
many and so able, this exclusion makes itself felt. A Jew may
hold a medical or mathematical professorship in the Prussian
universities, but he may not hold a professorship of history or
philosophy. France is in all these matters a model of reason and
justice, and as much ahead of Germany as she is of England.
The religious instruction in her schools is given by ministers
of religion, and the State asks no other instructor any questions
about his religious persuasion.

Restrictions such as that which I have just described are
said to be contrary to the provisions of the Prussian Constitution of 1850. The Prussian Parliament has begun to occupy
itself with them, and it is probable they will not long be
maintained.

A master on his appointment takes the title of *ordentlicher
Lehrer*, ordinary master (the title of under-master is not used
in the Prussian schools), or of *Oberlehrer*, upper master. The
Oberlehrer is so either by post or by nomination. The posts
conferring the title of *Oberlehrer*, posts in the upper part of
the school, can only be held by a teacher whose certificate
entitles him to give instruction in one of the two highest classes.
Oberlehrer by nomination are masters of long standing, who
as *ordinarii* or general class-masters have done good service,
and have the title of upper-master given to them in acknowl-
edgment of it; but the title so conferred does not enable them
to give instruction in any class for which their certificate
does not qualify them. The regulations direct that there shall
be not more than three *Oberlehrer*, exclusive of the director,
for every seven *ordentliche Lehrer;* but in schools with a larger
staff of *ordentliche Lehrer* than this, the proportion of *Oberlehrer* to *ordentliche Lehrer* may become much larger. The

minister confers the title of professor upon masters distinguished by their attainments and practical success. The directors rank as full professors of the universities, the masters with the title of professor rank as assistant professors of the universities. It should be said that in Germany the title of professor confers on its holder a fixed rank, as a few official titles do here in England. The director is more like one of our head-masters than he is like a French *proviseur*, but he does not, like our head-masters, give the whole of the instruction, or even the whole of the classical instruction, to the head class. Often he is not its *ordinarius*. He, like other masters, cannot give any part of the instruction for which he has not at some time proved his qualification. In general he has some special branch in which he is distinguished, and in this branch he gives lessons in *prima*, and usually in other classes too; governing also, as his name implies, the whole movement of the school, and appearing, much oftener than our head-masters, in every class of it.

Formerly few masterships had fixed incomes assigned to them, but it has more and more become a rule of administration in Prussia to give to all directors and teachers fixed incomes, and to do away with their sharing the school fees. Neither the proceeds of these, nor the proceeds of foundations, are in any case abandoned to the school staff, to do what they like with. On the school estimates which I have described, all salaries appear, and all receipts from endowments or from school fees; the surplus of receipts over salaries and other school expenses is funded, and becomes available for enlarging or improving the school. There are few large endowments; in one or two cases, as at Schulpforta, the endowment is allowed to create for the director and the teachers a position above the average, and at Berlin, where the proceeds of the school-fees are very great, the masters of the public schools have also a position above the average; but all this is kept within strict regulation, and is settled, as I have said, by administrative boards of public composition, or under public supervision, and is not left to the disposition of the school staff itself. Schulpforta has a yearly income of more than 8,000*l.*, but of

this sum, less than 2,000*l.* goes in salaries to the rector and masters. The yearly sum funded, after all the expenses of this noble
foundation are paid, is not much smaller than the sum spent
in salaries.

5   By a *Normaletat,* or normal estimate, there is fixed for the
staff of State gymnasiums the following scale of payments,
which is above rather than below the average scale in *Realschulen,* or in any kind of secondary school not of State patronage. The scale has three classes: the first class is for nine places

10   in Prussia, exclusive of Berlin and Schulpforta, which stand
on an exceptional footing of their own; the second class is for
thirty-four places; the third class for fifty-eight. Of course
the nine places in the first class, being the principal towns in
Prussia except the capital, have far more than nine gymnasiums.

15   In all the State gymnasiums of these nine places, the scale of
salaries is, for the director, 270*l.* a year; for the masters, according to their post and their length of standing, from 90*l.*
a year to 195*l.* In the thirty-four places of the second class,
the scale is, for a director, 240*l.* a year; for the masters, from

20   82*l.* 10*s.* to 172*l.* 10*s.* In the fifty-eight places of the third, for
a director, 195*l.;* for the masters, from 75*l.* to 150*l.* The salaries
thus fixed are meant to represent the whole emoluments of the
post; when a house is attached to a post, the rule is that a
deduction of 10 per cent. shall be made from the salary to

25   balance the gain by the house. In some places there are special
endowments for augmenting masters' salaries; thus the *Streitsche Stiftung* gives 455*l.* a year to augment the masters'
salaries at the Greyfriars gymnasium, in Berlin; but nowhere
probably in Prussia does a school salary reach 350*l.* a year,

30   and the rector of Schulpforta, whose post is perhaps the most
desirable school post in the Prussian dominions, has, I understand, about 300*l.* a year, and a house. To hold another employment (*Nebenamt*) along with his school post, is not absolutely forbidden to the public teacher; thus Dr. Schopen, the

35   excellent Latin scholar at the head of the Bonn gymnasium, is
at the same time professor in the philosophical faculty of the
University there; but the *Nebenamt* must not interfere with
his school duty, and the supervising authorities take good care

that it shall not. So far as it does not interfere with his school duty, the public teacher may give private tuition, and in this manner increase his income; but to give private tuition for fee to the pupils of his own form in the public school, he needs the director's consent. Even when every possible addition to it has been allowed for, the salary of a Prussian schoolmaster will appear to English eyes very low.

The whole scale of incomes in Prussia is, however, much lower than with us, and the habits of the nation are frugal and simple. The rate of schoolmasters' salaries was raised after 1815, and has been raised again since; it is not exceptionally low as compared with the rates of incomes in Germany generally. The rector of Schulpforta with his 300*l.* a year and a house, has in all the country round him,—where there is great well-doing and comfort,—few people more comfortably off than himself; he can do all he wants to do, and all that anybody about him does, and this is wealth. The schoolmasters of the higher school enjoy, too, great consideration; and consideration, in a country not corrupted, has a value as well as money. As a class, the Prussian schoolmasters are not, so far as I could find out, fretting or discontented; they seem to give themselves heartily to their work, and to take pride and pleasure in it.

What I have yet to say about Prussian schools, their scholars, and their teachers, may perhaps be best said in connection with two or three of those institutions which I visited. In this manner I shall have an opportunity of rendering, by the help of particular illustrations, general results and statements more interesting to the English reader, and more intelligible to him.

Chapter XIX

The Prussian System Seen in Operation in Particular Schools

Berlin has four royal gymnasiums, one with a *Realschule* annexed; four municipal gymnasiums, one with a *Realschule* annexed; four other municipal *Realschulen*, and one higher Burgher School. All these are full; there were, in 1863, 6,864
5 scholars in them, without counting the children in the *Vorschulen* or preparatory schools which several of them have as appendages; but the supply of higher schools in Berlin is not sufficient for the demand, and the municipality, which was spending in 1863 more than 40,000*l*. a year on the secondary
10 and primary schools of the city, is about to provide several higher schools more. All through Prussia one hears the same thing: the secondary schools are not enough for the increasing numbers whom the widening desire for a good education (*der weiter verbreitete Bildungstrieb*) sends into them. The
15 State increases its grants, and those grants are met by increased exertions on the part of the communes, but still there is not room for the scholars who come in, and the rise which has taken place in the rate of school-fee has in no degree stopped them. To obtain the State's consent to the formation of a
20 new school with the name and rights of a public secondary school, a commune must satisfy the State authority both that

its municipal schools for the poor will not be pinched for the sake of the new establishment, and also that it can provide resources to carry on the new establishment properly, and in conformity with the requirements of the *Lehrplan*. This is being done in all directions.

Perhaps the most remarkable of the higher schools at Berlin is the *Friedrich-Wilhelms Gymnasium*. The Greyfriars gymnasium (*Gymnasium zum grauen Kloster*) has about the same number of scholars, but with the *Friedrich-Wilhelms Gymnasium* is connected a *Realschule;* a *Vorschule*, or preparatory school, common to the gymnasium and the *Realschule* both; and a girls' school, called from the then Crown Princess of Prussia who gave it her name in 1827, the *Elisabetschule*. There were, at the end of 1863, 2,200 scholars in the whole institution together; 581 in the Gymnasium, 601 in the *Realschule*, 522 in the preparatory school, and 496 in the girls' school. The gymnasium is remarkable as being the only higher school in Prussia, except the *Realschule* on the Franck foundation at Halle, where the receipts from the scholars cover the expenditure of the school. The annual expenditure for the gymnasium, *Realschule*, preparatory school, and *Elisabetschule* together, is in round figures 65,000 thalers; the receipts from the scholars' fees are in round figures 53,000 thalers. The property of the institution is very small, producing about 400*l.* a year only, so the deficiency is made up by a State grant of about 10,000 thalers; this deficiency, however, arises not in the gymnasium, where the school-fees more than cover the expenses, but in the schools allied with it.

The history of this institution is the history of many public schools in Prussia. It owes its origin to the Church, and has then in course of time passed under the superintendence of the State. I have mentioned the establishment by Johann Hecker in 1747 of the first *Realschule* at Berlin. Hecker was preacher at the Trinity Church in the Friedrichsstadt, and he grouped together several small schools in his parish under the name of a *Realschule*. The institution throve from the first; in 1748 it had 808 scholars, and 20 years afterwards it had 1,267. It was governed by the curators of the Trinity Church and by inspectors of their appointment; and it was supported, having no endowment except a very trifling house-property, by voluntary contributions and by school-fees. The Latin school, which was one of the grouped schools, grew in importance, and at the fiftieth anniversary of the institution it received the name of *Friedrich-Wilhelms Gymnasium*, and in 1803 was rebuilt with a grant from the king of nearly 10,000*l.* towards the rebuilding. At the great reforming epoch of 1809 it passed with the other public secondary schools of Berlin under the administration of the Education Department; this change being sanctioned, not only by public opinion, but by the governing bodies of the schools themselves, with the view of giving to these great and important metropolitan establishments the benefit of a common and intelligent direction. The *Friedrich-Wilhelms Gymnasium* is now, therefore, both for *interna* and *externa*, under the School Board of the province of Brandenburg, to which, as soon as the School Boards were constituted, the central department transferred its direct charge of the public schools.

The gymnasium is by foundation Protestant, and out of the 600 boys whom I found there, only 20 were Catholics and 15 were Jews. The united schools have a joint director and a joint administration of their affairs. They have altogether 66 teachers, of whom 21 are for the gymnasium. Of these 21, 11 are *Oberlehrer*, and of these 11, six or seven have the title of professor. The director is Dr. Ferdinand Ranke, a brother of the historian; he has been nearly twenty-five years director here, and more than forty years in the profession. He and seven of the upper masters of the gymnasium are lodged in the school buildings, which are very plain; but in the school-court is one of those relics of the past, so far more common in the German schools, as in ours, than in the French,—the inscription on Hecker's original school-house: *Scholæ Trinitatis ædes in Dei honorem, regis gaudium, civium salutem, juventutis institutioni dicatæ.* There are no boarders, a boarding establishment which originally formed part of the institution having been done away with in 1842. The scholars all through the school pay the same fee, 26 thalers a year (3*l.* 18*s*).

In the *Vorschule* the fee is the same; in the *Realschule* it is
only two thalers a year lower. In one gymnasium at Berlin the
scholars pay four thalers a year more than in the *Friedrich-
Wilhelms Gymnasium;* in all the others they pay one thaler
less. There is very considerable variety in the rate of school-fees
in Prussia, the circumstances of the school and locality being
always taken into account in fixing it. The rate in the metropolitan schools is of course a comparatively high one, low as
it seems to us. Many schools have a rate rising with the class
or division; thus in the gymnasium at Wetzlar the boys in
sexta and *quinta* pay 16 thalers, those in *quarta* and *tertia* pay
18 thalers, those in *secunda* and *prima* pay 20 thalers. In some
schools the rate is as low as eight or ten thalers for the lower
classes, and 14 or 16 thalers for the higher. As an average rate
for all the gymnasiums of Prussia, 20 thalers (3*l.*) a year, would
certainly be rather above the mark than under it. The rates in
the *Realschulen* and the higher Burgher Schools do not in
general range below those of the classical schools. Moderate
as these present rates appear to us, they are much higher than
they used to be; in the *Friedrich-Wilhelms Gymnasium* the
school-fee forty years ago was only 16 thalers in *sexta* and
quinta, and 20 thalers in the other classes. In many provincial
schools it was astonishingly low, as low as two, two and a
half, and three thalers. In a gymnasium I have already mentioned, the *Magdalenen-Gymnasium* at Breslau, there was, in
1824, a uniform fee of 8 thalers, and there is now a uniform
fee of 24 thalers.

In the *Friedrich-Wilhelms Gymnasium* I found that 10 per
cent. of the 600 scholars had free schooling. The number of
free posts as they are called (*Freistellen*) varies in different
schools; in some it goes up to 25 per cent., but I think 10 per
cent. may be taken as a fair average. These free posts are given
on the ground of need and public claim. There are also a few
exhibitions in the *Friedrich-Wilhelms Gymnasium*, but it will
be best to notice the subject of exhibitions when I am speaking
of some older and richer establishment.

Of course in the very large schools it is not possible to actually group and teach the scholars in six classes, nor yet is

it always possible to observe the rule which enjoins that there shall not be more than forty scholars in either *secunda* or *prima*, or more than fifty in any of the other classes. The supply of class-rooms falls short, even more than the supply of teachers. The highest class, however, always remains *prima*, as in our great schools it always remains the *sixth;* and in the higher classes the Germans, as I have already mentioned, follow, when it is necessary, the plan of having an upper and lower division (*oberprima, unterprima*), and in other classes both this plan and the plan of having two groups or assemblages (*cœtus*) at the same stage of school work, and advancing parallel to one another.

The first lesson I heard was Dr. Ranke's own lesson to *prima*, on the *Philoctetes* of Sophocles. He spoke Latin to his class and his class spoke Latin in answer; this is still a common practice in the German schools, though not so common as formerly. The German boys have certainly acquired through this practice a surprising command of Latin; Dr. Schopen's lesson at Bonn to his *prima* in extemporaneous translation into Latin,—a lesson which has a deserved celebrity,—I heard with astonishment; a much wider command of the Latin vocabulary than our boys have, and a more ready management of the language, the Germans certainly succeed in acquiring. On the other hand, the best style of the best authors is not, to my mind, so well caught in Latin composition by their boys as by ours. This is more particularly the case in verse, where their best scholars often show, I cannot but think, not only a want of practical skill (that of course is nothing), but a want of tact for what is uncouth and inadmissible, which one would not have expected of people who know the Latin models so well. The same is true, in a less degree, of their prose; the best scholars in the best schools of England or France, if set to write a speech or a character in the style of Cicero or Tacitus, would, I think, in general acquit themselves of the task more happily than the corresponding boys of a German school.

But the feeling which was strongest with me in the Berlin *Philoctetes* lesson was the feeling that one seemed to be back in the sixth form at Rugby again, as I remember it nearly thirty years ago. After the lecture rooms at Oxford, and the French *lycées,* and the Italian *licei,* here was at last a body of pupils once more who had worked at their lessons, had learnt Greek, and were at home in a Greek play. What the Berlin boys knew about the scope of the play, its chief personages, and the governing idea and character of each, was more than the Rugby boys would have known; but the quantity of lines done, the style of doing them, and the extent of scholarship expected in the boys and found in them, seemed to me as nearly as possible the same thing at Berlin and at Rugby. I thought the same in the afternoon when I heard Professor Zumpt (a son of the famous Latin scholar) take *unterprima* in Cicero's speech *Pro Sex. Roscio Amerino.* The boys had been through the oration during the early part of the half-year; they were now going very rapidly through it again, translating into fluent German without taking the Latin words. The master let the boys be the performers, and spoke as little as possible himself, but every good or bad performance was noticed. Just the same with lessons in Thucydides, Livy, and Horace, which I heard at other gymnasiums in Berlin. The lessons had been well prepared by the pupils, the master made few comments, and only on really noteworthy matters, or to cite some parallel passage which was not likely to have come within his pupils' reading; in general, when he spoke it was to question, and he questioned closely. I was struck with the exact knowledge of the Horatian metres which the *unterprima* boys at Greyfriars showed when questioned on them. I found that the practice was to begin by taking eleven odes as specimens of metre, and carefully studying these before proceeding further. Then they commence the *Odes* at the beginning and go right through them. The portion of a Latin or Greek author got through at a lesson is about the same as in the corresponding form in one of the best English schools, but either in school or by private study the boys have certainly read more than our boys or the French; it is the general rule that a boy who goes in for the leaving examination has read Homer all through. A larger number of the boys, too, seem to have really benefited by the instruction, and to be in the first flight of their class,

than with us. But the great superiority of the Germans, and
where they show how much farther they have gone in *Alterthumswissenschaft* than we have, is in their far broader notion
of treating, even in their schools, the ancient authors as *litera-*
5 *ture*, and conceiving the place and significance of an author
in his country's literature, and in that of the world. In this
way the student's interest in Greek and Latin becomes much
more vital, and the hold of these languages upon him is much
more likely to be permanent. This is to be set against the
10 superior finish and elegance of the best of our boys in Latin
and Greek composition; above all, in Latin and Greek verse.
Greek verse, indeed, can scarcely be said to be a school exercise at all, so far as I could see or hear, in the foreign schools.

Instead of having to write Greek iambics, the boys in *prima* at
15 the *Friedrich-Wilhelms Gymnasium*, on one of the days when
I was there, had had to write a summary of Lessing's essay
on the epigram. The summaries were handed to the professor,
who then made a boy stand up and give in his own words
the substance of Lessing's essay, beginning at the beginning,
20 the professor commenting and asking questions as the boy
proceeded. Presently another boy was set on, and in this way
they went through the essay. The lesson was as much out of
the range of my English school experience as the lesson on the
Femmes Savantes of Molière, which I heard, as I have already
25 said, with so much interest in the *École Normale* at Paris. The
Berlin lesson, like the Paris one, was very interesting.

In the lower division of *tertia* (about the middle of the
school) I had another opportunity of observing a way, not, I
think, in use in England, of practising the boys in Latin. The
30 lesson was Ovid; the boys had had to translate at home a certain portion of Ovid into German, and then to bring their
translation with them to school. This they had then, in school,
to turn back into Latin, not metrical. After this, boys were
called upon one after another, as in England, to say a few
35 lines of Ovid by heart; but then, again, each boy had also to
say in German prose the passage he had just recited in Ovid's
verse.

In *quinta* I heard the religious instruction. For boys still so

near the primary school stage, religious instruction, as a part
of the school lessons, seems to me to be still, as in the primary
school, in place, and still useful; in the higher classes of the
secondary school it seems to me, I confess, unprofitable and
inappropriate. Anything more futile and useless than the lesson in the *Galatians* which I heard given to *secunda* at Bonn
cannot possibly be imagined. In *quinta* here at Berlin, it was
different; the boys were first questioned in Bible narratives
from a text-book; a good text-book and good questioning; then
they said Luther's Short Catechism, and then they repeated
hymns. The two or three Catholic and Jewish boys belonging
to the class did not come to this lesson.

The mention of a text-book reminds me to say a word about
the rule in the Prussian public schools for school-books. The
masters choose the books, but the approval of the Provincial
Board must be obtained for their choice; before approving for
the first time any new book, the Provincial Board must refer
to the Education Minister and his Council. When a book has
once been approved for a gymnasium, it may be used in any
other gymnasium or progymnasium of the same province; but
approval for a gymnasium does not count for a *Realschule,* and
vice versa.

I must in passing observe how greatly some intelligent cen-
sorship like that of the Provincial Boards and the Minister in
Prussia, or that of the Council of Public Instruction in France,
is needed for school-books in England. Many as are the absurdities of our state of school anarchy, perhaps none of them
is more crying than the book-pest which prevails under it.
Every school chooses at its own discretion; many schools make
a trade of book-dealing, and therefore it is for their interest
to have books which are not used elsewhere, and which the
pupil will not bring with him from his last school; so that a boy
who has been at three or four English schools has often had to
buy a complete new set of school-books for each. The extravagance of this is bad enough; but then, besides, as there exists
no intelligent control or selection of them, half at least of our
school-books are rubbish, and to the other defects of our school
system we may add this, that in no other secondary schools

in Europe do the pupils spend so much of their time in learning such utter nonsense as they do in ours.

I have mentioned the Greyfriars gymnasium, where I also
heard lessons, and where they were of the same character as at
the *Friedrich-Wilhelms Gymnasium,* a character much more
like that of the lessons in our best English public schools than
of the lessons in the French *lycées.* The history of Greyfriars
is this. It occupies the site of a Franciscan convent abolished
at the Reformation; in 1574 the third part of the convent
premises was assigned by the elector, at the instance of the
town magistracy, for use as a public school. The magistracy
endowed it, and the elector made it over to them, but with
an electoral *Schulordnung.* Here from the earliest times of
the school there was a *convictorium* (the Italian *convitto*).
The robust appetite of the sixteenth century for the humanities appears in the original plan of work; Greek had thirteen
hours a week, Latin ten, logic two, arithmetic two, singing
five. In 1655 the school had 400 scholars. In the second quarter of the eighteenth century the mother-tongue and its literature first appear as part of the school course; the German public schools having thus the start of ours, in this particular, by
about 125 years. In 1793 the school got the benefit of a great
endowment which I have already mentioned, the *Streitsche
Stiftung;* the capital of this endowment is now 33,000*l.* It is
administered by a *Directorium* composed, not of Sigismund
Streit's descendants, but as follows: the provost of St. Nicholas
(parish minister), the director and the prorector of the school,
a councillor of the Education Department, a merchant or
tradesman, and a lawyer. The financial administration of this
Directorium is controlled, in the manner I have already described, by the public finance officers of the *Regierung* or governmental district in which Berlin stands.

Streit's endowment maintains at Greyfriars teachers of the
modern languages, of astronomy, and of music, provides a
Wohncommunität (lodging, bedding, fire and lights) for
twelve scholars, and a *Freitisch* (board) for twenty-four more;
and keeps improving the school library (now 20,000 volumes),
the observatory, collections, &c. It also augments the salaries

of the director and a number of the masters. Other benefactions provide the widows of masters who die in office with a sum for their husbands' funeral expenses, and a pension of 45*l.* a year. There is an endowment of nearly 450*l.* a year for exhibitions to be enjoyed at the school, and of 150*l.* a year for exhibitions at the universities. Every two years is held a school-festival in honour of founders and benefactors. The school premises had an important enlargement by Crown grants of land in 1819 and 1831, and great additions have since that time been made to the buildings. I found about 550 boys, with a director and twenty-five masters. On an average, twenty-five boys pass the *Abiturientenexamen* from this school every year. Here, too, as at the *Friedrich-Wilhelms Gymnasium*, the number of free posts is ten per cent. They are provided by the municipality. The school gets a grant of about 100*l.* a year from the State and 1,000*l.* a year from the city of Berlin.

By original foundation and by endowment this school too is Protestant. Hardly any Catholic boys are here, but of Jewish boys there are seventy or eighty. About a third of the whole number of the scholars are *Auswärtige*, boys who come from a distance, and cannot, therefore, live with their parents. The great *internats* of the French *lycées* are unknown in Germany; the *Alumnate* or *Convicte* of the German schools are properly establishments like *college* at Eton or Winchester, and are for foundationers; for establishments like the School House and the masters' boarding-houses at Rugby, or Commoners at Winchester, the strict designation would in Germany be *Pensionat, Pensionsanstalt*, and not *Alumnat*. The practice of having one's son live at home and go to school for his lessons only, obtains much more widely in Germany than with us; 40,000 of the 66,000 boys in the Prussian higher schools are day scholars. Still this leaves 26,000 who are not; and of these the vast majority live with some respectable family in the place where they go to school. The household with which their son is to board or lodge is designated by the parent, but must, by the school regulations of Prussia, be approved by the director of the boy's school, who holds the householder responsible

for the boy's conduct out of school. The family life in North
Germany is in general decent, kindly, and God-fearing; and a
boy is, I think, much better placed as a boarder in this way than
as an *interne* of a French *lycée*. Still the school authorities in
5 Prussia are of opinion that the provision of boarding establishments in immediate connection with the public schools needs
increasing, and they design to increase it.

The patron at Greyfriars, for matters that do not come
within the province of the *Directorium* of Streit's charity, is
10 still, as the elector John George originally appointed, the city
of Berlin, the municipality. The reader will remember that for
the *interna* of a Prussian gymnasium the intervention of the
Provincial Board always subsists.

I must give a word in passing to the great *Alumnat* of Berlin,
15 the *Joachimsthalsche Gymnasium*. Here I found 404 scholars;
120 of them were collegers (*Alumnen*), 12 were boarders in
the establishment (*Pensionaire*); the rest were boys who came
for the lessons only (*Hospiten*). Ten per cent. of these have
free schooling. The *Pensionaire* pay only 24*l.* a year; the
20 *Alumnen* are not all of them free of all cost; 25 of them pay
8*l.* 14*s.* a year, 75 of them pay 4*l.* 10*s.* There are 20 places
with board, lodging, and instruction all entirely free, for 20
proved scholars of the highest forms.

The *Joachimsthalsche Gymnasium* is a royal foundation,
25 endowed with lands by the elector Joachim Frederick in 1607.
It is Protestant. The school has now an income of over 3,000*l.*
a year from land, and of over 2,000*l.* a year from money in the
funds. The Crown is the patron; the property is administered,
owing to its connection with the Crown domain, by the *Re-*
30 *gierung* at Potsdam.

This is an interesting school, for the list of its masters contains the names of Buttmann, Schneider, Passow, Zumpt,
Krüger, and Bergk. The director is Dr. Kiessling, a son of the
editor of Theocritus. Constantly in the rolls of the German
35 schools one is coming upon a well-known name of this kind;
on the roll of former teachers at Greyfriars are to be found
the names of Heindorf, Spalding, Droysen. Nor are other recollections, as interesting as any school in the world can boast,

wanting to the Prussian schools. The Joachimsthal School had a scholar of *quarta* who, like so many German schoolboys, joined the army in the great uprising against the French in 1813. This boy was wounded at Leipzig, made the campaign of France, was at Waterloo, received the decoration of the Iron Cross, and finally, with the decoration on his breast, took his place again on his old school-bench as a scholar of *quarta*.

But no *Alumnat* in Prussia, or indeed in Germany, can compare with Schulpforta, which by its antiquity, its beauty, its wealth, its celebrity, is entitled to vie with the most renowned English schools. The Cistercian abbey of St. Mary's, Pforta, dates from 1137. It was secularised in 1540; and Duke Maurice of Saxony, in 1543, established in its place and endowed with its revenues a Protestant school for 100 scholars. It stands near the Saale, in the pleasant country of Prussian Saxony; and the venerable pile of buildings rising among its meadows, hills, and woods, is worthy of the motto borne on the arms of the old abbey: '*Hier ist nichts anderes denn Gottes Haus, und hier die* Pforte *des Himmels*.' * It has a beautifully restored chapel, regular commemorative services, and a host of local usages. A Latin grace is sung in hall every day before dinner by the whole body of scholars. Every scholar has by ancient institution his *tutor*, every master his *famulus*. This is the German school where Latin verse has been most cultivated, and the *Musæ Portenses*, like those of Eton, have been published.

The property is very large, and considerable Church patronage is attached to it. Up to 1815, when it passed into the possession of Prussia, the old abbey estate had still its feudal privileges, and enjoyed full civil and criminal jurisdiction. The property is now entirely under the superintendence of the School Board of the province of Saxony, which appoints a procurator for it. The revenues of Pforta are from 8,000*l.* to 9,000*l.* a year.

The great head-master of Schulpforta was Ilgen, whose name every one who has read the Homeric Hymns ought to respect. Ilgen was rector for nearly thirty years, from 1802 to 1831,

* 'This is none other but the house of God, and this is the gate (*porta, Pforte*) of heaven.'—*Gen.* xxviii. 17.

and his reforms make this period an epoch in the school's history. Few schools can show such a list of old scholars. Grævius, Ernesti, Klopstock, Böttiger, Mitscherlich, Fichte, Dissen, Thiersch, Spitzner, Döderlein, Spohn, were all of them school-boys here.

There are now about 205 pupils: 180 *Alumnen* proper, or collegers, 20 boarders (*Pensionaire, Extraneer*), and four or five half-boarders (*Semi-Extraneer*). These half-boarders have, in fact, all the advantages of collegers, except board, for a payment of 7*l*. 10*s*. a year; their board they get at a master's. The real *Extraneer* board and lodge with a master; they pay him about 45*l*. a year for their board and lodging, and the school 5*l*. 8*s*. a year for their instruction.

The *Alumnen* proper have all of them certain payments to make; those exacted, however, from the 140 who hold *Freistellen* are very trifling. There are 30 old *Koststellen*, or posts with board, the holders of which pay about 3*l*. a year each, and 20 new *Koststellen*, the holders of which pay 7*l*. As a general rule, a boy is not admitted at once to a *Freistelle*. The right of nominating to about half the posts on the foundation belongs to the Crown, that to the other half to different municipalities. Of the Crown appointments a certain number is reserved, by convention with the Saxon Government when Pforta passed into Prussia's possession, for natives of the duchy of Saxony. The rest are given, on grounds of public claim, by the Minister of Justice and the Home Secretary. No boy is admitted till he is twelve years old; he must be able to pass for *tertia*. The school begins with *tertia*, but it has six forms, because there is an upper and a lower division of each class. There are 77 boys in the two divisions of *tertia*, 79 in the two of *secunda*, 49 in the two of *prima*. For some of the posts several boys are nominated, and the one who passes the best examination gets admitted; but the candidates here, the English reader will observe, must all of them be over twelve years of age. The school is well provided with exhibitions, in general of from 10*l*. to 15*l*. a year in value, to the universities.

There is a noteworthy usage here of making one day in the week a *Studientag*, in which the boy is free from all school lessons that he may pursue his private studies. In the same spirit, in the *Gymnasien* generally, promising boys in *prima* are excused certain of the school lessons, that they may work at matters which specially interest them. Results of this private study are to be produced at the *Abiturientenexamen*, and are taken into account for the leaving certificate. Nothing could better show the freedom of Germany, as compared with France, in treating school matters, than a practice of this kind, which to the French authorities would appear monstrous. In England the school authorities would have a belief, in general too well justified, that hardly any one of our boys has any notion of such a thing as systematic private study at all.

At Schulpforta they are very proud of their playing-field, which is indeed, with the wooded hill rising behind it, a pleasant place; but the games of English playing-fields do not go on there: instead of goals or a cricket-ground, one sees apparatus for gymnastics. The Germans, as is well known, now cultivate gymnastics in their schools with great care. Since 1842, gymnastics have been made a regular part of the public-school course; there is a *Central-Turnanstalt* at Berlin, with 18 civilian pupils who are being trained expressly to supply model teachers of gymnastics for the public schools. The teachers profess to have adapted their exercises with precision to every age, and to all the stages of a boy's growth and muscular development. The French are much impressed by what seems to them the success of the Germans in this kind of instruction, and certainly in their own *lycées* they have not at present done nearly so much for it. Nothing, however, will make an ex-schoolboy of one of the great English schools regard the gymnastics of a foreign school without a slight feeling of wonder and compassion, so much more animating and interesting do the games of his remembrance seem to him. This much, however, I will say: if boys have long work-hours, or if they work hard, gymnastics probably do more for their physical health in the comparatively short time allotted to recreation than anything else could. In England the majority of public schoolboys work far less than the foreign schoolboy, and for this majority the English games are delightful; but for the few

hard students with us there is in general nothing but the *constitutional*, and this is not so good as the foreign gymnastics. For little boys, again, I am inclined to think that the carefully taught gymnastics of a foreign school are better than the loung-
5   ing shiveringly about, which in my time used often at our great schools to be the portion of those who had not yet come to full age for games.

All the schools I have hitherto described are denominational schools. Before I conclude, I must describe a mixed (*simultan*)
10   school, or the nearest approach to it to be found. Such a school is the *Friedrich-Wilhelms Gymnasium* at Cologne. Cologne, as every one knows, is Catholic; up to 1825 it had only one gymnasium, a Catholic one. It has now two Catholic gymnasiums, one with 382 scholars, the other with 281; it has also
15   a *Realschule* of the first rank, with 601 scholars.* Besides these schools it has a Protestant gymnasium, with *real* classes; as we should say, with a modern school forming part of it. This is the *Friedrich-Wilhelms Gymnasium.* An old Carmelite college, which had become the property of the municipality, was
20   in 1825 made into a public gymnasium, in order to relieve the overcrowding in the Catholic gymnasium and to provide special accommodation for the Protestants. In 1862 this school was, by the subscriptions of friends, both Catholic and Protestant, provided with *real* classes up to *secunda*, the two lowest
25   classes (*sexta* and *quinta*) being common to both classical and *real* scholars. There are, therefore, in fact, three special classes for *real* scholars; or, as we should say, a modern school of three classes. There are 356 boys in the classical school, and about 100 in the modern school. Of the boys in the classical
30   school 125 only are Protestants, though the school is by foundation *evangelisch;* 215 are Catholics and 16 are Jews. Nothing could better show how little the 'religious difficulty' practically exists in Prussian schools, than this abundance of Catholic scholars in a Protestant school, where the director and the
35   majority of the 15 masters are Protestants. The regular religious instruction of the school is of course Protestant; but the Catho-

* Cologne is a town of 120,570 inhabitants.

lics being in such numbers, a special religious instructor has
been provided for them, as, too, there is a special religious
instructor provided for the Protestants in the two Catholic
gymnasiums. It will be remembered that where the boys not
of the confession for which the school is founded are very few   5
in number, the parents have to make private arrangements for
their religious instruction, and the school does not provide it.
The school-fee is from 18 to 22 thalers a year, according to the
form a boy is in.

The property of the school brings in less than 200*l.* a year.   10
The State contributes about 900*l.* a year. School-fees produce
almost exactly the same sum. The municipality gave in the
first instance the school premises, and now contributes about
50*l.* a year to keep them up. It is a Crown patronage school,
but the *externa*, or property concerns, of this school, as of all   15
the gymnasiums and school endowments of Cologne, are managed by a local *Verwaltungsrath*, or council of administration.
This *Verwaltungsrath* is thus composed: a representative of
the Provincial School Board, the directors of the three gymnasiums, with a lawyer, a financier, an administrator, and two   20
citizens of Cologne; these last five chosen, on the presentation
of the Common Council, by the Provincial School Board. For
the *Studienfonds*, which are endowments general for education
in Cologne, and not affected to particular institutions, a Catholic ecclesiastic is added to the *Verwaltungsrath*. These *Studien-*   25
fonds are very considerable, producing close upon 60,000
thalers a year (9,000*l.*). The *Verwaltungsrath* has a staff of
seven clerks, office-keepers, &c., and both council and staff are
paid for their services.

The director was the personage already mentioned, whose   30
nomination to a school * the Education Minister had refused
to confirm, because of the nominee's politics. I had much conversation with him, and he struck me as a very able man. He
said, and his presence in this Cologne school confirmed it, that
the Government found it impossible to treat their school   35
patronage politically, even so far as the directors or head-

* The school was the gymnasium at Bielefeld.

masters were concerned. The appointment of the professors
and teachers, he declared, it never even entered into the Government's head to treat politically. We went through the school
admission-book together, that I might see to what class in so-
5   ciety the boys chiefly belonged. We took a class in the middle
of the school, and went through this boy by boy, both for
the classical school and the modern school. As it happened,
the social standing of the *real* scholars was on the whole somewhat the highest, but there was very little difference. There
10 were a few peasants' children, picked boys from the elementary schools in the neighbourhood, but these were all of them
bursars. There were a good many sons of Government officials. But the designation I found attached to by far the greater
number of parents' names was *Kaufmann,*—'trader.' I heard
15 several lessons, and particularly noticed the English lesson
in the third class of the modern school. This lesson was given
by a Swiss, who spoke English very well, and who had been,
he told me, a teacher of modern languages at Uppingham. I
thought here, as I thought when I heard a French lesson at
20 Bonn, that the boys made a good deal more of these modern
language lessons in Germany than in England; the Swiss master
at Cologne said this impression of mine was quite right. Even
in France I thought these lessons better done,—with better
methods, better teachers, and more thoroughly learned,—than
25 in England. In Germany they were better than in France. The
lessons in the natural sciences, on the other hand, which in
France seemed to me inferior to the mathematical lessons, I
thought less successfully given in Germany than even in France.
But of this matter I am a very incompetent judge, and England,
30 besides, supplied me here with no standard of comparison, for
in the English schools, when I knew them, the natural sciences
were not taught at all. The classical work in the Cologne gymnasium was much the same that I had seen in other Prussian
gymnasiums, and calls for no particular remark.
35   Dr. Jäger, the director of the united school,—well placed,
therefore, for judging, and, as I have said, an able man,—
assured me it was the universal conviction with those competent to form an opinion, that the *Realschulen* were not, at

present, successful institutions. He declared that the boys in the
corresponding forms of the classical school beat the *Realschule*
boys in matters which both do alike, such as history, geography, the mother-tongue, and even French, though to French
the *Realschule* boys devote so far more time than their com-   5
rades of the classical school. The reason for this, Dr. Jäger
affirms, is that the classical training strengthens a boy's mind
so much more.

This is what, as I have already said, the chief school authorities everywhere in France and Germany testify: I quote   10
Dr. Jäger's testimony in particular, because of his ability and
because of his double experience. In Switzerland you do not
hear the same story, but the regnant Swiss conception of secondary instruction is, in general, not a liberal but a commercial
one; not culture and training of the mind, but what will be   15
of immediate palpable utility in some practical calling, is there
the chief matter; and this cannot be admitted as the true scope
of secondary instruction. Even in Switzerland, too, there is a
talk of introducing Latin into the *Realschule* course, which at
present is without it; so impossible is it to follow absolutely the   20
commercial theory of education without finding inconvenience
from it. But I reserve my remarks on this question for my conclusion.

Chapter XX

Superior or University Instruction in Prussia

Passage from Secondary to Superior Instruction—Special Schools and Universities—Universities of Prussia—Proportion of University Students to Population—German Universities State Establishments —University Authorities—University Teachers—1. Full Professors —2. Assistant Professors—3. Privatdocenten—Students—Fees— Certificates of Attendance at Lectures—Degrees—the Staatsprüf- ung—Character of the German University System.

The secondary school has essentially for its object a general liberal culture, whether this culture is chiefly pursued through the
group of aptitudes which carry us to the humanities, or through
the group of aptitudes which carry us to the study of nature.
5   It is a mistake to make the secondary school a direct professional school, though a boy's aims in life and his future profession will naturally determine, in the absence of an over-
powering bent, the group of aptitudes he will seek to develope.
It is the function of the special school to give a professional
10   direction to what a boy has learnt at the secondary school,
at the same time that it makes his knowledge, as far as possible, systematic,—developes it into science. It is the function of
the university to develope into science the knowledge a boy
brings with him from the secondary school, at the same time
15   that it directs him towards the profession in which his knowledge may most naturally be exercised. Thus, in the university,
the idea of science is primary, that of the profession, secondary; in the special school, the idea of the profession is primary,
that of science, secondary. Our English special schools have
20   yet to be instituted, and our English universities do not perform the function of a university, as that function is above
laid down. Still we have, like Germany, great and famous
universities, and those universities are, as in Germany, in im-

mediate connection with our chief secondary schools. It will be well, therefore, to complete my sketch of the Prussian school system by a sketch of the university system with which it is co-ordered.

Prussia has now six complete universities, with all the four faculties of theology, law, medicine, and philosophy; and two incomplete universities, with only the faculties of theology and philosophy. The complete universities are Berlin, Bonn, Breslau, Greifswald, Halle, and Königsberg; the incomplete ones are Münster and Braunsberg. In both of these last the faculty of theology is Catholic.

These eight Prussian universities had, in 1864, 6,362 students and 600 professors. But this number does not represent the number of Prussians who come under university instruction, because many Prussians go to German universities out of Prussia, such as Heidelberg, Göttingen, Leipzig, Jena. There is very free circulation of the German students through the universities of the fatherland; and to estimate the proportion, in any German State, who come under superior instruction, the fairest way is to take the proportion which the whole number of students in Germany bears to the whole population. For else, while we get for Prussia but about one student to every 2,800 inhabitants, we shall get for Baden, and for the three Saxon duchies, Weimar, Coburg, and Altenburg, about one student to every 1,100 inhabitants; yet it is not that in these territories more of the population go to the university than in Prussia, but Baden has the University of Heidelberg, and the three Saxon duchies have in common the University of Jena, and to these two universities students from all parts of Germany come. Taking, therefore, the whole of Germany, exclusive of the non-German States of Austria, we get about one matriculated student for every 2,600 of population; and this proportion is probably pretty near the truth for Prussia, and for most of the single States. In England the proportion is about one matriculated student to every 5,800 of the population.

The universities of the several German States differ in many points of detail, but in their main system and regulations they are alike. I shall continue, in speaking of universities, to have Prussia in immediate view; but the English reader will understand that what I say of the Prussian university system may be applied in general to that of all Germany.

The German university is a State establishment, and is maintained, so far as its own resources fall short, by the State. A university's own resources are both the property it has and the fees it levies. The two most important of the Prussian universities, Berlin with its 2,500 students and Bonn with its 1,000, date from this century, and foundations of this century are seldom very rich in property. For the year 1864, the income of the University of Berlin was 196,787 thalers (29,518*l.*); of this sum, the real and funded property of the university produced 161 thalers, fees produced 7,557 thalers. The State gave all the rest,—189,069 thalers (about 28,842*l.*). And the State which does this is the most frugal and economical State in Europe.*

The Minister of Public Instruction appoints the professors of a university, the academical senate having the right of proposing names for his acceptance; and he has also his representative in each university,—the *curator*,—who acts as plenipotentiary for the State, and whose business it is to see to the observance of the laws and regulations which concern the universities. Thus, for instance, a full professor (*Professor ordinarius*) is bound by regulation to give throughout the *Semester*, or half-year, at least two free lectures a week on his subject; if he tried to charge fees for them, it would be the curator's business to interfere. And the university authorities cannot make new regulations for the government of the university without

* For further details respecting the University of Berlin see the Appendix. I have there given, also, a list of all the universities of Germany, with the numbers of their students and teachers. For valuable information on this subject, and for excellently composed tables in which that information is exhibited, I am indebted to M. [Jean-Frédéric] Minssen's clear and useful *Étude sur l'Instruction secondaire et supérieure en Allemagne* (Paris, Librairie Internationale, 1866). M. Minssen was sent by M. Duruy to see the universities and gymnasiums of Germany, and was in that country at the same time that I was. [The appendices are not printed in this edition.]

obtaining for them the sanction of the minister and of Parliament. Still the university authorities practically work, in Germany just as much as in this country, their own university; the real direction of the university is in their hands, and not, as in France, in those of the minister.

These university authorities are the following. First comes the rector, or, in cases where the sovereign is the titular rector, as at Halle and Jena, the pro-rector, who answers to our vice-chancellor, only he is elected for one year only, instead of four. His electors are the full professors. The rector or pro-rector is the visible head of the university, and is charged with its discipline. Like our vice-chancellor, he has an assessor, or judge, who sits with him whenever there is a question of inflicting fines, or whenever one of the parties appearing before him is not a member of the university. The academical senate is also chosen by the full professors, and for one year, its members consisting of the actual rector (or pro-rector), the outgoing rector, and a full professor of each faculty. In some universities all the full professors are members of the academical senate. The rector is president, and the internal affairs of the university are brought before it for its discussion and regulation of them.

Next come the faculties. The faculties in nearly all German universities are four in number: * theology, law, medicine, and philosophy. Philosophy embraces the humanities, and the mathematical and natural sciences. As a university authority, a faculty consists only of its full professors, headed by the dean, whom these professors elect for one year. It is the business of the faculty thus composed to see that the students attend regularly the courses of lectures for which they are entered, to summon defaulters before it, to reprimand them, and to inflict on them, if it think proper, a slight penalty.

The last university authority to be mentioned is the *quæstor*. He has to collect from the students the fees for the courses for which they have entered themselves, and to pay those fees

* In one or two universities there is a separate faculty for political economy; in general this science is comprehended in the faculty of philosophy.

to the professors to whom they are due, a small deduction being made for the quæstor's salary and for the university chest.

And now to take the university, not as an administrative but as a teaching body. Of the university, considered in this capacity, the *faculty* is a very different thing from the limited faculty above described. The university faculty, as a teaching body, comprehends not only all the full professors of that faculty, but all its professors extraordinary, or assistant professors, and all its *Privatdocenten*. The dean of faculty ascertains from all the full professors, all the professors extraordinary, and all the *Privatdocenten* of his faculty, what subject each of them proposes to treat in the coming *Semester:* there is perfect liberty of choice for each lecturer, but by consent among themselves they so co-order their teaching that the whole field of instruction proper to their faculty may be completely covered. Then the dean calls together the full professors, who make the administrative faculty; and the programme of lectures is by them drawn up from the data collected by the dean, and is promulgated by their authority.

All full professors must have the degree of doctor in their faculty. Each of them is named for a special branch of the instruction of his faculty; and in this branch he is bound, as I have said, to give at least two public lectures a week without charging fees. He receives from the State a fixed salary which is sometimes as much as 350*l.*, or even 400*l.*, a year; he has also a share in the examination fees, and he has the fees for what lectures he gives besides his public lectures. The regular number of full professors in each university is limited, but the State can always, if it thinks fit, nominate an eminent man as full professor in a faculty, even though the faculty may have its complement of full professors; and the State then pays him the same salary as the other full professors. Both from the consideration which attaches to the post and from its emolument, a full professor's place is in Germany the prize of the career of public instruction, and no schoolmaster's place can compare with it. At Heidelberg several professors have, I am told, an income, from fixed salary and fees together, of 1,000*l.* a year, and one an income of 1,500*l.*

The professors extraordinary, or assistant professors, are also named by the State, but they have not in all cases a fixed salary. Their main dependence is on fees paid by those who   5 come to their lectures. They are in general taken from the most distinguished of the *Privatdocenten*, and they rise through the post of professor extraordinary to that of full professor.

Other countries have full professors and professors extraordinary. France, for instance, has her *professeurs titulaires* and   10 her *professeurs suppléants;* but the *Privatdocent* is peculiar to Germany, and is the great source of vigour and renovation to her superior instruction. Sometimes he gives private lessons, like the private tutors of our universities; these lessons have the title of *Privatissima.* But this is not his main busi-   15 ness. His main business is as unlike the sterile business of our private tutors as possible. The *Privatdocent* is an assistant to the professorate; he is free to use, when the professors do not occupy them, the university lecture-rooms, he gives lectures like the professors, and his lectures count as professors' lec-   20 tures for those who attend them. His appointment is on this wise. A distinguished student applies to be made *Privatdocent* in a faculty. He produces certain certificates and performs certain exercises before two delegates named by the faculty, and this is called his *Habilitation.* If he passes, the faculty   25 names him *Privatdocent.* The authorisation of the minister is also requisite for him, but this follows his nomination by the faculty as a matter of course. He is then free to lecture on any of the matters proper to his faculty. He is on his probation, he receives no salary whatever, and depends entirely on his   30 lectures; he has, therefore, every motive to exert himself. In general, as I have said, the professors and *Privatdocenten* arrange together to parcel out the field of instruction between them, and one supplements the other's teaching; still a *Privatdocent* may, if he likes, lecture on just the same subject that   35 a professor is lecturing on; there is absolute liberty in this respect. The one precaution taken against undue competition

is, that a *Privatdocent* lecturing on a professor's subject is not
allowed to charge lower fees than the professor. It does honour
to the disinterested spirit in which science is pursued in Germany, that with these temptations to competition, the relations
5 between the professors and the *Privatdocenten* are in general
excellent; the distinguished professor encourages the rising
Privatdocent, and the *Privatdocent* seeks to make his teaching
serve science, not his own vanity. But it is evident how the
neighbourhood of a rising young *Privatdocent* must tend to
10 keep a professor up to the mark, and hinder him from getting
sleepy and lazy. If he gets sleepy and lazy, his lecture-room is
deserted. The *Privatdocent*, again, has the standard of eminent
men before his eyes, and everything stimulates him to come
up to it.

15   In the faculty of philosophy at Berlin the number of *Privatdocenten* is almost exactly the same as the number of full professors. There are 28 full professors and 29 *Privatdocenten*. The
professors extraordinary are more numerous than either. They
are 33 in number. The whole number of teachers in the Uni-
20 versity of Berlin is 183.

Now I come to the students. The university course in theology, law, and philosophy, takes three years; in medicine it
takes four or five. A student in his *triennium* often visits one
or two universities, seldom more. Lachmann (to take an emi-
25 nent instance) first went for half-a-year to Leipzig to hear
Hermann; then he passed on to Göttingen, where he afterwards
got his *Habilitation*. To become a member of a university, the
student has to be entered on the university register (*Matrikel*),
and then on the register of the faculty in which he means to
30 follow lectures; for inscription on the university register the
production of the school leaving certificate (*Maturitätszeugnis*), of which I have already said so much, is indispensable.
You may get leave to attend lectures without being a member
of the university, and without any school certificate; but such
35 attendance counts nothing for any purpose for which a university course is by law or official rule required. The university entrance fee is about 18s. The matriculating student signs
an engagement to observe the laws and regulations of the uni-

versity. The penalties for violating them are enforced by the rector. These penalties are, according to the nature of the offence, reprimand; fine; imprisonment for a period not exceeding one month in the university *carcer; consilium abeundi,* or dismissal from the particular university to which the student belongs, but with liberty to enter at another; and finally, *Relegation,* or absolute expulsion, notice being sent to the other universities, which then may not admit the student expelled.

The lecture fees range from 16s. to 1l. 14s. for every course which is not a public and gratuitous one. They are somewhat higher at Berlin than in most German universities. In the faculty of medicine they are highest; here they go as high as 1l. 14s. a *Semester* for a course of about five hours a week. A course of the same length in theology or philosophy costs at Berlin about 17s. a *Semester.* The fees are collected, as I have said, by the university quæstor, and they must be paid in advance. But every professor has the power to admit poor auditors to his lectures without fee, and often he does so. Poor students are also, by a humane arrangement, suffered to attend lectures on credit, and afterwards, when they enter the public service,—which in Prussia means not only what we in England call the public service, but the learned professions as well,— their lecture fees are recovered by a deduction from their salary. Each university has besides, for the benefit of poor scholars, a number of exhibitions ranging from 12l. to 60l. a year; and it is common to allow the holders of school exhibitions, which are of smaller amount, and range from 6l. to 30l. a year, to retain them at the university.

Certificates of having followed certain courses of lectures are required both for the university degree and for the subsequent examination for a public career (*Staatsprüfung*) which almost every university student has in view. It is said that the professors whose lectures are very numerously attended have difficulty in ascertaining who is there and who is not, and that they give the certificates with too much laxity. In general, however, it is certain that a student who has his way to make, and who is worth anything, will attend regularly the lectures for which he has entered himself and paid his money.

There are, of course, many idlers; the proportion of students in a German university who really work I have heard estimated at one-third; certainly it is larger than in the English universities. But the pressure put upon them in the way of com-
5 pulsion and university examinations is much less than with us. The paramount university aim in Germany is to encourage a love of study and science for their own sakes; and the professors, very unlike our college tutors, are constantly warning their pupils against *Brodstudien*, studies pursued with a view
10 to examinations and posts. The examinations within the university course itself are far fewer and less important in Germany than in England. It is Austria, a country which believes in the things of the mind as little as we do, which is the great country for university examinations. There they are applied
15 with a mechanical faith much like ours, and come as often as once a month; but the general intellectual life of the Austrian universities is lower, though Vienna and Prague are good medical schools, than that of any other universities of Germany. '*Le pays à examens, l'Autriche,*'—exclaims an eminent
20 French professor, M. Laboulaye, who has carefully studied the German university system with a view to reforming that of France,—'*Le pays à examens, l'Autriche, est précisément celui dans lequel on ne travaille pas;*' and every competent authority in Germany will confirm what M. Laboulaye says.
25 I do not say that in countries like Austria and England, where there is next to no real love for the things of the mind, examinations may not be a protection from something worse.* All I say is that a love for the things of the mind is what we want, and that examinations will never give it.
30 Each faculty in a German university examines for degrees in that faculty and confers them. The *Maturitätszeugnis* which the student brings with him from school answers to our grade of bachelor of arts. The degree of licentiate, answering to our degree of master, is only given in theology
35 and philosophy, and is not often sought for. The great faculty

* Although I am no very ardent lover of examinations, I am inclined to think the non-Austrian universities of Germany might with advantage make a somewhat greater use of them.

degree is the degree of doctor. For this a certificate of university studies, an oral examination, and a written dissertation, are required. The dissertation is in Latin or German, and is usually published. A doctor's degree in philosophy costs 17*l.* at Berlin; there are faculties and universities in which a doctor's degree costs as much as 22*l.* 10*s.* A poor student who passes a brilliant examination has sometimes his degree given him without fees. I have already said that the degree of doctor is given much more easily and carelessly in some German universities than in others. But in none is the degree examination in itself such as to make it what the degree examination is with us,— the grand final cause of the university life. '*Der Zweck des Lebens ist das Leben selbst,*' says the German poet; and this is certainly true, in Germany, of the university life.

The *Staatsprüfung,* however, supplies a bracing examination test; but this examination falls outside the sphere of the university itself. As I have again and again begged the English reader to remark, the examination test is never used in Prussia as sufficient in itself; it is only used to make the assurance of a really good education doubly sure; the really good education is regarded as the main assurance, and no one who has not had this may present himself for the *Staatsprüfung.* The student who leaves a university receives from the rector a certificate mentioning what lectures he has attended, and what the character of his university career has been. With this certificate, and with the leaving certificate of his school, the future civil servant, clergyman, lawyer, or doctor, presents himself before an examining commission (*Prüfungscommission*) such as I have described in an earlier part of this volume. He is then examined, having three or four days of paper work, and six or eight hours of *viva voce.* For lawyers and for clergymen there is a double examination, the second coming three years after the first.

Such, sketched in the briefest possible outline, is the system of the German universities. *Lehrfreiheit* and *Lernfreiheit,* liberty for the teacher and liberty for the learner; and *Wissenschaft,* science, knowledge systematically pursued and prized in and for itself, are the fundamental ideas of that system.

The French, with their ministerial programmes for superior instruction, and their ministerial authorisations required for any one who wants to give a course of public lectures,—authorisations which are by no means a matter of form,—are naturally most struck with the liberty of the German universities, and it is in liberty that they have most need to borrow from them. To us, ministerial programmes and ministerial authorisations are unknown; our university system is a routine, indeed, but it is our want of science, not our want of liberty, which makes it a routine. It is in science that we have most need to borrow from the German universities. The French university has no liberty, and the English universities have no science; the German universities have both.

IV

Switzerland

Chapter XXI

The Schools of Switzerland

Resemblance of the Swiss Schools to Those of Germany—The Zurich Schools to be Taken as Representatives of Those of Switzerland—Communal Schools—Common Popular Schools—Obligatory Attendance—School Authorities—The School Partnership—The Communal School Committee—The District School Committee—The Education Council—Higher Popular Schools (Secundarschulen) —School Committees for Secondary Schools—Cantonal Schools—The Gymnasium and the Industrieschule—Their Government, Course, Fees, and Instruction—Municipal Schools at Winterthur —Associations of Teachers—Private Schools—The University—The Federal School, or Polytechnicum—Merits and Defects of Swiss Schools—The Swiss and the Scotch Conception of Education—Superiority of the German Conception of It—Excellent Foundations Laid by the Swiss.

What is most important in the Swiss secondary schools is so closely akin to what is to be found in Germany, that the sketch I have given of the higher schools of Prussia might serve in the main for those of the most notable Swiss cantons also. But I will take the opportunity which Switzerland gives me to notice the secondary schools, which in Germany I have chiefly noticed by their classical side, by that side of them which is not classical, and also in connection with the primary schools.

Nowhere is the continuity between the primary and the higher schools so complete as in Canton Zurich, which I therefore will take as a representative of Switzerland, in the same way that I took Prussia as the representative of Germany. Zurich is, no doubt, an eminently favourable representative to take; it is on the whole the best provided with schools of all the Swiss cantons. Its schools, however, are scarcely better, even as a whole, than those of Canton Aargau and Canton

Basle; in the classical school, Canton Basle probably surpasses Canton Zurich. Even in cantons which are generally spoken of as backward, Lucerne, for instance, my astonishment was, and the astonishment of every Englishman accustomed to the unhappy deficiencies of our own school system must be, not to find the Lucerne schools no better than they are, but to find them so good as they are. Zurich, therefore, though a very favourable specimen, is not unique, is still representative; and every day, as the great movement of education goes on which has for the last thirty years made the force of Switzerland, the cantons which are behind Zurich are more and more exerting themselves to emulate her example.

Canton Zurich has about 260,000 inhabitants, the immense majority of whom are of German stock and Protestants. Nearly a third of the whole public expenditure of the canton is directed to education, and one in five of the population are in school.

The schools in the canton are communal, cantonal, or federal. The system begins with the communal school. By the school law of the canton, instruction is obligatory on all children between the ages of six and sixteen. The communal day-school takes the child at six. It is a school of six classes, three of them *Elementarclassen,* and three of them *Realclassen;* each class takes the child a year to pass through it. By the time he has passed through the communal day-school he has, therefore, completed his twelfth year. He has still three years more of obligatory instruction before he arrives at his confirmation;—this, which answers to the *première communion* of the Catholics, being for Zurich Protestants the epoch to which the term of obligatory school-attendance is reckoned, and this epoch being reached when the child is sixteen. If he does not pass from the communal day-school into a school of a higher order, two courses are open to him. Either he attends the *Ergänzungsschule,* or finishing school, which is in fact a department of the communal day-school for his benefit and that of others like him, with eight hours' instruction a week, the eight being generally taken in two mornings; or, if he cannot spare time for even so much as this, he becomes a *Sing-*

und Unterweisungsschüler. He is a pupil of the *Singschule*, to keep up by one hour's practice in the week that knowledge of church music and singing which in Protestant Germany is thought so important; and he is a pupil, for *Unterweisung*, or religious instruction, of the pastor of the place, who has him for an hour and a half in the week to keep up his religious instruction preparatory to his confirmation. The instruction comes to much the same in amount as the instruction of our Sunday-schools. One of these two courses is obligatory, from the age of thirteen to the age of sixteen, upon every child who does not go to some higher school.

I have seen many of the Swiss primary day-schools, and think them in general better than even the inspected schools of this class with us now are. The programme of work for them is fixed by the Education Council of the canton, and embraces religious instruction, the mother-tongue, arithmetic and geometry, the elements of natural philosophy, history and geography, singing, handwriting, drawing, gymnastics; and, for girls, needlework. Needlework is taught in the day-school to the three elementary classes only; for girls in the *real* classes of the day-school, and for girls in the *Ergänzungsschule*, there are special schools, *weibliche Arbeitschulen,** to which they have to go for their instruction in needlework. The needlework of girls in the elementary schools of Germany and Switzerland is very much better than that of girls in ours. The *Arbeitschulen* are of course taught by women, but the immense majority of the Zurich day-schools are mixed schools, and taught by men. The canton has a Normal School at Küssnacht to train its teachers, who have of course to pass an examination and to obtain a certificate.

From seven to thirteen, therefore, every child in Canton Zurich has the instruction of such a day-school as I have described. In 1864 there were 365 day-schools in the canton, with 515 departments under separate teachers (*Einzelnschulen*). The moment the number of scholars in a school exceeds 100, the law compels the school to have a second teacher and a second

* There were, in 1864, 322 *Arbeitschulen* of this kind in Canton Zurich.

school-room. But the Education Council may order this relief when there are more than 80 scholars, and, in fact, as soon even as there are more than 40 or 50, the commune of its own motion frequently bestows it; providing, if not a second school-master, at least a trained assistant with the title of *Adjunct*. The school hours in the day-school are from 18 hours a week in the lowest classes to 27 hours a week in the highest, and there are eight weeks of holidays in the year.

I have said that every child in Canton Zurich has, from the age of seven to that of thirteen, the instruction of such a day-school as I have described. Not that every child is obliged to go to the communal day-school; but at the beginning of every school year the pastor of the commune furnishes a list of all the children of the commune who have reached the legal school age; the school committee of the commune issues a notice that all such children must be brought to school; and if any of them are taught at home or sent to private schools, their parents must satisfy the school committee that they receive an instruction at least equal to that of the communal day-school, and meanwhile must pay to this school the fee for them just the same as if they attended. This being so, and the public day-schools being really good, few children go elsewhere, and one finds all classes of society mixed in them. In the school district of Zurich, comprising the city itself and its environs, there were in 1864 only two private schools for boys, with forty boys of school age divided between the two establishments.

The 365 communal day-schools of Canton Zurich had, in 1864, 25,797 scholars between the ages of seven and thirteen. The number of school absences in the year was 13·12 per scholar. But school absences are distinguished into *verant-wortete*, those of which a satisfactory explanation (illness, death in the family, &c.) is given, and *strafbare*, those which are unallowed and punishable. The latter were only 1·04 per scholar. In different places the mode of dealing with punishable absences differs. In the town of Zurich the school authority warns the offending parent or guardian after three punishable absences, cites him after three more, fines him after three more. This applies to absences from the day-school; for absences from the *Ergänzungsschule* or *Singschule* the warning is after the second punishable absence, the citation after the fourth, the fine after the sixth. But in all cases the law which makes non-attendance penal is enforced, the Education Council repaying to the local school authorities the costs of any proceedings against defaulters. The same authorities are also empowered to see that the half-timers, as we might call them, of their locality, the pupils of the *Ergänzungsschule*, are not overtaxed out of school hours by their employers, or rendered unfit for the school work still required of them.

Of children between thirteen and sixteen, 10,441 attended in 1864 the *Ergänzungsschulen* of Canton Zurich, and 11,428 were only *Sing- und Unterweisungsschüler*. It is noteworthy that almost one-half of the scholars whose day-school obligation had ended took the greater rather than the less amount of schooling assigned for their last three years of educational nonage. The law fixes three francs a year as the school fee *
of a day-scholar, and a franc and a half as the fee of all scholars not day-scholars. No distinction is made between a scholar of the *Ergänzungsschule* and a scholar of the *Singschule*. This of course constitutes an inducement to the parent to send his son if he can to the finishing school rather than the singing school, to get as much as he can for his school money.

I have several times spoken of the school authorities. These form a closely connected series. The authority nearest to the elementary school (*allgemeine Volksschule*) is the *Schulgenossenschaft*, or school partnership, composed of the school's immediate tributaries. Each school has its own *Schulgenossenschaft*, to abridge or to extend the limits of which, or to unite it with another *Schulgenossenschaft*, the intervention of the Council of State, the high governing body of the canton, is requisite. Each school has likewise its own *Schulfond*, or school fund, and *Schulverwalter*, or steward of this fund. The school

* The local school authority may increase this up to double the amount. In the great communal day-school of Zurich, with nearly 1,400 scholars, and with fifteen or sixteen teachers in each of its two departments, the school fee is six francs a year.

partnership elects its steward, who is then its representative
in the management of the school finances. It also elects, if it
pleases, its schoolmaster; fixes, within the limits left to it by
the law, the rate of school fee; and decides what poor scholars
5   shall be admitted gratuitously, and what at reduced rates. Pau-
per children are paid for out of the poor's fund of that whole
commune of which the *Schulgenossenschaft* forms a part.*
The school partnership is charged with providing, fitting,
maintaining, and warming the school premises, with the pay-
10 ment of 8*l.* a year towards the schoolmaster's salary, and with
finding him a house, ground, and firing, or an equivalent in
money. The schoolmaster takes half the school fees; the other
half goes into the school chest. If the schoolmaster's half of
the school fees, with his fixed salary from the school partner-
15 ship, does not reach a certain minimum, the State, if necessary,
makes his income up to that minimum. But the school partnership, or the whole commune, often provides out of its own resources schoolmasters' salaries much above the legal minimum;
in the more important communes this is more particularly
20 the case. In the town of Zurich the fifteen teachers of the boys'
division of the elementary school all receive an income from the
commune of from 8o*l.* to 104*l.* a year. In the small country
communes 4o*l.* is about the average of a teacher's salary. The
revenues from the *Schulfond*, which consists of the landed or
25 funded property with which the school is endowed, of settlement dues paid by all new settlers in the commune, and of dues
paid on all marriages in the commune, are, with the proceeds
of school fines and of half the school fees, with what the school
partnership raises among its own members and with what the
30 State grants, the means of providing for the yearly support of
the school. In the town of Zurich the commune rates itself to

* Though our English National schools date from George the Third's
reign only, their constitution has a mediæval character. But in some
parts of England the supporters of a Methodist day-school afford a
35 specimen of a genuine *Schulgenossenschaft*, providing, maintaining and
managing the school they require for their own children. But they are
not, as in Switzerland, co-ordered with a regular graduated series of
school authorities; they have nothing between them and the central
Education Department in London.

make up the sum it requires for its schools; in the country, the school partnerships raise by voluntary contributions among their members the amount they need. The *Schulfonds* of the elementary schools of Canton Zurich amount altogether to nearly 5,550,000 francs; to the yearly income from this source the State adds about 300,000 francs,—35,000 francs for school buildings in poor communes, and 275,000 francs for teachers' salaries; for the rest of the expenditure on the elementary schools, school-fees and the contributions of the local bodies provide.

The school partnership is not charged with the duty of superintending the discipline and teaching of its school. This duty belongs to the next authority in the series, to the school administration of the commune (*Gemeindeschulpflege*). This body represents the whole *Schulkreis*, or school circle, in which the school partnership falls; it represents the commune in fact, for the school circles of Canton Zurich coincide as a general rule with its communes. The canton has 162 school circles, and 367 school partnerships. The school administration of the school circle or commune is a body of four or more members elected by the commune; the *Pfarrer*, or parson,* being *ex officio* their president. The other members are elected by universal suffrage, but no one under twenty-five may be on the *Schulpflege*, and two near relations or connections may not be on it together. The meetings of this *Gemeindeschulpflege* are attended by all the teachers of the school circle, but they have a consultative voice only. Whenever the financial affairs of a school are under consideration by the *Schulpflege*, the steward representing the school partnership of that school attends. The

---

* In Canton Geneva the lay tendencies of modern democracy have so far prevailed that the pastor, or the curé, is not *ex officio* a member of the communal school committee; but all the communal schools have a dogmatic religious instruction, Catholic or Protestant. Many people in England seem to have a notion that a State system of education must of necessity be undenominational and secular. So far is this from being the case, that in all the countries to which the present work relates,—France, Italy, Germany, and Switzerland,—there is a State system of education, and that system is both denominational and religious. Only the different denominations are not suffered to persecute one another.

duties of the communal *Schulpflege* are to see that in all the elementary schools of the *Gemeinde,* or commune, the school law is properly obeyed, the teacher properly paid, the rules issued from time to time by the Education Council of the can-
5 ton properly followed, the teaching and discipline properly maintained. The members inspect by rotation the schools of their commune, and make a yearly report to the body next above them in the chain of school authorities,—the school administration of the district (*Bezirksschulpflege*).
10 Canton Zurich has eleven *Bezirke,* or districts. Each district, like each commune, has its *Schulpflege.* The district *Schulpflege* is composed of from nine to thirteen members, of whom three are chosen by the teachers of the *Bezirk,* the rest by the inhabitants of the district by universal suffrage. The members
15 choose their own president and secretary. This higher *Schulpflege* sees that the communal *Schulpflege* properly fulfils its functions, that the law and the Education Council's rules are observed, that the children are sent regularly to school, and the school premises kept in good condition. Plans for new
20 school buildings have to be submitted to this *Schulpflege* for approval, with appeal from its decision to the Education Council. It names each of its members visitor (*Visitator*) for certain schools for a certain period; the visitor has to visit twice a year each of the schools assigned to him, to be present at the
25 yearly examination by which in every school the pupils pass from one class to another, and to report to his *Schulpflege.* The district *Schulpflege* itself reports annually to the Education Council.

A small allowance of from three to six francs is made to
30 the visitors of this *Schulpflege* for days on which they are actually employed in inspecting, and the school partnerships generally pay their stewards; with these exceptions, all the functions I have been describing are performed gratuitously.

The supreme authority, to which we now come, is the Edu-
35 cation Council (*Erziehungsrath*). This represents the State. The Director of Education for the canton, who is president of the Education Council, is a member of the government of the canton, the Council of State. The Education Council has

six members besides its president. Four of the six are chosen by the Great Council of the canton, that is, by universal suffrage; two are chosen by the School Synod, a body which consists of all the teachers of the canton, those of the higher schools as well as those of the popular schools. One teacher elected must be chosen from among the masters of the higher schools, the other from among those of the popular schools. The members of this Council are appointed for four years, and half of them go out every two years; the other bodies I have been describing, and in general all public councils and committees in Canton Zurich, follow the like course.

The superintendence and promotion of education, higher and lower, throughout the canton, is the business of the *Erziehungsrath*. It is the centre to which the reports of the district committees and the communal committees converge, and to which appeals are brought. It selects the commissions of superintendence for the cantonal schools, of which I have yet to speak; of each of these commissions the Director of Education is president, if he chooses; if not he, then some other member or members of the Education Council must be on each commission. The Council has also the power of ordering special inspections, and has a credit opened to it for this purpose. It can, also, suspend or interdict teachers.

Such is the series of authorities by which popular education in Canton Zurich is managed. The spirit in which they have been contrived, balanced, and organised, is, as the English reader will perceive, an intensely democratic and an intensely local spirit; yet not insanely democratic, so that the idea of authority, nor insanely local, so that the idea of the State, shall be lost sight of.

But the obligatory three years of the finishing school or the singing school, are not the proper completion of the six years of the elementary or common popular school (*allgemeine Volksschule*), though they are a completion which the law accepts. The proper completion is three years of the higher popular school (*höhere Volksschule*), or, as it is also called (the school nomenclature of Switzerland being somewhat different from that either of Germany or of France), the secondary school (*Secundarschule*). This is the *Mittelschule* of Germany, the *école élémentaire supérieure* of M. Guizot's law; but what is important to be observed is that it is still a school for the people, or *Volksschule,* and also a school which the public provides for them. The Council of State divides the canton into *Secundarschulkreise,*—school circles for the higher popular school, as the commune is the school circle for the common popular school. Of these *Secundarschulkreise* there are 57; the communes which compose each circle undertaking to maintain, with aid from the State, a secondary school in it. Each of these schools, too, has its *Schulfond;* the aggregate value of their property was in 1864, in round numbers, 470,000 francs. The school-fee is 24 francs a year, but the school is bound to take one scholar in eight as a free scholar. The regular State grant to each of the 57 secondary schools is 42*l.* a year; this is increased, however, when the school is considerable enough to need more than one teacher. These teachers are trained, like the primary teachers, in the Normal school at Küssnacht, which has special lessons for them, and special certificates. In 1864 there were 74 teachers in the 57 secondary schools, and 2,398 scholars. The studies are in general the same as those of the primary school, but each branch is carried further, and French is added. The school has a three years' course, is held for about twenty-eight hours in each week, and there are eight weeks of holidays in the year. It is evident, therefore, that this is no supplementary or half-time school, and can take no children who are not able to give their whole time to it. None are admitted who have not passed the examination which guards the exit from the primary school. Some special preparation for the business of agriculture or of trade is attempted in the secondary school.

The master of a secondary school gets on an average about 60*l.* a year, with house, ground, and firing. In the town of Zurich, where the secondary school, established, like the primary school, in a really splendid building, is excellent, his position is far better than this; the income of the five or six masters in the boys' department averaging there from 100*l.* to 110*l.* a year. I saw both departments of this school at work;

the girls were more numerous than the boys, about 250 to the boys' 150. In both schools almost all the teaching is done by masters; nor, indeed, does the American preference of women as teachers get in general any sanction from the practice of the Continent.* I found in this Zurich girls' school ten masters employed and nine mistresses, but eight of the nine mistresses were for needlework. The children were of the class that one finds in the better British or Wesleyan schools in England, but they receive an instruction such as can be got in no British or Wesleyan school. I was particularly struck with the thorough way in which French was taught and learnt. The introduction of a foreign language, as an obligatory part of the school course for every scholar, marks sufficiently the broad difference between the instruction in the Zurich secondary school and that in any British or Wesleyan school of ours; but the essential difference is in the abundance of teachers, and in their training and culture. Scholars who show eminent promise are passed on, with free posts if necessary, into the higher schools of the canton.

Every secondary school has its *Schulpflege*, of from seven to eleven members, two of whom are chosen by the *Bezirks-schulpflege* of the district in which the school stands, the rest by the *Schulpflegen* of the communes which make up the secondary school circle. Their functions for the secondary school are like those of the communal *Schulpflege* for the primary school, and they report to the *Bezirksschulpflege*.

The child who after completing his twelfth year goes neither to the finishing school (*Ergänzungsschule*), nor to the singing school (*Singschule*), nor to the secondary school (*Secundar-schule*), has still three years of *Schulzwang*, or obligation to be under instruction. But such a child must be of a class to do

---

* I may say that competent foreign observers who have studied the American schools, report that, as a general rule, though something is to be learnt from them as to providing and maintaining schools, little or nothing is to be learnt from them as to teaching. Nor is this the slightest reproach to America, which has inherited from us our preference of business to learning, and up to the present time has had a thousand reasons more than we for following this preference.

more than satisfy this obligation, and he goes to the gymnasium,
where the school course lasts six years and a half, or to the
Industrieschule (so at Zurich a *Realschule* is called), where it
lasts five years and a half. These are *cantonal* schools, at the
5   charge of the whole canton. Each of them has its own *Auf-
sichtscommission*, or commission of superintendence, of nine
members, chosen, as I have said, by the Education Council. A
delegate from this commission attends and controls, as in
Prussia, the yearly examinations at which leaving certificates
10 are issued. The rectors of the cantonal schools are always
members of the commission of superintendence, but they never,
of course, represent it at examinations. Nor do they represent
it at inspections, which the other members of the commission
perform by monthly rotation, the inspector having to visit each
15 class and hear lessons given in it, in the course of the month.
The rectors are nominated by the Council of State; the masters by the Education Council, reinforced by a certain number
of members of the commission of superintendence for the
school concerned. The commission for the gymnasium and
20 that for the *Industrieschule* have a joint meeting once a quarter,
to ensure the harmonious working of the two schools.

    The instruction in the gymnasium is classical, and the pas-
sage to the university lies through it. It is in all important
respects modelled on a German gymnasium such as those
25 which I have so fully described in speaking of Prussia. It is
divided into a lower gymnasium (*unteres Gymnasium*), with
a course of four years, and an upper gymnasium (*oberes
Gymnasium*), with a course of two and a half years. In the
lower gymnasium the school-fee is thirty francs a year. A boy
30 passes the sixth year's examination of the elementary school,
and then enters at the bottom of the gymnasium. He cannot,
—and this is the general rule in the Swiss and German schools,
—be put above his age. If for any reason he does not come to
the gymnasium till he is fourteen or fifteen, he is still not placed
35 by examination, but goes to the form which at fourteen or
fifteen he would have reached had he entered the gymnasium
in due course after twelve. He is not admitted at all unless he
is up to the work of the class to which his age assigns him. The

graduation of the school programme, according to which the fit work is supposed to be assigned for each age in fit proportions, is the ground for these rules, which seem to me to be on the whole judicious.

In the lower gymnasium the boys have religious instruction,* Latin, Greek, French and the mother tongue, history, geography and natural history, arithmetic and mathematics, free-hand drawing, writing, singing, gymnastics, and military exercising. In the upper gymnasium the fee is forty-eight francs a year. Here they of course carry the studies of the lower gymnasium further, and they add to them Hebrew besides, and logic. Enumerations of this kind are not in themselves very instructive; the English reader will get a clearer notion of the Zurich gymnasium by bearing in mind that whereas in Prussia the *Volksschule* is, as I mentioned, not regarded as the right preparation for the gymnasium, the Swiss law expressly assigns to both sides, the classical as well as the *real*, of the cantonal school, an immediate connection with the popular school. Then for scholars who enter above the second class of the lower gymnasium, and for all scholars in the upper gymnasium, Greek is not obligatory. But what is most noteworthy is that not only is no Latin or Greek verse done in the gymnasium at all, but no original Latin or Greek composition in prose is done there; a translation once a week,—into Greek one week and into Latin another,—is all the Greek and Latin composition done; and this translation is little more than a grammatical exercise. Composition in French is carried as far as the essay, and much beyond composition in the old classical languages. Greek, however, gets from five to eight hours a week in every class of the gymnasium above the lowest, and Latin ten hours in the lowest class, and from six to eight hours in the rest. It may be noticed that in the highest class of the gymnasium Greek gets only five hours a week, an hour less than it gets in the *prima* of a Prussian gymnasium.

There are about 180 scholars in the Zurich gymnasium, and fourteen of them in 1864 obtained the certificate of ripeness

* The regulations with respect to this are in Canton Zurich, and in Protestant German countries generally, as. in Prussia.

(*Zeugnis der Reife*) which here, as in Germany, is required
for matriculation at the university.

The *Industrieschule* is more fully attended than the gymnasium, and has about 250 scholars. Like the gymnasium, it
5 has an upper and a lower division. The lower division has a
three years' course, and the fee, thirty francs a year, is higher
than in the corresponding division of the gymnasium. There
is not, as in the German *Realschule*, Latin. Latin and Greek being left out and geometrical drawing added, the list of matters
10 of instruction is nearly identical with that of the lower gymnasium, and it is in the proportion of time allotted and the
development given to the several matters of instruction, that
the two schools, the one designed to lead to the university,
the other to what the school law calls 'technical and business
15 lines,' differ. The school course of the lower *Industrieschule*
is, as a general rule, the same for all scholars there, and is
obligatory in all its parts for all of them. In the upper division
it is not so; there is one programme, but no scholar goes
through the whole of it; the lessons composing it fall into
20 three groups, that for the mechanical line, that for the chemical line, and that for the business line; and each boy, according
to the line of life he intends to follow, is assigned by the rector
to the group of lessons suitable for him. Of eighty-four scholars in the upper *Industrieschule* in 1864, thirty-four were in
25 the mechanical group, thirteen in the chemical, and thirty-
seven in the business group. The Education Council urges the
masters not to let the school be turned into a place for mere
professional study; but this organisation gives, of course, a
bias which it is hard to resist. English and Italian make part
30 of the regular school course in this division.

The moment instruction becomes professional it becomes
saddled with special expenses, and in the upper *Industrieschule*
the school-fee is 60 francs a year, a high school-fee for Switzerland. The pupils who follow the chemical line pay 60 francs
35 a year for the expenses of the laboratory.

The lessons in the upper *Industrieschule* are excellent, and
qualified pupils from other public establishments are allowed,
if the rector of the *Industrieschule* and their own master con-

sent, to attend particular lessons which are better given at the *Industrieschule* than anywhere else. Young men who have left school, but are following an occupation for which these lessons are useful, are also allowed, if properly qualified for profiting by them, to attend. Such hearers take the title of *Auditoren*, and pay five francs a week for each lesson they follow. Of the 84 pupils in the three groups of the upper *Industrieschule* in 1864, 12 were *Auditoren* of this kind.

There are ten weeks' holiday for the cantonal schools in the year. These holidays were going on when I was at Zurich; but the town of Winterthur has established higher schools both for boys and girls,* which, though not cantonal but municipal, emulate the higher schools of Zurich in their organisation and far excel them in their school buildings; these I saw at work, and I saw also those of Basle. Winterthur is, I think, for its school establishments the most remarkable place in Europe. It is the second town for importance in Canton Zurich, and thrives by its manufacture of muslins; but it has not more than 8,000 inhabitants. The schools of this small place recall the municipal palaces of Flanders and Italy. They are the objects of first importance in the town, and would be admirable anywhere; besides the elementary schools there is a *Mittelschule*, an *Industrieschule*, and a gymnasium, all built within the last twenty-five years, and which have cost the town not less than 100,000*l*. I found about eighty scholars in the gymnasium, about two-thirds of them Winterthur boys; the rest come from a

---

* I have found it impossible to include in this work an account of the girls' schools of the Continent. I visited several of them, but in the boys' schools I had already more on my hands than I could well manage, and the girls' schools well merit a separate enquiry, and by an enquirer who has first thoroughly acquainted himself, as I have not, with the working of our girls' schools at home. I will just mention, as places where the girls' schools will richly reward the future enquirer's attention, Naples, Weimar and Zurich. And I will add, that Italian girls seem to me those in all Europe who are best suited for school education as distinguished from home education; who derive most benefit from it, and with the fewest drawbacks of any kind. On the other hand, I doubt whether there is any German or English girl for whom there are not grave drawbacks to balance its benefits.

distance, and board, under regulations similar to those in Prussia, with the masters or with families in the town. I heard a lesson in Livy in the class which with us would have been the fifth form; the performance was quite as good as that which I
5　remember in the fifth form of Winchester or Rugby. In the *Industrieschule* I found about 200 scholars; in the upper division of this there is the same grouping of scholars for different lines (*Richtungen*) which obtains at Zurich. The teaching is said by competent judges to be particularly well organised in
10　these higher *Realschulen* of Switzerland. The Winterthur higher schools, though not cantonal schools, have, and deservedly, an exceptional position; they are under the inspection of a cantonal commission, and in immediate relation with the Education Council. The burghers of Winterthur seek
15　competent advice and superintendence with as much zeal as in England a batch of local people show in resisting it. Nor is it to get money that they have recourse to the State; the grant from the State to these Winterthur establishments is 80*l.* a year, and the town of Winterthur itself spends 3,200*l.*
20　a year on them. This sum is supplied from the *Bürgergut* or communal property, and it is to be observed that generally in a Swiss parish it is the commune that is the great proprietor, as in England it is the squire. The sons of Winterthur burghers have free schooling; others pay much the same rates as at
25　Zurich. As at Zurich, too, half of the school-fees is divided among the teachers; the other half goes to the school chest.

The teachers in Canton Zurich form a sort of guild, and exercise considerable influence. I have already said how they are represented on the local *Schulpflegen*. In the higher schools
30　they form *Convente* and *Specialconvente*, the *Convent* being for each school, the *Specialconvent* for each division, upper or lower, of each school. They are in fact masters' meetings, as at Rugby we used to call them; but in Switzerland they have a legal status, and report regularly to the commissions of
35　superintendence. They are said to be of great service in keeping the school work properly graduated, and in maintaining uniformity of standard. New rules they can only make for points which the school law and the regulations of the Educa-

tion Council have not already settled, but changes cannot be introduced without their opinion being taken upon them. In the same way, the teachers of the primary and secondary schools of each *Bezirk*, or district, form a *Schulcapitel*, or school chapter, which meets four times a year, forms sections for the discussion of any special matters in which schools and teachers are interested, reports to the Education Council, and has a right to be heard before any change in the work-plan or in the regulations of the popular schools are adopted. These chapters, again, unite with the whole body of teachers of the higher schools of the canton to form a School Synod, having for its business the promotion of education in the canton, and to convey the wishes and proposals of the teaching body to the authorities. This Synod meets once a year, its business and method of proceeding being always prepared beforehand by a Pro-Synod.

I have already said that private schools must, if they are schools for popular education, give an instruction at least equal to that of the public popular school. All private schools are entirely open to State inspection and must furnish yearly reports of themselves to the authorities. But besides this, for the opening of any private school the consent of the State, and an official approval of the work-plan, are necessary. The great development of the public schools in the last thirty years, however, and the increasing favour they enjoy, tend to make the Swiss private schools of less and less importance, so far as the Swiss themselves are concerned. The better status of the public school teacher is an attraction for masters; the better guarantees of the public school are an attraction for parents. I met at Basle an excellent teacher, the son of a Swiss private schoolmaster of European celebrity; the son had given up his father's establishment when it came, at his father's death, into his hands, in order to take the more interesting and honourable functions of a public teacher. I was told by Swiss gentlemen of authority and standing, who had themselves been brought up in Fellenberg's famous school at Hofwyl, that they would not send their own sons to any but a public school, and that even a man of Fellenberg's special gifts could not now,

since the improvement of the public schools, establish a private
school to vie with them successfully. When it was the habit
of the young Swiss cadet of family to enter into foreign service, he had a special inducement to go to a famous school like
that at Hofwyl, where, by meeting Austrians or Bavarians who
had been attracted thither by Fellenberg's reputation, he
formed connections which were useful to him in after life.
This habit having been stopped, a considerable attraction
which a private school like Fellenberg's offered to the Swiss
of the last generation has ceased; and the best informed Swiss
will tell you that the Swiss private schools, of which we hear
so much in England, now exist mainly *pour exploiter les
Anglais,* who do indeed invite *exploitation.*

At the apex of the school system of Canton Zurich stands the
Hochschule, or university. This is in all important respects a
German university, and many of the professors come from
Germany; the famous Dr. Strauss was, as is well known, a
professor here. The canton pays the professors, of whom there
are five for each of the three faculties of theology, law and
medicine, and fourteen for that of philosophy. Here, as in
Germany, the professors are divided into *ordinarii* and *extraordinarii,* full professors and assistant professors; and their
teaching is powerfully supplemented by that of the *Privatdocenten.* The Education Council proposes professors, the
Council of State appoints them, the opinion of the faculty
concerned being always taken. That of the Church Council
(*Kirchenrath*) is also taken on the appointment of a theological
professor. The professors, *ordinarii* and *extraordinarii,* of each
faculty, form a body who elect their own dean; the deans of
faculty and the ordinary, or full, professors compose the *senatus
academicus,* which chooses the rector, who must be confirmed
by the Council of State. The academical senate is charged with
the discipline of the university, and has a right to be heard
before the Education Council can introduce any changes in
academical matters.

At the end of 1864 there were in the *Hochschule* of Zurich
200 matriculated students, besides seven who were not matriculated. Of the 200, twenty-seven were in the faculty of theology,

thirty-seven in that of law, seventy-eight in that of medicine, and fifty-eight in that of philosophy. The Swiss students were 138 out of the 200; of these 138 the Zurichers were sixty-three. But of the fifty-eight students in philosophy the Swiss numbered only twenty-six, and of these twenty-six the Zurichers were only eight. The remaining thirty-two came chiefly from Germany and Russia; two were from England.

But more noteworthy than the university at Zurich is the Polytechnicum, or high school for forming civil engineers, for teaching the applied sciences, and for training teachers for all departments of technical instruction. This is a federal and not a cantonal institution. It was established by the Federal Council for the benefit of the whole of Switzerland, and a commission appointed by the Federal Council administers it. It was placed at Zurich, where it occupies a commanding position on a slope above the town, and is one of the first objects that attracts a stranger's notice.

This Polytechnicum was in vacation when I visited Zurich, but I saw at work another admirable institution of the same kind, the Polytechnicum at Stuttgart, of which the object and the methods are very much the same. That of Zurich has six divisions; the school of construction, the school of civil engineering, the school of mechanics, the school of chemistry, the school of woodcraft, and the school of mathematical and natural sciences, of literature, and of moral and political sciences. The course in the different divisions varies in length from two to three years. The fees are low, and the staff of professors excellent; some of the most distinguished scientific men of Germany have been brought here by the Swiss Government. A professor may in his lessons use the German, French, or Italian language, as suits him best. The yearly cost of the institution is about 340,000 francs (13,600*l.*), of which 16,000 fr. are given by the town of Zurich, 10,000 fr. come from the *Schulfond*, 64,000 fr. from the students' fees, and the remaining 250,000 fr. from the Swiss Confederation. There are about fifty professors and five hundred students.

The Polytechnicum, though not specially belonging to Canton Zurich, worthily crowns by its presence the astonish-

ing series of schools which this canton exhibits, and which I
have endeavoured to describe to the English reader. A terri-
tory with the population of Leicestershire possesses a university, a veterinary school, a school of agriculture, two great
5 classical schools, two great *real* schools, a normal school for
training primary and secondary teachers, fifty-seven secondary schools, and three hundred and sixty-five primary schools;
and many of these schools are among the best of their kind in
Europe.

10   The primary, secondary, and *real* schools, are those of which
this can be affirmed most decidedly. I can well understand
that M. Baudouin, who was sent by the French Minister of
Public Instruction to see the schools for the middle and trading classes in countries which have any such schools to show,
15 and who has published an elaborate and invaluable report *
of what he saw, should have imagined himself in Paradise
when he came to Zurich, and should have thought no words
too strong to express his admiration. The *Realstudien* of the
Swiss schools are prosecuted without any of the misgivings
20 and hesitations which hang about them in Germany. Switzerland does not much trouble her head with ideas such as haunt
a German Education Minister in genuine Germany, that '*die
unwissenschaftliche Praxis des Nützlichkeitsprincips den Char-
akter einer allgemeinen höheren Bildungsanstalt aufhebe;*' or
25 share his concern because, do what he will, the programme of
a *Realschule* possesses less *innere Geschlossenheit* than that of
a gymnasium. The aim which Swiss education has before it,
is not, I think, the highest educational aim. The idea of what
the French call *la grande culture* has not much effect in
30 Switzerland, and accordingly it is not in her purely literary
and scientific high schools, and in the line of what is specially
called a liberal education, that she is most successful. Her
highest teachers are Germans from Germany; but large as are
the salaries paid to draw these distinguished foreigners to
35 Zurich, a genuine German, I am told, does not much like the

* *Rapport sur l'état actuel de l'enseignement spécial en Belgique, en
Allemagne et en Suisse,* par J. M. Baudouin. Paris, Imprimerie Impériale,
1865.

atmosphere in which he finds himself there; he sighs for the more truly scientific spirit, the *wissenschaftlicher Geist*, of the universities of his own country, and will not in general stay long at Zurich. The spirit which reigns at Zurich, and in the thriving parts of German Switzerland, is a spirit of intelli- 5
gent industrialism, but not quite intelligent enough to have cleared itself from vulgarity. At Lausanne and Geneva the French language and the traditions of a high intellectual life introduce other elements; but even at Lausanne and Geneva, the effect of the great movement of the last thirty years, has 10
been to develop, as the principal power there, the same sort of intelligent industrialism as is the principal power in German Switzerland. The representatives of the old high culture and intellectual traditions of French Switzerland are not now masters of the situation there, and the course of events pushes them 15
more and more aside.

But the grand merit of Swiss industrialism, even though it may not rise to the conception of *la grande culture*, is that it has clearly seen that for genuine and secure industrial prosperity, more is required than capital, abundant labour, and 20
manufactories; it is necessary to have a well-instructed popu-
lation. So far as instruction and the intelligence developed by instruction are valuable commodities, the Swiss have thoroughly appreciated their market worth, and are thoroughly employing them. 25

They seem to me in this respect to resemble the Scotch. The Scotch, too, as the state of their universities shows, have at present little notion of *la grande culture*. Instead of guard-
ing, like the Germans, the *wissenschaftlicher Geist* of their uni-
versities, they turn them into mere school-classes; and instead 30
of making the student, as in Germany, pass to the university through the *prima* of a high school, Scotland lets the Univer-
sity and the High School of Edinburgh, with a happy spirit of independence worthy of their neighbours south of the Tweed, compete for schoolboys; and the University recruits 35
its Greek classes from the third or fourth forms of the High School. Accordingly, while the aristocratic class of Scotland is by its bringing up, its faults, its merits, much the same as

the aristocratic class in England, the Scotch middle class is in
la grande culture not ahead of the English middle class. But
so far as intellectual culture has an industrial value, makes a
man's business-work better, and helps him to get on in the
5 world, the Scotch middle class has thoroughly appreciated
it and sedulously employed it, both for itself and for the class
whose labour it uses; and here is their superiority to the English, and the reason of the success of Scotch skilled labourers
and Scotch men of business everywhere. In this they are like
10 the Swiss, though the example and habits of England have, as
was inevitable, prevented the Scotch from developing their
school institutions, even for their limited purpose, with the
method and admirable effectiveness shown by the Swiss.

What I admire in Germany is, that while there too indus-
15 trialism, that great modern power, is making at Berlin, and
Leipzig, and Elberfeld, the most successful and rapid progress,
the idea of culture, culture of the only true sort, is in Germany
a living power also. Petty towns have a university whose teaching is famous through Europe; and the King of Prussia and
20 Count Bismarck resist the loss of a great *savant* from Prussia,
as they would resist a political check. If true culture ever becomes at last a civilising power in the world, and is not over-
laid by fanaticism, by industrialism, or by frivolous pleasure-
seeking, it will be to the faith and zeal of this homely and much
25 ridiculed German people, that the great result will be mainly
owing.

Meanwhile let us be grateful to any country, which, like
Switzerland, prepares by a broad and sound system of popular
education the indispensable foundations on which a civilising
30 culture may in the future be built; and do not let us be too
nice, while we ourselves have not even laid the indispensable
foundations, in canvassing the spirit in which others have laid
them.

Chapter XXII

General Conclusion. School Studies

Probable Issue of the Conflict Between Classical and Real Studies —New Conception of the Aim and Office of Instruction—The Circle of Knowledge Takes in Both the Humanities and the Study of Nature—This Not Enough Recognised at Present—Tyranny of the Humanists—Tyranny of the Realists—Our Present School-Course—How to Transform It—Excessive Preponderance of Grammatical Studies, and of Latin and Greek Composition—The Ancient Languages to be More Studied as Literature—And the Modern Languages Likewise—Summing Up of Conclusions.

The reader will probably expect that at the end of this long history I should offer some opinion as to the lessons to be drawn from all which I have been describing. This I shall attempt to do; although I can hardly hope, perhaps, to communicate to him the weight of conviction with which I myself am left by what I have seen. Two points, above all, suggest matter for reflection: the course of study of foreign schools, and the way in which these schools are established and administered. I begin with the first.

Several times in this volume I have touched upon the conflict between the gymnasium and the *Realschule*, between the partisans of the old classical studies and the partisans of what are called real, or modern, or useful studies. This conflict is not yet settled, either by one side crushing the other by mere violence, or by one side clearly getting the best of the other in the dispute between them. We in England, behindhand as our public instruction in many respects is, are nevertheless in time to profit, and to make our schools profit, by the solution which will certainly be found for this difference. I am inclined to think that both sides will, as is natural, have to abate their extreme pretensions. The modern spirit tends to reach a new conception of the aim and office of instruction; when this conception is fully reached, it will put an end to conflict, and will probably show both the humanists and the realists to have been right in their main ideas.

5   The aim and office of instruction, say many people, is to make a man a good citizen, or a good Christian, or a gentleman; or it is to fit him to get on in the world, or it is to enable him to do his duty in that state of life to which he is called. It is none of these, and the modern spirit more and more dis-
10   cerns it to be none of these. These are at best secondary and indirect aims of instruction; its prime direct aim is to enable a man *to know himself and the world*. Such knowledge is the only sure basis for action, and this basis it is the true aim and office of instruction to supply. To know himself, a man must
15   know the capabilities and performances of the human spirit; and the value of the humanities, of *Alterthumswissenschaft*, the science of antiquity, is, that it affords for this purpose an unsurpassed source of light and stimulus. Whoever seeks help for knowing himself from knowing the capabilities and per-
20   formances of the human spirit, will nowhere find a more fruitful object of study than in the achievements of Greece in literature and the arts during the two centuries from the birth of Simonides to the death of Plato. And these two centuries are but the flowering point of a long period, during the whole
25   of which the ancient world offers, to the student of the capabilities and performances of the human spirit, lessons of capital importance.

This the humanists have perceived, and the truth of this perception of theirs is the stronghold of their position. It is a vital
30   and formative knowledge to know the most powerful manifestations of the human spirit's activity, for the knowledge of them greatly feeds and quickens our own activity; and they are very imperfectly known without knowing ancient Greece and Rome. But it is also a vital and formative knowledge to
35   know the world, the laws which govern nature, and man as a part of nature. This the realists have perceived, and the truth of this perception, too, is inexpugnable. Every man is born with aptitudes which give him access to vital and formative

knowledge by one of these roads; either by the road of studying man and his works, or by the road of studying nature and
her works. The business of instruction is to seize and develope
these aptitudes. The great and complete spirits which have
all the aptitudes for both roads of knowledge are rare. But 5
much more might be done on both roads by the same mind,
if instruction clearly grasped the idea of the entire system of
aptitudes for which it has to provide; of their correlation, and
of their *equipollency*, so to speak, as all leading, if rightly
employed, to vital knowledge; and if then, having grasped this 10
idea, it provided for them. The Greek spirit, after its splendid
hour of creative activity was gone, gave our race another
precious lesson, by exhibiting, in the career of men like Aristotle and the great students of Alexandria, this idea of the
correlation and equal dignity of the most different departments 15
of human knowledge, and by showing the possibility of uniting them in a single mind's education. A man like Eratosthenes
is memorable by what he performed, but still more memorable
by his commanding range of studies, and by the broad basis of
culture out of which his performances grew. As our public 20
instruction gets a clearer view of its own functions, of the relations of the human spirit to knowledge, and of the entire circle
of knowledge, it will certainly more learn to awaken in its
pupils an interest in that entire circle, and less allow them to
remain total strangers to any part of it. Still, the circle is so vast 25
and human faculties are so limited, that it is for the most part
through a single aptitude, or group of aptitudes, that each individual will really get his access to intellectual life and vital
knowledge; and it is by effectually directing these aptitudes on
definite points of the circle, that he will really obtain his com- 30
prehension of the whole.

Meanwhile neither our humanists nor our realists adequately
conceive the circle of knowledge, and each party is unjust to
all that to which its own aptitudes do not carry it. The humanists are loth to believe that man has any access to vital 35
knowledge except by knowing himself,—the poetry, philosophy, history which his spirit has created; the realists, that he
has any access except by knowing the world,—the physical

sciences, the phenomena and laws of nature. I, like so many others who have been brought up in the old routine, imperfectly as I know letters,—the work of the human spirit itself, —know nothing else, and my judgment therefore may fairly
5   be impeached. But it seems to me that so long as the realists persist in cutting in two the circle of knowledge, so long do they leave for practical purposes the better portion to their rivals, and in the government of human affairs their rivals will beat them. And for this reason. The study of letters is
10 the study of the operation of human force, of human freedom and activity; the study of nature is the study of the operation of non-human forces, of human limitation and passivity. The contemplation of human force and activity tends naturally to heighten our own force and activity; the contempla-
15 tion of human limits and passivity tends rather to check it. Therefore the men who have had the humanistic training have played, and yet play, so prominent a part in human affairs, in spite of their prodigious ignorance of the universe; because their training has powerfully fomented the human force in
20 them. And in this way letters are indeed *runes*, like those magic runes taught by the Valkyrie Brynhild to Sigurd, the Scandinavian Achilles, which put the crown to his endowment and made him invincible.

Still, the humanists themselves suffer so much from the igno-
25 rance of physical facts and laws, and from the inadequate conception of nature, and of man as a part of nature,—the conduct of human affairs suffers so much from the same cause,—that the intellectual insufficiency of the humanities, conceived as the one access to vital knowledge, is perhaps at the present
30 moment yet more striking than their power of practical stimulation; and we may willingly declare with the Italians * that no part of the circle of knowledge is common or unclean, none is to be cried up at the expense of another. To say that the fruit of classics, in the boys who study them, is at present

---

35   *'Essendo diverse le parti dell'insegnamento, nessuno mostri di spregiare le altre, esaltando troppo quella cui è addetto. Nessun ramo del sapere è meno necessario; di tutte le scienze si avvantaggia l'umana società; tutte cospirano al suo bene.'—*Sulle Condizioni,* &c. p. 384.

greater than the fruit of the natural sciences, to say that the realists have not got their matters of instruction so well adapted to teaching purposes as the humanists have got theirs, comes really to no more than this: that the realists are but newly admitted labourers in the field of practical instruction, and that while the leading humanists, the Wolfs and the Butt-manns, have been also schoolmasters, and have brought their mind and energy to bear upon the school-teaching of their own studies, the leaders in the natural sciences, the Davys and the Faradays, have not. When scientific physics have as recognised a place in public instruction as Latin and Greek, they will be as well taught.

The Abbé Fleury, than whom no man is a better authority, says of the mediæval universities, the parents of our public secondary schools: *Les universités ont eu le malheur de commencer dans un temps où le goût des bonnes études était perdu.* They were too late for the influences of the great time of Christian literature and eloquence, the first five centuries after Christ; they were even too late for the influences of the time of Abelard and Saint Bernard. And Fleury adds: *De là* (from these universities founded in a time of inferior insight) *nous est venu ce cours réglé d'études qui subsiste encore.* He wrote this in 1708, but it is in the main still true in 1867. All the historical part of this volume has shown that the great movements of the human spirit have either not got hold of the public schools, or not kept hold of them. What reforms have been made have been patchwork, the work of able men who into certain departments of school study which were dear to them infused reality and life, but who looked little beyond these departments, and did not concern themselves with fully adjusting instruction to the wants of the human mind. There is, therefore, no intelligent tradition to be set aside in our public schools; there is only a routine, arising in the way we have seen, and destined to be superseded as soon as ever that more adequate idea of instruction, of which the modern spirit is even now in travail, shall be fully born.

That idea, so far as one can already forecast its lineaments, will subordinate the matter and methods of instruction to the

end in view;—the end of conducting the pupil, as I have said,
through the means of his special aptitudes, to a knowledge
of himself and the world. The natural sciences are a necessary
instrument of this knowledge; letters and *Alterthumswissen-*
schaft are a necessary instrument of this knowledge. But if
school instruction in the natural sciences has almost to be
created, school instruction in letters and *Alterthumswissen-*
schaft has almost to be created anew. The prolonged philological discipline, which in our present schools guards the access to *Alterthumswissenschaft,* brings to mind the philosophy
of Albertus Magnus, the mere introduction to which,—the
logic,—was by itself enough to absorb all a student's time of
study. To combine the philological discipline with the matter
to which it is ancillary,—with *Alterthumswissenschaft* itself,
—a student must be of the force of Wolf, who used to sit up
the whole night with his feet in a tub of cold water and one
of his eyes bound up to rest while he read with the other,
and who thus managed to get through all the Greek and Latin
classics at school, and also Scapula's Lexicon and Faber's
Thesaurus; and who at Göttingen would sweep clean out of the
library shelves all the books illustrative of the classic on which
Heyne was going to lecture, and finish them in a week. Such
students are rare; and nine out of ten, especially in England,
where so much time is given to Greek and Latin composition,
never get through the philological vestibule at all, never arrive
at *Alterthumswissenschaft,* which is a knowledge of the spirit
and power of Greek and Roman antiquity learned from its
original works.

But many people have even convinced themselves that the
preliminary philological discipline is so extremely valuable
as to be an end in itself; and, similarly, that the mathematical
discipline preliminary to a knowledge of nature is so extremely
valuable as to be an end in itself. It seems to me that those
who profess this conviction do not enough consider the quantity of knowledge inviting the human mind, and the importance to the human mind of really getting to it. No preliminary
discipline is to be pressed at the risk of keeping minds from
getting at the main matter, a knowledge of themselves and

the world. Some minds have such a special aptitude for philology, or for pure mathematics, that their access to vital knowledge and their genuine intellectual life lies in and through those studies; but for one whose natural access to vital knowledge is by these paths, there will be ten whose natural access 5
to it is through literature, philosophy, history, or through some one or more of the natural sciences. No doubt it is indispensable to have exact habits of mind, and mathematics and grammar are excellent for the promotion of these habits; and Latin, besides having so large a share in so many modern 10
languages, offers a grammar which is the best of all grammars for the purpose of this promotion. Here are valid reasons for making every schoolboy learn some Latin and some mathematics, but not for turning the preliminary matter into the principal, and sacrificing every aptitude except that for 15
the science of language or of pure mathematics. A Latin grammar of thirty pages, and the most elementary treatise of arithmetic and of geometry, would amply suffice for the uses of philology and mathematics as a universally imposed preparatory discipline. By keeping within these strict limits, absolute ex- 20
actness of knowledge,—the habit which is here our professed aim,—might be far better attained than it is at present. But it is well to insist, besides, that all knowledge may and should, when we have got fit teachers for it, be so taught as to promote exact habits of mind; and we are not to take leave of 25
these when we pass beyond our introductory discipline.

But it is sometimes said that only through close philological studies and the close practice of Greek and Latin composition, can *Alterthumswissenschaft* itself, the science of the ancient world, be truly reached. It is said to be only through these 30
that we get really to know Greek and Latin literature. For all practical purposes this proposition is untrue, and its untruth may be easily tested. Ask a good Greek scholar, in the ordinary English acceptation of that term, who at the same time knows a modern literature,—let us say the French literature, 35
—well, whether he feels himself to have most seized the spirit and power of French literature, or of Greek literature. Undoubtedly he has most seized the spirit and power of French

literature, simply because he has read so very much more of it. But if, instead of reading work after work of French literature, he had read only a few works or parts of works in it, and had given the rest of his time for study to the sedulous practice of French composition and to minutely learning the structure and laws of the French language, then he would know the French literature much as he knows the Greek; he might write very creditable French verses, but he would have seized the spirit and power of French literature not half so much as he has seized them at present. No doubt it is well to know French philology like M. Littré, and to know French literature too; or to write Italian verse like Arthur Hallam, and to know Italian literature too; just as it is well to know the Greek lexicographers and grammarians as Wolf did, and yet to know, also, Greek literature in its length and breadth. But it needs a very rare student for this; and as, if an Englishman is to choose between writing Italian sonnets and knowing Italian literature, it is better for him to know Italian literature, so, if he is to choose between writing Greek iambics and knowing Greek literature, it is better for him to know Greek literature. But an immense development of grammatical studies, and an immense use of Latin and Greek composition, take so much of the pupil's time, that in nine cases out of ten he has not any sense at all of Greek and Latin literature as *literature*, and ends his studies without getting any. His verbal scholarship and his composition he is pretty sure in after life to drop, and then all his Greek and Latin is lost. Greek and Latin *literature*, if he had ever caught the notion of them, would have been far more likely to stick by him.

I was myself brought up in the straitest school of Latin and Greek composition, and am certainly not disposed to be unjust to them. Very often they are ignorantly disparaged. Professor Ritschl, I am told, envies the English schools their Latin verse, and he is no bad judge of what is useful for knowing Latin. The close appropriation of the models, which is necessary for good Latin or Greek composition, not only conduces to accurate verbal scholarship; it may beget, besides, an intimate sense of those models, which makes us sharers of their spirit and power; and this is of the essence of true *Alterthumswissen-schaft*. Herein lies the reason for giving boys more of Latin composition than of Greek, superior though the Greek litera-ture be to the Latin; but the power of the Latin classic is in *character*, that of the Greek is in *beauty*. Now character is 5 capable of being taught, learnt, and assimilated; beauty hardly; and it is for enabling us to learn and catch some *power* of antiquity, that Greek or Latin composition is most to be valued. Who shall say what share the turning over and over in their mind, and masticating, so to speak, in early life as models 10 for their Latin verse, such things as Virgil's

    'Disce, puer, virtutem ex me, verumque laborem'—

or Horace's

      'Fortuna sævo læta negotio'—

has not had in forming the high spirit of the upper class in 15 France and England, the two countries where Latin verse has most ruled the schools, and the two countries which most have had, or have, a high upper class and a high upper class spirit? All this is no doubt to be considered when we are judging the worth of the old school training. 20

But, in the first place, dignity and a high spirit is not all, or half all, that is to be got out of *Alterthumswissenschaft*. What else is to be got out of it,—the love of the things of the mind, the flexibility, the spiritual moderation,—is for our present time and needs still more precious, and our upper class suffers 25 greatly by not having got it. In the second place, though I do not deny that there are persons with such eminent apti-tudes for Latin and Greek composition that they may be brought in contact with the spirit and power of *Alterthums-wissenschaft*, and thus with vital knowledge, through them, 30 —as neither do I deny that there are persons with such emi-nent aptitudes for grammatical and philological studies, that they may be brought in contact with vital knowledge through *them*,—nevertheless, I am convinced that of the hundreds whom our present system tries without distinction to bring 35 into contact with *Alterthumswissenschaft* through composition and philology almost alone, the immense majority would have a far better chance of being brought into vital contact with it through literature, by treating the study of Greek and Latin as we treat our French, or Italian, or German studies. In other words, the number of persons with aptitudes for being carried to vital knowledge by the literary, or historical, or philosophical, or artistic sense,—to each of which senses we give a chance by treating Greek and Latin as literature, and not as mere scholarship,—is infinitely greater than the number of those whose aptitudes are for composition and philology.*

I cannot help thinking, therefore, that the modern spirit will deprive Latin and Greek composition and verbal scholarship of their present universal and preponderant application in our secondary schools, and will make them, as practised on their present high scale, *Privatstudien,* as the Germans say, for boys with an eminent aptitude for them. For the mass of boys the Latin and Greek composition will be limited, as we now limit our French, Italian, and German composition, to the exercises of translation auxiliary to acquiring any language soundly; and the verbal scholarship will be limited to learning the elementary grammar and common forms and laws of the language with a thoroughness which cannot be too exact, and which may easily be more exact than that which we now attain with our much more ambitious grammatical studies. A far greater quantity of Latin and Greek literature might, with the time thus saved, be read, and in a far more interesting manner. With the Latin and Greek classics, too, might be joined, as a part of the literary and humanistic course for those whose

---

* Since the above remarks were in print they have received powerful corroboration from the eminent authority of Mr. Mill, in his inaugural address at St. Andrews. The difference of my conclusions on one or two points from Mr. Mill's only makes the general coincidence of view more conspicuous; Mr. Mill having been conducted to this view by independent reflection, and I by observation of the foreign schools and of the movement of ideas on the Continent.

Mr. Farrar's very interesting lecture has still more recently come to show us this movement of ideas extending itself to the schools of England, and to distinguished teachers in the most distinguished of these schools.

aptitude is in this direction, a great deal more of the classics of the chief modern languages than we have time for with our present system.

We have still to make the mother tongue and its literature a part of the school course; foreign nations have done this, and we shall do it; but neither foreign nations nor we have yet quite learnt how to deal, for school purposes, with modern foreign languages. The great notion is to teach them for speaking purposes, with a view to practical convenience. This notion clearly belongs to what I have called the commercial theory of education, and not the liberal theory; and the faultiness of the commercial theory is well seen by examining this notion and its fruits. Mr. Marsh, the well-known author of the *History of the English Language,* who has passed his life in diplomacy and is himself at once a *savant* and a linguist, told me he had been much struck by remarking how, in general, the accomplishment of speaking foreign languages tends to strain the mind, and to make it superficial and averse to going deep in anything. He instanced the young diplomatists of the new school, who, he said, could rattle along in two or three languages, but could do nothing else. Perhaps in old times the young diplomatists could neither do that nor anything else, so in their case there may be now a gain; but there is great truth in Mr. Marsh's remark that the speaking several languages tends to make the thought thin and shallow, and so far from in itself carrying us to vital knowledge, needs a compensating force to prevent its carrying us away from it. But the true aim of schools and instruction is to develop the powers of our mind and to give us access to vital knowledge.

Again: if the speaking of foreign languages is a prime school aim, this aim is clearly best reached by sending a boy to a foreign school. Great numbers of English parents, accordingly, who from their own want of culture are particularly prone to the more obvious theory of education,—the commercial one, —send their boys abroad to be educated. Yet the basis of character and aptitudes proper for living and working in any country is no doubt best formed by being reared in that country, and passing the ductile and susceptible time of boyhood there;

and in this case Solomon's saying applies admirably: '*As a bird that wandereth from her nest, so is a man that wandereth from his place.*' That, therefore, can hardly be a prime school aim, which to be duly reached requires from the scholar an almost irreparable sacrifice. So the learning to speak foreign languages, showy as the accomplishment always is, and useful as it often is, must be regarded as a quite secondary and subordinate school aim. Something of it may be naturally got in connection with learning the languages; and above all, the instructor's precept and practice in pronunciation should be sound, not, as in our old way of teaching these languages through incompetent English masters it too often was, utterly barbarous and misleading; but all this part is to be perfected elsewhere, and is not to be looked upon as true school business. It is as literature, and as opening fresh roads into knowledge, that the modern foreign languages, like the ancient, are truly school business; and far more ought to be done with them, on this view of their use, than has ever been done yet.

To sum up, then, the conclusions to which these remarks lead. The ideal of a general, liberal training is, to carry us to a knowledge of ourselves and the world. We are called to this knowledge by special aptitudes which are born with us; the grand thing in teaching is to have faith that some aptitudes of this kind everyone has. This one's special aptitudes are for knowing men,—the study of the humanities; that one's special aptitudes are for knowing the world,—the study of nature. The circle of knowledge comprehends both, and we should all have some notion, at any rate, of the whole circle of knowledge. The rejection of the humanities by the realists, the rejection of the study of nature by the humanists, are alike ignorant. He whose aptitudes carry him to the study of nature should have some notion of the humanities; he whose aptitudes carry him to the humanities should have some notion of the phenomena and laws of nature. Evidently, therefore, the beginnings of a liberal culture should be the same for both. The mother tongue, the elements of Latin and of the chief modern languages, the elements of history, of arithmetic and geometry, of geography, and of the knowledge of nature, should be the studies of the lower classes in all secondary schools, and should be the same for all boys at this stage. So far, therefore, there is no reason for a division of schools. But then comes a *bifurcation*, according to the boy's aptitudes and aims. Either the study of the humanities or the study of nature is henceforth to be the predominating part of his instruction. Evidently there are some advantages in making one school include those who follow both these studies. It is the more economical arrangement; and when the humanistic and the real studies are in the same school, there is less likelihood of the social stamp put on the boy following the one of them, being different from that put on a boy following the other. Still the *bifurcation* within one school, as practised in France, did not answer. But I think this was because the character of the one school remained so overwhelmingly humanistic, because the humanist body of teachers was in general much superior to the realist body, and because the claims of the humanities were allowed to pursue a boy so jealously into his *real* studies. In my opinion, a clever *Realschüler*, who has gone properly through the general grounding of the lower classes, is likely to develop the greater taste for the humanities the more he is suffered to follow his *real* studies without let or stint. The ideal place of instruction would be, I think, one where in the upper classes (the instruction in the lower classes having been the same for all scholars) both humanistic and *real* studies were as judiciously prosecuted, with as good teaching and with as generous a consideration for the main aptitudes of the pupil, as the different branches of humanistic study are now prosecuted in the best German *Gymnasien;* where an attempt is certainly made, by exempting a pupil from lessons not in the direction of his aptitudes, and by encouraging and guiding him to develope these through *Privatstudien,* to break through that Procrustean routine which, after a certain point, is the bane of great schools. There should, after a certain point, be no cast-iron course for all scholars, either in humanistic or naturalistic studies. According to his aptitude, the pupil should be suffered to follow principally one branch of either of the two great lines of study; and, above all, to interchange the lines

occasionally, following, on the line which is not his own line, such lessons as have yet some connection with his own line, or, from any cause whatever, some attraction for him. He cannot so well do this if the *Gymnasium* and the *Realschule* are
5 two totally separate schools.

His doing it at all, however, is, it will be said, only an ideal. True, but it is an ideal which the modern spirit is, more and more, casting about to realise. To realise it fully, the main thing needful is, first, a clear central conception of what one can and
10 should do by instruction. It is, secondly, a body of teachers, in all the branches of each of the two main lines of study, thoroughly masters of their business, and of whom every man shall be set to teach that branch which he has thoroughly mastered, and shall not be allowed to teach any that he has not.

Chapter XXIII

General Conclusion Continued. School Establishment

England and the Continent—Civil Organisation in Modern States —Civil Organisation Transformed Not Only in France but Also in Other Continental States—Not in England—A Result of This in English Popular Education—English Secondary and Superior Instruction Not Touched by the State—Inconveniences of This—The Social Inconvenience—The Intellectual Inconvenience—Their Practical Results—Science and Systematic Knowledge More Prized on the Continent than in England—Effect of This on Our Application of the Sciences, and on Our Schools and Education in General— A Better Organisation of Secondary and Superior Instruction a Remedy for our Deficiencies—Public and Private Schools—Necessity for Public Schools—With Public Schools, an Education Minister Necessary—A High Council of Education Desirable—Functions of Such a Council—Provincial School Boards Requisite— How to Make Public Schools—Defects of Our University System —Oxford and Cambridge Merely Hauts Lycées—London University Merely a Board of Examiners—Insufficient Number of Students Under Superior Instruction in England—Special Schools Wanted, and a Reorganised University System, Taking Superior Instruction to the Students, and Not Bringing These Students to Oxford and Cambridge for It—Centres of Superior Instruction to be Formed in Different Parts of England, and Professors to be Organised in Faculties—Oxford, Cambridge, and London to Remain the Only Degree-Granting Bodies—Education Minister Should Have the Appointment of Professors—Probable Co-operation of Existing Bodies with the State in Organising this New Superior Instruction—How, When Established, It Should be Employed—Final Conclusion.

I come next to the second point for consideration: the mode of establishing and administering schools. I have now on two occasions, first in 1859 and again in 1865, had to make a close study, on the spot and for many months together, of one of

the most important branches of the civil organisation of the most civilised states of the Continent. Few Englishmen have had such an experience. If the convictions with which it leaves me seem strange to many Englishmen, it is not that I am dif-
5 ferently constituted from the rest of my countrymen, but that I have seen what would certainly give to them too, if they had seen it with their own eyes as I have, reflections which they never had before. No one of open mind, and not hardened in routine and prejudice, could observe for so
10 long and from so near as I observed it, the civil organisation of France, Germany, Italy, Switzerland, Holland, without having the conviction forced upon him that these countries have a civil organisation which has been framed with forethought and design to meet the wants of modern society; while our
15 civil organisation in England still remains what time and chance have made it. The States which we really resemble, in this respect, are Austria and Rome. I remember I had the honour of saying to Cardinal Antonelli, when he asked me what I thought of the Roman schools, that for the first time
20 since I came on the Continent I was reminded of England. I meant, in real truth, that there was the same easy-going and absence of system on all sides, the same powerlessness and indifference of the State, the same independence in single institutions, the same free course for abuses, the same confusion, the
25 same lack of all idea of *co-ordering* things, as the French say, —that is, of making them work fitly together to a fit end; the same waste of power, therefore, the same extravagance, and the same poverty of result, of which the civil organisation of England offers so many instances. To the like effect
30 a French publicist said the other day with great truth to the Austrian Government:—'La cour de Vienne comprendra-t-elle qu'il n'y a point de salut pour les états européens en dehors des idées modernes, c'est-à-dire des libres institutions populaires *et des organisations administratives positives et stricte-*
35 *ment contrôlées?*' We have in England the *libres institutions populaires,* so for us the point is in the last words of the sentence. Modern States cannot either do without free institutions, or do without a rationally planned and effective civil organi-

sation. Unlike in other things, Austria, Rome, and England are alike in this, that the civil organisation of each implies, at the present day, a denial or an ignorance of the right of mind and reason to rule human affairs. At Rome this right is sacrificed in the name of religion; in Austria, in the name of loyalty; in England, in the name of liberty. All respectable names; but none of them will in the long run save its invoker, if he persists in disregarding the inevitable laws which govern the life of modern society.

Every one is accustomed to hear that France paid the horrors of her great Revolution as the price for having a *tabula rasa* upon which to build a new civil organisation. But what one learns when one goes upon the Continent and looks a little closely into these things, is, that all the most progressive states of the Continent have followed the example of France, and have transformed or are transforming their civil organisation. Italy is transforming hers by virtue of the great opportunity which the events of the last eight years have given her. Prussia transformed hers from 1807 to 1812, by virtue of the stern lesson which her disasters and humiliation had then read her. Russia is at this moment accomplishing a transformation yet more momentous. The United States of America came into the world, it may be said, with a *tabula rasa* for a modern civil organisation to be built on, and they have never had any other. What I say is, that everywhere around us in the world, wherever there is life and progress, we find a civil organisation that is modern; and this in States which have not, like France, gone through a tremendous revolution, as well as in France itself.

Who will deny that England has life and progress? but who will deny also that her course begins to show signs of uncertainty and embarrassment? This is because even an energy like hers cannot exempt her from the obligation of obeying natural laws; and yet she tries to exempt herself from it when she endeavours to meet the requirements of a modern time and of modern society with a civil organisation which is, from the top of it to the bottom, not modern. Transform it she must, unless she means to come at last to the same sentence as the Church of Sardis: '*Thou hast a name that thou livest,*

and art dead.' However, on no part of this immense task of
transformation have I now to touch, except on that part which
relates to education. But this part, indeed, is the most important
of all; and it is the part whose happy accomplishment may ren-
5   der that of all the rest, instead of being troubled and difficult,
gradual and easy.

About popular education I have here but a very few words
to say. People are at last beginning to see in what condition
this really is amongst us. Obligatory instruction is talked of.
10 But what is the capital difficulty in the way of obligatory instruction, or indeed any national system of instruction, in this
country? It is this: that the moment the working class of this
country have this question of instruction really brought home
to them, their self-respect will make them demand, like the
15 working classes on the Continent, *public* schools, and not
schools which the clergyman, or the squire, or the mill-owner,
calls 'my school.' And what is the capital difficulty in the way
of giving them public schools? It is this: that the public school
for the people must rest upon the municipal organisation of
20 the country. In France, Germany, Italy, Switzerland, the public elementary school has, and exists by having, the commune
and the municipal government of the commune, as its foundations, and it could not exist without them. But we in England have our municipal organisation still to get; the country
25 districts, with us, have at present only the feudal and ecclesiastical organisation of the Middle Ages, or of France before the Revolution. This is what the people who talk so glibly
about obligatory instruction, and the Conscience Clause, and
our present abundant supply of schools, never think of. The
30 real preliminary to an effective system of popular education
is, in fact, to provide the country with an effective municipal
organisation; and here, then, is at the outset an illustration of
what I said, that modern societies need a civil organisation
which is modern.*

35   * France has now 37,500 communes, and nearly 37,500,000 inhabitants;
about one commune, therefore, to every 1,000 inhabitants. The mayor
of the commune is named by the Crown, and represents the State, the

We have nearly all of us reached the notion that popular education it is the State's duty to deal with. Secondary and superior instruction many of us still think should be left to take care of themselves. Well, this is what was generally thought, or at any rate practised, in old times, all over Europe. I have shown how the State's taking secondary instruction seriously in hand dates, in Prussia, from Wilhelm von Humboldt in 1809; in the same year, a year for Prussia of trouble and anxious looking forward, he created the University of Berlin. In Switzerland the State's effective dealing with all kinds of public instruction dates from within the last thirty years; in Italy it dates from 1859. In all these countries the idea of a sound civil organisation of modern society has been found to involve the idea of an organisation of secondary and superior instruction by public authority, by the State.

The English reader will ask: What inconvenience has arisen in England from pursuing the old practice? The investigations of the Schools Enquiry Commission, I feel sure, will have made it clear that we have not a body of 65,000 boys of the middle and upper classes receiving so good an instruction as 65,000 boys of the same classes are receiving in the higher schools of Prussia, or even of France. The English reader will not refuse to believe, though no Royal Commission has yet made enquiries on this point, that we have not a body of 6,300 university students in England receiving so good an instruc-

---

central power; the municipal council, of which the mayor is president, is elected by universal suffrage of the commune.

We have in England 655 unions and about 12,000 parishes; but our communes, or municipal centres, ought at the French rate to be 20,000 in number. Nor is this number, perhaps, more than is required in order to supply a proper basis for the national organisation of our elementary schools. A municipal organisation being once given, the object should be to withdraw the existing elementary schools from their present private management, and to reconstitute them on a municipal basis. This is not the place to enter into details as to the manner in which such a withdrawal is to be effected; I will remark only that all reforms which stop short of such a withdrawal and reconstitution are and must be mere patchwork.

tion as the 6,300 matriculated students in the Prussian universities, or even as the far more numerous students in the French
faculties, are receiving. Neither is the secondary and superior
instruction given in England on the whole so good, nor is it
given, on the whole, in schools of so good a standing. Of course,
what good instruction there is, and what schools of good
standing there are to get it in, fall chiefly to the lot of the
upper class. It is on the middle class that the inconvenience,
such as it is, of getting indifferent instruction, or getting it in
schools of indifferent standing, mainly comes. This inconvenience, as it strikes one after seeing attentively the schools
of the Continent, has two aspects. It has a social aspect, and it
has an intellectual aspect.

The social inconvenience is this. On the Continent, the
upper and middle class are brought up on one and the same
plane. In England the middle class, as a rule, *is brought up on
the second plane.* One hears many discussions as to the limits
between the middle and the upper class in England. From an
educational point of view these limits are perfectly clear.
Half-a-dozen famous schools, Oxford or Cambridge, the army
or navy, and those posts in the public service supposed to be
posts for gentlemen; these are the schools all or any one of
which give a training, a stamp, a cast of ideas, which make
a sort of association of all those who share them, and this association is the upper class. Except by one of these modes of
access an Englishman does not, unless by some special play
of aptitude or of circumstances, become a vital part of this
association, for he does not bring with him the cast of ideas
in which its bond of union lies. This cast of ideas is naturally
for the most part that of the most powerful and prominent
part of the association, the aristocracy. The professions furnish
the more numerous but the less prominent part; in no country, accordingly, do the professions so naturally and generally
share the cast of ideas of the aristocracy as in England. This
cast of ideas, judged from its good side, is characterised by
a high spirit, by dignity, by a just sense of the greatness of
great affairs,—all of them governing qualities; and the professions have accordingly long recruited the governing force

of the aristocracy, and assisted it to rule. Judged from its bad side, this cast of ideas is characterised by its indisposition and incapacity for science, for systematic knowledge. The professions are on the Continent the stronghold of science and systematic knowledge; in England, from the reason above assigned, they are not. They are also in England separate, to a degree unknown on the Continent, from the commercial and industrial class with which in social standing they are naturally on a level. So we have amongst us the spectacle of a middle class cut in two in a way unexampled anywhere else; of a professional class brought up on the first plane, with fine and governing qualities, but without the idea of science; while that immense business class, which is becoming so important a power in all countries, on which the future so much depends, and which in the leading schools of other countries fills so large a place, is in England brought up on the second plane, cut off from the aristocracy and the professions, and without governing qualities.

If only, in compensation, it had science, systematic knowledge! The stronghold of science should naturally be in a nation's middle class, who have neither luxury nor bodily toil to bar them from it. But here comes in the intellectual inconvenience of the bad condition of the mass of our secondary schools. On the Continent, if the professions were as aristocratic in their indifference to science as they are here, the business class, educated as it is, would at once wrest the lead from them, and would be fit to do so. But here in England, the business class is not only inferior to the professions in the social stamp of its places of training, it is actually inferior to them, maimed and incomplete as their intellectual development is, in its intellectual development. Short as the offspring of our public schools and universities come of the idea of science and systematic knowledge, the offspring of our middle class academies probably come, if that be possible, even shorter. What these academies fail to give in social and governing qualities, they do not make up for in intellectual power.

If this is true, then that our middle class does not yet itself see the defects of its own education, perceives no practical

inconvenience to itself from them, and is satisfied with things as they are, is no reason for regarding this state of things without disquietude. '*He that wandereth out of the way of understanding shall remain in the congregation of the dead;*' sooner
5 or later, in spite of his self-confidence, in spite of his energy, in spite of his capital, he must so remain, by virtue of nature's laws. But if the English business class can listen to testimonies that in the judgment of others, at any rate, its inferior education is beginning to threaten it with practical inconvenience,
10 such testimonies are formidably plentiful. A diplomatist of great experience, not an Englishman but much attached to England, who in the course of the acquisition and the construction of the Italian lines of railroad, had been brought much in contact with young men of business of all nations,
15 told me that the young Englishman of this class was manifestly inferior, both in manners and instruction, to the corresponding young men of other countries. That is, he had been brought up, as I say, on a lower plane. And the Swiss and Germans aver, if you question them as to the benefit they
20 have got from their *Realschulen* and Polytechnicums, that in every part of the world their men of business trained in those schools are beating the English when they meet on equal terms as to capital; and that when English capital, as so often happens, is superior, the advantage of the Swiss or the German
25 in instruction tends more and more to balance this superiority. M. Duruy, the French Minister of Public Instruction, confirms this averment, not as against England in especial, but generally, by saying that all over the Continent the young North German, or the young Swiss of Zurich or Basle, is seiz-
30 ing, by reason of his better instruction, a confidence and a command in business which the young men of no other nation can dispute with him. This confidence, whether as yet completely justified or not by success, is a force which will go far to ensure its own triumph.
35   But the idea of science and systematic knowledge is wanting to our whole instruction alike, and not only to that of our business class. While this idea is getting more and more power upon the Continent, and while its application there is leading

to more and more considerable results, we in England, having done marvels by the rule of thumb, are still inclined to disbelieve in the paramount importance, in whatever department, of any other. And yet in Germany every one will tell you that the explanation of the late astonishing achievements of 5 Prussia is simply that every one concerned in them had thoroughly learnt his business on the best plan by which it was possible to teach it to him. In nothing do England and the Continent at the present moment more strikingly differ than in the prominence which is now given to the idea of science 10 there, and the neglect in which this idea still lies here; a neglect so great that we hardly even know the use of the word science in its strict sense, and only employ it in a secondary and incorrect sense. The English notion,—for which there is much to be said if it were not pushed to such an excess,—is, 15 that you come to do a thing right by doing it, and not by first learning how to do it right and then doing it. The French, who in the extent and solidity of their instruction are, as a nation, so much behind the Germans, are yet in their idea of science quite in a line with the Germans, and ahead of us. 20 That is because there is in France a considerable highly instructed class into whose whole training this idea of science has come, and whose whole influence goes to procure its application. We have no considerable class of this kind. We have, probably, a larger reading class than the French, but 25 reading for amusement, not study; occupied with books of popular reading that leave the mind as inaccurate, as shallow, and as unscientific as it was before. The French have a much more considerable class than we have which really studies. A good test of this is the description of foreign books which 30 get translated. Now the English reader will perhaps be surprised to hear that a German scientific book of any sort,— on philosophy, history, art, religion, &c.,—is much more sure of being translated into French than it is into English. A popular story or a popular religious book is sure enough of being 35 translated into English; there is a public for a translation of that; but in France there is a public, not large certainly, but large enough to take an edition or two, for a translation of

works not of this popular character.* In Germany, of course, there is a yet far larger public of such a kind. The very matter of public instruction suggests an illustration on this point, and an illustration at my own expense. It has been quite the
5 order of the day here, for some years past, to discuss the subject of popular education. This is a subject which can no more be known without being treated comparatively, than anatomy can be known without being treated comparatively. When it was under discussion in foreign countries, these countries pro-
10 cured accounts of what was done for popular education elsewhere, which were published, found a public to study them for their bearing on the general question, and went through two or three editions. But I doubt whether two hundred people in this country have read Mr. Pattison's report, or mine,
15 on the popular schools of the Continent; simply because the notion of treating a matter of this kind as a matter of scientific study hardly occurs to any one in this country; but almost every one treats it as a matter which he can settle by the light of his own personal experience, and of what he calls his prac-
20 tical good sense.

Our rule of thumb has cost us dear already, and is probably destined to cost us dearer still. It is only by putting an unfair and extravagant strain on the wealth and energy of the country, that we have managed to hide from ourselves the incon-
25 venience we suffer, even in the lines where we think ourselves most successful, from our want of systematic instruction and science. I was lately saying to one of the first mathematicians in England, who has been a distinguished senior wrangler at Cambridge and a practical mechanician besides, that in one
30 department at any rate,—that of mechanics and engineering, —we seemed, in spite of the absence of special schools, good instruction, and the idea of science, to get on wonderfully well. 'On the contrary,' said he, 'we get on wonderfully ill.

* There is nothing like an illustration, so let me name these three
35 standard works, [G. F.] Creuzer's *Symbolik*, [Ludwig] Preller's *Römische Mythologie*, and [J.] von Hammer[-Purgstall]'s *Geschichte des Osmanischen Reiches*, of each of which there is a translation in French, and none in English.

Our engineers have no real scientific instruction, and we let them learn their business at our expense by the rule of thumb; but it is a ruinous system of blunder and plunder. A man without the requisite scientific knowledge undertakes to build a difficult bridge; he builds three which tumble down, and so learns how to build a fourth which stands; but somebody pays for the three failures. In France or Switzerland he would not have been suffered to build his first bridge until he had satisfied competent persons that he knew how to build it, because abroad they cannot afford our extravagance. The scientific training of the foreign engineers is therefore perfectly right. Take the present cost per mile of the construction of an English railway, and the cost per mile as it was twenty years ago; and the comparison will give you a correct notion of what rule-of-thumb engineering, without special schools and without scientific instruction, has cost the country.'

Our dislike of authority and our disbelief in science have combined to make us leave our school system, like so many other branches of our civil organisation, to take care of itself as it best could. Under such auspices, our school system has very naturally fallen all into confusion; and though properly an intellectual agency, it has done and does nothing to counteract the indisposition to science which is our great intellectual fault. The result is, that we have to meet the calls of a modern epoch, in which the action of the working and middle class assumes a preponderating importance, and science tells in human affairs more and more, with a working class not educated at all, a middle class educated on the second plane, and the idea of science absent from the whole course and design of our education.

On popular education I have already touched so far as is proper for my present purpose. Secondary, and superior instruction remain. It is through secondary instruction that the social inconvenience I spoke of is to be remedied. The intellectual inconvenience is to be remedied through superior instruction, at first acting by itself, and then, through the teachers whom it forms and its general influence on society, acting on the secondary schools. I will sketch, guided by the com-

parative study of education which I have been enabled to make,
the organisation of schools which seems to me required for
this purpose. My part is simply to say what organisation seems
to me to be required; it is for others to judge what organisation
seems to them possible, or advisable to be attempted. The times,
however, are moving; and what is not advisable to-day, may
perhaps be called for to-morrow.

But the English reader will hardly, I think, have accompanied
me through my long course, without sharing the conclusion
that at any rate a public system of schools is indispensable
in modern communities. From the moment you seriously desire to have your schools efficient, the question between public
and private schools is settled. Of public schools you can take
guarantees, of private schools you cannot. Guarantees cannot
be absolutely certain. It is possible for a private school, which
has given no guarantees, to be good; it is possible for a public
school, which has given guarantees, to be bad. But even in
England the disbelief in human reason is hardly strong enough
to make us seriously contend that a rational being cannot
frame for a known purpose guarantees which give him, at any
rate, more numerous chances of reaching that purpose than
he would have without them.

If public schools are a necessity, then an Education Minister
is a necessity. Merely for administrative convenience he is,
indeed, indispensable. But what is yet more important than
administrative convenience is to have, what an Education Minister alone supplies, *a centre in which to fix responsibility.**

The country at large is not yet educated enough, political
considerations too much overbear all others, for a minister with
a board of six or seven councillors, like the minister at Berlin,
to be left alone to perform such a task as the reconstruction
of public education in this country must at first be. A High
Council of Education, such as exists in France and Italy, comprising without regard to politics the personages most proper
to be heard on questions of public education, a consultative

* I need hardly point out that at present, with our Lord President,
Vice-President, and Committee of Council on Education, we entirely
fail to get, for primary instruction, this distinct centre of responsibility.

body only, but whose opinion the minister should be obliged
to take on all important measures not purely administrative,
would be an invaluable aid to an English Education Minister,
an invaluable institution in our too political country.

One or two matters on which I have already touched in   5
the course of this work are matters on which it would be the
natural function of such a Council to advise. It would be its
function to advise on the propriety of subjecting children
under a certain age to competitive examination, in order to
determine their admission to public foundations. It would be   10
its function to advise on the employment of the examination
test for the public service; whether this security should, as
at present, be relied on exclusively, or whether it should not
be preceded by securities for the applicant having previously
passed a certain time under training and teachers of a certain   15
character, and stood certain examinations in connection with
that training. It would be its function to advise on the organisation of school and university examinations, and their
adjustment to one another. It would be its function to advise
on the graduation of schools in proper stages, from the ele-   20
mentary to the highest school; it would be its function to
advise on school books, and, above all, on studies, and on the
plan of work for schools; a business which, as I have said, is
more and more inviting discussion and ripening for settlement. We have excellent materials in England for such a Coun-   25
cil. Properly composed, and properly representing the grave
interests concerned in the questions it has to treat, it would not
only have great weight with the minister, but great weight,
as an illustrious, unpaid, deliberative, and non-ministerial body,
with the country, and would greatly strengthen the minister's   30
hand for important reforms.

Provincial School Boards, too, we have in this country very
good materials for forming, and this institution of Germany is
well suited to our habits, supplies a basis for local action, and
preserves one from the inconveniences of an over-centralized   35
system like that of France. Eight or ten Provincial School
Boards should be formed, not too large, five or six members
being the outside number for each Board, and one member

being paid. This Board would be administrative; it would represent the State in the country, keeping the Education Minister informed of local requirements and of the state of schools
in each district; being the direct public organ of communica-
5 tion with the schools, superintending the execution of all public regulations applied to them, visiting them so far as may be
necessary, and representing the State by the presence of one
of its members at their main annual examinations. An elaborate
system of inspection, modelled on that of primary schools, is
10 out of place when applied to higher schools; the French school
authorities complained to me that they were over-inspected,
and no doubt there are evident and solid objections to putting
a *lycée* on the same footing, as regards inspection, with an elementary school. The Prussian system is far better, which re-
15 solves inspection, for higher schools, mainly into a concert
of the State with the school authorities in great examinations,
—as effective a way of inspection, in real truth, as can be found.
What special visits may happen to be required are best made,
as in Prussia, by members of the Provincial Boards, or by
20 councillors of the Central Department; and a staff of school
inspectors for higher schools is neither requisite nor desirable.

Where are the English higher schools, it will be asked, with
which this Minister, this Council, and these School Boards
are to deal? Guided by the experience of every country I
25 have visited, I will venture to lay down certain propositions
which may help to supply an answer to this question. Wherever there is a school-endowment, there is a right of public
supervision, and, if necessary, of a resettlement of the endowment by public authority. Wherever, again, there is a school
30 endowment from the Crown or the State, there is a right, to
the State, of participation in the management of the endowment, and of representation on the body which manages it.
These two propositions, which in ten years' time will even
in England be admitted on all hands to be indisputable, supply
35 all that is necessary for a public system of education. School
endowments will certainly be dealt with ere long, and the
extraordinary immunity which from the peculiar habits and
isolation of this country the corporations or private trustees

administering them have hitherto enjoyed, is really a reason for applying the principles of common sense and public policy, when they are at last applied to these matters, the more stringently instead of the less stringently. Endowments enough have merited an absolute withdrawal from their present bad application, and an absolute appropriation by public authority for the purposes of a better application, to furnish the State with means for creating, as a commencement, a certain number of Royal or Public schools, to be under the direct control of the Education Department and the Provincial Boards; and in which all the regulations for management, fees, books, studies, methods, and examinations, devised by public authority as most expedient, should have force unreservedly. Other schools would be found offering to place themselves under public administration, as soon as this administration began to inspire respect and confidence; and organised rightly, it would immediately inspire respect and confidence. A body of truly public schools would thus be formed, offering to the middle classes places of instruction with sound securities and with an honourable standing. Nor would these new schools long be in antagonism with our present chief schools, and following a different line of movement from them. Some of our present chief schools, like Eton and Westminster and Christ's Hospital, are royal foundations. Here the right of the State to have a share in the whole administration of the institution, and a voice in the nomination of the masters, immediately arises. Others, like Winchester, Rugby, and Harrow, are not royal foundations, but all of them are foundation schools, and therefore to all of them, as such, a right of public supervision applies. The best form this supervision can possibly take is that of a participation, as in Germany, by the public authority represented through the Provincial School Boards or through members of the High Council of Education, in their main examinations. On these examinations matriculation at the university,* and access to all the higher lines of public employment, should

* But there should be a different matriculation examination for each faculty, and, except for the faculties of theology and arts, Greek should not be required.

be made to depend. The pupils of private schools should be
admitted to undergo them. In this way every endowed school
in the kingdom would have yearly an all-important examination following a line traced or sanctioned by the most com-
5 petent authority, the Superior Council of Education; and
with a direct or indirect representation of this authority taking part in it. The organisation of studies in our very best
schools could not fail to gain by this; in all but the very best,
it would be its regeneration. Even in England, where the gen-
10 eral opinion would be opposed to requiring, as in Germany,
for the appointment of all public schoolmasters the sanction
of a public authority, there could be no respectable objections
urged to such a mode of public intervention as this; the one
bulwark, to repeat Wilhelm von Humboldt's words, which
15 we can set up against the misuse of their patronage by private
trustees. And we should at the same time get the happiest
check put to the cram and bad teaching of private schools,
by compelling them either to adjust their studies to sound and
serious examinations, or to cease to impose upon the credulity
20 of ignorant parents.

The mention of the matriculation examination brings me
to superior or university instruction. This is, in the opinion
of the best judges, the weakest part of our whole educational
system, and we must not hope to improve effectually the
25 secondary school without doing something for the schools
above it, with which it has an intimate natural connection.
The want of the idea of science, of systematic knowledge, is, as
I have said again and again, the capital want, at this moment, of
English education and of English life; it is the university, or the
30 superior school, which ought to foster this idea. The university
or the superior school ought to provide facilities, after the general education is finished, for the young man to go on in the
line where his special aptitudes lead him, be it that of languages
and literature, of mathematics, of the natural sciences, of the
35 application of these sciences, or any other line, and follow
the studies of this line systematically under first-rate teaching. Our great universities, Oxford and Cambridge, do next
to nothing towards this end. They are, as Signor Matteucci

called them, *hauts lycées;* and though invaluable in their way
as places where the youth of the upper class prolong to a very
great age, and under some very admirable influences, their
school education, and though in this respect to be envied by
the youth of the upper class abroad and if possible instituted   5
for their benefit, yet, with their college and tutor system, nay,
with their examination and degree system, they are still, in
fact, *schools*, and do not carry education beyond the stage
of general and school education. The examination for the degree of bachelor of arts, which we place at the end of our   10
three years' university course, is merely the *Abiturientenexamen* of Germany, the *épreuve du baccalauréat* of France,
placed in both those countries at the entrance to university
studies instead of, as with us, at their close. Scientific instruction, university instruction, really begins when the degree   15
of bachelor (*bas chevalier*, knight of low degree) is taken,
and the preparation for mastership in any line of study, or for
doctorship (fitness to teach it), commences. But for mastership
or doctorship, Oxford and Cambridge have, as is well known,
either no examination at all, or an examination which is a mere   20
form; they have consequently no instruction directed to these
grades; no real university instruction, therefore, at all. A machinery for such instruction they have, indeed, in their possession; but it is notorious that they do not practically use it.

    The University of London labours under a yet graver defect   25
as an organ of scientific or superior instruction. It is a mere
collegium, or board, of examiners. It gives no instruction at
all, but it examines in the different lines of study, and gives
degrees in them. It has real university examinations, which
Oxford and Cambridge have not; and these examinations are   30
conducted by an independent board, and not by college tutors.
This is excellent; but nevertheless it falls immensely short of
what is needed. The idea of a university is, as I have already
said, that of an institution not only offering to young men facilities for graduating in that line of study to which their apti-   35
tudes direct them, but offering to them, also, *facilities for
following that line of study systematically, under first-rate
instruction*. This second function is of incalculable impor-

tance; of far greater importance, even, than the first. It is
impossible to overvalue the importance to a young man of
being brought in contact with a first-rate teacher of his matter
of study, and of getting from him a clear notion of what the
systematic study of it means. Such instruction is so far from
being yet organised in this country, that it even requires a
gifted student to feel the want of it; and such a student must
go to Paris, or Heidelberg, or Berlin, because England cannot
give him what he wants. Some do go; an admirable English
mathematician who did not, told me that he should never recover the loss of the two years which after his degree he
wasted without fit instruction at an English university, when
he ought to have been under superior instruction, for which
the present university course in England makes no provision. I
dare say he *will* recover it, for a man of genius counts no
worthy effort too hard; but who can estimate the loss to the
mental training and intellectual habits of the country, from
an absence,—so complete that it needs genius to be sensible
of it, and costs genius an effort to repair it,—of all regular
public provision for the scientific study and teaching of any
branch of knowledge?

England has twenty millions of inhabitants, and the matriculated students in England number about 3,500. Prussia,—the
Prussia of this volume,—has 18,500,000 inhabitants, and 6,362
matriculated students. France has at least as large a proportion
of her population coming under superior instruction. England, with her wealth and importance, has barely one-half the
proportion of her population coming, even nominally, under
superior instruction, that Prussia and France have. But this
comparison by no means gives the full measure of her disadvantage, because, as I have just shown, Oxford and Cambridge being in reality but *hauts lycées*, and London University being only a board of examiners, the vast majority of
even the 3,500 students of superior instruction whom England nominally possesses, do not, in fact, come under superior
instruction at all. This entire absence of the crowning of the
edifice not only tends to give us, as I have said, a want of scientific intellect in all departments, but it tends to weaken and

obliterate, in the whole nation, the sense of the value and importance of human knowledge; to vulgarise us, to exaggerate
our estimate, naturally excessive, of the importance of material
advantages, and to make our teachers, all but the very best of
them, pursue their calling in a mere trade spirit, and with an 5
eye to little except these advantages.

Exactly the same effect which in the field of university teaching our want of any real course of superior instruction produces, is produced, in the field of the applied sciences, by our
want of special schools like the School of Arts and Trades in 10
Paris, or the *Gewerbe-Institut* of Berlin, or the Zurich Polytechnicum. It is the same crowning of the edifice of instruction
which is wanting in both cases; the same bad intellectual habits
and defective intellectual action, which are in both cases fos-
tered by this want. Our Science and Art Department at South 15
Kensington is a new experiment in this country, and has been
a mark for much obloquy here. I am totally unconnected with
that department; I am barely acquainted with Mr. Cole who
directs it, and I have not the special knowledge requisite for
criticising its operations. But I am bound to say that every- 20
where on the Continent I found a strong interest directed to
this department, a strong sense of its importance and of the
excellent effect it had already produced on our industry, with
a conviction that in the mere interests of this industry we
should be obliged to go on and give to this idea of a special 25
school greater development. I, too, believe that we must have
a system of special schools; but this is a subject which well
deserves a separate study, and some one to treat it who is better qualified for the business than I am. I touch on it here
merely as a branch of the great subject of superior instruction, 30
—the instruction which is properly, and in all but special cases,
to be given by universities.

To extend this amongst us is the great matter. Considering
the wealth and occupations of the middle and upper classes
of this country, we ought to have at least 8,000 students com- 35
ing under this instruction. The Education Department, by the
leaving examination which I have mentioned,—an examination
to be held at the different schools and to represent the present

matriculation examination,—should take the admission of university students entirely out of the hands of the colleges, and
thus save Oxford and Cambridge from the absolute *non-
valeurs* (to use M. Duruy's term) of which at present, owing
5 to the laches of many of the colleges, they have far too many.
The degree examination should be taken out of the hands of
the college tutors, and entrusted, for reasons which I will
give presently, to a board of examiners named by public authority. Beyond these changes, it is not in Oxford and Cam-
10 bridge that the great work to be done is to be accomplished.
All around me I hear people talking of university reform, university extension; all these projects end in Oxford or Cambridge, and the most liberal of them with a year's residence
there. If there is one thing which my foreign experience has
15 left me convinced of,—as convinced of as I am of our actual
want of superior instruction,—it is this: that we must take
this instruction to the students, and not hope to bring the
students to the instruction. We must get out of our heads all
notion of making the mass of students come and reside three
20 years, or two years, or one year, or even one month, at Oxford
or Cambridge, which neither suit their circumstances nor offer
them the instruction they want. We must plant faculties in the
eight or ten principal seats of population, and let the students
follow lectures there from their own homes, or with what-
25 ever arrangements for their living they and their parents
choose. It would be everything for the great seats of population to be thus made intellectual centres as well as mere places
of business; for the want of this at present, Liverpool and
Leeds are mere overgrown provincial towns, while Strasbourg
30 and Lyons are European cities. Oxford and Cambridge would
contribute in the noblest and most useful way to the spread of
university instruction, if they placed a number of their professors,—of whom they themselves make little use owing to
the college system,—in these new faculties, to be established
35 in London or the provinces, where they might render incalculable service, and still retaining the title of Oxford or Cambridge professors, unite things new and old, and help in the
happiest manner to inaugurate a truly national system of su-

perior instruction. Oxford and Cambridge can from the nature of things be now-a-days important schools only in theology, arts, and the mathematical and natural sciences. Owing to their college system, which for certain purposes, as I have said, and for a certain class, works well, they do not really need half their professors in even these three faculties, and could spare half of them for use elsewhere. They are actually bad places for schools in law and medicine, and all their professors in these faculties they might with advantage employ where there would be a better field for their services. All future application of Oxford and Cambridge emoluments to national purposes might, with advantage to the country, and honour to Oxford and Cambridge themselves, be made in this direction of endowing chairs for professors and exhibitions for students in university faculties to be organised in the great towns of England. The University of London should be re-cast and faculties formed in connection with it, in order to give some public voice and place to superior instruction in the richest capital of the world; and for this purpose the strangely devised and anomalous organisations of King's College and University College should be turned to account, and *co-ordered*, as the French say, with the University of London. Contributions from Oxford and Cambridge, and new appointments, might supply what was wanting to fill the faculties, which in London, the capital of the country, should, as at Paris or Berlin, be very strong. London would then really have, what it has not at present, a university.

It is with our superior instruction as with so much else; we have plenty of scattered materials, but these materials need to be co-ordered, and made, instead of being useless or getting in one another's way as at present, to work harmoniously to one great design. This design should be, to form centres of superior instruction in at least ten different parts of England, with first-rate professors to give this instruction. These professors should of course be grouped in faculties, each faculty having its dean. So entirely have Oxford and Cambridge become mere *hauts lycées*, so entirely has the very idea of a real university been lost by them, that the professors there are not

even organised in faculties; and their action is on this account alone, if it were not on other accounts also, perfectly feeble and incoherent. The action of professors grouped in faculties, and concerting, as the professors and *Privatdocenten* of a
5　faculty concert in Germany, their instruction together, is quite another thing. In a place like London all the five faculties of arts, mathematical and natural sciences, theology, law, and medicine, should of course be represented; but it is by no means necessary that each centre of superior instruction should have
10　all these five faculties. Durham, for instance, ought probably to have, as I think a Royal Commission once proposed, but two faculties,—a faculty of theology, and a faculty of mathematical and natural sciences. The requirements of different localities, and the facilities they offer for certain lines, must be taken into
15　account. It is evident, for example, that faculties of medicine are best placed in very large towns, where hospitals and hospital patients are numerous.

Neither is it by any means necessary, or even expedient, that each centre of faculties should have the power of conferring
20　degrees. To maintain a uniform standard of examination and a uniform value for degrees is most important, and this is impossible when there are too many bodies examining for degrees and giving them. Germany suffers from having too many universities granting degrees, and from these degrees bearing
25　a very unequal value. We have two old and important universities, Oxford and Cambridge; one new and important university, London, and we want no more degree-granting bodies than these. The different centres of faculties throughout the country should be in connection with one or other of the
30　universities, according as they may have received professors from them, or may be nearest to one or the other of them; and each of these three universities should have its board of examiners, composed of professors holding chairs in its district, and with the Superior Council of Education represented on
35　each board. Thus composing your examining board substantially of professors, you would avoid the objection urged against the present examinations of the London University, that they are *in the air*, and that their standard fluctuates;

composing it from among the professors of a third part of England, you would avoid the inconveniences of letting the teachers of any set of students have the sole decision of the degrees to be granted to them. All lesser examinations, such as should at the end of each year be held in order to deter-   5
mine whether the student makes progress and is to be allowed to go on with his course, belong naturally, in each centre, to the professors in that centre.

Such a system as that of which I have thus given the bare outline, can be properly organised only by an Education Min-   10
ister, with the concert and advice of a Superior Council of Public Instruction, and, if necessary, with the help of a public grant. The intervention of the State becomes especially neces-sary in superior instruction, because here the body of public opinion educated enough to discern what is wanted gets smaller   15
than ever, while the importance of organising your instruction well and committing it to first-rate men becomes greater than ever. It is not from any love of bureaucracy that men like Wilhelm von Humboldt, ardent friends of human dignity and liberty, have had recourse to a department of State in organ-   20
ising universities; it is because an Education Minister supplies you, for the discharge of certain critical functions, the agent who will perform them in the greatest blaze of daylight and with the keenest sense of responsibility. Convocation made me a professor, and I am very grateful to Convocation; but Con-   25
vocation is not a fit body to have the appointment of pro-fessors. It is far too numerous, and the sense of responsibility does not tell upon it strongly enough. A board is not a fit body to have the appointment of professors; men will connive at a job as members of a board who single-handed would   30
never have perpetrated it. Even the Crown, that is, the Prime Minister, is not the fit power to have the appointment of professors, for the Prime Minister is above all a political func-tionary, and feels political influences overwhelmingly. An Education Minister, directly representing all the interests of   35
learning and intelligence in this great country, a full mark for their criticism and conscious of his responsibility to them, *that* is the power to whom to give the appointment of professors,

not for his own sake, but for the sake of public education. Even if the appointment of professors at Oxford and Cambridge be left as at present, the appointment of every professor in the new faculties should be vested in the Education Minister, and he should be responsible for it; though the faculties should have the right, as they have abroad, of themselves proposing to him candidates they may think proper.

Putting Oxford and Cambridge out of the question, all other places in England, even London, would have so much to gain by a regular public organisation being given to superior instruction in them, and by their professors acquiring the status and authority of public functionaries, that I cannot doubt that bodies like the Senate of the London University, the Council of London University College, or the trustees of Owens College at Manchester, would gladly co-operate with an Education Minister in transforming and co-ordering their institutions so as to give them a national character and an increased effectiveness. Several of the personages in the Senate of the London University are personages who would naturally have a place in any Superior Council of Public Instruction. Following the Prussian division of school interests into *externa* and *interna*, trustees might remain charged with *externa*, the management of property; while *interna*, the appointment of professors and the organisation of faculties, devolved upon the Education department. The great towns chosen to be the seats of the new faculties would most of them gladly charge themselves with providing a fit habitation for a public establishment adding so much to their resources and importance. Many of them would furnish an annual contribution to the expenses of the faculties. I believe there would be more chance of a brisk competition among the chief towns for the honour of being made seats of university faculties, than of their undervaluing it. At any rate, no such town would be the seat of them long without learning to value them. The important thing is to establish them.

Once established, they should be employed as in a country which, relying on its good intentions, its industry, and its wealth, has too long set at nought Solomon's warning: '*They that hate instruction love death.'* The end to have in view is, that every one who presents himself to exercise any calling, shall have received for a certain length of time the best instruction preliminary to that calling. This is not, it must be repeated again and again, an absolute security for his exercising the calling well, but it is the best security. It is a thousand times better security than the mere examination-test on which with such ignorant confidence we are now, in cases where we take any security at all, leaning with our whole weight. The Civil Service Examination should be used in strict subordination to this better and ampler security, and with a view of keeping it real. For some classes of post in the public service the having passed the leaving examination of a public school ought to be demanded; for others, the having gone through the appointed courses and passed the appointed examinations in certain faculties or in certain special schools; for all, one or the other. Then, and not till then, may come in, as a confirmatory and supplementary test, a rationally regulated civil service examination. No minister of religion, to whom, as such, any public functions are assigned, no magistrate, no schoolmaster of a higher school, no lawyer, no doctor, should be allowed to exercise his function without having come for a certain time under superior instruction and passed its examinations. The Pharmaceutical Society should be co-ordered with the faculties of medicine, and no druggist should be allowed to practise without its instruction and certificates. It is with the industrial class that the great difficulty of applying superior instruction arises; this class so large, wealthy, and important, and which needs superior instruction so much just because it feels that it needs it so little. Owens College at Manchester with its 100 students, and London University with its 450 students (even if these, who have no appointed faculty instruction, are to be called university students at all), sufficiently show, what is well known, that practically the English industrial class cannot be said to come under superior instruction at all. Their present indifference to it, however, affords no true criterion for judging of their probable willingness to accept it if it were properly organised, brought home to their

doors, and made compatible with the necessary conditions of
their lives.

Thus I have attempted to sketch in outline the plan of
reorganisation for English instruction which is suggested almost irresistibly by a study of public instruction in other
European countries, and of the actual condition and prospects
of the modern world. To make that study and to render an
account of it has been a long and laborious task. The reader
will, I hope, be indulgent to the many imperfections which
he will find in my performance of it. It was a task for many
parts of which I was ill qualified; and it was a task almost beyond any one man's powers, however qualified. He will also
pardon anything which may seem too trenchant and absolute
in the manner in which I have conveyed my criticisms and suggestions. In the first place, the pressure of matter and space
almost obliged me to use great plainness and shortness, and to
cut off all accompaniments of deprecation and apology. In
the second place, I have a profound conviction that if our country is destined, as I trust it is destined, still to live and prosper,
the next quarter of a century will see a reconstruction of English education as entire as that which I have recommended in
these remarks, however impossible such a reconstruction may
to many now seem.

Seven years ago, having been sent by a Royal Commission
to study the primary schools on the Continent, I was so much
struck by all I then saw, and by the comparison of it with
what I had left behind me in England, that looking beyond
the immediate scope of my errand, I said to my countrymen
on my return: *Organise your secondary instruction.* That advice passed perfectly unheeded, the hubbub of our sterile
politics continued, ideas of social reconstruction had not a
thought given them, our secondary instruction is still the chaos
it was; and yet now, so urgent and irresistible is the impression left upon me by what I have again seen abroad, I cannot help presenting myself once more to my countrymen with
an increased demand: *Organise your secondary and your superior instruction.*

German and English Universities

Professor Von Sybel, with whom English readers have lately been made acquainted through Dr. Perry's valuable translation of his work on the French Revolution, made the other day at Bonn, his own university, a speech about the German universities, and those of France and England, which he has   5
since printed as a pamphlet, and which has in it much to interest English people at the present moment.

For the first time the public of this country is beginning to look with some attention at the schools and universities of foreign countries. But he who turns for the first time his   10
attention to a subject of this kind needs much practice and much experience before he rightly learns what to look at and how to look at it. The report of M. Duruy's Commissioners on our secondary schools, which has lately attracted so much notice here, supplies, by the sort of comments it has called   15
forth, a good illustration of the want of this discriminating point of view. English critics read this report with Eton, Harrow, Rugby, and our other chief public schools before their minds, and, finding that the French Commissioners discover much to admire and envy in these great schools, come to the   20
conclusion that "foreign schools," as, lumping them all together, they call them, are not by any means so good as we have been told, and that we ought not to be in too great a hurry to make root-and-branch reforms in our own schools. Now the right way for us in England to regard the public   25
secondary schools of France is not as objects of comparison with our half-dozen great public schools, but as establishments educating some 65,000 of the youth of France, while our only schools of equal status educate but some 5,000 of

the youth of England. The study of the Greek language and
literature goes so little way in the French schools that probably
the French Commissioners themselves could neither well appreciate the difference, in respect of this study, between the best
5   scholars turned out every year by Harrow or Rugby, and the
best scholars turned out by a French *lycée,* nor adequately
measure the superiority which this far better knowledge of
Greek, this directer hold upon the great tradition of antiquity,
confined though it even be to our best schoolboys only, must,
10 in the eyes of every true lover of the humanities, confer upon
the English public schools. No German humanist would have
any doubt about this matter. He would be astounded, and
so must every well-informed man be astounded, to see that the
notions of English school reformers seem almost limited to
15 an eternal canvassing of the merits and demerits of our half-
dozen best schools, and our five thousand luckiest schoolboys,
while the condition of the unhappy mass of our secondary
schools, to which a French *lycée* is almost what Heidelberg
or Berlin are to Mr. Spurgeon's new Baptist College, can
20 hardly win from us more than a passing notice.

An Englishman ought, therefore, to regard above all, in
the public secondary and superior instruction of France, the
quantity of work done, and not to spend too much of his
time in canvassing its quality. A great deal of work is there
25 done of a tolerable quality; but the remarkable point is that it
is such a great deal, not that it is of such new and noteworthy
quality. With Germany it is different. There too, indeed, as
in France, the quantity of service rendered to the nation by
its public establishments of secondary and superior instruction
30 may well fix an Englishman's attention; there, too, as in
France, thousands and thousands of middle-class boys are
under competent and tested instructors, who with us would
be a prey to mercenary and ignorant pretenders. But in
Germany the quality of the teaching and training deserves
35 careful attention from us as well as its quantity. In its quality,
also, we shall find much that is new to us, much that is the
best of its kind in Europe, and either unique, or the model
of whatever is best of the same kind elsewhere; much, there-

fore, from which we may get valuable suggestions for our own use.

Above all is this the case with superior or university instruction. Of the German secondary schools, as of ours, the aim is a preliminary general training and strengthening of the mind, and a giving to it the materials to work with. This process Harrow or Rugby effect, on the whole, as well as a Prussian *gymnasium;* in some respects they may be inferior to the foreign institution, but in others they are certainly superior. The important difference between us and Germany comes later. It comes in the universities. With us the universities are, at best, but the continuation of the sixth form of Eton, Harrow, or Rugby; they are, as the French report calls them, *hauts lycées;* as Dr. Von Sybel says, "nothing else but the *gymnasium* still, the formal cultivation of the spirit being now, as before, the dominant problem." In a German university, on the other hand, the aim, the dominant problem, is no longer the formal cultivation of the spirit; it is *science*— the concentration of the spirit upon a definite branch of knowledge, the systematic study of this branch, and, finally, the sense of a first-hand, independent, sure mastery of it. This is, in German eyes, as indispensable a preparation for practical life as the formal preliminary training of the secondary school, and is, indeed, the due crown and complement of that. In this way alone can the young German, to quote Dr. Von Sybel's own words, "qualify himself, through the strict service of science, to be of avail in the service of his country."

One thing, however, Dr. Von Sybel envies the English universities, and we shall all be curious to know what it is. It is not their discipline, or their studies, or their exclusion of Nonconformists, or their shelter to orthodoxy. It is their endowments. At a moment when every one in England has a hard word for our endowments, when Mr. Gladstone would tax them, Mr. Lowe pitch them into the sea, when Mr. Bright invites them to compare their stunted fruits with the majestic produce of voluntaryism, when Professor Seeley shakes his head at them as hindrances to knowledge, when Mr. Hobhouse, the Charity Commissioner, proclaims that "the shade of the pious founder stands in the path and blights every suggestion for improvement," at this moment stands forth a Prussian professor to say that "here, indeed, Germany may well cast her eyes over towards England in humble admiration, and envy an endowment of learning which exceeds the German endowment of it three times as much as the national wealth of England exceeds that of Germany."

The reason, too, which makes Dr. Von Sybel thus envious of our endowments at this moment will surprise us. Just when we are straining our ingenuity to shorten the terms and expedite the cuts for our votaries of knowledge, in order to keep them as little while as possible from the field of their invaluable practical activity, comes this dauntless German professor, saying that the sum of knowledge, in every line of study, has doubled during the last fifty years, that the worth and force of the nation will suffer if its youth perform their studies superficially and incompletely, that three years is no longer enough for a university student who wants to master his branch of study thoroughly, and that the university course ought to be five years long instead of three. It is to make this prolongation of their term of study possible and tolerable for students who now bear pinching of poverty and straining of health to an extent of which we in England have little notion, that Dr. Von Sybel casts longing eyes towards our scholarships and fellowships.

We know by experience that endowments will not of themselves create or keep alive the scientific spirit and the love of the things of the mind. But we do an injustice to our endowments if we impute to them our prevalent want of the scientific spirit and our indifference to the things of the mind. These shortcomings are due to a far different cause, and if they are ever removed and the love of the things of the mind awakens amongst us, our endowments of learning will be invaluable, and their worth will be deeply felt by us. This is a reflection which Dr. Von Sybel's remarks may well suggest to us. But his speech may do us a yet greater service by putting clearly before us the true aim and office of a university, as Germany conceives them. Only what is attractive and has

promise of good persuades us; what is aggressive and nega-
tive rouses our opposition, and at last can only conquer us,
not persuade us; yet our adhesion is only worth having when
we are persuaded, not conquered. We confess to having some
sympathy with Dr. Pusey and Mr. Liddon in their resistance 5
to Mr. Goldwin Smith and most of the Oxford reformers, in
whom party and political excitement annuls, or at least ob-
scures, the scientific spirit. Dr. Pusey has, indeed, far beyond
most Oxford professors, and far beyond most Oxford reformers, done in his own line of study the proper work of a uni- 10
versity man; but putting this out of the question, the old
Oxford which he and Mr. Liddon defend, the place of discipline, authority, and shelter, the continuation of the public
school, is a thing which they know and are used to, which
has its merits, which has its attractiveness, and which may 15
well be defended and even loved. They will not love it less
because the House of Commons gives Mr. Goldwin Smith the
satisfaction of mustering his Ironsides under Dr. Pusey's window, or lets the Positivist priest take his turn at St. Mary's
with Mr. Liddon. The victory of one set of political and 20
religious partisans over another will do nothing to improve
Oxford; what both sides need, what Oxford needs, is to love
science more than politics and partisanship. It is because the
German universities love science that Dr. Von Sybel, in spite
of a passing fear about the dangers which threaten the thor- 25
oughness of studies, accepts for the German universities the
praise which the best-informed foreigners—M. Renan, Mr.
Pattison, Mr. Grant Duff—shower upon them, and begins
and ends his speech by asserting their "incomparable advantages." The true, persuasive, and fruitful answer to the Bishop 30
of Oxford and the lovers of our old university system is not
a diatribe against their bigotry and obstructiveness; it is such
a conception of the functions of a university, and of the
worth of science, as is presented by the following words of
Dr. Von Sybel:— 35

If the German nation has in the last hundred years found strength
to make the most powerful advance in every direction, the most
important impulse to its progress has probably been given here.

It is impossible to rate too highly the advantage of our highest places of learning having in their inmost nature the tendency to the complete freeing of the human spirit. In the secondary school which precedes them authority does and must rule the whole man;
5 a little later, practical life, and again authority along with it, gets a considerable part of him. *But at least one moment in his life every educated man on German soil is to have, when the organs of authority, when nation, State, and teachers themselves, as the first and foremost of their injunctions to him, lay upon him this com-*
10 *mand—to be spiritually free.* In the strength of his own soul, by the light of independent knowledge, to cut the way of life for himself—that is the aim which the university system of Germany sets up before its scholars. The individual may, as the result of his studies and labours here, follow this line or that; he may be
15 liberal or conservative, reactionary or progressive, orthodox or heretical: *for us, the essential thing is only, that whatever he be, he be it not out of youthful habit, vague disposition, traditional obedience, but that he be it, from this time forward, upon scientific appreciation, critical verification, independent decision.*

Glossary

aggregation: the acquisition of the certificate, after examination, without which one cannot hold the higher teaching posts in the French secondary schools or universities. See pp. 65–66, 134.

bifurcation: the division of students at the upper levels of the French secondary schools into a scientific section and a literary section. See p. 83.

bursar: one who holds a bursarship or bursary; that is, an endowment given to a student at a school or university.

commoner: a student at a school or university who is not on the foundation; that is, who does not hold a scholarship or an exhibition.

commune: the unit of municipal government in France: either a town or city or a territorial division of the countryside, in which latter sense it corresponds to the American township.

consistory: originally a bishop's court; in protestant Germany "a board of clerical officers, local, provincial, or national, usually appointed by the sovereign, and charged with the supervision of ecclesiastical affairs."—*N.E.D.*

estimate: the annual budget (in this case, of a school).

exhibition: "a fixed sum given for a term of years from the funds of a school, college, or university, generally upon the result of a competitive examination."—*N.E.D.* It is the same as a bursarship and in American usage is embraced in the term "scholarship"; in England, a scholarship is generally larger than an exhibition, carries greater distinction, and may give some legal status in the government of the foundation.

form: "one of the numbered classes into which the pupils of a school are divided according to their degree of proficiency." —*N.E.D.* In American usage, a "grade." The highest form in an English school is the sixth; in a Continental school, it is the first.

foundationer: "one who is 'on the foundation' of an endowed school or college" (*N.E.D.*); that is, an exhibitioner or scholar.

franc: the unit of currency in France and Switzerland, in 1865 worth 9½*d.* or nearly 20¢. Arnold uses the term also for the Italian *lira*, which had the same value.

ordinary: the archbishop in a province, bishop or bishop's deputy in a diocese, viewed as having immediate jurisdiction in cases at ecclesiastical law.

preparatory school: in British usage a junior school, one that comes before the grammar school or public school. Boys customarily left it about the age of twelve.

thaler: the unit of currency in Prussia, in 1865 worth about three shillings or 75¢.

usher: an assistant to a schoolmaster.

Critical and Explanatory Notes

References to Arnold's diary-notebooks are drawn from H. F. Lowry, K. Young and W. H. Dunn, eds., *The Note-Books of Matthew Arnold* (London, 1952), supplemented by W. B. Guthrie, ed., *Matthew Arnold's Diaries: the Unpublished Items* (Ann Arbor, 1959). Most quotations from Arnold's letters, unless otherwise identified, are taken from the collection edited by G. W. E. Russell, where they can be found under their dates; the collection has been published in so many editions that page references are not helpful. A very few quotations are from unpublished letters.

[EDUCATION AND THE STATE]

"You ask for the Pall Mall Gazette with my letter," Arnold wrote to his mother on December 21, 1865. "I sent it to K [his sister Mrs. Forster] and did not ask for it back. Last night there was a leading article on the subject of my letter, and now I have written another letter, which I will send you, if it appears. They give me three guineas for a letter, so it is a correspondence which pays; however I would gladly not write, but the subject interests me so much that I do not like to lose any chance of making an impression.... If you take the Evening Star still, I advise you to drop it and take the Pall Mall Gazette—it is well worth the extra penny." And nine days later he wrote to her, "There was a second letter of mine in the Pall Mall Gazette; I don't know whether you saw it. It took a line you would say was after Papa's own heart, and opened with quoting a passage from Wither, in Coleridge's Church and State, of which Papa was very fond."

The two letters to which he referred, published December 11 and 22, 1865, were his first contributions to the daily newspaper to which he continued to send most of his ephemeral work for the next nineteen years. The *Pall Mall Gazette* was founded in February,

337

1865, under the proprietorship of George Smith (of Smith, Elder), proprietor also of *The Cornhill Magazine* (to which by this time Arnold sent most of his serious essays) and from 1867 publisher of most of Arnold's successive volumes of prose. Payment for contributions to the *Gazette* was by the length of the contribution; Professor Neiman has established that it was usually two guineas a column, and thus Arnold's accounts for 1865 show that though he received three guineas for the first letter, the second brought him only two guineas. His diary has the memorandum on Friday, December 8, "finish P.M.G. art." and on Thursday, December 21, "write P.M.G. letter."—ed. W. B. Guthrie (Ann Arbor: University Microfilms, 1959). The pseudonymous signature "A Lover of Light" was one Arnold used for a letter in the *Daily News* of March 25, 1862 (*Prose Works*, ed. Super, II, 244–46). The two letters were first attributed to Arnold by J. P. Kirby in an unpublished dissertation on *Friendship's Garland* (Yale University, 1937), and first publicly by Marion Mainwaring, "Notes Toward a Matthew Arnold Bibliography," *Modern Philology* XLIX, 191 (February, 1952); they were edited with valuable notes by Fraser Neiman, *Essays, Letters, and Reviews by Matthew Arnold* (Cambridge, Mass.: Harvard University Press, 1960), pp. 102–7.

The Committee of Council's Revised Code of 1862 drastically reduced the government grants to the colleges set up for the training of teachers and a minute of March 21, 1863, made them "retrospective" rather than "prospective"—that is, instead of basing them on the number of students at the college, it based them on the number who actually entered and continued in the teaching profession. It provided also that the government grants should not exceed seventy-five per cent of the approved annual expense of a training college. A further provision of the Revised Code (article 22b), the so-called "conscience clause," was understood to compel the managers of schools built with the aid of grants to exempt from dogmatic instruction and worship the children of all parents who could not, because of their religious beliefs, conscientiously allow their children to receive such instruction. This clause, formerly applied only to non-conformist schools, was now applied to Church of England schools in districts where there were more than a few dissenters; its application led to a rupture between the Committee of Council and the National Society (the Church of England school society).

On December 4, 1865, the Bishop of Oxford (Samuel Wilber-

force) distributed prizes to successful students at the diocesan training college at Culham, near Abingdon, then presided over a lunch-
eon in the college hall at which he spoke of the impact of the
Revised Code upon the income of the college and of the efforts being made to compensate for the reduction in grants by voluntary
contributions. Two other speakers were the Duke of Marlborough
and the Rev. Alfred Pott, later Archdeacon of Berkshire; the former
was especially bitter against the conscience clause. The proceedings
were given a full column of the *Times* on December 5, 1865 (p. 7,
col. 5).

Among the guests invited but unable to attend was John Walter,
proprietor of the *Times*, member of Parliament, and vigorous op-
ponent of government control of education. On the day the proceedings at Culham were reported, the *Times* printed a leading
article (pp. 8–9) justifying the Revised Code and turning the
Bishop's lament into eloquent praise of the voluntary support of
this and other training colleges. Two days later R. R. W. Lingen,
secretary to the Committee of Council, explained in the *Times*
(December 7, p. 9, col. 5) the new principle of grants to training
colleges, and added that in 1864 Culham had received from the government £2,611 10s. out of a total expenditure by the college of
£3,143 13s. 8d. A letter to the *Times* by the principal of Culham
College, James Ridgway, in reply to Lingen (December 9, p. 5, col.
6) appeared after Arnold wrote his article.

The *Pall Mall Gazette* on December 20 (pp. 1–2) devoted a leading article to "Popular Education," in which it characterized as fallacious Arnold's concept of "the State." Since this concept was at
the heart of Arnold's educational doctrine, he replied the next day.

1:7–21. The Bishop of Oxford (lines 7–13), the Rev. Alfred Pott
(lines 14–18, 20–21) and the Duke of Marlborough (lines 18–20),
speaking at Culham and reported in the *Times*, December 5, 1865, p.
7, col. 5.

1:25–2:17. A summary, frequently using the exact words, of the
leading article in the *Times*, December 5, pp. 8–9.

2:18–23. Robert Lowe, as vice-president of the Committee of
Council on Education, was the chief proponent of the Revised Code.
R. R. W. Lingen, secretary to the Committee, was his principal subordinate officer. Arnold quotes the conclusion of Lingen's letter in
the *Times* on December 7, p. 9, col. 5.

2:29. The word "trammels" is the Duke of Marlborough's, speaking at Culham; so too is the sentence attributed to him, p. 3:3–6.

2:34–36. Quoted by Arnold in *The Popular Education of France* and printed as an appendix to that volume; for the former, see *Prose Works*, ed. Super, II, 69, 154. Arnold wrote from memory, hence inexactly, in his letter.

4:20–21. In their defence of the Revised Code in 1862, both Lowe and the *Times* advocated the application of the principles of free trade, of the law of supply and demand, to education. See Arnold, *Prose Works*, ed. Super, II, 232, 243, 349, 360.

4:32–34. "We were fast developing a colossal system of official education after the model of Continental countries, which would soon have left no place for that local diversity and independent energy which in every other instance are such vital characteristics of our national life."—*Times*, December 5, p. 9, col. 1. This sentence was aimed directly at Arnold's *Popular Education of France* and *A French Eton*.

5:21–28. George Wither, *Vox Pacifica* (1645), canto IV, p. 199, quoted by Coleridge, *On the Constitution of the Church and State*, end of Chapter XI (*Complete Works*, ed. W. G. T. Shedd [New York, 1853], VI, 90). The italics are Arnold's, and he slightly altered the language to compensate for the omission of four lines.

6:9. Arnold remembered that the *Saturday Review* had called him a transcendentalist; see *Prose Works*, ed. Super, III, 289.

6:16–17. G. Shaw Lefevre, "The Conscience Clause," *Fortnightly Review* III, 165–80 (December, 1865). The quotation from Lord Granville, Lord President of the Privy Council, is on p. 172.

7:15–28. "The power which the clergy, nobility, and gentry have at present over the education of the poor accurately represents the degree of interest which they have taken in the subject and the indifference shown about it by the poor themselves. Nothing could be better for the whole nation than the general diffusion of such a sense of the importance of the subject as would induce the parents to insist in a practical and effectual way on both paying for and managing the education of their own families, but so long as they do not do so things will remain much as they are."—"Popular Education," *Pall Mall Gazette*, December 20, 1865, p. 1442.

[THE MANSION-HOUSE MEETING]

This letter to the *Pall Mall Gazette* on January 17, 1866, signed, like the two preceding, "A Lover of Light," was first attributed to Arnold by J. P. Kirby in an unpublished dissertation on *Friend-*

ship's Garland (Yale University, 1937), and first publicly by Fraser Neiman, "Some Newly Attributed Contributions of Matthew Arnold to the *Pall Mall Gazette*," *Modern Philology* LV, 87 (November, 1957); it was reprinted by Neiman in *Essays . . . by Matthew Arnold* (1960). There is no indication in Arnold's diary of his working on the article, but he received three guineas payment from the *Pall Mall Gazette* in January, 1866. He in effect acknowledged his authorship in a passage, later cancelled, in "My Countrymen," *Cornhill Magazine* XIII, 155 (February, 1866). It was in any case an open secret to his contemporaries. "I mean to do hardly anything for the *Pall Mall Gazette* [from now until Easter]," Arnold told his mother on February 3, "partly because it is not much use writing letters when I am immediately guessed, and so what I urge does not get the benefit of coming with the weight of impersonal newspaper authority—partly because the habit of newspaper writing would soon become too fascinating and exciting."

On January 20 the *Pall Mall Gazette* published a reply to Arnold's letter, headed "Secondary Education" and signed "A British Philistine." It is hardly to be doubted that the writer guessed Arnold to be the author of "The Mansion-House Meeting," both because he used the Arnoldian designation of his class as "Philistine" and because he referred rather pointedly to "Mr. Matthew Arnold's valuable work on the subject" of the establishment of French secondary education (though his memory was not good: neither *The Popular Education of France* nor *A French Eton* contained any significant discussion of the point to which he referred). That the "British Philistine" was in fact Arnold himself, writing ironically—and this is the position argued at length in an appendix to Kirby's dissertation—is much more doubtful; the letter in fact contains no marks of irony at all: its position is reasonable enough, and on the matter of school inspection and certification of teachers the "Philistine" agreed so heartily with Arnold's firmest convictions that Arnold would not have dared to put these opinions into the mouth of an ironically conceived antagonist. There is none of the wonderful self-depreciation of Arnold's irony in *Friendship's Garland*, nor is there any other unmistakable note of Arnold's style (though the attribution is not stylistically preposterous). So far as external evidence goes, it is against Arnold's authorship of the "Secondary Education" letter: his recorded payment of three guineas from the *Gazette* in January was precisely the right sum for "The Mansion-House Meeting," but less than half the payment for two letters. At present, therefore, the "British Philistine" cannot be identified with Arnold.

On November 7, 1865, upon the instigation of the Rev. William Rogers, rector of St. Botolph's, Bishopsgate and a man of some wealth, a group of influential persons from the City (the commercial district of London) met at the Mansion House (the Lord Mayor's residence) to set in motion a scheme for providing education for the children of clerks with small salaries, of small tradesmen, and of the best class of mechanics—men with an income of £200–£300 a year. A committee was set up, and at first it was believed that a start could be made by persuading the trustees of unused endowments to direct their superfluous income to this end. But the complexities of dealing with charitable endowments were so great that the committee resolved on a direct appeal to wealthy men and business establishments for contributions. By the time of a second meeting at the Mansion House on January 12, 1866, the committee was able to report thirty-three subscriptions of £1000 and another seven of £500. Among the subscribers was the house of Rothschild and one of the speakers at this second meeting was Arnold's friend Sir Anthony de Rothschild. Rogers himself, a few years older than Arnold, was still an undergraduate at Balliol when Arnold was a freshman there and was a close friend of such men as John Duke Coleridge, Frederick Temple, and A. C. Tait. He had been a member of the Newcastle Commission on elementary education. The general proposal discussed at the January meeting was the building of a day school near Finsbury Circus to provide nonsectarian secondary education (initially for boys only, to the number of 800–1000) of a sort appropriate to the class from which the pupils came—not a classical education, that is—at a fee of about £4 a year. The efforts of the committee prospered; a Middle Schools Corporation was formed and the Central School, Finsbury (on Cowper Street, still in operation) was already flourishing by the time the Schools Inquiry Commission made its report on December 2, 1867 (see that report, I, 185). The problem of educating this class was of course the principal subject of Arnold's *A French Eton* (see *Prose Works*, ed. Super, II, 280–81), but his solution was not that of the London committee.

Arnold draws for his letter principally upon the account of the meeting in the *Times*, January 13, 1866, p. 6, cols. 4–6, and the leading article in the same number (pp. 8–9).

8:10–12. *Times*, January 13, 1866, p. 8, col. 6.

8:13–16, 20–23. *Morning Star* (London), January 13, 1866, p. 4, cols. 3–4.

8:23–25. Charles Kaye Freshfield, M.P., whose firm, solicitors to the Bank of England, had subscribed £1000, was a member of the sub-committee to draw up specific proposals. He reminded the meeting that "they would have proceeded but a short way towards realizing the object which they had in view, when they had merely succeeded in organizing the first school. They would, nevertheless, have made a good beginning in a cause which would never flag when it had once been fairly set on foot."—*Times*, January 13, p. 6, col. 5. The sub-committee's report recommended "That as far as funds and other considerations will permit, other schools should be established, as branches of or in communication with the first or central school, in other parts of London and the suburbs."—*ibid.*, col. 4.

8:26–9:2. From the sub-committee's report.—*ibid.*

9:2–3. John Peter Gassiot, a member of the sub-committee whose firm of wine merchants, Martinez, Gassiot and Co., had subscribed £1000, spoke at the meeting.—*ibid.*, col. 5.

9:8–25. The speech of the architect William Tite, M.P., member of the sub-committee, who had subscribed £1000, and the comment of the *Times* leading article.—*ibid.*, p. 6, col. 5, and p. 9, col. 1. The question of endowments was a very active one in the public eye at this time.

10:5–6. When Rogers was Curate of St. Thomas's, Charterhouse, he organized an elementary school for the children of the poor.

10:6–7. Tite remarked at the meeting, "The great necessity there was for such education had long been understood and felt by the heads of banking and mercantile houses." Gassiot said, "The proposal was one which struck home to the heart of every man who kept a clerk. . . . The poor clerk, striving to maintain the position of a gentleman, was obliged to send his boys to the cheapest schools or, by straining every nerve, to pay £30 or £40 a year out of his salary to provide them with an education which, after all, was not of so good a kind as it was desirable they should receive."—*Times*, January 13, p. 6, col. 5.

10:12–14. Gassiot said, "As there were many trustees of charitable trusts who would be glad to be relieved from the necessity of having to administer them, clauses would, he hoped, be introduced into the Act of Parliament for which it was proposed to apply, enabling the promoters of the present scheme, having obtained the assent of those trustees, to go before the Charity Commissioners and get their sanction to the laying out of the money on the new schools,"—or, as the *Times* leading article put it, to "facilitate ... the prospective arrangements with the trustees of charities."—*ibid.*, p. 6, col. 5 and p. 9, col. 1.

10:22. Perhaps an allusion to the mythological Danaë's shower of gold.

10:24–25. For a more complete description of the Superior (or Imperial) Council of Public Instruction, see Arnold, *Prose Works*, ed. Super, II, 80–81 and index.

11:15–20. Tite reported that "the committee disclaimed all intention to interfere in any way with such schools as those of St. Paul's and Merchant Taylors'. They were admirably managed, and Dean Collett, the founder of St. Paul's School, was right when he said to Erasmus, who, while his guest, had expressed his surprise at the management of the school being intrusted to a trading company, 'I know of nothing more perpetual than a trading company in the city of London, nor any body of men more likely to be honest.' Most nobly had the Mercers' Company redeemed that pledge."—*Times*, January 13, p. 6, col. 5.

[SCHOOLS AND UNIVERSITIES ON THE CONTINENT]

On his visit to France in 1859 Arnold found time to look not only at the elementary schools he was commissioned to report on, but at a few representative secondary schools, and he ventured both in his official report of 1861 and at greater length in his articles on "A French Eton" to urge the great need for reform of English secondary education in the interest of the middle class. It was no doubt inevitable that after the Newcastle Commission (1858–61) had reported on the elementary education of the poor and the Clarendon Commission (1861–64) on the secondary education of the aristocracy, a third royal commission should be set up to investigate the secondary education of the middle class, but there is no doubt also that *A French Eton* helped give impetus to the new investigation. The third of Arnold's articles on that subject appeared in May, 1864; on May 19 his friend M. E. Grant Duff, M.P., was calling public attention "to the expediency of making the Secondary Endowed Schools throughout the country more available for the purposes of those who wish to give their children a liberal but not a learned education," and on July 29, in reply to Grant Duff's question in the Commons, the Government declared that a new education commission would shortly be announced.

Before this date, of course, there were firm rumors, and Arnold had his eye set on the post he wanted. "There will certainly be a Middle Class School Commission, and I cannot but hope they will send me abroad next spring," he told his mother on July 22. On August 7 he reported to her, "I have received a confidential letter from [H. A.] Bruce [Lowe's successor as vice-president of the Committee of Council], saying the Govt. have to name this Middle-Class Commission, and he is desired to ask me in strict confidence to give the names of those whom I consider best fitted to serve on such a Commission. I consider this really gratifying.... I would not be on the Commission myself, if they asked me, but should much like to be sent abroad by them." A second letter from Bruce asked Arnold's opinion as to the scope which should be given to the inquiry. "I would sooner write in this way than be stuck personally forward in fifty Commissions." On October 12 he told his mother, "Lingen thinks it certain I shall be offered the Secretaryship to the new Commission, and thinks I ought not to decline it; for my own part I would rather go abroad."

In the end, the secretaryship went to H. J. Roby; the commission, as formed, had Lord Taunton as its chairman and included (with others) Lord Lyttelton, who had served on the Clarendon Commission; Arnold's brother-in-law W. E. Forster; the headmaster of Rugby Frederick Temple, and the leading voluntaryist in school matters, the dissenter Edward Baines. "The Middle Class Commission will be full of people who have declared themselves beforehand against State-intervention," Arnold wrote on December 1. "I shall not be on it; to be on it I did not expect, or, indeed, wish: I see many objections to it, and indeed I do not suppose Ld. Granville [Lord President of the Privy Council] ever entertained any notion of it. But I wish it was a better and more open-minded Commission. But this, like all else which happens, more and more turns me away from the thought of any attempt at direct practical and political action, and makes me fix all my care upon a spiritual action, to tell upon people's minds, which after all is the great thing, hard as it is to make oneself fully believe it so." There was, however, a personal overtone that distressed him: he had urged Bruce to name Temple to the commission, "*if* he could be there without offence to the private schoolmasters," and then Temple told Walter Arnold "that he had used all his influence with Ld. Granville to prevent his putting me on the Commission—for fear I should promote my 'State-views,'" as Matthew Arnold wrote to his sister Jane Forster on January 6, 1865. "You know I have never wavered in thinking that the Commission was much better without me, but this of Temple is a good instance of the violent partisanship, the indisposition to anything like a disinterested search for the truth, which is the bane of our action in England." Temple soothed Arnold's personal wound by writing most kindly to accept his son Budge into the School House at Rugby.

It remained for Arnold to get his appointment to the mission abroad. He addressed a letter to Lord Lyttelton urging the necessity of the foreign investigation, and Lyttelton replied, "strongly approving." "I would not for the world have asked William [Forster], connected as we are, to start the matter in the Commission," Arnold wrote to his sister Mrs. Forster; "besides, Lord Lyttelton knew what had passed about it in the last Commission; but now, when Lord Taunton brings the matter before the Commission and reads my letter, I daresay William will support it. I think I have made out a strong case for sending some one, and perhaps even the Anti-State Members of the Commission will be willing enough to collect *information* as to the State systems. I must talk to William before the Commission meets, because I think some one should go to America also. France, Germany, Switzerland, Lombardy, and the United States of America are the important countries. Holland is said to be still, as it was in Cuvier's time, not up, in its middle class schools, to the mark of its primary schools."

Arnold met with the Commission at Forster's on February 27. By that time it seemed certain that he would be sent abroad. He received his letter of appointment on March 9. "It is a great satisfaction to me," he wrote to his mother, "to be going on this errand. You know how deeply the Continent interests me, and I have here an opportunity of seeing at comparative leisure, and with all possible facilities given me, some of the most important concerns of the most powerful and interesting States of the Continent." But there was a final delay. Lingen, Arnold's superior, though a friend, was the type of a perfect administrator: he proposed that Arnold's salary at the Council Office be stopped while he was abroad. As Arnold could not then have afforded to go, he protested vigorously and won his point.

He left London on April 8 and established himself at the Hotel Meurice in Paris. He renewed his acquaintance with Guizot and Jean-Jacques Rapet, who had been most helpful to him six years earlier, and he called on the Minister of Public Instruction, Victor Duruy. Then he returned to England for a week at Easter (April 14–21). For the next four weeks he devoted himself rather strenuously to the visiting of the Paris *lycées;* certainly this was the most successful month of his mission, for from the time he left Paris on May 17 he met little but frustration. Arrived at Turin, he discovered that the Minister of Public Instruction had gone to Florence, and in Florence, to which all the government offices were being transferred, he found nothing but confusion when he arrived on May 21. And so he spent a few days sightseeing, went on to Rome for more sightseeing (May 25–29), and finally in Naples, where the inspector-general was a man he had met and entertained in London in 1862, he was able to visit a few schools. In Rome again after June 4 he was hampered by holidays. By June 12 he was back in Florence; he may have stopped at Pisa, and on the 18th he reached Genoa. He visited schools there for a few days, then returned to Turin, where he had a useful meeting with Carlo Matteucci, former Minister of Public Instruction, "who knows the subject better than almost anybody in Europe. I like him more than any Italian I have seen—he is more like a Frenchman or Englishman." He visited schools for four hours in Milan on June 24, then set out on the 25th for Germany. He reached Berlin only a little more than a week before the schools closed for the summer, went to Rolandseck (on the Rhine near Cologne) in time to see a little of the schools of Rhenish Prussia, then was forced into idleness by the long vacation. His wife and children joined him about July 12, and he took them to Kiefernadel Bad, Gernsbach, near Baden-Baden for a holiday that lasted until the end of August. Again in Baden he was disappointed in his hopes of finding the schools in operation.

He travelled across Germany, visited Schulpforta (near Naumburg), then went on to Dresden, Prague (September 14–15) and Vienna. But the Austrian schools were not to open until October 1; on he went to Switzerland, only to discover in Bern on September 30 that the Swiss schools would not open until October 15. He moved about a good deal in Switzerland, saw schools in Zurich and Lucerne, was back in France (Strasbourg) on October 28, and at home once more on November 1. He had seen Lingen in Vienna and found a sympathetic ear for his difficulties, but a proposal made through Forster that his commission be extended a month to let him visit the schools of Württemberg came to nothing.

In each country he visited Arnold set himself diligently to improve his knowledge of the language.* But under the circumstances the greater part of his information had to be based on official or quasi-official reports rather than observation. "Every one floods me with books and documents which I am obliged to send home for the most part, or I must have ten portmanteaus; but I shall want them," he wrote to his mother on July 5. "I am in arrear at Oxford and getting fined, and with this foreign report and its ocean of documents on my hands I do not see how I am even, within the next year, to make up my Oxford arrears [the lectures on poetry]," he complained on September 30.

The writing of the report was a long and oppressive task. His school inspection began almost at once upon his return, and he had three lectures on Celtic literature to write and deliver (on December 6 and 7 and February 24). On March 17, 1866, he told his mother he was getting on "as badly as possible" with his report, "but done it will be in the course of the next six weeks, and I daresay when it is done it will not be so bad. But it scarcely ever happens to me that anything I am about runs smooth or gives me satisfaction while I am about it. This makes me shrink from setting to work till the last minute." On May 24, the report was only one item on a list of tasks that included, besides his inspecting, the looking over thirty sacred poems, thirty poems offered for the Newdigate, ten Latin prize poems and several English prize essays, the delivering a final lecture on Celtic literature, and the writing and delivering the Crewian oration in Latin. By that time he had taken (from May 1) a house for the summer at West Humble, near Dorking. "My Report plagues me dreadfully," he wrote on June 30. On July 27 he inspected his last school for the summer; his plan was to have the

---

* There exists a sheet of note-paper on which he has written some fifty German phrases and their translations—not only *"Bitt' um Entschuldigung—Wo geht man hier nach dem Berliner Bahnhof?"* but *"Muss ich mich zum Concert besonders anziehn*—must I dress for the concert?" *"Möchten Sie langsamer sprechen*—Would you speak slower?" *"Von allen Deutschen ist er am leichtesten zu verstehen.* Of all Germans he is the easiest to understand." *"Ich hatte nicht die Absicht die Schulcarriere zu machen*—I never meant to take to school-master-work." *"ich bin zu schlecht abgenommen worden*—(in photography)" and *"Damals* at that time. *Ich war damals um die Gesundheit meines Kindes besorgt."*

report done by August 27. In September he complained that his movements were constricted by the task that still hung over him; on October 13 he wrote that he had "just read two quartos on Italian universities and schools; severe work, but improving." "The style of modern Italian is so diffuse and tedious, has so entirely lost the good habits of Latin and French, that I would almost as soon have had to read two quartos of German. Germany comes next, but most of what I have to read for Germany is already read; however, till the end of the year I shall be hampered and worried, and unable to pay a single visit, or even to go to Oxford to give my lecture." "Italy is done at last," he wrote on November 9, "and now for Germany and Switzerland. I shall have a pretty clear month to work at them in." To escape the holiday demands, he retreated from his family during the day and worked at Forster's house in Eccleston Square. "I have not yet done the general summing up, which is a very troublesome business," he told his mother in a belated New Year's letter about January 5, 1867, when she prematurely congratulated him on completing his task, "and then I have to correct the press of Germany and Switzerland, and to put in a number of things I have left out, and then to draw up the tables and statistics for the whole, so I am not out of the wood yet. However on Tuesday, or at latest on Wednesday [the 9th], I hope the drawing up will be finished, and the rest, the *cadre* or framework being complete, will be merely child's play. It is odd how much easier I find it to write a thing for insertion in a particular place when what is before and behind it stands finished, than to write it when I come to it in its regular course. The afternoons and evenings I have to give to looking over examination papers, so I have fully employed days." And on the 10th he completed his draft, to his great satisfaction. "I have many things to do to it still, but the framework of the whole now stands finished. I hope and think it will be useful; it has cost me much time and trouble, and even money,—all these are well spent if the good cause is any gainer by them. I do not consider that my last report on foreign schools effected anything; the time, however, was not come for it; there are signs that this new report will be born at a better moment."

But of course it was not really done. There were proof-reading and appendix-making, so that "it sometimes seems as if I should never be able to get it fairly off my hands." On February 2 he hoped to "finish the last important insertion I have to make; all then left will be mere corrections of words and single sentences." Finally, on the 21st, he finished reading the second proofs. "It now stands as it will finally appear. I hope by the end of next week to have pretty well got the appendix off my hands." On March 2, he still had, he thought, a week's work on the appendix—"work I must do at home, because it has to be compiled out of a number of documents that I cannot bring here [to the Athenaeum Club], and to come in at three in the afternoon at home and work for three or four hours I find the hardest thing in the world, though I can do it here.... However, manage this appendix I must." At last, on April 8, "My appendix has gone in, and now I have only to correct the proofs of it. I feel rather stupid after my long labours on this Report, but I daresay I shall gradually get clear and fresh again." Proofs of the appendix were corrected about the middle of May.

As the end drew closer, also, he began to have increased hopes for its effect on the public. "Young George Trevelyan," Macaulay's nephew, told both Arnold and his wife that "he was reading my French Report of seven years ago with the greatest attention, and could repeat passages of it by heart. So perhaps that Report will not in the end be so useless as at one time it seemed likely to be." He sent first proofs to Temple, who delighted him by "saying how strong an effect [it had] produced on him; in many things he agreed with me, he says, beforehand: and in almost all the things where he did not agree with me, I have, he says, converted him. As he must necessarily be the most influential man in determining the Commission's report, I consider his adhesion of the greatest possible value to the cause which I really care more about than I do about my own success." On August 2, 1867, Grant Duff asked on the floor of the Commons if Arnold's report might be laid promptly upon the table of the House as Fraser's report on American schools had been, and was told that although Arnold's report was on hand, it would not be available until the entire report of the Commission was presented (as it was on December 2).

The refusal of the Government to comply was compensated for Arnold by the decision of Macmillan, to whom he had given a copy, to bring it out as a book at the publisher's expense. "This makes all clear," Arnold told his mother on August 8; "it will come out as a book in November when the Commission reports, and coming as a book is sure to receive sufficient attention. But after burning my fingers with the last report I had determined not to touch the publishing of this at my own risk." Like the earlier book, this one required a Preface, but this time, having laid down his general principles in the report itself, Arnold made his Preface far more topical. It was finished by November 8, corrected by November 16, 1867. "I ... am well pleased with it; part of it, where I touch on the Revised Code, needed very delicate handling." The book appeared about March 14, 1868, priced at half a guinea; Dr. Frank J. J. Davies has ascertained from the publishers that, whereas *The Popular Education of France* (1861) sold only somewhat more than 300 copies, this volume sold an entire edition of 750.—*Matthew Arnold and Education*, unpublished dissertation, Yale University, 1934, p. 198n. Reviewers were generally very high in their praise, except for the *Quarterly Review*, which objected in October that Arnold drew so much of his report from printed documents that the Commission could have got as good a statement "without paying a sixpence for travelling expenses," that he was entirely unfit for his task, and that he was utterly ignorant of the English public schools except for "his hazy recollections of thirty years since." "Of this we are sure, that any one who is intimately acquainted with the education of France, Switzerland, and Germany, and with the best phases of our public schools, will, without hesitation, award the palm to England." (Arnold got his own back at the reviewer, Oscar Browning, a master at Eton, in the original version of his Preface to *Culture and Anarchy*.) On the other hand, a reviewer in a journal to which Arnold often contributed, good-naturedly acknowledging Arnold's sympathy with some aspects of state authority in France under Napoleon III, wrote: "We should not be surprised, if some good and far-seeing despot were to find himself endowed with absolute power in this country, to see him placing Mr. Arnold in such a position as that of M. Duruy in France, and banishing Mr. Robert Lowe to Cayenne."—*Pall Mall Gazette*, March 24, 1868, p. 12.

Arnold himself regarded the German portion of his report as the most useful (and it may be said that though he was not fond of the German people, his visit to their country gave him a high regard for their intelligence and may have been partly responsible for his increasing preference for their government and administration, just as it certainly provided him with the character of Arminius, who began to appear in Arnold's letters to the *Pall Mall Gazette* on July 21, 1866). Bismarck's handling of the religious problem in connection with higher education gave some timeliness to a new edition of the German chapters (with the chapters of general conclusion) in 1874, for which a new Preface pointed the moral as regarded Ireland. *Higher Schools and Universities in Germany* was published at

6s. about March 7 of that year. An edition of 1500 copies was exhausted. The book was still useful enough to go through an edition of 1000 copies, without the Irish Preface, in 1882, when it was stereotyped, and another reprint of 1000 copies ten years later. The former was published about April 29, and sold at 6s. In 1892 Macmillan also reprinted "A French Eton," the French chapters of the 1868 volume, and the 1874 Preface.

It is not surprising, and no discredit to Arnold, that he had some notion of his central thesis even before he went to the Continent. "[No] countries are more worth studying, as regards secondary instruction, than those in which intellectual life has been carried farthest—Germany first, and, in the second degree, France," he told his sister Mrs. Forster early in January, 1865. "Indeed, I am convinced that as *Science*, in the widest sense of the word, meaning a true knowledge of things as the basis of our operations, becomes, as it does become, more of a power in the world, the weight of the nations and men who have carried the intellectual life farthest will be more and more felt; indeed I see signs of this already. That England may run well in this race is my deepest desire; and to stimulate her and to make her feel how many clogs she wears, and how much she has to do in order to run in it as her genius gives her the power to run, is the object of all I do."

As in his earlier books on continental education, Arnold foresaw the way things must go in England, though he undoubtedly hoped they would move faster than they did. He remained firmly convinced that no group, however wealthy, could by voluntary measures significantly move to a solution of England's educational needs; the State, through a Minister of Education, must provide the schools and ensure that they are adequately taught. The 1861 report had dealt essentially with "popular education"; the new report, directed at a level of schooling that was still closed to the great mass of Englishmen, necessarily invited some consideration of class distinctions, and it is significant that in his Preface of 1868 Arnold looked back to elementary education to insist (as he did also when he glanced at the new demand for technical education) that the State would never do the best for its people if it regarded the education of the lower classes as a distinct problem from that of the upper. In England today Arnold's book must seem in many ways merely to call for what now actually exists; in America, where class distinctions were never reflected on a large scale in the schools, the incorrigible anarchy of local authority must still make the book a difficult one even to comprehend. Historically, at least, Americans will sense the nature of the impact of the German university ideal upon their own universities in the nineteenth century. It is not likely that anyone who has a curiosity about European education in the nineteenth century—in itself or as a background of modern education—can find a more lucid, intelligent account than this book, nor is there a better statement of the aim of liberal education than the first of Arnold's two chapters of general conclusion, which states a theme Arnold continued to repeat in his writings, perhaps most notably in the lecture he delivered again and again in America, "Literature and Science."

The appendixes which gave Arnold so much trouble are not reprinted in this edition. There were statistical tables showing the number and population of the French *lycées* and communal colleges, the entire budget of state expenditure for education in France in 1865 (nearly twenty million francs), the number and population of public secondary schools in Italy and of the higher schools and universities in Prussia, a summary of the budgets of the Prussian higher schools and universities and the budget in greater detail of the University of Berlin, and the population and budgets of the schools of Canton Zurich. He gave in detail the programs of school work in the French *lycées* (this required thirty-eight pages) and briefer summaries of the curriculum in other French schools and German schools. A long description of the work, grade by grade, at a combined *Gymnasium* and *Realschule* in Cologne paralleled the description of the program of the *lycées*, then came the program at Schulpforta and at the Gewerbeschule of Basle. Finally he listed all the courses of lectures by professors, *Privatdocenten*, and readers at the University of Berlin in the winter semester of 1865–66. In *Schools and Universities on the Continent*, the statistical tables were all retained, but of the courses of study only the list of university lectures at Berlin remained. In 1874 and 1882 the only appendix was the last of these.

P. 14: Epigraph. See p. 209:36–38.

16:9–15, 28–34. Arnold quotes from the report of the Rev. Alexander Wilson at the 56th annual general meeting of the National Society for Promoting the Education of the Poor in the Principles of the Established Church, on May 8, 1867.—*Times*, May 9, p. 8, col. 5.

16:16–19. J. W. Pease, M.P., spoke in seconding the adoption of the annual report at the meeting of the British and Foreign School Society on May 6, 1867.

16:20–24, 35–38. The Congregational Union closed its autumn

session in Manchester with a conference on popular education on October 11, 1867. Edward Baines presided and indicated, in a long opening address, that the tide of opinion in England had gone against voluntaryism, and that he himself thought they as a group might achieve more for the education of the people if they accepted government grants than if they held staunchly to "the purely voluntary system, which had done such immense service in former years, [but which was now] obviously overmatched and undermined." Samuel Morley reluctantly seconded the view that they must alter their course, however strongly he himself believed that "the true wisdom of Englishmen was to lessen rather than to increase the functions of government."—*Daily Telegraph,* October 14, 1867, p. 3, col. 1. Spencer's remark is quoted from the fuller report of the session in the *Nonconformist* XXVIII, 850 (October 16, 1867). In June, 1868, the Congregational Board at last applied for a share of the Parliamentary grant for their elementary schools and their training college at Homerton. Arnold thereupon was requested to make a preliminary inspection of the latter; his account is reprinted in his *Reports on Elementary Schools,* ed. F. Sandford (London, 1889), pp. 285–91.

16:24–27. At a banquet of the London and Westminster Working Men's Constitutional Association in the Crystal Palace on November 11, 1867, to celebrate the passing of the Reform Act, Lord John Manners told the 2000 members, "Figures, which no one doubts and everybody admits, show that during the last half century the most extraordinary progress has been made in popular education. The last census shows that with the single exception of Prussia, where education may be said to take place, not at the point of the birch, but of the bayonet (laughter), our primary education is ahead of all the countries of the world."—*Times,* November 12, p. 12, col. 4.

17:14–15. The report of the Newcastle Commission describes the method of obtaining statistics both in its Introduction and with its statistical tables.—House of Commons, *Sessional Papers,* 1861, XXI, part I, pp. 11–13, 591. For the proportion of students to population (1 in 7.83 for 1858), see p. 635.

18:36–19:2. The table at I, 672 of the Newcastle Commission report shows 917,255 students in inspected schools that received grants from the government.

19:17–20. John Flint, in a letter to the *Times* on April 23, 1867 (p. 12, cols. 5–6), cited the same figures and drew the same conclusion that Wilson drew for the National Society: "We are, therefore, educationally in advance of France and Holland, and but a very little way behind Prussia, if at all, at the present moment." "As I hope I have shown, the numerical progress of education in this country and its present state as regards quantity (I say nothing as to its quality) are not such as to justify the querulous strain in which persons have lately written, and the sweeping statements they have made." His letter is indeed remarkable: he dispels the arguments of those who find "a large number of children in the streets playing or at their homes idling, and . . . at once assume that these are uneducated and are permanently absent": the average rate of absence is 24%, "but they are only temporarily absent. The 24 who are in the streets to-day may be all, or for the most part, at school to-morrow, to be replaced in the streets by a different 24." See also p. 167n.

20:35. James Fraser, later Bishop of Manchester, was an assistant commissioner to both the Newcastle Commission and the Schools Inquiry Commission. His good friend J. P. Norris, an inspector of Church of England schools, was a warm defender of the Revised Code, which had been sponsored by Robert Lowe as vice-president of the Committee of Council on Education.

21:1–7. Lowe's speech at Edinburgh on November 1, 1867, was reported in the *Times* on November 4, p. 8, col. 4. Arnold made further use of Lowe's speech in the second chapter of *Culture and Anarchy*, published January, 1868.

21:29–31. The Marquis of Hartington, speaking before the Accrington Mechanics' Institution in North Lancashire on October 18, 1867, first cited Lowe's speech on the Reform Bill to the effect that "it was absolutely necessary 'our masters' should learn their letters," then remarked that "he believed that education owed more to Mr. Lowe than to any single man in the country; and . . . there was no man whom they could look forward to with more hope for the future of education than him."—*Times*, October 22, p. 6, col. 1.

22:6–8. Fraser, in the first of a series of letters in the *Times* on "The Education of the People," reminded his readers of his own report to the Newcastle Commission: "Even if it were possible, I doubt whether it would be desirable, with a view to the real interests of the peasant boy, to keep him at school till he is 14 or 15 years of age. But it is not possible. We must make up our minds to see the last of him, as far as the day-school is concerned, at 10 or 11." His own conviction favored 10.—*Times*, April 16, 1867, p. 7, col. 2.

22:29–23:11. Arnold dealt with this aspect of Lowe's reforms in "The Twice-Revised Code," *Fraser's Magazine* LXV, 347–65 (March, 1862). See especially *Prose Works,* ed. Super, II, 232–35, 239, 350.

23:22–24. Fraser, who reported to the Newcastle Commission on popular education in certain agricultural districts of the West of England, went to America for the Schools Inquiry Commission to report on schools in the United States and Canada. Anticipating his report in the third of a series of letters in the *Times* on "The Education of the People," he said: "If people suppose that every American rate-supported school is in a condition of efficiency, they are simply labouring under an entire misconception. There are as many degrees of goodness and badness in schools there as here."—*Times,* April 18, 1867, p. 4, col. 4.

23:35–24:6. Arnold discussed this argument in his article on "Mr. Walter and Schoolmasters' Certificates," *London Review* VI, 374–75 (April 11, 1863). See *Prose Works,* ed. Super, II, 257–61 and notes.

24:15–18. See note to p. 21:1–7.

25:1. Emmanuel-Joseph, Abbé Sieyès (1748–1836) was one of the most influential leaders in the early days of the French Revolution, a member of the Directory, and for a short time consul with Napoleon. His most famous pamphlet is *Qu'est-ce que le Tiers État?,* a question to which he replied "*Tout.*"

25:19–25. Arnold alludes to the verdict of the Newcastle Commissioners, who thus (somewhat misleadingly) summarized Pattison's verdict and quoted from Arnold's own.—House of Commons, *Sessional Papers,* 1861, XXI, part I, p. 195. The actual text of Pattison's report will be found in part IV, pp. 202, 204–5; of Arnold's, in *Prose Works,* ed. Super, II, 171–72. In his fourth letter to the *Times* on "The Education of the People" (April 20, 1867, p. 7, col. 3), James Fraser cited these opinions of Pattison and Arnold.

26:5. "Awake to righteousness, and sin not."—I Corinthians 15:34.

26:8. "Throughout my district I find the idea of compulsory education becoming a familiar idea with those who are interested in schools," Arnold wrote in his general report as inspector of schools in 1867. "I imagine that with the newly awakened sense of our shortcomings in popular education—a sense which is just, the statistics brought forward to dispel it being, as every one acquainted with the subject knows, entirely fallacious—the difficult thing would not be to pass a law making education compulsory; the difficult thing would be to work such a law after we had got it. In Prussia, which is so often quoted, education is not flourishing because it is compulsory, it is compulsory because it is flourishing. Because people there really prize instruction and culture, and prefer them to other things, therefore they have no difficulty in imposing on themselves the rule to get instruction and culture. In this country people prefer to them politics, station, business, money-making, pleasure, and many other things; and till we cease to prefer these things, a law which gives instruction the power to interfere with them, though a sudden impulse may make us establish it, cannot be relied on to hold its ground and to work effectively. When instruction is valued in this country as it is in Germany it may be made obligatory here; meanwhile the best thing the friends of instruction can do is to foment as much as they can the national sense of its value. The persevering extension of provisions for the schooling of all children employed in any kind of labour is probably the best and most practicable way of making education obligatory that we can at present take. But the task of seeing these provisions carried into effect should not be committed to the municipal authorities, less trustworthy with us than in France, Germany, or Switzerland, because worse chosen and constituted." Two years later he wrote in his general report: "The questions of compulsory schooling, gratuitous schooling, secular schooling, are rapidly passing out of the sphere of abstract discussion, and entering into the sphere of practical politics. In that sphere, however they may be settled, it will not and cannot be on their merits; and it seems vain to repeat the considerations proper to one sphere when the matter is about to be settled in another. As to compulsory schooling, I will only say that in no country is the text '*The bread of the needy is their life: he that depriveth them thereof is a man of blood,*' felt with so much force as here; that a law of direct compulsion on the parent and child would therefore, probably, be every day violated in practice; and that, so long as this is the case, to a law levelled at the parent and child, a law levelled at the employer is preferable."—Arnold, *Reports on Elementary Schools*, ed. F. S. Marvin (London, 1908), pp. 117–18, 138.

28:12. Arnold took his figure from the *Public Schools Calendar* for 1866, by adding the number of students at the "Nine Schools" that had been studied by the Public Schools Commission of 1861–64, at forty old endowed grammar schools, and at twenty-four schools of modern foundation. The figure was about 15,690 students, which here he rounded down to 15,000, and on p. 106 up to 16,000. See also p. 195:22–25.

29:1. Addressing his constituents at Elgin on October 3, 1867,

M. E. Grant Duff said: "It seems to me that the first thing we have got to do, in point of time, as well as in point of importance, is to reorganise our education." He spoke of the need for passing the Public Schools Bill, and for making elementary education compulsory. "Our educational edifice will not, however, be such as befits the times in which we live, until we thoroughly modernise and revivify our higher education [i.e., the universities]."—*Daily News*, October 7, 1867, p. 2, col. 6.

29:4–7. The Schools Inquiry Commission, while unable to consider technical education in detail, submitted to Parliament in July, 1867, a brief *Report Relative to Technical Education*. A few months after Arnold wrote his Preface, Professor Lyon Playfair proposed a resolution at a conference on technical education held at the council-chamber of the Society of Arts (January 23, 1868): "Special institutions for technical instruction, adapted to the wants of various classes of society and to the industries of the country, should be established and maintained in the United Kingdom," and Lord Russell's speech in support of the resolution expressed the kind of sentiment to which Arnold alludes.—*Times*, January 24, p. 5, col. 6.

29:21–23. The "shell"—a term that originated at Westminster School—was an intermediate level of the upper school, usually between the fourth and fifth forms; the maximum age for boys in the shell was ordinarily fifteen. (At Westminster itself, however, the shell was intermediate between the fifth and sixth forms, and the boys therefore were a little older.) In the edition of 1874, Arnold altered "from the shell" to "from the fourth form." For Ritschl, see note to p. 224:20.

29:36–37. The philosopher John Stuart Mill, and Frederick Temple, Headmaster of Rugby and later Archbishop of Canterbury.

30:35–37. Ecclesiastes 10:10.

36:8. Anthony à Wood (1632–95) was historian of the University of Oxford.

36:10–17. For the historical sketch of French higher education, Arnold drew once more (but not exclusively) upon a book he had used in preparing *The Popular Education of France:* Auguste Vallet de Viriville, *Histoire de l'Instruction Publique en Europe* (Paris, 1849); see pp. 139, 231, 191–93, 118, 130.

38:3–19. Vallet de Viriville, pp. 69–72.

38:26–34. Vallet de Viriville, pp. 96, 89–90, 92, 96–97, 95.

39:6–25. Vallet de Viriville, pp. 116, 118, 101, 122–24, 143, 147.

39:32–38. Vallet de Viriville, pp. 123, 131, 133.

40:6–35. Vallet de Viriville, pp. 129, 135–36, 142, 230–31.

41:2–14. Vallet de Viriville, pp. 118, 125n., 152–53.

41:22–35. Vallet de Viriville, pp. 163–67, 232, 193.

41:36. Johann Reuchlin (1455–1522) was the leading German humanist and Hebraist of his day.

Theodore Beza (1519–1605), French theologian, was associated with Calvin in Geneva and became his biographer.

41:37–42:6. Vallet de Viriville, pp. 143–44.

44:13–17. Vallet de Viriville, p. 248.

45:3–25. Vallet de Viriville, pp. 223–30, 245–53, 274. Charles Rollin (1661–1741), three times Rector of the University, was a rhetorician and historian who significantly reformed studies there to give larger place to history and the use of the vernacular.

45:32–38. Vallet de Viriville, pp. 235–39.

46:6–47:6. Vallet de Viriville, pp. 273–79, 283–84, 280–81. Condorcet, in the name of the committee of public instruction, delivered his plan to the Legislative Assembly on April 20, 1792.

47:7–48:12. Vallet de Viriville, pp. 282, 284, 286–87, 291–92.

49:1–50:36. Vallet de Viriville, pp. 292–93, 301, 297–98, 301–4.

53:13. The *Cour des Comptes* is the Exchequer and Audit Department.

61:19. Victor Duruy (1811–94), Minister of Public Instruction from 1863 to 1869, was one of the most distinguished men to hold that post and seems to have been in every way worthy of the esteem in which Arnold held him. After his retirement he devoted himself to writing voluminous histories of Greece and Rome.

62:1. Paul-Henri-Ernest de Royer (1808–77) was a magistrate and politician who held a succession of high offices under Napoleon III.

62:7–9. Adolphe Franck (1809–93), professor at the Collège de France, director of and contributor to the *Dictionnaire des sciences philosophiques* and author of a learned treatise on the religious philosophy of the Hebrews, was remarkable for his talented *vulgarisation* of esoteric subjects.

Samuel-Ustazade Silvestre de Sacy (1801–79) was elected to the Academy for his distinction as writer for the *Journal des Débats*.

Joseph-Daniel Guigniaut (1794–1876) was a hellenist and archaeologist, permanent secretary of the Academy of Inscriptions.

Henri Milne-Edwards (1800–1885), naturalist, was author of a classic four-volume *Elements of Zoology*.

Michel Chevalier (1806–79), early a Saint-Simonian, became an influential free-trade economist, well known in England as author (with Cobden) of the Anglo-French commercial treaty of 1860 and as representative of his nation on the jury of awards at the Exposition of 1862 in London.

Félix Ravaisson (1813–1900), philosopher and archaeologist, held numerous posts under the Minister of Public Instruction; from 1853 he was inspector general of higher education.

Jean-Baptiste Dumas (1800–1884), pioneer in organic chemistry, turned from the academic to the practical world in the latter part of his life and devoted much of his energy to problems of sanitation in Paris.

Urbain-Jean-Joseph Leverrier (1811–77) was discoverer of the planet Neptune.

Désiré Nisard (1806–88), anti-romantic critic of literature, was director of the École normale supérieure from 1857 to 1867 and editor of a series of Latin classics accompanied by French translations.

63:13. Athanase Coquerel (1795–1868) was the most distinguished Protestant pastor in Paris.

63:14. Adrien-Marie Devienne (1802–84). The *Cour impériale* was a court of appeal, lower than the *Cour de Cassation*, of which Devienne became *premier président* in 1869.

68:18. Carlo Matteucci (1811–68) was a well-known chemist, physicist, and electro-physiologist who became Minister of Public Instruction to Victor Emmanuel II in 1862.

72:18. Louis Pasteur (1822–95) in 1857 was made director of scientific studies at the École normale, where he had formerly been a pupil.

72:20. Gaston Boissier (1823–1908), a distinguished archaeologist and Roman historian, later became professor at the Collège de France and was elected to the Academy in 1876. Arnold read Boissier's two articles on Caesar and Cicero in November, 1864.—*Note-Books*, ed. Lowry, pp. 575, 631.

72:24. Charles Hermite (1822–1901), who has been described as one of the most profound analysts in the field of pure mathematics in the nineteenth century, became *maître de conférences* at the École normale in 1864.

72:31–33. Charles-Auguste-Albert Briot (1817–82), mathematician, became *maître de conférences* at the École normale in 1855.

Julien-François-Adolphe Berger (1810–69) was *maître de conférences* in rhetoric.

Charles Bénard (1807–98) was professor of philosophy at the *lycées* Bonaparte and Charlemagne.

Jules-Augustin Girard (1825–1902) was *maître de conférences* for Greek literature from 1854.

Louis Étienne, professor at the *lycée* Saint-Louis, published a review of *Essays in Criticism* in the *Revue des Deux Mondes* on April 1, 1866; at the time, Arnold described Étienne as a man "of whom I know nothing." He asked Macmillan to send a copy of *Schools and Universities on the Continent* to Étienne in May, 1868, as a man "who is likely to review it."—W. E. Buckler, *Matthew Arnold's Books* (Geneva, 1958), p. 112.

Victor Cousin (1792–1867), philosopher, professor at the Sorbonne and director of the École normale from 1835 to 1840, was Minister of Public Instruction for the few months of 1840 when Villemain was out of office.

Abel-François Villemain (1790–1870) became *maître de conférences* at twenty, professor of French literature at the Sorbonne at twenty-six, and member of the Academy at thirty-one. He was Minister of Public Instruction, except for a few months, from 1839 to the end of 1844. He was a distinguished critic and literary historian.

72:37–38. Hippolyte Taine (1828–93), philosopher, critic and historian, was one of the most influential writers of his day, best known now, no doubt, for his *History of English Literature* (1863).

Lucien-Anatole Prévost-Paradol (1829–70), well-known journalist and author of a monograph on Swift, was named ambassador to Washington in 1870 and shot himself soon after his arrival.

83:14. The *bifurcation*, established by a decree of April 10, 1852, when Fortoul was Minister of Public Instruction, had political overtones that stirred up violent opposition; Larousse's *Dictionnaire universel* describes it as "an institution as barbarous as the word by which it was called." Duruy abolished it in successive steps from June 29, 1863, to December 4, 1864.

86:28–87:12. Vallet de Viriville, pp. 237n., 289.

87:20–23. The commission of inquiry appointed in 1861 reported three years later on Eton, Winchester, Westminster, Charterhouse, St. Paul's, Merchant Taylors', Harrow, Rugby, and Shrewsbury Schools. The first three and the last three were presumably the ones Arnold placed in the higher rank.

87:32. Arnold had some difficulty getting permission to visit the classes at the *lycées*. "They wanted me to be content with going over the buildings, and having a statement of what was done," he wrote to his wife. Once he persuaded the authorities, however, he found himself very well treated at the schools—"but their morning hours for their classes—eight to ten—are rather trying." His visits to them took place between April 28 and May 17.

89:30. The Sisters of Charity were a nursing order founded by St. Vincent de Paul in 1633.

92:1. The report of the Public Schools Commission remarked that "a school rifle-corps is like a volunteer corps at a University or elsewhere, with the difference that it does not form part of the defensive force of the country.... It is ... of some use in affording to boys who do not care for cricket and do not row, a healthy and social employment for their leisure—in giving them, in short, something to do."—House of Commons, *Sessional Papers*, 1864, XX, 41.

92:32. I.e., all the scholarships, or places in the school drawing benefits from the charitable endowment under which the school was set up.

93:29. See note to p. 325:30.

97:9. A ticket-of-leave man is a convict who has been given "his liberty under certain restrictions before his sentence has expired," on the basis of his conduct and industry.—*N.E.D.*

98:5. When the Collège Sainte-Barbe, which dated from 1460, was threatened with financial disaster in 1831, it was rescued by vigorous action of its former pupils, who placed it in 1838 under the direction of Alexandre Labrouste (1796–1866). He held the post with notable success until his death. Sainte-Barbe-des-Champs, established at Fontenay-aux-Roses in 1852, was the model for the establishment at Vanves, not its imitator.

99:6. The Marais is the district roughly between the Hôtel de Ville and the Place de la Bastille, east of the central city; it contains more ancient buildings than any other part of Paris.

101:29. A "sister" is a nurse, not necessarily a member of a religious order.

104:27–32. The Communal College of Boulogne attempted to attract an English clientele by advertising in the London papers (e.g., *The Athenaeum*, January 5, 1867, p. 2); it added an Anglo-French School with two English professors (for mathematics, classics, and English language and literature) to its normal complement of French professors. The leaflet describing this innovation in somewhat unidiomatic English is among the mementos of his continental tour that Arnold preserved.

105:16. Oxford, Cambridge, London, and Durham were the only English universities that granted degrees when Arnold wrote, and Durham was very small.

105:27. See note to p. 28:12.

106:32. The "metropolitan department" is Seine, of which Paris is the chief city.

109:16. A Maronite is a member of a Lebanese Christian community that is in communion with the Roman Catholic Church.

113:30. See note to p. 72:20.

114:14. "Piles of exercise-books are sent to me to look through," Arnold wrote to John Conington, Professor of Latin at Oxford, on May 17, 1865, "and I wish you could see them with me. The Latin verse is certainly very good; but it is clear that Latin and Greek are cultivated almost entirely with a view to giving the pupil a mastery over his own language: a mastery which has always been the great object of intellectual ambition here, and which counts for more than a like mastery does with us. Perhaps, because it does not count for so much with us, a like mastery is, in fact, scarcely ever attained in England—certainly never at school."

115:13–14. The students were reading the first sentence of Cicero's first oration against Catiline: "Quo usque tandem abutere, Catilina, patientia nostra?"

116:6. *Poeta nascitur, non fit.*—Latin proverb.

118:8. Charles Vacquant (born 1829) was the author of several elementary textbooks in geometry and of a monograph on the program of studies for the baccalaureate in science.

118:15. William de La Rive (1827–1900), son of the Swiss physicist Auguste de La Rive, had published a volume of reminiscences of his relative Cavour and brief monographs on the Savoy question and on Swiss law. The first was translated into English by Edward Romilly in 1862. La Rive was chief literary editor of the *Bibliothèque universelle de Genève*. His address ("rue de l'Hôtel de Ville, 14") is jotted on an early page of Arnold's pocket diary for 1865.

118:32–33. "We absolutely reject all theories which, as disconnected with our globe, are by that fact at once mere idle questions, even granting them to be within our reach. This leads us finally to eliminate, not merely the so-called sidereal astronomy, but also all planetary studies which concern stars invisible to the naked eye, and which have consequently no real influence on the earth."—Auguste Comte, *The Catechism of Positive Religion*, translated from the French by Richard Congreve (London, 1858), p. 211. Arnold

quoted from the *Catechism* with devastating ridicule in "Anarchy
and Authority" (1868).

119:11–12. "Les Anglais ont conservé religieusement l'antique
traité d'Euclide. ... Les élèves récitent par coeur les propositions; le
maître écoute, et, de mémoire, les ramène, s'il est besoin, au texte
sacramental," wrote E. Marguerin and J. Motheré, *De l'enseignement des classes moyennes et des classes ouvrières en Angleterre*
(Paris, 1864), pp. 92–93. The same criticism of the English teaching
of arithmetic and Euclid was made in the report published almost
simultaneously with Arnold's, J. Demogeot and H. Montucci, *De
l'enseignement secondaire en Angleterre et en Écosse* (Paris, 1868),
pp. 113–21, 588: "En un mot, [l'élève anglais] ne comprend pas
l'esprit de la science, il n'en saisit que le côté purement matériel.
C'est à faire sourire tout élève français d'une intelligence même
moyenne" (p. 120).

120:25–28. *Enseignement secondaire spécial* (Paris, 1866), p. 388.

120:36–121:1. The Collège Chaptal was established in 1842 to give
vocational education (in industry, commerce, and agriculture) to
the children of the bourgeoisie; it became a municipal institution
two years later. The École Turgot, founded in 1839 to give an education that fell between the primary schools and the colleges, attracted much the same clientele and prided itself on its success in
placing its students in commerce and industry. Its director from
1853 to 1870 was Émile Marguerin, whose report on English education is cited in the note to p. 119:11.

121:12–32. *Enseignement secondaire spécial*, pp. 389–91, 434.

121:34–122:17. *Ibid.*, pp. 387–88, 392–93.

122:34. The Benedictine Abbey at Cluny, some fifty miles north
of Lyons, was founded in 910 and became, by the middle of the
twelfth century, the head of an order that embraced 314 monasteries
in all parts of Europe. It was dissolved in 1790 and many of its
buildings were destroyed.

123:36–124:12. *Enseignement secondaire spécial*, pp. 435–36.

125:35–126:2. "A stumbling-block in the way of the *enseignement
secondaire spécial, i.e.* of the new modern schools of which the programme was given in the last number of *The Museum*, has arisen in
the amount of the school-fees proposed by Government, viz. six
guineas per annum. It is objected that, at this rate, only the children
of the wealthier middle classes will seek admission into these schools,
and that those of even the best paid working men will remain unprovided for. ... There are two classes in France clamouring for a
new set of schools, viz. a wealthy but not numerous class of capital-

ists, who wish for their sons a non-classical yet thorough mental training, and then a numerous but not wealthy class of aspiring operatives, who wish for their sons a more or less technical course of instruction, which may fit them for their future apprenticeships and business in life."—"Education Abroad," *The Museum: and English Journal of Education,* n.s. III, 155 (July, 1866). Arnold's admiration for *The Museum* was amply returned: in 1868 that journal reprinted the Conclusion of *Schools and Universities on the Continent* (July, 1868, pp. 138–43) and the whole of Arnold's General Report for 1867 (November, 1868, pp. 296–302), and prefixed to both the very highest praise for their author: Arnold was the best qualified, most intelligent writer upon English education, and his judgments were invariably right even when at first sight they might seem questionable.

128:23. Chambéry was capital of the Duchy of Savoy, which was ceded to France (along with Nice) in 1860; the conquest of Algiers was completed about 1847.

132:9; 133:17–24. At the meeting of the British Association for the Advancement of Science held at Nottingham on August 23, 1866, the president of the Chemistry Section, Dr. H. Bence Jones, attacked the requirement of Latin (and *a fortiori* Greek) in the education of medical men and pharmaceutists, but remarked of the latter: "All our druggists in England ought to be what they are in Germany and in France, chemists capable of any analysis that might be required of them, and able to satisfy themselves and the medical men that the substances they sell are what they profess to be, pure, unadulterated chemical compounds."—*Report,* part II, p. 32; also reported in the *Times,* August 24, p. 6, col. 2. Bence Jones the preceding October invited Arnold to lecture at the Royal Institution, but Arnold, just returned from his Continental mission, declined.

134:1–2. The eight inspectors-general for *secondary* instruction included four for sciences and four for letters; Arnold's pen slipped here (see Textual Notes).

134:4–6. Félix Ravaisson became inspector general of superior instruction in 1853, Désiré Nisard and Leverrier in 1852. See note to p. 62:7–9.

Adolphe-Théodore Brongniart (1801–76), botanist and founder of the science of plant paleontology, became inspector-general of the University for sciences in 1852 and member of the superior council of public instruction in 1866. His sister was the wife of Jean-Baptiste Dumas.

Charles Giraud (1802–82), jurist, became inspector-general of the faculties of law in 1842, held the portfolio of public instruction for five months in 1851, and became inspector-general for instruction in law in 1861.

135:16. Jules-Augustin Girard (1825–1902) in due course became Professor of Greek Poetry in the Faculty of Letters at Paris. His *Mémoire sur l'île d'Eubée* was published in 1852.

135:18. The great Bibliothèque Nationale is in the Rue de Richelieu.

135:34–37. Jean-Baptiste Élie de Beaumont (1798–1874) became Professor of Geology at the Collège de France in 1832. Pierre-Jean-Marie Flourens (1794–1867), physiologist, became Professor of Natural History in 1835. Victor Coste (1807–73), embryologist, occupied a chair especially created for him at the Collège de France. For Adolphe Franck and Michel Chevalier, see note to p. 62:7–9. Édouard-René Lefebvre-Laboulaye (1811–83) became Professor of Comparative Law in 1849. Alfred Maury (1817–92), historian and archaeologist, was Professor of History and Ethics from 1862. Salomon Munk (1805–67) was a Silesian-born orientalist and student of Hebrew and Arab antiquities, remarkably productive though blind for his last fifteen years; he held the chair of Hebrew from 1864. Armand-Pierre Caussin de Perceval (1795–1871) succeeded his father as Professor of Arabic in 1822. Jules de Mohl (1800–1876), German-born but naturalized in France, became Professor of Persian about 1847. Stanislas Julien (1799–1873) became Professor of Chinese in 1832. The critic Sainte-Beuve (1804–69) was named Professor of Latin Poetry in 1854. Alexis Paulin Paris (1800–1881) was Professor of Medieval French, a chair created for him in 1853 and in which he was succeeded by his son Gaston Paris in 1872.

136:26–137:9. The stringent qualifying examination for the civil service was instituted in 1855. Arnold was one of the examiners in July, 1864. In August, 1866, a 75-page document was printed by order of the House of Commons to make available the correspondence of the previous year and a half between Anthony Panizzi (while he was Principal Librarian at the British Museum) and the Civil Service Commissioners, whose secretary was Arnold's friend Theodore Walrond, respecting the effectiveness of the Commission's examinations and certificates in determining the fitness of candidates for posts in the Museum.—House of Commons, *Sessional Papers*, 1866, XXXIX, 241–318. The correspondence was reviewed in the *Athenaeum*, October 20, 1866, pp. 489–91.

137:23–24. Joseph Garcin de Tassy (1794–1878) was one of the most prolific of French orientalists, especially in the field of Hindustani. For Julien and Caussin see note to p. 135:34–37.

138:16. Either "altogether disreputable" or legally deprived of his civic rights because of criminal conviction.

142:1–17. Carlo Matteucci, *Raccolta di Scritti varii intorno all' istruzione pubblica* (Prato, 1867), I, 255–56. The official report cited by Arnold has not been available to the present editor; the section dealing with universities was here reprinted by Matteucci along with other writings on education, and sufficiently shows the extent of Arnold's dependence upon his work.

142:19–21. *Ibid.*, I, 254.

142:33–143:6,12–36. Ernest Renan, *Averroès et l'Averroïsme* (new ed.; Paris, n.d.), pp. 322–23, 52, 324–26, 425–26. Cremonini died in 1631.

144:2–15,28–145:2. *Ibid.*, pp. 364–65, 411–16.

145:4–5. The Barnabites are members of an order (the Regular Clerics of St. Paul) founded in 1530 and devoted especially to learning and education. The Regular Poor Clerics of the Pious Schools ("Escolapios"), a teaching order established in 1621, set up the first genuinely popular, free primary schools in Italy.

145:14–27. Matteucci, *Istruzione pubblica*, I, 255–59.

145:31–33. Gabriele Falloppio (1523–62), anatomist at Ferrara, Pisa, and Padua, did pioneer work on the head and uterus.

Evangelista Torricelli (1608–47), mathematician and physicist at Florence, was amanuensis to Galileo at the very close of the latter's life and was discoverer of the principle of the barometer.

Marcello Malpighi (1628–94), physiologist at Pisa, Messina, and Bologna, was founder of microscopic anatomy, whose most important work was done on capillary circulation, the lungs, secreting glands, and the brain.

Antonio Vallisnieri (1661–1730), physiologist at Bologna and Padua, made significant advances in the study of reproduction of insects and aquatic plants; he finally disproved the possibility of spontaneous generation of the former.

Lazzaro Spallanzani (1729–99), physiologist at Reggio, Modena, and (after 1769) Pavia, demonstrated the necessity of spermatozoa for fertilization in animals and disproved the notion of spontaneous generation of microscopic organisms.

Luigi Galvani (1737–98), physiologist and anatomist at Bologna, was best known for his experiments in the action of electricity upon the muscles of frogs.

Alessandro Volta (1745-1827), physicist at Como and Pavia (1779-1814), was a pioneer in electrical science, after whom the "volt" was named.

Antonio Scarpa (1752-1832), anatomist and surgeon at Modena and (1783) Pavia, and friend of Spallanzani and Volta, was one of the founders of the nineteenth-century study of surgery; his own principal work was in neurology, but his range of valuable observations was very wide.

145:36. Giambattista Vico (1668-1744) was a professor of rhetoric at Naples, best known as philosopher of law and of cultural history.

145:36-146:32. Matteucci, *Istruzione pubblica*, I, 259-60, 265-67, 253.

146:34. Amedeo Peyron (1785-1870) of Turin, pioneer in the study of Greek papyri of the Ptolemaic period and of the Coptic tongue, may have been best known to Arnold as editor of the fragments of Empedocles and Parmenides (1810).

147:9-15. Matteucci, *Istruzione pubblica*, I, 261.

147:27-28. The left bank of the Rhine was annexed to France as early as 1795 and the Rhenish districts were left in possession of their liberal institutions when they were assigned to Prussia by the Congress of Vienna. But to the east, in Westphalia, which was set up as a separate kingdom under Jerome Bonaparte in 1807, French rule was ineffective and the province returned to Prussia on its old terms after the Battle of Leipzig in 1813. The German civil code was to supplant both legal systems after the establishment of a unified German Reich in 1871.

148:1-6. Matteucci, *Istruzione pubblica*, I, 257.

148:14-19. *Ibid.*, I, 261. Matteucci says that the men Arnold lists (and others he names) "nello stesso tempo furono Professori in quella Università" (Pavia), but they were not in fact all there at quite the same time.

Johann Peter Frank (1745-1821), German born, was professor of medicine at Pavia from 1785; he was called to Vienna in 1795 and to Vilna in 1804, where he organized the instruction in medicine. His special interests were hygiene and legal medicine.

Ugo Foscolo (1778-1827), poet and prose writer, was professor of Italian eloquence at Pavia for a short time in 1808-9.

Vicenzo Monti (1754-1828), neoclassical poet, was appointed professor of poetry at Pavia by Napoleon in 1802 and held the post for two years.

148:19–149:2,4–10. Matteucci, *Istruzione pubblica*, I, 262, 361–62, 257–58, 367.

150:19–20. Gabrio Casati (1798–1873), a Milanese leader of the Italian revolt against Austria, was Minister of Instruction from July 18, 1859 to January 21, 1860.

151:11–12. Matteucci was Minister of Instruction for most of the year 1862.

162:1–163:19. Matteucci, *Istruzione pubblica*, I, 392–97, 365–66, 448.

163:20–164:29. *Ibid.*, I, 388, 391, 283, 450–51, 281–82. Matteucci asserted that the German, Belgian, and French faculties lectured "no less than thirty-two, thirty-four, thirty-six weeks."

164:29–165:12. *Ibid.*, I, 408, 342–44.

165:13–166:13. *Ibid.*, I, 294–95, 297–98, 302, 310, 405, 402–3, 408–10.

166:14–35. *Ibid.*, I, 296, 412–13.

167:15–18. In a letter to the *Times* on October 24, 1866, p. 2, col. 6, "One of the Royal Commissioners" (of the Newcastle Commission) pointed out the unanimous testimony of the English Assistant-Commissioners in 1861 that though the managers of schools with religious support attached great importance to educating in such schools all the children of their churches and sects, the parents were far more interested in the quality of the schools than in their religious attachments. The Commissioner then cited a new report of the London Diocesan Board of Education to the effect "that more than 150,000 children, of age to be at school, are not under education of any sort or denomination in London alone," and concluded, "Surely it is not a time for disputes about catechisms and dogmas, but for action." On October 30, p. 8, col. 5, John Flint challenged the Board's report on the ground that it had inadequately surveyed attendance in non-conformist schools and "totally ignore[d] the thousands upon thousands of private schools to which people, acting in the spirit of self-respect and independence, send their children," "private adventure schools" that "literally swarm in almost every street."

169:22. The Concordat of 1855 placed Catholic education in Austria under the supervision of the bishops. Its educational provisions were set aside by the new laws of 1868, and the Concordat itself was annulled by the Austrian government in 1870.

173:20–21. Edoardo Fusco (1824–73) lived in London as a political exile from Naples from 1853 to 1860, contributed to many of the best English journals, and taught Italian at Eton and at Queen's

College, London. Early in 1861 he was appointed inspector of primary and secondary schools in Naples. Matteucci, as Minister of Public Instruction, sent him to London in 1862 to study English education. "At Naples the Inspector-General is, oddly enough, a man whom the Italian Government sent over to our great Exhibition, whom a French inspector [presumably J.-J. Rapet] introduced to me, and who dined at my house," Arnold wrote to his mother on May 24, and his letters from Naples are full of Fusco's attentive care. In the summer of 1866 Fusco visited London and Ireland on his own account and was given the privileges of the Athenaeum Club "as distinguished foreigner" at Arnold's behest. When Fusco's widow published one of his lectures at Queen's College, "Italian Art and Literature Before Giotto and Dante," Arnold wrote a brief biographical account of Fusco by way of preface (*Macmillan's Magazine* for January, 1876). See G. I. Fusco, *Della Vita e delle opere di Edoardo Fusco* (Naples, 1880), I, 40; II, 149–50.

175:7–12,22–176:15. Matteucci, *Istruzione pubblica*, II, 10–15; I, 311.

177:20–178:31. *Ibid.*, I, 454–55, 264, 253, 458–59, 485–86, 477–78.

179:4–36. *Ibid.*, I, 478–79, 470–73, 489–90, 486, 467–69. "Gli esami speciali o per materia durante il corso" are contrasted with "gli esami generali o di laurea" at the end of the student's university career (p. 415). The American university student is accustomed to being examined *per materia*, at the completion of each term's work.

179:37–180:14. *Ibid.*, I, 457–60, 474–76.

181:19–22. Arnold's pocket diaries, which do contain some memoranda for this chapter, do not contain the entry he here quotes. He wrote to his wife about June 3, 1865: "The professors [of the Lyceum at Naples] are very inferior to those in France, and generally, I must say, the impression of plain dealing, honesty, and efficiency, according to their own system, which one gets in France, is very different from what one gets here."

182:17–34. Matteucci, *Istruzione pubblica*, I, 367, 264–65. "De toutes les louanges que Winkelmann prodigue à l'Italie, il n'en est pas de plus fréquente dans sa bouche que d'appeler l'Italie la terre des sentiments humains."—Hermann Hettner, "Winkelmann et la Renaissance du goût antique au XVIIIᵉ siècle," *Revue moderne* XXXVI, 79 (January, 1866). Arnold copied the key phrase at the end of his note-book for 1866 (ed. Lowry, p. 41).

186:16. Johann Matthias Gesner (1691–1761), professor at Göttingen, one of the most learned men of his day, edited a number of classical texts, revised Estienne's *Thesaurus,* and reformed classical instruction in the German universities.

Johann August Ernesti (1707–1781), Gesner's sub-rector and then successor as rector of the Thomasschule in Leipzig, and later professor of the university there, edited a number of classical texts (most notably Cicero) and laid the foundation of the "higher criticism" of the Bible by establishing the principle that biblical texts should be subject to the same philological scrutiny as the Greek and Roman classics.

Christian Gottlob Heyne (1729–1812), professor at Göttingen after 1763, editor of Tibullus, Vergil, Pindar, the *Iliad,* and Epictetus, was distinguished for the breadth of his learning in all aspects of classical antiquity, especially mythology, art, and cultural history.

186:21–26. [Mark Pattison], "F. A. Wolf," *North British Review* XLII, 245–99 (June, 1865). Arnold quotes the reviewer's summary of Wolf's principles (pp. 262–63), not Wolf's actual words. The article was among those his *Note-Books* show he planned to read in November, 1865, and he quotes another passage from the same page in his lecture on "Literature and Science" (1882).

186:27. Karl Abraham von Zedlitz (1731–93) was Minister of Church and School Affairs from 1771 to 1788.

188:11. Frankfurt-am-Main, a free city for centuries, sided with the Austrians in the war of 1866, was occupied by Prussian troops, and on October 18 was formally incorporated into the Prussian state.

189:1–192:10. Ludwig Wiese, *Das höhere Schulwesen in Preussen* (Berlin, 1864), pp. 1, 20–26. But Wiese gives three years to *prima,* and hence ten years to the gymnasial course.

192:16–194:35. Wiese, pp. 26–30.

192:20. Johann Amos Comenius (1592–1670), the last bishop of the old church of the Moravian Brethren, gained a European reputation for his method of teaching languages and for his advocacy of balanced, broad education in practical and modern subjects. He was invited to England to aid in a projected reform of education there in 1641 and in 1642 went to Sweden to supervise the regulation of Swedish schools according to his own method.

192:23–27. Johann Bernhard Basedow (1723–90), after holding a professorship of moral philosophy and belles-lettres in an academy in Denmark, devoted himself to a project of general educational reform in Germany under the strong influence of Comenius, with the coloring of Rousseau's *Émile.* He established his Philanthropinum at Dessau, near Magdeburg, about 1774; it had only a decade of activity, but was imitated throughout Germany.

192:34–38. Ludwig Wiese (1806–1900) was in the Prussian Ministry of Public Worship and Education from 1852 to 1875; the first volume of his *Deutsche Briefe über englische Erziehung* (Berlin, 1852, 1877) was translated into English by Arnold's brother William Delafield Arnold in 1854 and both volumes were the subject of an article by Matthew Arnold in the *Pall Mall Gazette* of May 3, 1877. The influence of Dr. Thomas Arnold upon his early education was very great. It was Dr. Wiese who on July 1, 1865, signed the official letter of introduction Arnold carried with him on his visits to the Prussian schools.

194:36–195:26. Wiese, p. 32 and statistical tables on pp. 437, 446–53. See also p. 58:27–28 and note to p. 28:12.

195:8. The war between Prussia and Austria in 1866.

196:1–197:18. Wiese, pp. 13–15.

198:7–199:5. Wiese, pp. 2–5, 15.

198:29. Karl von Stein zum Altenstein (1770–1840) was summoned to government service in Berlin under Hardenberg and Stein, and was head of the Ministry of Public Worship and Education from 1817 to 1838.

198:32. Heinrich von Mühler (1813–74), son of a Prussian Minister of Justice, held various posts in the Ministry of Public Worship and Education from 1840, and was Minister from 1862 to 1872. He was the object of much hostility for his bigoted stand in religious matters.

199:6–201:20. Wiese, pp. 5–8.

200:16–17. Johann Wilhelm Süvern (1775–1829), a professor at Königsberg and author of books on the Greek drama, was attached to the Prussian ministry in Berlin from 1809 on.

Georg Heinrich Ludwig Nicolovius (1767–1839), Protestant theologian, was in the Prussian office of education from 1808 to 1839. His primary concern was religious education and worship: it was his firm conviction that the King, though Protestant, must make the same provision for his Catholic subjects as for his Protestant subjects in the practice of their faith and religious education.

Johann Peter Friedrich Ancillon (1767–1837), pastor of the French community in Berlin and a writer on political theory, became tutor of Crown Prince Friedrich Wilhelm (IV) in 1810; four years later he was attached to the Ministry of Foreign Affairs and became its head in 1832.

Friedrich August Wolf (1759–1824), a pupil of Heyne's at Göttingen, became professor at Halle and a leader in the reform of instruction at the *Gymnasien* of Prussia. In 1807 he moved to Berlin and became a professor at the university there. He is best known for his *Prolegomena ad Homerum* (1795), in which he tried to demonstrate the multiple authorship of the Homeric poems. See note to p. 186:20.

Friedrich Ernst Daniel Schleiermacher (1768–1834), Protestant theologian and philosopher, was professor at Halle, 1805–9, and one of the most distinguished of the professors at the University of Berlin after 1810.

201:21–202:38. Wiese, pp. 8–10, 649–50. Arnold omits the province of the seventh member of the Examination Commissions, modern languages.

203:1–205:33. Wiese, pp. 38–42, 474–75, 606–7, 88–89, 87.

208:11–214:28. Wiese, pp. 478–85, 487–88, 492–504.

211:32–39. J. F. Minssen, *L'Instruction ... en Allemagne* (Paris, 1866), pp. 41–42n.

212:32–39. The dissertation on the Cissoid was by Buchbinder of Schulpforta (Minssen, p. 14); the others are not listed by Minssen.

214:37–38. "Recte studet qui sibi et vitae studet. ... Perverse studere qui examinibus studeant."—*North British Review* XLII, 266 (June, 1865).

214:35–217:5. Wiese, pp. 504–11, 699–700, 618–21, and statistical tables on pp. 515, 521–22, 524.

218:1–222:31. Wiese, pp. 545–54.

219:18–22. See p. 186:20–31.

219:31. Arnold himself held an Oriel fellowship from 1845 to 1852.

219:23–222:15. In his report on English training colleges for 1867, Arnold wrote: "I am bound to record my opinion, founded on my experience of the foreign training schools, that with our mode of conducting these examinations and of marking the papers, uniformity of standard and trustworthy unity of impression are very hard to attain, and that these results are much better attained when the whole examination is conducted and the papers marked, as abroad, by an examining commission."—*Reports on Elementary Schools,* ed. Marvin, p. 254.

223:12–224:2. Wiese, p. 539, and [M. Pattison], "F. A. Wolf," *North British Review* XLII, 263, 266–67 (June, 1865). The number of new seminarists each year was twelve, so that the total number at any one time was twenty-four.

223:20–21. Immanuel Bekker (1785–1871) became professor at

374 *Schools and Universities on the Continent*

the University of Berlin in 1810 on Wolf's recommendation; he made new collations and published greatly improved editions of an impressive number of Greek and Roman texts, as well as some texts in Old French and Provençal.

224:2–21. Wiese, pp. 526, 532–33, 543.

224:17–18. August Boeckh (1785–1867), a pupil of Wolf's at Halle, moved from a professorship at Heidelberg to a chair at the University of Berlin in 1811; there he conducted the philologic seminar and (after 1819) the pedagogic seminar also. His studies were in economic history of ancient times and in methodology.

Philipp Buttmann (1764–1829) was a classical grammarian.

Gottfried Bernhardy (1800–1875) was the author of histories of Greek and Latin literature and a study of Greek syntax, and was editor of the *Lexicon* of Suidas.

Karl Lachmann (1793–1851), professor of Germanic philology at Berlin after 1825, was (next to Jacob Grimm) the most distinguished scholar in his field; he applied the critical methods of Wolf to the *Nibelungenlied* and other antique German texts and to the New Testament.

Moritz Haupt (1808–74) succeeded Lachmann in the chair of Germanic philology in Berlin in 1853.

224:20–21. August Ferdinand Näke was a classical philologist, editor of the *Rheinisches Museum für Philologie* at Bonn from 1833 to 1839.

Friedrich Gottlieb Welcker (1784–1868) was professor of ancient literature and archaeology at Bonn from 1819 to 1861, co-editor with, then successor to Näke as editor of the *Rheinisches Museum*, and author of studies in the Greek epic cycle, Greek tragedy, and Greek mythology.

Friedrich Wilhelm Ritschl (1806–76), classical philologist, was professor at Bonn from 1839 to 1865, then at Leipzig. He laid the foundation for the study of early Latin, and edited numerous texts and inscriptions.

Otto Jahn (1813–69), professor of classical philology and archaeology at Bonn after 1855, applied the rigorous critical methods of the philologists to the examination of ancient monuments and handicraft, and published the standard edition of Juvenal in his day.

224:24–227:37. Wiese, pp. 530–44, 528–29, 10–12, 564–65, 574–79.

224:30. Heinrich von Sybel (1817–95), German political historian, pupil of Ranke's and author of a monumental *History of Europe during the French Revolution*. See p. 329.

228:15–26. Wiese, pp. 562–63.

229:16. See p. 251:30 and note.

230:3–231:13. Wiese, pp. 37–38, 455; and see p. 243:5–7.

231:17–19. In 1817 Frederick William III of Prussia decreed the Union of Lutheran and Reformed Churches into the "United Evangelical" Church and forbade any body that called itself Lutheran to separate from this Union. By 1827 the two confessions had been united also in Nassau, Baden, Saxe-Weimar, and Württemberg.— A. L. Drummond, *German Protestantism since Luther* (London, 1951), pp. 194–97, 200.

231:22–28. Wiese, p. 22. For the Dutch schools, see Arnold, *Prose Works*, ed. Super, II, 195–98, 192.

232:1–21. Wiese, pp. 563–64. The movement of *Lichtfreunde* or *protestantische Freunde* began in revolt against the Protestant state church in 1841; their "free religious communities" were given liberty to practice their religion in Prussia in 1847. The movement was joined in 1859 by the "German Catholics," a group that separated from the Roman Catholic Church in 1844 and denied the divinity of Christ, faith in miracles, and the doctrine of the Trinity.

232:22–233:7. Wiese, pp. 568–70. At one point Arnold clearly misunderstood Wiese, whose tortured language gives ample justification of Arnold's verdict upon the German tongue (*Prose Works*, ed. Super, III, 351–52): "Für jedes Gymnasium und jede zu Entlassungsprüfungen berechtigte Realschule sollen diejenigen Lehrerstellen, deren Inhabern das Prädicat Oberlehrer als mit dem Amte verbunden beizulegen ist, fest bestimmt, und dabei als Regel angenommen werden, dass an diesen Anstalten bei 7 ordentlichen Lehrern (mit Ausschluss des Directors) 3 Stellen als Oberlehrerstellen zu bezeichnen sind. Bei umfangreicheren und mit einer grösseren Zahl von ordentlichen Lehrern versehenen Anstalten kann die Zahl der Oberlehrerstellen den Verhältnissen nach angemessen vermehrt werden."

233:19–235:5. Wiese, pp. 581–83, 271, 93, 572–73. Ludwig Schopen (1799–1867) edited several Latin and Byzantine texts.

236:1–239:36. Wiese, pp. 88, 427–30, 31, 97–99, 610–13. The inspectors (p. 238:1) were appointed by the founder, not the vestry. One other gymnasium (p. 239:4–5) had in fact the same fees as the Friedrich-Wilhelms; five were one thaler lower.

238:27. Leopold von Ranke (1795–1886) had perhaps the highest reputation of any nineteenth-century historian of modern Europe; he was founder of a school which aimed at rigorous objectivity and

the ferreting out of recondite sources. For nearly fifty years he held
a chair at the University of Berlin.

241:11–12. Karl Gottlob Zumpt (1792–1849) was author of a
Latin grammar and other school texts in the classics; like his nephew
(not son) August Wilhelm (1815–77), he was a teacher in a Gymnasium in Berlin (see p. 246:32). The nephew translated several of
Cicero's treatises into German, edited a number of Cicero's orations
with valuable commentaries, and wrote on Roman law. He became
professor at the Friedrich-Wilhelms Gymnasium in 1851.

242:16–17. "Zerstreute Anmerkungen über das Epigramm und
einige der vornehmsten Epigrammatisten" (1771).

243:1–11. "There remains the question of secular schooling," Arnold wrote in his general report as inspector of schools for 1869,
"and this is a question of which the solution is above all likely to be
governed by politics, lay or religious, and, by being so governed,
may do serious harm to education. I address myself on this point to
the managers of British schools, with many of whom I have an
acquaintance of now nearly twenty years. One of the main objects
for which their schools were instituted was to promote the knowledge of the Bible. That this or any other branch of instruction will
be really provided for by the Sunday school no serious educationist
believes; but neither is it really provided for if it is withdrawn from
inspection. My own observation, my inquiries, and the entries of the
teachers in their log-books, all convince me that the knowledge of
the Bible in British schools is not what their managers would wish it
to be. The other day, in a school where the managers were so solic-
itous for this instruction that they begged me to hear and take part
in an examination in it, the question was asked in the boys' school,
'Of whom was it said, *Behold an Israelite indeed in whom is no
guile,* and who said it?' Not a boy could tell. The same question was
asked in the girls' school in the afternoon with the same result. This
does not surprise me, for it follows naturally from the Bible knowledge of the children being wholly excluded from the matters which
appear in the school's inspection. Let the managers of British schools
set an example which other managers also, if they are wise, may follow. Let them make the main outlines of Bible history, and the getting by heart a selection of the finest Psalms, the most interesting
passages from the historical and prophetical books of the Old Testament, and the chief parables, discourses, and exhortations of the
New, a part of the regular school work, to be submitted to inspection and to be seen in its strength or weakness like any other. This
could raise no jealousies; or, if it still raises some, let a sacrifice be

made of them for the sake of the end in view. Some will say that what we propose is but a small use to put the Bible to; yet it is that on which all higher use of the Bible is to be built, and its adoption is the only chance for saving the one elevating and inspiring element in the scanty instruction of our primary schools from being sacrificed to a politico-religious difficulty. There was no Greek school in which Homer was not read; cannot our popular schools, with their narrow range and their jejune alimentation in secular literature, do as much for the Bible as the Greek schools did for Homer?"—*Reports on Elementary Schools*, ed. Marvin, pp. 139–40.

243:13–22. Wiese, p. 34.

243:23–244:2. "With the increase of schools, the supply of books designed to meet the requirements of the examination instituted by the Education Department increases, and becomes a lucrative and important business," Arnold wrote in his general report for 1867. "These books are very often compiled by persons quite incompetent for the undertaking. It seems to me very desirable that the Education Department should here, as in other countries, exercise some control over school books in aided schools; and all the more so because, with our present system of grants, these books profess to be in immediate correspondence with our requirements. It is very usual for the scholar to have to purchase his reading book, which is often the only book of secular literature in his possession; it is important to do what we can to ensure its being a good one." He printed "a specimen of popular poetry from the Fifth Standard book of a series much in vogue," and commented: "When one thinks how noble and admirable a thing genuine popular poetry is, it is provoking to think that such rubbish as this should be palmed off on a poor child for it with any apparent sanction from the Education Department and its grants."—*Reports on Elementary Schools*, ed. Marvin, pp. 119–21. See also Arnold, *Prose Works*, ed. Super, II, 341–42.

244:3–246:13. Wiese, pp. 90–93, 30–31, 455, 632–33. Johann Georg was Elector of Brandenburg from 1571 to 1598, his eldest son Joachim Friedrich from 1598 to 1608. A *convitto* is a boarding school. Collegers at Eton were educated and lodged in the College at the expense of the foundation; oppidans at Eton, commoners at Winchester, and most inmates of the School House and masters' boarding houses at Rugby paid for their maintenance.

246:14–37. Wiese, pp. 94–96, 92. For Buttmann, see p. 224:18; for K. G. Zumpt, see p. 241:11–12.

246:32–33. Arnold may have confused the Conrad Schneider who was master at Joachimsthal from 1809 to 1821 with the much more distinguished scholar Karl Ernst Christoph Schneider (1786–1856), who edited Aesop, Caesar, and Plato. He spent the greater part of his academic career at the University of Breslau. Likewise the Carl Passow who was master at Joachimsthal from 1828 to 1860 was not the more famous Franz Passow (1786–1833), a pupil of Hermann and Wolf who made the Greek lexicon on which Liddell and Scott based theirs. He too was professor at the University of Breslau.

Karl Wilhelm Krueger (1796–1874) was professor at Joachimsthal from 1827 to 1838, author or editor of a great many texts for the study of Greek.

Theodor Bergk (1812–81), best known for his edition of the Greek lyric poets, was at Joachimsthal from 1838 to 1840.

The editor of Theocritus (and of Iamblichus' life of Pythagoras and of Tacitus) was Theophilus Kiessling; the director of Joachimsthal was Friedrich Gustav Kiessling.

246:37. Ludwig Friedrich Heindorf (1774–1816) edited various Greek and Latin authors and wrote a commentary on the Satires of Horace.

Georg Ludwig Spalding (1762–1811) was best known for his edition of Quintilian.

Johann Gustav Droysen (1808–84) was distinguished for his comprehensive histories of the Hellenistic world.

247:8–249:1. Wiese, pp. 267–71. *Musae Portenses* was published in 1843.

247:34–35. Karl David Ilgen (1763–1834) published his edition of the Homeric Hymns in 1796.

248:2–4. Johann Georg Grävius (1632–1703), professor at Utrecht, published editions of classical texts and two large Thesauri of Roman and Italian antiquity.

For Ernesti, see p. 186:15.

Friedrich Gottlieb Klopstock (1724–1803) was author of an epic poem in hexameters, the *Messias* (1748–73); his significance is great in the history of German literature for his breaking loose from the shackles of barren rationalism.

Karl August Böttiger (1760–1835), director of the Gymnasium at Weimar for thirteen years and an acquaintance of the literary group there, then curator of the museum of antiquities in Dresden, was best known for a lively study of the private life of the Romans, *Sabina; or, Morning Scenes in the Dressing Room of a Rich Roman Lady* (1803).

Christoph Wilhelm Mitscherlich (1760–1854) was editor of Horace and of the Greek romances and great uncle of the famous chemist Eilhard Mitscherlich.

Johann Gottlieb Fichte (1762–1814) was the well-known philosopher.

Georg Ludolf Dissen (1784–1837), professor at Göttingen, won his reputation for editions of Pindar and Tibullus.

Friedrich Thiersch (1784–1860), professor at Munich and Göttingen, was author of a Greek grammar and of significant studies of German public education.

Franz Spitzner (1787–1841) was a scholar in Homeric and post-Homeric Greek heroic verse.

Ludwig Döderlein (1791–1863), director of the Gymnasium at Erlangen and professor at the university there, edited Tacitus and Horace and compiled works on Latin synonymy and etymology.

Friedrich August Wilhelm Spohn (1792–1824), professor of ancient literature at Leipzig, was an ardent scholar of ancient geography whose interest then turned to the deciphering of hieroglyphics; he made an early attempt at reading the Rosetta stone.

249:18–22. Wiese, pp. 32–33.

249:22–250:7. In his report on English training colleges for 1867, Arnold wrote: "The Stockwell students have regular lessons in callisthenics, to their great advantage. At the Borough Road College gymnastics are not taught, and there are neither room nor appliances for teaching them. To one who has recently seen the training schools of Germany and Switzerland, and who knows the value there attached to cultivating, through gymnastics and outdoor exercises, the physical development of the future schoolmaster—above all, of the future primary schoolmaster—this omission cannot but be a matter of regret. No public normal school for primary teachers would in Germany or Switzerland be allowed to exist without adequate provision for teaching gymnastics to the students. The buildings of Küssnacht, the primary normal school for Canton Zurich, would make a poor show beside those of the Borough Road College, but attached to them is a good gymnasium and a good garden for the students. The students there have one hour's instruction in gymnastics every week, and two hours' military exercising; all through the fine time of the year they have three hours a week of gardening. In great towns in Germany, where there can be no garden and gardening, the time given to gymnastics is proportionably augmented."—*Reports on Elementary Schools,* ed. Marvin, pp. 254–55.

250:8–251:32. Wiese, pp. 337–44, 611.

251:30. Oskar Jäger (1830–1910) was author of textbooks in history and in the method of teaching history. Jäger's predecessor at the Cologne Gymnasium took the post at Bielefeld for which Arnold says Jäger was not confirmed.

252:18. The grammar school at Uppingham, in Rutland, was founded in 1584; at the time Arnold was writing it had achieved a place of considerable distinction among English public schools through the exertions of Edward Thring, headmaster from 1853 to 1887. The study of modern languages especially flourished there.

Pp. 254–64. The whole of Arnold's Chapter XX (with the single exception of the description of the office of Quaestor, pp. 257–58) depends very closely on J. F. Minssen, *L'Instruction ... en Allemagne* (Paris, 1868), pp. 57–100. Arnold also drew his Appendixes Nos. 7–10 from Minssen.

260:24. For Lachmann, see p. 224:18.

260:26. Gottfried Hermann (1772–1848), professor at Leipzig from 1798, was acknowledged head of the school of grammarian-critics of ancient literatures, a brilliant pioneer in the study of ancient metrics, and a distinguished editor of Greek drama.

262:19–23. Édouard Laboulaye, "Quelques réflexions sur l'enseignement du droit en France," *Revue de Législation et de Jurisprudence* XXIV, 322 (November, 1845), quoted by Minssen, *L'Instruction ... en Allemagne*, p. 86n.

263:12–13. Goethe in a letter to Johann Heinrich Meyer, Weimar, February 8, 1796.—*Werke* (Weimar, 1892), IV. Abtheilung, XI, 22. Arnold found the sentence in F. W. Riemer, ed., *Briefe von und an Goethe* (Leipzig, 1846), p. 24, and recorded it in his Note-Books for August 19, 1868 (ed. Lowry, p. 80).

272:32. That is, the schools of the National Society for Promoting the Education of the Poor in the Principles of the Established Church throughout England and Wales.

276:2. See Arnold, *Prose Works*, ed. Super, II, 68, 86–87, 90.

280:6. The fee Arnold gives here is in fact the same as that on p. 278:29. The editor is unable to make the correction.

283:36. Philipp Emanuel von Fellenberg (1771–1844), a Swiss philanthropist with a passion for educating the poor, established at Hofwyl, about six miles north of Bern, an agricultural and industrial institute (1807), a boarding school for children of the nobility on Pestalozzian principles (1808), a free school for poor children, and a normal school for the training of rural teachers (1809). The institution attracted pupils from all Europe, even from America.

284:17. David Friedrich Strauss (1808–74), author of *Das Leben*

Jesu, was named to the chair of dogma and ecclesiastical history at the University of Zurich in 1839 but because of the controversy aroused by his book never was able to take up the post. His appointment caused the overthrow of the liberal regime.

286:12–18. "Zurich peut montrer ses écoles avec orgueil, comme Cornélie montrait ses enfants."—Baudouin, *Rapport*, p. 459.

290:5–27. This doctrine is the basis of Arnold's Rede Lecture at Cambridge in 1882, "Literature and Science."

291:17. Eratosthenes (c.275–194 B.C.) succeeded Apollonius Rhodius as head of the Alexandrian Library, was the first to call himself a "philologist," and wrote books of literary criticism, history, mathematics, geography, philosophy, and original poetry. He was the most versatile of the Alexandrian scholars.

291:22–23. Arnold knew well the series of textbooks by Charles Baker called *Graduated Reading, Comprising a Circle of Knowledge in 200 Lessons* (London, 1855 and later), or simply *The Circle of Knowledge*. See his *Diaries* for 1863, p. 97 (ed. Guthrie, II, 422).

292:20–23. In Chapter XX of the *Völsunga Saga*.

292:32. Acts 10:28.

293:13–23. Claude Fleury, *Discours sur l'histoire ecclésiastique* (Paris, 1747), p. 194 (Discourse V, part iv: "Cours d'études").

294:15–22. See [M. Pattison], "F. A. Wolf," *North British Review* XLII, 249, 252–54 (June, 1865).

296:11. Émile Littré (1801–81) published his *Dictionnaire de la langue française* from 1863 to 1872.

296:12. Arthur Henry Hallam's *Remains in Verse and Prose* (1853) contained six poems in Italian, a long college oration on the influence of Italian literature on English literature, and a review of Gabriele Rossetti's *Disquisizioni sullo spirito antipapale* (1832). The editor, Hallam's father, commented in his Preface on Arthur's surprising competence in the Italian language.

297:12. Vergil *Aeneid* xii. 435.

297:14. Horace *Odes* III. xxix. 49.

298:29–35. In his *Inaugural Address* [as Rector] *delivered to the University of St. Andrews Feb. 1st 1867* (London, 1867), John Stuart Mill surveyed what he considered to be the whole province of university instruction. The classics would be better learned as a child learns a modern foreign language, "by acquiring some familiarity with the vocabulary by practice and repetition, before being troubled with grammatical rules" (p. 15), and there is no room in general education for "the laborious idleness in which the school-time is wasted away in the English classical schools," irreparably squandering "the most precious years of early life ... in learning to write bad Latin and Greek verses" (p. 39). Mill paid tribute to the "practical reformers of school tuition, of whom [Dr.] Arnold was the most eminent" (p. 14), and may have been echoing Matthew Arnold when he concluded: "Let us strive to keep ourselves acquainted with the best thoughts that are brought forth by the original minds of the age" (p. 98).

298:36–39. F. W. Farrar, then an assistant master at Harrow (where Arnold was to live from April, 1868, to June, 1873), more than once attacked the practice of Greek and Latin verse composition in the English public schools. Arnold alludes to his lecture delivered at the Royal Institution on February 8, 1867, *On Some Defects in Public School Education* (London, 1867). There may be in this lecture a passing allusion to Arnold's doctrine: "If English people ... are indifferent to knowledge, scorn ideas, and despise *Geist* as a continental importation—then there is an end of the matter" (p. 23). But Arnold's was not the first use of the term "Geist" in England. On January 10, 1868, Arnold wrote to Farrar: "I shall ask Macmillan to send you my foreign Report in its more readable *book*-form. You must bear in mind that it has all been written some while ago,—even the Preface some two or three months ago. I have made an opportunity to mention in a note your lecture of last winter, but many important contributions to the discussion of the Education question,—such for instance as the recent 'Essays' [*on a Liberal Education*, ed. Farrar (London, 1867)],—did not come into my hands till my own book was fairly out of them." Farrar reviewed Arnold's book briefly but most admiringly in the *Fortnightly Review* IX, 709–11 (June, 1868).

299:13–15. George P. Marsh was named by Lincoln in 1860 as the first United States Minister to the Kingdom of Italy and held that post until his death in 1882. His *Origin and History of the English Language, and of the Early Literature it Embodies* was published in 1862. Arnold cited his *Lectures on the English Language* in *On Translating Homer:* see *Prose Works,* ed. Super, I, 132. "I am going a walk this evening with Mr. Marsh the American Minister here," Arnold wrote to his sister Jane Forster from Turin on June 21, 1865; "I like him, too, but he is redeemed from Yankeeism rather by being a student than by his natural temper and timing—and of course that is not quite so well as to have the merit by nature."

300:1–3. Proverbs 27:8.

304:18. Giacomo Antonelli (1806–76), though not a priest, was created cardinal by Pius IX in 1847 and held the post of secretary of state from 1850 until his death. This office placed him in general control of the papal states so long as they existed (until 1870) and of the diplomatic relations of the pope. Arnold was presented to Cardinal Antonelli by Odo Russell on June 6, 1865.

305:38–306:1. Revelation 3:1.

307:28–38. In the eighteenth century, the parish was a main unit of local government in England; ecclesiastical in origin, it retained such functions as the relief of the poor (which had initially been the duty of the church) and became the territorial unit for other functions not originally ecclesiastical. The Poor Law Amendment Act of 1834 set up three Poor Law Commissioners to unite parishes into unions for general administration and the building of workhouses. Initially there were 618 unions and 126 single parish units under this law for a total of 14,610 parishes in England and Wales. The number of unions fluctuated throughout the century as the population shifted. The Elementary Education Act of 1870, sponsored by Arnold's brother-in-law W. E. Forster, set up school districts and provided for the election of school boards by the rate-payers, but only to supplement the voluntary system where there was a deficiency.—John J. Clarke, *A History of Local Government of the United Kingdom* (London, 1955), pp. 9, 41–42, 57. Except in the boroughs, the civil parish ordinarily constituted the school district.

310:3–4. Proverbs 21:16.

310:10–14. Perhaps George Perkins Marsh, American Minister to the Kingdom of Italy; see p. 299:13.

312:14–15. Arnold reported on "The Systems of Popular Education in Use in France, Holland, and the French Cantons of Switzerland" and Mark Pattison on "The State of Elementary Education in Germany" as assistant commissioners for the Newcastle Commission (1861). Arnold published his report separately as *The Popular Education of France* (London, 1861), and its sale was so poor that in October, 1862, he was obliged to pay its publisher, Longman, £80.16.4 to make up the deficit. This report is published in *Prose Works*, ed. Super, II, 30–211.

312:27–29. Arnold's description would fit Arthur Cayley (1821–95), senior wrangler in 1842 and Sadlerian Professor of Pure Mathematics at Cambridge after 1863.

312:34–38. One volume of Von Hammer appeared in English translation in 1835; the others remain untranslated.

314:36–38. By an Order in Council of April 10, 1839, the superintendence of parliamentary grants in aid of education was given to a committee of the Privy Council named for the purpose, with the lord president of the Council (customarily a peer) as its chairman. In 1856 Parliament provided for a vice-president of the Committee of Council of ministerial rank who should· be a member of the House of Commons. The latter was the nearest equivalent to a minister of education in nineteenth-century England.

319:16. This conjectural etymology of "bachelor" is not accepted by the *N.E.D.*, but the origin of the word is unknown.

320:9–14. Perhaps Henry John Stephen Smith (1826–83), who won the Balliol scholarship from Rugby in 1844, was mathematical lecturer at Balliol from 1850 to 1873, and Savilian professor of geometry at Oxford from 1860. Arnold certainly knew Smith personally.

321:15–20. The Science and Art Department was established under the Board of Trade in 1853 and transferred to the newly formed Education Department in 1856. It significantly encouraged, through classes and grants, the teaching of science and art, and especially the former, throughout England. Henry Cole (later Sir Henry, 1808–82) was the leading member of the executive committee for the Great Exhibition of 1851, general adviser to the exhibition of 1862, and secretary of the Science and Art Department from its establishment until 1873.

322:3–4. See p. 126:17.

323:16–22. A non-sectarian "London University" was founded in 1828 in Gower Street, but not chartered because of opposition to its complete secularization. The Church of England replied by establishing King's College in the Strand in 1831, with a royal charter. Neither institution could grant degrees. In 1836, by a compromise, the Gower Street institution was re-named University College, London, and a new body, the University of London, was chartered to grant degrees to candidates from either college. By a charter of 1858 the University of London examined all who presented themselves, without inquiry into their training or affiliation with any college. It offered no instruction on its own account. Not until 1898 were University College, King's College, and twenty-two other institutions made constituent schools of a teaching university. Arnold's remarks led to Walter Bagehot's article, "Matthew Arnold on the London University," which carried Arnold's suggestions somewhat further.—*Fortnightly Review* IX, 639–47 (June, 1868).

324:10–13. The University of Durham was established in 1832, and gave its only degrees in arts; theological students as such received no degrees and the medical degree was seldom requested, though available. It did not flourish for several decades, and was subject of a commission appointed in 1861 to draw up ordinances for the university; their proposals included the granting of degrees in three separate schools, Arts (classics and mathematics), Theology, and Physical Science.—House of Commons, *Sessional Papers*, 1863, XVI, 11.

325:24–27. The House of Convocation at Oxford consists of all masters of arts and doctors of the higher faculties who have their names on the university books; it has final control over all acts of the university and it elects the Professor of Poetry, but by its nature it is little informed about university affairs.

325:30. The *N.E.D.* defines "job" as "a transaction in which duty or the public interest is sacrificed for the sake of private or party advantage." See also Arnold's use of the verb "job" on p. 93:29.

325:31–34. Nearly a fourth of the professors at Oxford and Cambridge were appointed by the Crown—i.e., the Prime Minister.

326:15. Owens College, Manchester, founded from a huge bequest of a Manchester merchant and intended as the nucleus of a new university, opened in 1851. Until 1880, when it became the Victoria University, it prepared its students for the University of London degrees.

326:38–327:1. See Proverbs 8:1, 33, 35–36.

327:24. The Pharmaceutical Society was founded in 1841.

328:24–29. See Arnold, *Prose Works*, ed. Super, II, 90.

[GERMAN AND ENGLISH UNIVERSITIES]

A few weeks after the publication of *Schools and Universities on the Continent*, Professor Heinrich von Sybel (whom Arnold may have met at Bonn in 1865) delivered a lecture at the university there (March 22, 1868) and published it as a pamphlet, *Die deutschen und die auswärtigen Universitäten* (Bonn, 1868). The pamphlet is not mentioned in Arnold's diaries nor in his surviving correspondence, but the former do record the receipt from the *Pall Mall Gazette* on June 1 of three and a half guineas in payment of some article. There can be no question, on grounds of style and content, that the anonymous review in the *Gazette* on May 5 of von Sybel's pamphlet is Arnold's, a re-affirmation of some of the principal doctrines of his newly published book. In view of the promptness with which the review followed the publication of the pamphlet, it is more than probable that Arnold received a copy either from the author himself or from some other Bonn acquaintance such as Dr. Perry (to whom von Sybel alludes in his lecture).

329:1–3. Von Sybel's *Geschichte der Revolutionszeit von 1789 bis 1795* was translated by Walter Copland Perry as *History of the French Revolution* (London, 1867–69). Perry (1814–1911), the son of a Congregationalist and Unitarian minister, took his doctorate in philosophy at Göttingen in 1837. For six years he was a dissenting minister in Exeter, but in 1844 he went to Bonn as schoolmaster and remained there some thirty years (though he returned to England each summer). Like Arnold, he was a member of the Athenaeum Club and he had been a friend of Arnold's brother William. He published a book on German universities in 1845, and he testified on their operation before a Select Committee on the Oxford and Cambridge Universities Education Bill, July 26, 1867.

329:13–15. Jacques Claude Demogeot and Henri Montucci, *De l'Enseignement secondaire en Angleterre et en Écosse. Rapport adressé à son exc. M. le Ministre de l'Instruction publique* (Paris, 1868). The report was critical of English instruction in the classics because composition in the ancient languages was an end in itself and contributed neither to an understanding of the authors read (for composition and reading were separate disciplines in the English schools) nor to a sense of modern style, and because the explication of a classical author altogether ignored his literary merits. "Un tel exercice, prolongé pendant une heure, captiverait difficilement l'attention d'une classe de jeunes Français" (p. 105).

330:19. The very popular Baptist preacher Charles Haddon Spurgeon in 1856 founded a pastors' college to prepare young men for the ministry under his active guidance. The college still exists, as Spurgeon's College.

331:14. If the French report does not use the precise term "*hauts lycées*," it does say: "En Écosse comme en Angleterre une partie de l'instruction que nous appelons *secondaire* est réservée à l'université" (p. 591). "Dans l'organisation générale des études classiques, l'école n'est que le vestibule de l'université" (p. 586). In England, the student got all his degrees—bachelor's as well as master's and doctorate—from the university and got nothing when he completed his secondary education; in France, the bachelor's degree was awarded at the completion of the course at the *lycée*. "The foreign universities attach little importance to examinations; and they have

invented for the English universities the nickname of 'high gram-
mar-schools'—*hauts lycées; verlängerte gymnasien.*"—J. R. Seeley,
"A Plea for More Universities," *The London Student,* No. 1, p. 4
(April, 1868). See also p. 68:20.

331:14–16. "Der eigentliche Unterricht geschieht... in den Colleges, und hier ganz in den Formen unserer Gymnasien. Der
leitende Zweck, welcher die Richtung und den Lehrstoff der Ox-
forder Studien bestimmt, ist allerdings nicht die Abrichtung des
Schülers zu einem praktischen Berufe, aber auch nicht die Einfüh-
rung desselben in speciellere und tiefere Wissenschaftlichkeit:
sondern es ist die Entwicklung und Formirung der allgemeinen
Geisteskraft, der Fähigkeit zu denken und zu sprechen, der Leich-
tigkeit der Combination, der Sicherheit des Urtheils, der Fertigkeit
des Ausdrucks; es ist, wie gesagt, die Aufgabe unserer Gymnasien,
nur höher gefasst und reicher entwickelt nach dem reiferen Alter
und vorgeschrittenen Bildungsstufe des Studirenden.... In England, wie wir sehen, ist... die Universität nichts anderes als ein
fortgesetztes Gymnasium, die formale Bildung des Geistes ist nach
wie vor die herrschende Aufgabe des Unterrichts."—Von Sybel,
pp. 8, 15. The view was a commonplace. On December 22, 1866,
Dr. Ignaz von Döllinger, upon entering the office of Rector at the
University of Munich, delivered an address on *Die Universitäten
sonst und jetzt* (Munich, 1867), in which he remarked (p. 29):
"Aber [die englischen Universitäten] sind von dem was wir eine
Universität nennen, himmelweit verschieden. Ich möchte sie als
verlängerte Gymnasien, verbunden mit geistlichen Collegien und
einer Beigabe von etwas Theologie bezeichnen."

331:18–27. "Der Schüler soll vor Allem dadurch gebildet werden,
dass er an diesem Entstehungsprocesse des Gedankens anschauend
Theil nimmt; was auch im späteren Leben sein Beruf sein möge, in
seinen akademischen Jahren soll er Jünger der Wissenschaft sein,
und nichts anderes, weil die beste Vorbereitung für jeden Beruf die
Erlangung wissenschaftlicher Reife, Gelenkigkeit und Selbstständig-
keit des Geistes ist.... Unsere akademischen Fachschulen [verfol-
gen] das Ziel, ihre Zöglinge so tief wie möglich in die Arbeit ihrer
Wissenschaft einzuführen und dadurch ihrem Geiste die letzte
männliche Entfaltung zu geben. Sie setzen damit die Wirksamkeit
der Gymnasien fort, nur freilich nicht, wie die englischen Colleges
in bloss erweitertem Umfang, sondern auf einer neuen höhern
Stufe.... Es ist die Pflicht und das Interesse der Nation, ihre Söhne
in den Stand zu setzen, durch strengen Dienst der Wissenschaft sich

zum Dienste des Vaterlandes geschickt zu machen."—Von Sybel, pp. 14–16, 32.

331:32–33. Since private schools could be approached by the Schools Inquiry Commission only if they volunteered to give information, by far the greatest part of the Commission's investigation was directed to nearly 800 schools supported by charitable endowment. Not only, therefore, were schools under investigation, but the whole question of endowments as well. See Arnold's long note on pp. 53–55.

331:33–34. An attempt by Gladstone to subject charitable endowments to an income tax was defeated by the vigorous opposition of the House of Commons in committee on May 4, 1863.

331:34. Robert Lowe, testifying before the Schools Inquiry Commission on June 13, 1865, said: "I look upon endowments as a great evil.... I am hostile to the principle of the endowment of schools. I look upon it as a premium to continue teaching things after the spirit of the age has got beyond them." Asked whether he would prefer applying the endowment to some other purpose, and not to education, he replied, "I would rather throw it into the sea."— House of Commons, *Sessional Papers*, 1867–68, XXVIII, pt. 3, 645 (Schools Inquiry Commission, *Report*, IV, 637).

331:36–37. "[The London University] wants unity and organization; it possesses everything else which the age requires in a university—a vast assemblage of learned men, vast museums and libraries, variety of instruction, cheapness, absence of great endowments, and lastly, religious comprehensiveness."—Seeley, "Plea for More Universities," p. 16. J. R. Seeley was Professor of Latin in University College, London.

331:37–332:2. "And so the shade of the Pious Founder stands in the path, and blights every suggestion for improvement.... [But] few are pious;... fewer still are wise; [and] none however wise or pious has a right to dictate to posterity how they shall employ the property which was his while he lived."—Arthur Hobhouse, *A Lecture on the Characteristics of Charitable Foundations in England* (London, 1868), pp. v–vi. Hobhouse (1819–1904), a very successful barrister, became Charity Commissioner in 1866 and immediately set himself to the task of reforming the law governing charitable endowments. The Endowed Schools Act of 1869 was the first step in this direction. He retired from his commissionership in 1872.

332:3–7. "Hier dürfen wir mit demüthiger Bewunderung hinüber nach England blicken.... Und ich betone es, all diese kolossale Dotirung, welche die unsrige in dreifach höherem Masse übertrifft, als der englische Nationalreichthum den unsrigen, ist zum grössten Theile nicht Zuschuss der Staatsregierung, auf die wir bei eigener Unthätigkeit zu blicken lieben, sondern successive Stiftung einzelner Bürger, welche damit sich Denkmäler wissenschaftlichen Sinnes gesetzt haben, wie wir sie leider in dem wissenschaftlichen Deutschland vergebens suchen."—Von Sybel, pp. 26–27.

332:8–25. See Von Sybel, pp. 24–28.

333:5–6. The Oxford University Act of 1854 abolished all religious tests for matriculation and for the degrees of bachelor of arts, law, and medicine. But the M.A. and higher degrees still required subscription to the Thirty-Nine Articles and to the forms prescribed in the Book of Common Prayer. Since nearly all college fellows were obliged to take such higher degree, teaching posts at the university were still hedged by a religious test. Residents at the university repeatedly petitioned Parliament for relief from 1862 onwards, and bills were introduced annually in the Commons from 1863 to 1870 without avail. Tests were finally abolished by the University Tests Act of 1871.

Edward Bouverie Pusey (1800–1882) joined Newman and Keble in the Tractarian Movement in its first year, 1833; after Newman left the Church of England Pusey became the leader of the Oxford movement and as Regius Professor of Hebrew was a vigorous and somewhat thorny defender of the university's position as the seat of orthodox Christian education under clerical tuition. He was a frequent preacher in the university church (St. Mary's), as was his friend and future biographer Henry Parry Liddon (1829–90), select preacher to the university from 1863 to his death. Like Pusey, Liddon regarded abandoning tests as the triumph of irreligion in Oxford. On the other hand Goldwin Smith (1823–1910), Regius Professor of Modern History from 1858 to 1866, was leader of the campaign for the abolition of tests at the university; in 1864 he published *A Plea for the Abolition of Tests in the University of Oxford* and in 1868 a pamphlet on *The Reorganization of the University of Oxford*.

333:19. Smith mentioned (*Plea*, p. 58) that J. S. Mill, among the authors in constant use in the university, was a follower of "the atheistic theory of Comte," but Arnold's allusion may have been suggested by an article he read in June, 1863: "Bien des doctrines ont trouvé asile à Oxford; il n'y a pas, m'a-t-on assuré, jusqu'au positivisme d'Auguste Comte qui n'y soit représenté par une petite école très-fervente, quoique très-discrète.... Bien loin de craindre pour l'Université les résultats qu'amenèrait la suppression de ce que j'appellerais volontiers le monopole anglican, je suis convaincu qu'elle trouverait tout avantage à l'écarter.... Qu'on y fasse entrer l'esprit de liberté moderne, et elle secouera bientôt la vieille poussière des âges, son enseignement sera rajeuni, la science et la critique moderne y élèveront de nouvelles chaires ou y trouveront des auditoires plus attentifs; les controverses sortiront du cercle étroit où elles se tiennent renfermées et deviendront les luttes viriles et fécondes."—Auguste Laugel, "L'Université d'Oxford," *Revue germanique et française* XXV, 506–7 (May, 1863). See Arnold, *Note-Books,* ed. Lowry, pp. 571, 629.

333:27–30. Von Sybel began his lecture by quoting Grant Duff and Renan ("L'Instruction supérieure en France," *Questions contemporaines* [Paris, 1868], p. 84) in praise of German universities, and a few pages later (9–11) cited Pattison to the effect that in contrast to the German university student, the Oxford lad seemed to be trained only in the method of writing a graceful leading article in a newspaper. For "die unvergleichlichen Vorzüge," see his p. 33.

333:30–31. Samuel Wilberforce (1805–73) was bishop of Oxford from 1845 to 1869. Zealous for the good of religion and the church, he was not himself a Tractarian, nor was he sympathetic with ritualism, but he was on the side of Pusey and Liddon on the matter of university religious tests and in the House of Lords defended their imposition.

333:36–334:19. Von Sybel, pp. 21–22; the italics are Arnold's.

P. 341:9. (*Add:*) —*Prose Works,* ed. Super, V, 488.

P. 351:22. (*Add:*) —*Prose Works,* V, 530–31.

P. 351:41. (*Add:*) —*Prose Works,* VII, 90–130.

P. 353:10. (*Add:*) —*Prose Works,* X, 53–73.

P. 353, *note to Epigraph:* (*Add:*) Arnold's source, Wiese, does not attribute this statement to Humboldt personally, merely to his ministry.

21:1–7. (*Add:*) —*Prose Works,* V, 126.

118:32–33. (*Add:*) —*Prose Works,* V, 505–6.

P. 370:15. (*Add:*) —*Prose Works,* VIII, 7–8.

186:21–26. (*Add:*) —*Prose Works,* X, 57.

P. 372:8. (*Add:*) —"German Letters on English Education," *Prose Works,* VIII, 208–15.

P. 385:32–33. *Cancel* nor in his surviving correspondence. (*Insert:*) Arnold wrote to his mother on June 2: "I have received today £3..13ˢ..6ᵈ for the page and a half on German Universities I wrote for the Pall Mall three weeks ago."

Textual Notes

[EDUCATION AND THE STATE]

PMG Pall Mall Gazette, December 11, 1865, p. 4, and December 22, 1865, p. 3. Signed "A Lover of Light."
Not reprinted by Arnold.

5:12.   of the county. *mispr. PMG; corrected by ed.*

[THE MANSION-HOUSE MEETING]

PMG Pall Mall Gazette, January 17, 1866, pp. 2–3. Signed "A Lover of Light."
Not reprinted by Arnold.

[SCHOOLS AND UNIVERSITIES
ON THE CONTINENT]

68r.*   Schools Inquiry Commission. | Vol. VI. | General Reports | of | Assistant Commissioners. | Burgh Schools in Scotland, and Secondary | Education in Foreign Countries. | Presented to both Houses of Parliament by Command of Her Majesty. | London: | Printed by George E. Eyre and William Spottiswoode, | Printers to the Queen's Most Excellent Majesty. | For Her Majesty's Stationery Office. | 1868.
"Report on the System of Education for the Middle and Upper Classes in France, Italy, Germany, and Switzerland, by M. Arnold, Esq., M.A., one of H.M. Inspectors of Schools," pp. 441–712.

68s.   Schools and Universities | on the Continent | By | Matthew

* For 68 read 1868, etc.

Arnold, M.A. | Foreign Assistant Commissioner to the Schools Enquiry Commission; One of Her | Majesty's Inspectors of Schools; Formerly Foreign Assistant Commissioner | to the Commission for Enquiring into the State of Popular Education | in England, and Professor of Poetry in the University of Oxford | London | Macmillan and Co. | 1868 | (*Right of translation reserved.*)

The earliest edition with the "Preface [1868]."

74. Higher Schools and | Universities in | Germany | By | Matthew Arnold, D.C.L. | *Formerly Foreign Assistant Commissioner to the Schools Enquiry Commission* | London | Macmillan and Co. | 1874 | *All rights reserved*

"Preface to the Second Edition," pp. v–lxx.
"Preface to the First Edition. (1868.)" pp. lxxi–lxxxi.
The text reprints Chapters xiv–xx and xxii–xxiii and Appendix 10 of 68s.

80. Passages from | the Prose Writings | of | Matthew Arnold | London | Smith, Elder, & Co., 15 Waterloo Place | 1880 | [*All rights reserved*]

Also issued with the imprint: New York | Macmillan and Co., | 1880

82. Higher | Schools & Universities | in Germany | By | Matthew Arnold, D.C.L. | Formerly Foreign Assistant Commissioner to the Schools | Enquiry Commission | London | Macmillan and Co. | 1882 | *All rights reserved.*

"Preface [1882]," pp. v–vii.
"Preface to the First Edition (1868)," pp. ix–xxi.
The text reprints Chapters xiv–xx and xxii–xxiii and Appendix 10 of 68s.
Reprinted from the stereotyped plates in 1892.

92f. A French Eton | or | Middle-class Education and the State | to which is added | Schools and Universities in France | being part of a volume on 'Schools and Universities | on the Continent' published in 1868 | by | Matthew Arnold | London | Macmillan and Co. | and New York | 1892 | *All rights reserved*

Includes "Preface to the Second Edition [1874]" and Chapters i–viii of 68s.
This edition has no textual authority and is not collated.

The following passage appears in 80: 308:3–310:3 (pp. 125–28, headed "Our Middle-Class Education").

*68r is divided into sections on France, Italy, Germany, and Swit-
zerland, and a Conclusion, but there are no other chapter divisions.
The pages of 68r have marginal topic-headings that were assembled
at the heading of each chapter of 68s. The Preface is not in 68r, but
the report there is preceded by the following Introduction:*

SIR,   London, 1866.

Having been charged by the Schools Inquiry Commission with
the task of investigating the system of education for the middle and
upper classes which prevails in France, Germany, Switzerland, and
Italy, I proceeded to Paris on the 8th of April last year. I remained   5
on the Continent nearly seven months, and during that time I
visited the four countries named, and made as careful a study as I
could of the matters to which the Commission had directed my attention. In prosecuting my inquiries I received the most ready and
full help both from the representatives of Her Majesty in the for-   10
eign countries which I visited, and from the governments to which
Her Majesty's representatives recommended me. I gladly take the
opportunity of expressing, at the outset of this Report, my sincere
gratitude for the abundant kindness and assistance which I thus received.   15

At the outset, also, let me state the interpretation which I found
myself obliged to put upon the Commissioners' instructions to me
to investigate "the system of instruction of the middle and upper
classes." The system of instruction of the upper classes, at any rate,
includes, if it is taken in its widest sense, the whole of university in-   20
struction. University instruction is in itself a very large subject; the
Commission which sent me does not concern itself with university
instruction in England; and in order to avoid attempting more than
I could perform, I thought it best to limit, in a great degree, my
inquiry to that kind of education which forms the object of the   25
present Commission's Inquiry in this country. That kind of education is on the Continent generally known by the name of *secondary
instruction*. The Schools Inquiry Commission deals with the secondary instruction of England, except so far as relates to a few large
schools which had already been subjected to a special investigation,   30
and which were therefore withdrawn from the field of this Commission's inquiry. The secondary instruction, therefore, of France,
Germany, Switzerland, and Italy was that to which I directed my
attention. University instruction, the instruction given by the different faculties, goes generally on the Continent by the name of supe-   35
rior instruction. Superior instruction I treated as for the most part

beyond the scope of my inquiry; I touched it directly only at the point where secondary instruction touches it—at the school-boy's passage out of the school-boy stage of his instruction and entrance upon another, through his matriculation. My Report therefore will
5   be found to deal only incidentally, and not in any complete manner, with the instruction of the Universities.

The four countries to which I was sent I visited in the following order:—France, Italy, Germany, Switzerland. I propose to take them in the order in which I visited them.

P. 14, Motto. *not in* 68r

Pp. 15–30. *not in* 68r. *Entitled* Preface 68s; Preface to the First Edition (1868). 74, 82

15:8–20:19. *not in* 74, 82

19:37. 1 in 9 *mispr.* 68s

20:20. ¶It is expedient 74, 82

20:21. those educational 74, 82

20:24–25:5. *not in* 74, 82

25:6. *no* ¶. As to compulsory education, denominational 74, 82

25:7–8. precedents are to be studied, and they are to be studied for the sake 74, 82

25:10–11. ¶Most English Liberals 74, 82

25:13. with a system of public elementary schools it cannot 82

25:14. us clearly 82

25:17. ¶Then, again, as to compulsory 74, 82

26:3. conduct. But in general, 74, 82

26:6–7. what patriotic people say, I 74, 82

26:31–32. from school, and left to run idle at home. He is not 74, 82

27:28. any final law 82

27:30–31. here, for the following work is devoted to that subject. Secondary and higher education is not, like 74, 82

27:33. It is their 74, 82

28:5. the fact that on the Continent 74, 82

28:8–9. or France some 65,000 of 74, 82

29:1. who, I must say, directed 74, 82

29:3. everybody's thoughts as 74, 82

29:20. school. To 82

29:21–22. from the fourth form at one of our classical public 74, 82

29:31. matter. Our 82

30:4. matters affecting public instruction in this country,—our system 74, 82

30:20. which sets this 74, 82

30:30. energy and prosperity. 74, 82

30:31,32. our energy and our prosperity 74, 82

30:33. them. Here, if 82

30:36. must be put *mispr.* 68s; forth more 74, 82

35, heading. Development of present system of secondary instruction in Europe. This development best 68r

43:6–7. Priscian, coming 68r

45:29. alone; by 68r

50:11–12. about 2½ millions of francs. 68r

51:12–13. State. The teaching staff was paid 68r

53:16–17. suppressed, the collection 68r

56:15. law of the 15th of March 1850, 68r

58:10–11. State contribution for 68r

58:33–34. have 15,000 more 68r

62:6. among them, not 68r

64:26–27. But, in general, the 68r

66:3,11,12,14. science 68r

66:26. authority; in an appendix I will print one or two of them, to enable the Commissioners to judge for themselves what the examination in mathematics, for instance, or in physics and natural science, must be. I will 68r

67:10–11. in a mathematical or scientific class, nor can 68r

68:10–11. like these, taking 68r

69:33. science 68r

70:2. the Commissioners will 68r

70:6. scientific, which is represented by the programmes printed in the appendix to this report. In 68r

70:8–9. calculus, and the Commissioners know what advanced 68r

70:29,36. science. 68r

72:16–17. the well-known author of a history 68r

72:19. Europe; among 68r

72:28–29. country as borne by men of mark 68r

72:30. science 68r

72:33. of living Frenchmen, 68r

72:34–35. they have both also been Ministers 68r

72:35. Instruction, and M. Duruy 68r

74:24,27. science 68r

74:34. them; of course 68r

76, heading. *68r has no marginal headings for the paragraphs included in this chapter.*

77:25. each. The programmes regulating this instruction I print at the end of my report. Drawing   68r

77:35. 24 hours   68r, 68s; *corrected by ed.*

78:25,26. science   68r

79:28. philosophy.* [*footnote:*] * See the programme in full at the end of this report.   68r

79:36-37. *philosophie*, its design being   68r

79:38. share in the classes. In the ten classes they   68r

80:15. are now added   68r

81:1. the paper examination   68r

81:7. geography, and science.   68r

81:10. one, science for two.   68r

81:13-14. mathematics and science (for convenience sake I frequently follow, in this report, our bad and incorrect use of the word science) in an   68r

81:16,24,36,37. science   68r

81:30. mathematics and science.   68r

82:3,25. science   68r

82:12. leaves Greek altogether on one side,   68r

82:14-15. given to physical science, five   68r

82:17-18. mathematics, science has the same share   68r

82:19. ten, but physical science gets   68r

83:27,30,31. science   68r

84:21,32. science   68r

84:37. degree,   68r

86:9. given; all   68r

86:10. *exercice;* of the   68r

86:11. are so; the rest   68r

86:15. Bonaparte, Bourbon,   68r, 68s; *a slip of the pen; these were two names for the same* lycée. *See p. 86:28.*

87:26. all England, nay, of all   68r

88:15. rightly, of such   68r

90:27. dinner at 12,   68r

91:8. rise from five to   68r

91:28-29. more last and a tougher   68r

92:16. amusement; the   68r

93:11-12. tends to a broad   68r

93:24. wish the Commission to remark   68r

94:15-16. have seen; even supposing   68r

95:20. prosperity; it   68r

96:13. sleeping there; these   68r

96:14. a year for it. 68r
96:21. all the day scholars of 68r
97, heading. The *séminaires*. 68r
97:1. *no* ¶. They are not free 68r
97:2. likes; to 68r
103:19. *no* ¶ 68r
105:1. science, 68r
105:5–6. classics; the 68r
106:2. think the Commissioners will 68r
106:6. So private education 68r
106:7–8. cannot give the Commissioners any accurate 68r
108:14. am afraid in 68r
110:37. *not in* 68r
113:28–29. Greek; but even 68r
116:24–25. seemed to me considerably 68r
117:29; 118:3–4. mathematics and science 68r
118:18,22. in physical science; 68r
118:28. the Cambridge 68r
119:14. entirely agreed 68r
119:20. view to meeting all 68r
119:24. call the Commissioners' attention 68r
120:20. mathematics and science 68r
120:37. in 1793. 68r, 68s; *corrected by ed.*
121:10. mathematics, science, and 68r
121:22. sort or another 68r
121:37. 14 *mars* 68r, 68s; *corrected by ed.*
123:28. at present recruits for 68r
123:34. prolonged trainings, 68r
124:15. natural science 68r
124:18–19. Mathematics and science 68r
125:22–23. to me so well composed, 68r
125:23. omits, and so suggestive, that I reprint it at the end of this
    report for the Commissioners' information. 68r
125:30. and therefore it is not 68r
127:14. opportunity, at the end of my report, to 68r
127:16. it; all 68r
128, heading. *The word* Conclusion *not in* 68r
128:18. Of each 68r
128:19. are 16 faculties 68r
128:20. for science, 68r
129:11. science, 68r
129:19. seven faculties, 68r
130:1. and what it has 68r

130:3. has 11 faculties, 68r
130:7. other 10 faculties. 68r
130:8–9. the Commissioners may 68r
131:13–14. The Commissioners will doubtless compare 68r
131:16. they will bear 68r
131:20. three great faculties, 68r
131:28; 133:10. science 68r
133:18. declared the other day, at 68r
133:34. of that of medicine, 68r
134:1–2. four for letters, four for sciences, 68r, 68s; *corrected by ed.*
134:4. to the Commissioners: 68r
134:29. the academy-rector 68r
136:4. which come under 68r
136:10. leave the Commissioners, 68r
136:12. for themselves. 68r
137:3–5. The Commissioners have seen, no doubt, the recently published correspondence respecting 68r
137:8. of the examiners 68r
137:15. subject; at 68r
137:28. such institutions serve 68r
137:34. kind; a modern 68r
141:1. I said that 68r
141:11–12. attributes the foundation of 68r
143:1. humanists; the grand 68r
144:33. universities and the 68r
144:34. cause; it 68r
145:11. *no* ¶ 68r
145:16. fallen to 62. 68r, 68s; *corrected from Matteucci.*
145:22. Universities became regarded, 68r
145:35. name to match with this list— 68r
148:10. instruction; thus 68r
148:18. professors here at 68r
148:35. &c.; but 68r
150:15. first annexations 68r
151:10. in May last year the 68r
152:27. science, 68r
154:11. It is thus divided. 68r
154:17. every seven scholars and 68r
155:15. in physical science 68r
155:23. make this first 68r
156:10. it is considered 68r

156:33. as it is at present   68r
158:4, 6. physical science   68r
158:16. degree; in   68r
159:29. and carried, by   68r
163:10–11. faculty of natural sciences—   68r
163:21. are regular   68r
166:11–12. Germany, by supplementing the regular   **68r**
166:13. turn its cheapness to the   68r
166:32–33. The yearly sum which   68r
168:17. for their examinations,   68r
168:32. end of last year   68r
169:22. 1856,   68r, 68s; *corrected by ed.*
170:36. the total number   68r
173:10. Eighty-two have been closed, 40 in the past year alone. Then,   68r
173:11. of September, 1865, the   68r
173:15. gave back to the   68r
173:21–22. during this last spring.   68r
174, heading. supported by public   68r
174:23. element   68r
175:26. the whole kingdom. *Una*   68r
176:1. to give to each   68r
178:24. science,   68r
178:36. seminaries,   68r
178:37. to the three university faculties of letters,   **68r**
178:38. required of them.   68r
180:27. were no public   68r
180:29. but hardly anything   68r
180:31. the only substitute.   68r
180:35. *not in* 68r
181:7. Their school   68r
181:34–35. me. One who has been   68r
181:35–36. has a certain   68r
182:14. may, perhaps, flourish   68r
182:20. only seven were   68r
182:26–27. Intelligent their direction   68r
185, title. Secondary or Higher Schools.   74, 82
185, heading. The Renaissance and the Reformation   *not in* 68r. *In* 68s *the last sentence appears at the beginning of the heading of Chapt. XV; in* 74, 82 *it appears here.* schools to be representatives   68r; schools representatives   68s; schools representative   74, 82

185:2. Renascence. *So spelled throughout* 74, 82
185:3. operated, and produced 68r
185:21. and culture. 68r
186:3–4. reformers. In 74, 82
186:36–37. its writer (Mr. Pattison) touches, 74, 82
187:3. ¶Prussia was 74, 82
187:7–32. *not in* 74, 82
187:33. ¶As a rule 74, 82
188:11. Prussian. Prussia now, of course, stands for Germany in a
    degree, even, beyond what could have been anticipated when the
    above was written. 74, 82
189:24–26. *not in* 74, 82
190:30. which the Commissioners will 68r
191:7–8. as an *extra*. Geography 68r
191:14. them when there is no *Realschule* in the place and the boys
    68r
193:27. week.* [*footnote:*] *But see the appendix to this report for
    fuller details as to the course of study in the German higher
    schools of each kind. 68r
195:7–8. Before the Austrian war 74, 82
195:20, 22. The Commissioners will ... They will 68r
195:20–22. tried. We find in the year 1865, I will not say 74, 82
196, heading. Sources of public character of Prussian public schools.
    Common 68r; State intervention and regulation. 68r
196:1. *no* ¶ 68r
197:13–14. to found and to conduct 74, 82
198:14. were entrusted 68r, 68s, 74, 82
198:29. Medicine being now added 68r
198:32. The ... Mühler. *not in* 74, 82
199:19. *episcopus*, and 68r
199:21–22. in them, went in Protestant 68r
200:18. The Commissioners will 68r
204:32. But the Commissioners will 68r
204:36. for which I had complete 74, 82
205:4. the Commissioners may 68r
205:8. conducted; because for 74, 82
205:28. elsewhere; the 68r
205:34. schools abroad, because 68r
206:7. them; and 68r
207:2. merits; the 68r
207:5. is undoubtedly secured 68r

207:10. to civil   74, 82
208:9. the Commissioners will   68r
209:11. examination; the   68r
209:26. To Wilhelm von Humboldt is owing the most important
  68r
209:31. the examination   68r
210:23. different views   82
212:3. him; in   68r
213:7. The Commissioners will   68r
213:31. left in order   74, 82
213:34-35. gymnasium in *secunda*,   74, 82
214:26. are great matters   74, 82
215:12-13. show the Commissioners   68r
215:31-32. ancient history, and the history   68r
216:11-12. which a certificate,... is given,   74, 82
217:17. translation,   74, 82
217:21. the Commissioners themselves know   68r
218:20. the only defence   68r
219:31-32. candidates for many Oxford fellowships.   74, 82
221:33. two half years without   68r
222:22. so uses must   74, 82
223:7. there; the   68r
224:2. The later statutes   68r
225:27. gymnasiums for Berlin   74, 82
225:32. Boeckh was in 1865 the director   74, 82
227:10. All the directors and   74, 82
228:12. from the Commissioners.   68r
228:30. Mühler,* [*footnote:*] * He is now (1873) removed.   74, 82
228:32. not at all likely   68r
229:6-7. last year or two have   68r; last few years before 1865
  were a time   74, 82
229:8. height; I   68r
231:5. few in numbers,   68r
231:8. had, in 1864, 11,289,655   74, 82
231:8-9. Protestants, 6,901,023 Catholics.   68r
231:9. She had nearly   74, 82
231:9-10. inhabitants classed neither   74, 82
231:10-11. these were principally   74, 82
231:12-13. were Protestant ... were Catholic ... were Jews.   74, 82
232:10. at the Prussian   68r
235:28. to the Commissioners,   68r

235:29. to them. 68r
236, heading. Notice of particular schools. The Berlin schools. 68r
236:4. 6,874 scholars 68r, 68s, 74, 82; *corrected from Wiese.*
237:6. *no* ¶ 74, 82
238:37. done away in 1832. 68r; done away with in 1832. 68s, 74, 82; *year corrected from Wiese.*
239:12. 10 thalers, those 68r, 68s, 74, 82; *corrected from Wiese.*
239:12. and in *prima* 74, 82
239:21. twenty years ago 68r, 68s, 74, 82; *corrected from Wiese.*
239:28. *no* ¶ 68r
240:19. lesson at 68r, 74, 82; lessons at *mispr.* 68s
240:29. tact for judging what 74, 82
241:14. now they were 68r
241:20. Berlin; the 68r
242:6. world: in 68r
242:23. lesson on 68r; lessons on 68s, 74, 82
242:34. called up one 68r
243:23. in passing remark to the Commissioners how greatly 68r
243:29. chooses *ad libitum;* most schools make 68r
244:8. this: it 68r
244:20. first appears 68r
244:37. (now of 20,000 68r
246:11. The Commissioners will 68r
246:21. 10s.; there are 68r
246:26. It is also Protestant. 68r
248:2. scholars; Grævius, 68r
248:11–12. pay to him . . . and to the school 74, 82
248:33–34. the Commissioners will 68r
248:36. a year value, 68r
249:11. that none of our boys 68r
250:5. which used often 68r
250:9. schools; before 68r
250:13. In 1865, it had Catholic *mispr.* 74; In 1865 it had two Catholic 82
250:14, 16. it had also . . . it had a 74, 82
250:30. though this school 68r
250:37. *not in* 74, 82
251:20. financier and an administrator, and two 68r
253:22–23. *Last sentence not in* 68r, *which here introduces nearly the whole of what became Chapter XXII in* 68s
254, heading. German universities are State 68r

254:2. chiefly reached through   68r
254:4. the world of nature.   68r
255:5. Prussia had, in 1865, six   74, 82
255:8. universities were Berlin,   74, 82
255:9–10. incomplete ones, Münster and   74, 82
256:2. the Commissioners will   68r
256:30. more complete details   68r
256:30–39. *not in* 74, 82
256:31. appendix to this Report.   68r
257:10–11. He is the visible   68r
258:37–259:1. have an income,   68r
259:2. one has an   68r
259:15. *Privatissima;* but   68r
260:11. lazy; if he   68r
260:16. is about exactly   68r, 68s; is almost exactly   74, 82
260:20. is 183.* [*footnote:*] * All these numbers relate to the year
   1864. For full details respecting the provision of teaching in the
   University of Berlin, see the appendix.   74, 82
261:12. highest; they   68r; go up as high   74, 82
262:5–6. us; the   68r
262:26. there is so little real   74, 82
262:37. think the German universities might   68r
263:8. I think I have already   68r
263:9. more easily in some   68r
263:17–18. begged the Commissioners to   68r
263:29. of this Report.   68r
267, heading. government. Their course, fees, and   68r
267:1. I have already given the Commissioners so much to read that
   I am unwilling to occupy them for more than a short time longer,
   and indeed what is most   68r
269:15. Educational Council   68r
269:19–20. day-school only to the three elementary classes;   68r
270:1. school room, but the Education   68r
270:26–27. school age between them.   68r
272:6. of the whole   68r
273:5–6. from this the State   68r
273:36. to which this Report relates—   68r
274:4, 21. Educational Council   68r
275:8. are elected for   68r
275:12. *no* ¶   68r
275:19–20. some other members of   68r

275:23. purpose; and it can suspend   68r
275:26-27. as the Commissioners will   68r
275:35. accepts. But the proper   68r
275:37. school terminology of   68r
277:11. learnt; the   68r
277:31. But then he is of a class to do   68r
277:35. from any of them as to teaching.   68r
278:3-4. called) for five years and   68r
279:7. geography and natural philosophy,   68r
279:13. the Commissioners will get   68r
279:14. gymnasium from remarking that whereas   68r
279:32. It is remarkable that in   68r
280:8. Latin; Latin and Greek   68r
280:12. given to them, that   68r
280:34. pay another 60 francs   68r
281:5. They take the title   68r
281:27. impossible to comply with the Commissioners' wish that I
   should include in this Report an account   68r
282:10. Switzerland, and on that account I print the scheme of instruction for one of the best of them (that at Basle) in the appendix to my Report. The Winterthur   68r
282:14. These Winterthur burghers seek   68r
283:17. Private schools must, as I have said, if they   68r
283:18. an instruction corresponding to that   68r
283:19-23. popular school. But besides this, for the opening of any
   private school the consent of the State, and an official approval
   of the work-plan, are necessary; and all private schools are entirely open to State inspection and must furnish yearly reports
   of themselves to the authorities. The great   68r
283:24-25. 30 years, and the   68r
283:34-35. by several Swiss of great authority and   68r
286:2. to the Commissioners.   68r
286:3. maintains a university,   68r
286:14-15. to show (England, alas! is not of the number of these
   countries), and who has   68r
286:28. aim; the   68r
288:11. prevented them from   68r
288:17-18. is there a living   68r
288:21. culture becomes   68r
288:31. we have ourselves not even   68r
289, heading. issue of this conflict. New   68r

289:1–6. *not in* 74, 82
289:1–2. The Commissioners will . . . long Report I   68r
289:5. to the Commissioners   68r
289:6–9. *not in* 68r
289:6. ¶In what has been said, two points,   74, 82
289:10–302:14. *Placed between 253:22 and 254:1 in* 68r
289:10. in this Report   68r; in the foregoing chapters   74, 82
289:20. will have, as is natural, to   68r
290:5. *no* ¶   68r
292:24. *no* ¶   68r
292:38. bene."—Matteucci.   74, 82
293:24. of this Report   68r
293:36. travail, is fully   68r
296:35. But the close   68r
296:37. accurate and verbal   74, 82
297:5. *beauty;* and character is   68r
297:19. This is   68r
297:21. *no* ¶   68r
298:29. were written they   68r
298:36. A very interesting lecture from Mr. Farrar has still   74, 82
299:27. prevent it carrying   68r
299:30. *no* ¶   68r
301:33–34. is a bane to great   68r
301:37–38. the two lines of   68r
302:2. such studies as have   74, 82
302:6. *no* ¶   68r
302:7–8. is casting about   68r
303, heading. Provincial School Boards to be organized.   68r
303:1–2. *not in* 68r
303:2–328:37. ¶I have now   *follows 289:6 in* 68r
303:3. again last year,   68r
304:21. in plain truth,   68r
304:29–36. *not in* 74, 82
305:14. into things is,   68r
305:18. last seven years   68r; last fifteen years   74, 82
305:27. this is in States   74, 82
306:35. France had, in 1865, 37,500   74, 82
307:16. The Commissioners will   68r
307:17–19. Their inquiries in England, I feel sure, will have satisfied them that we have not   68r
307:22. They will not   68r

307:23–24. believe, though their inquiries have not gone to this point, that   68r

307:30. this number more   68r

308:4–5. England so good on the whole, if we regard the whole number of those to whom it is due, as that given in Germany or France, nor is it given in schools   80

308:8. that the injury,   80

308:9. getting inferior instruction, and of getting it   80

308:10. of inferior standing,   80

308:10–11. This injury, 80

308:14. social injury is   80

308:18–19. From a social and educational point   80

308:20. Ten or a dozen famous   80

308:20. Cambridge, the church or the bar, the army   80

308:22–23. are the lines of training, all or any of which give a cast of ideas, a stamp or habit, which make   80

308:30. in the main that of   80

308:34–309:7. England. Judged from its bad side, this cast of ideas is characterised by over-reverence for things established, by an estrangement from the powers of reason and science. Judged from its good side, it is characterised . . . to rule. But they are separate, to a degree   80

309:8. industrial classes with   80

309:12. qualities, but disinclined to rely on reason and science; while   80

309:15. which in the great public schools of other   80

309:19–22. systematic knowledge, reason! But here comes in   80

309:20. would naturally   68r

309:22. intellectual mischief of   80

309:24–28. schools. In England the business   80

309:28. professions and aristocracy in   80

309:30–31. and incomplete as their development of reason is, in its development of reason. Short   80

309:36. intellectual power. Their intellectual result is as faulty as their social result.   80

309:37. this be true,   80

309:38–310:1. education, is not conscious of the injury to itself from them, and is satisfied   80

310:26. Duruy, till lately the French   74, 82

311:1. more and more considerable   68r; more and considerable *mispr.*   68s, 74, 82

311:8. to teach it him. 68r
311:25. have a much larger reading class 68r
311:31. the Commissioners will 68r
313:8. till he had 68r
314:4. for the Commissioners to 68r
314:5. to be recommended. 68r
314:8. the Commissioners will 68r
314:9. accompanied me thus far, without 74, 82
314:32. will at first 68r
315:5. matters which I have already approached or touched in the 74, 82
315:6. course of my Report 68r; course of this volume 74, 82
315:20. advise on school books, on the graduation of 68r
315:21–22. highest school; and, above all, it would be its function to advise on studies, and on the plan 68r
316:8. annual examination. 68r
316:27–29, 30–32. there ... authority. there ... it. *italics* 68r
317:13. would have force 68r
318:13–14. the one dam, to repeat 68r
318:24. the Commissioners must not 68r
319:2–3. a very late age, 68r
319:13. in both of these countries 74, 82
320:11. two years after his 68r
320:22. England had, in 1865, twenty 74, 82
320:23. numbered then about 74, 82
320:24. Prussia of my Report— 68r
321:16. is a recent experiment 74, 82
321:17. am, as the Commissioners perhaps know, totally 68r
321:28. deserves a report to itself, and a reporter to treat 68r
322:1. examination (where such examination exists),—should 68r
322:7. or entrusted, 68r
323:17. and should have faculties formed 74, 82
325:4. All the lesser 74, 82
325:24. made me formerly a 74, 82
326:33. rate they would not be 68r
327:29. and which needs it so much 68r
328:7–18. world. The reorganisation proposed will to many people in England appear chimerical. Yet I have a profound conviction 74, 82
328:8–9. The Commissioners will, 68r
328:10. they will find 68r

328:12. They will also   68r

328:18. place, I am addressing in this Report a small body of select judges, who are certainly desirous to hear the plain truth, and capable of receiving it; not the general public, whose ignorance and prejudices require, perhaps, infinite management. To the Commissioners I owed the truth; and the blame I have applied and the changes I have suggested, are, in truth, too little rather than too much. And now I leave this question in the Commissioners' hands, with the profound and unalterable conviction that   68r

328:21–22. in this Report,   68r

328:24–37. *not in* 74, 82

328:24. a former Royal   68r

328:27. had just left in England,   68r

328:28–29. said to the Commission which sent me: 68r

328:35. myself before another Commission with an   68r

328:37. *68r has the following close:* I am, Sir, | Your obedient servant, | MATTHEW ARNOLD. | *To* | *The Secretary to the Schools Inquiry Commission.*

[GERMAN AND ENGLISH UNIVERSITIES]

PMG Pall Mall Gazette, May 5, 1868, p. 11. Anonymous. Not reprinted by Arnold.

Index

A reference to a page of text should be taken to include the notes to that page.